CHINA'S POLITICAL ECONOMY IN THE XI JINPING EPOCH

Domestic and Global Dimensions

Series on Contemporary China (ISSN: 1793-0847)

Series Editors: Joseph Fewsmith *(Boston University)*
Zheng Yong-Nian *(East Asian Institute, National University of Singapore)*

This series showcases the most significant and lasting contributions to scholarship in the studies of China's politics, society, and culture — whether for general readers or specialists. Each of the volumes is a quality work by a leading scholar or scholars in the field and may take the form of a research monograph, a multi-author edited volume, a conference proceeding, a textbook, or an annual review, among others. While the focus is on China, the series does not lose sight of the interplay of other regional and global forces and their influence and impact on China.

*Published**

Vol. 49 *China's Political Economy in the Xi Jinping Epoch: Domestic and Global Dimensions*
edited by Lowell Dittmer

Vol. 48 *Value Changes and Regime Stability in Contemporary China*
by Wei Shan

Vol. 47 *Political Economy of Agricultural Trade-Related Policies in China*
by Wenshou Yan

Vol. 46 *A Critical Decade: China's Foreign Policy (2008–2018)*
by Zhiqun Zhu

Vol. 45 *China's Omnidirectional Peripheral Diplomacy*
edited by Jianwei Wang & Tiang Boon Hoo

Vol. 44 *Reform and Development in China: After 40 Years*
edited by Wei Shan & Lijun Yang

Vol. 43 *The South China Sea Disputes and the U.S.–China Contest: International Law and Geopolitics*
by James C Hsiung

Vol. 42 *The South China Sea Disputes: Historical, Geopolitical and Legal Studies*
edited by Tsu-Sung Hsieh

Vol. 41 *Moralization of China*
by Xin Liu

Vol. 40 *Social Construction in Contemporary China*
by Xueyi Lu

*To view the complete list of the published volumes in the series, please visit:
http://www.worldscientific.com/series/scc

Series on Contemporary China – Vol. 49

CHINA'S POLITICAL ECONOMY IN THE XI JINPING EPOCH

Domestic and Global Dimensions

Editor

Lowell Dittmer

University of California at Berkeley, USA

World Scientific

NEW JERSEY • LONDON • SINGAPORE • BEIJING • SHANGHAI • HONG KONG • TAIPEI • CHENNAI • TOKYO

Published by

World Scientific Publishing Co. Pte. Ltd.
5 Toh Tuck Link, Singapore 596224
USA office: 27 Warren Street, Suite 401-402, Hackensack, NJ 07601
UK office: 57 Shelton Street, Covent Garden, London WC2H 9HE

Library of Congress Cataloging-in-Publication Data
Names: Dittmer, Lowell, editor.
Title: China's political economy in the Xi Jinping epoch : domestic and global dimensions / editor, Lowell Dittmer, University of California at Berkeley, USA.
Description: New Jersey : World Scientific, [2021] | Series: Series on contemporary China, 1793-0847 ; vol. 49 | Includes bibliographical references and index.
Identifiers: LCCN 2020048240 | ISBN 9789811226571 (hardcover) | ISBN 9789811226588 (ebook) | ISBN 9789811226595 (ebook other)
Subjects: LCSH: China--Economic policy--2000– | China--Economic conditions--2000– | China--Foreign economic relations.
Classification: LCC HC427.95 .C45649 2021 | DDC 330.951--dc23
LC record available at https://lccn.loc.gov/2020048240

British Library Cataloguing-in-Publication Data
A catalogue record for this book is available from the British Library.

For any available supplementary material, please visit
https://www.worldscientific.com/worldscibooks/10.1142/11999#t=suppl

Desk Editors: Balasubramanian Shanmugam/Lixi Dong

Typeset by Stallion Press
Email: enquiries@stallionpress.com

https://doi.org/10.1142/9789811226588_fmatter

About the Editor

Lowell Dittmer is Professor of Graduate Studies at the University of California at Berkeley. He has also served as visiting professor at universities in Malaysia, Taiwan, China, and Singapore. Recent works include *China's Asia: Triangular Dynamics Since the Cold War* (Lanham, MD: Roman & Littlefield, 2018); *Taiwan and China: Fitful Embrace* (Berkeley: University of California Press, 2017); with George Lin, *China, the Developing World, and the New Global Dynamic* (Boulder: Lynne Rienner, 2010); with Samuel Kim (eds.) *China's Quest for National Identity* (Cornell, 1993); *Liu Shaoqi and the Chinese Cultural Revolution* (rev. ed., 1997); with Haruhiro Fukui and Peter N.S. Lee, *Informal Politics in East Asia* (Cambridge, 2000), and numerous scholarly articles.

https://doi.org/10.1142/9789811226588_fmatter

About the Authors

Marc Blecher is the James Monroe Professor of Politics and of East Asian Studies at Oberlin College. His most recent book, coauthored with Philippe Schmitter, is *Politics as a Science: A Prolegomenon* (2020). He has also published *Tethered Deer: Government and Economy in a Chinese County*; *China Against the Tides: Restructuring Through Revolution, Radicalism and Reform*; and *Micropolitics in Contemporary China: A Technical Unit During and After the Cultural Revolution*; as well as dozens of articles on China's political economy, political sociology, and farmers' and workers' politics. His current project is a book manuscript entitled *A World to Lose: Working Class Formation and the Chinese State*, a longitudinal study tracing the political development of the Chinese working class and labor politics from its inception to the present.

Shaun Breslin is Professor of Politics and International Studies at the University of Warwick. He is also Senior Research Fellow at the Wong MNC Center and Co-Editor of *The Pacific Review*. His latest book, *China Risen? Studying Chinese Global Power*, has been published by Bristol University Press in early 2021.

Kang Chen is Professor of Economics at the National University of Singapore. His research specialties are China's economic reform and development, public choice and public policy, and macroeconomic modeling. His research has been published in professional journals for economics, including *Journal of Comparative Economics*, *China Economic Review*, *European Journal of Political Economy*, and *Economic Modelling*. He is the author of *The Chinese Economy in Transition: Micro Changes and Macro Implications*. He currently serves on the editorial board of the *European Journal of Political Economy*, and the advisory board of *China Economic Quarterly*. He was the Wang Yanan Chair Professor of Economics at Xiamen University, China. He has a BSc from Xiamen University and a PhD in economics from the University of Maryland.

Rou-Lan Chen is an assistant professor in the department of Political Economy at National Sun Yat-sen University, Taiwan. She received her Ph.D. in Political Science from U.C. Berkeley. Her research interests include political methodology and nationalism, with a specific focus on Hierarchical Linear Modeling. She has published articles on Taiwan's identity politics and Chinese nationalism in *Journal of Contemporary China*, *Nations and Nationalism*, *Journal of East Asian Studies*, *Asian Survey*, as well as in edited volumes. Her recent research centers on China's fandom nationalism and the rise of nationalist populism in Taiwan.

Martin K. Dimitrov is Professor of Political Science at Tulane University. His books include *Piracy and the State: The Politics of Intellectual Property Rights in China* (Cambridge University Press, 2009); *Why Communism Did Not Collapse: Understanding Authoritarian Regime Resilience in Asia and Europe* (Cambridge University Press, 2013); and *The Politics of Socialist Consumption* (Ciela Publishers, 2018).

Jane Du is Research Associate at SOAS China Institute, University of London. Du has specialized in the political economy of Chinese agriculture. Her research studies on Chinese agriculture have ranged from Mao's collectivization to Deng's agricultural reforms, and the role of agriculture in China's return to the market. Her publications have appeared in *European Review of Economic History*, *The China Quarterly*, and *Applied Economics*.

Barry Eichengreen is the George C. Pardee and Helen N. Pardee Professor of Economics and Professor of Political Science at the University of California, Berkeley, where he has taught since 1987. He is a Research Associate at the National Bureau of Economic Research (Cambridge, Massachusetts) and Research Fellow of the Centre for Economic Policy Research (London, England). In 1997–1998, he was Senior Policy Advisor at the International Monetary Fund. He is a fellow of the American Academy of Arts and Sciences (class of 1997).

Professor Eichengreen has held Guggenhim and Fulbright Fellowships and been a fellow of the Center for Advanced Study in the Behavioral Sciences (Palo Alto) and the Institute for Advanced Study (Berlin). From 2004 to 2020, he served as convener of the Bellagio Group of academics and officials. He is a regular monthly columnist for *Project Syndicate.*

Gang Chen is Assistant Director and Senior Research Fellow of the East Asian Institute (EAI), National University of Singapore. Since he joined the EAI in 2007, he has been tracing China's politics, foreign policy, environmental and energy policies and publishing extensively on these issues. He is the single author of P*olitics of Renewable Energy in China* (Cheltenham, UK: Edward Elgar, 2019), *The Politics of Disaster Management in China: Institutions, Interest Groups, and Social Participation* (New York: Palgrave Macmillan, 2016), *China's Climate Policy* (London and New York: Routledge, 2012), *Politics of China's Environmental Protection: Problems and Progress* (Singapore: World Scientific, 2009), and *The Kyoto Protocol and International Cooperation against Climate Change* (in Chinese) (Beijing: Xinhua Press, 2008). His research papers have appeared in internationally-refereed journals such as *Asian Survey*, *Asia Pacific Business Review*, *The Copenhagen Journal of Asian Studies*, *The International Spectator*, *The Polar Journal*, *China: An International Journal*, *The Chinese Journal of International Politics*, and *The Journal of East Asian Affairs.* He provides consultancy for the Singapore government on environmental and energy issues in East Asia. He is a member of the Association of Chinese Political

Studies based in the United States. He is frequently interviewed by media like Bloomberg TV, *The Wall Street Journal*, the BBC, NHK, Channel NewsAsia, and Xinhua News Agency. He sometimes gives lectures at the Business School of the National University of Singapore, the Ministry of Foreign Affairs of Singapore, and Singapore Environment Institute. He helps the Lee Kuan Yew School of Public Policy to design the "Public Sector Risk Management" curriculum for MPA students. He is a member of the Global Emerging Voices program jointly sponsored by The German Marshall Fund of the United States, Stiftung Mercator, Torino World Affairs Institute, and Australian National University. He has participated in various international research projects like the "EU–Asia Dialogue" co-funded by the European Union and the Konrad Adenauer Foundation (KAF) of Germany and the Asian Energy Program sponsored by the Lee Kuan Yew School of Public Policy.

Jonathan Holslag teaches international politics at the Free University Brussels. His research focuses on China, EU–Asia relations, and geopolitics. His latest books are *Silk Road Trap* (Polity, 2019) and *Political History of the World* (Penguin, 2018). Besides his academic work, Jonathan has worked for various institutions.

Scott L. Kastner is a Professor in the Department of Government and Politics at the University of Maryland, College Park, where he teaches courses on international relations, US–China relations, and East Asia. He is author of *China's Strategic Multilateralism: Investing in Global Governance* (Cambridge University Press, 2019; with Margaret Pearson and Chad Rector) and *Political Conflict and Economic Interdependence across the Taiwan Strait and Beyond* (Stanford University Press, 2009). He has also published articles in journals such as *International Security, International Studies Quarterly, Journal of Conflict Resolution, Comparative Political Studies*, and *Security Studies.*

Cheng King is Research Fellow at Sun Yat-sen University. His major research foci include fiscal management in China between the seventeenth and nineteenth centuries, the agricultural history of ancient

China, and the process of post-war economic catch-up in East and Southeast Asia. His publications on Chinese economy have appeared on *Journal of Policy Modeling*, *Journal of Contemporary China*, etc.

Dalton Lin is an Assistant Professor at the Sam Nunn School of International Affairs, Georgia Institute of Technology. Before joining Georgia Tech in 2016, he was a postdoctoral research fellow at Princeton University with the Princeton–Harvard China and the World Program. His current research interests center around explaining contemporary China's foreign policy and regional countries' responses to it. His most recent work includes "China's Soft Power Over Taiwan" (with YH Chu, in *Soft Power with Chinese Characteristics* (Routledge, 2019)). Dr. Lin is also the Executive Editor of the website Taiwan Security Research (http://taiwansecurity.org).

Guangtao Xia is the Assistant Director of both the Center for International Finance and Economics Research and Center for International Digital Capital Research at Tsinghua University, where he received his BA and PhD in economics with summa cum laude in 2012 and 2018, respectively. From 2016 to 2017, he was a visiting PhD student at the University of California, Berkeley. He was also a postdoctoral fellow at the PBC School of Finance, Tsinghua University, before joining the Institute of World Economics and Politics, Chinese Academy of Social Sciences, as a research fellow in 2020.

Guangtao's main research interests are international finance and macroeconomics. His recent research focuses on reform of the international monetary system and the renminbi internationalization, safe asset scarcity, and digital currencies competition.

Guangtao was the 2016 recipient of the National Scholarship for Visiting PhD Students and the 2015 recipient of the China Development Research Scholarship.

Zhu Zhang is a PhD candidate in the Department of Political Science at Tulane University and a pre-doctoral fellow (2019–2020) at the Center on Democracy, Development and the Rule of Law at Stanford University.

https://doi.org/10.1142/9789811226588_fmatter

Acknowledgments

Preliminary drafts of several of the chapters included here were first presented at an international conference on China's political economy under Xi Jinping at National Chenchi University, Taipei, on October 21–22, 2017. We wish to thank Tsai Chung-min and the NCCU Staff for successfully organizing the conference, and the Institute of East Asian Studies at the University of California in Berkeley and the Chiang Ching-kuo Foundation for their generous financial support. For helpful comments on early drafts of the papers, we are indebted to Professor Samuel Kim and two anonymous referees.

https://doi.org/10.1142/9789811226588_fmatter

Contents

Part I

Introduction

https://doi.org/10.1142/9789811226588_0001

Chapter 1

Transformation of the Chinese Political Economy in the New Era

Lowell Dittmer

dittmer@berkeley.edu

This book presents a fresh look at the nature of the Chinese political economy at a significant inflection point, namely the inauguration of what has been designated a "new era" of Chinese political economy, designed to achieve the "rejuvenation of the Chinese nation" and "Chinese dream" promised by Chairman Xi Jinping. We shall find that plans for this rejuvenation include both new policy ideas, such as Xi's boldly visionary "Belt and Road Initiative," and "upholding and improving" the synthesis of policies introduced by Xi's predecessors, such as the dual economic structure incrementally crafted since 1989 consisting of large state-owned corporate groups at the "commanding heights" engaged in strategically vital "lifeline" production along with a vast congeries of private and foreign-invested firms. It is an altogether eclectic synthesis, incorporating such diverse elements as a cult of the supreme leader and commitment to bureaucratic, legal and scientific rationality, ideological conformity and technological innovation, an assertive nationalism abroad and enforced harmony at home.

Part of what makes this a turning point is China's public realization that it has arrived as a great power in the world and that the Chinese Communist Party (CCP, also called Communist Party of China (CPC)) is determined to bring China's rise to a climactic crescendo in the foreseeable future.[1] But despite now having the largest army, navy and air force in the world (in quantitative and increasingly qualitative terms), China's great power identity can be almost entirely attributed to its unparalleled economic achievement. It no longer needs to accept foreign economic homilies, it can now invite other developing countries to consider a promising alternative.

This is so for at least two reasons. First, the economy *for itself* is enormous, the largest or second largest in the world depending on how one measures it, and its economic impact on the economies with which it interacts is correspondingly large and consequential. In addition to the economic impact *per se*, there is the impact of economics *for politics*. To an unusual degree, the economy is an expression of the interests of Party-state that controls it, and the usual economic data such as trade balances, exchange rates and so forth must be interpreted in terms of political-strategic logic as well as economically. Economics constitutes the basis for the Party-state's "performance legitimacy" and the fiscal foundation for its monopolization of force, domestically and abroad. It not only owns or controls the economy

[1]Overtaking the world's most developed economies has been one of China's core goals since at least 1957, when Mao enunciated it. And already China has surpassed the US in many aspects of political economy. The legendary workshop of the world, China is the world's largest producer of ships, aluminum, furniture, clothing, cell phones, semiconductors, pharmaceuticals, and computers. Chinese consumers bought 20 million cars in 2015 — three million more than were sold in the US. China imported more oil, consumed more energy, and installed more solar power. It now has the world's longest highway system and the biggest high-speed rail system, more high-speed rail tracks than the rest of the world combined. See Graham Allison (2017), *Destined for War: Can America and China Escape Thucydides' Trap?* (New York: Houghton Mifflin Harcourt), Chapter 1.

but identifies strongly with it — as illustrated most recently by its staunch defense and promotion of the private corporation Huawei.

At the time of Xi's ascent to the apex of China's rise, the need to confirm a sense of national identity seemed to call for a clear developmental choice: affirming socialism. But the success of that choice has been equivocal. As of 2019, international pushback and domestic slowdown find the country in an equipoise between continued adherence to Xi's turn to a more identifiably "socialist" industrial policy and a revival of Dengist market reform.

In this comprehensive and systematic overview of China's political economy in the new era of Xi Jinping, we focus on three basic questions: first, what is the essential nature of the Chinese political economy — what is "socialist" about it and what is "capitalist"? Second, what is distinctive (and what is not) about how such an economy interacts with other economies, whether socialist or non-socialist, in the international economic arena? Third, how well does it work? We begin with a brief discussion of definitions, followed by a series of chapters first on domestic political economy and then on the politics of China's economic relations with the world.

1. Domestic Political Economy

The arrival of a new great power in the global arena will always awaken interest. But, the relative suddenness and scale of China's rise has endowed it with a certain shock effect. By 2017, China was the world's biggest trading nation and the leading trade partner of over 130 countries in the world (and 16 Asian countries). Between 2004 and 2013, China's overseas investments had increased 13.7 times from $45 billion to $613 billion (about 10% of global OFDI flows). In 1990, the Chinese economy constituted less than 1% of the global economy, while by 2017 that number had surpassed 16% (meanwhile the US economy declined from 26% to 24%). In 2007, the United States' economy was four times as large as that of China; by 2012, it was but twice as large (and today, less than that). The US share of global high-tech exports has fallen from just below 20% in 1999 to barely over 5% in 2014, while China's share has risen from 3% to 26% during the same period.

One reaction has naturally been an undercurrent of American anxiety about the power-political consequences of such a power shift, which varies depending on the stakes existing stakeholders have to lose. But beyond the political dimension there is a more positive interest in the nature of the economy that has achieved such unprecedented success. To call it "socialism with Chinese characteristics" only begs further definition. What is still socialist about a country that has authorized private property, a stock exchange, and Asia's highest ranking (March 2020) on the Gini index? Defining China's political economy has been a moving target. China's political-economic institutions have changed over time in a constant scramble to keep up with spiraling GDP growth.

What is still socialist about a country that has legalized private property, integrated into global markets, and has quite a stratified class structure (with more billionaires than the United States)? According to Marx, political economic systems are defined by forces and relations of production. These relations are legally formalized in terms of property rights, as Yu-Shan Wu points out.[2] These he divides into two: ownership rights (defined as income power) and rights of control (or use power). The evolution of Chinese political economy progressed in phases, driven from the top in the form of legal changes. In the Maoist period, the Party-state saw its mission as "socialization of the means of production," thus it progressively moved (with some zigs and zags) to claim comprehensive ownership in what Western economists called a "command economy." With the reform and opening, it first adopted "market socialism," or marketization (i.e., the state owns the means of production but does not control market relations among them). From there, it moves to privatization, or "state capitalism" (the state no longer owns the means of production but tries to regulate them). China's "socialist market economy" today asserts ownership rights only over the "commanding heights" of upstream large-scale "strategic" industries while merely exercising "control" over the private sector. Xi Jinping's "socialism with Chinese

[2]Yu-Shan Wu (2019). "Grasp the Big Picture: China in State Capitalism," *Academia Sinica*, Taipei, Taiwan, unpublished paper.

characteristics in the new era" is a form of state capitalism indistinguishable from the East Asian developmental dictatorships of South Korea under Park or Taiwan under the Chiangs.

This is a keen conceptual insight, but with four caveats: First, the distinction between ownership and control is an analytic one that Chinese economic theorists are unlikely to recognize. The CCP uses rather a three-fold distinction between whole people's (state), collective, and individual ownership, in terms of the control that is vested in the Party-state as a sovereign representative of the people. Second, how meaningful is the distinction between ownership and control? Douglas Fuller contends that the only meaningful distinction is between those firms that are relevant to the CCP's political purposes (e.g., Huawei) and those that are not.[3] As we see in *Gang Chen's* chapter, the distinction is increasingly blurred under Xi, as CCP committees are ensconced on private and foreign-owned corporate boards and private and public corporations are invited into cross-stock holding arrangements. Third, the clarity of the distinction rests on the rule of law. China has historically never had a strong legal tradition, and while the People's Republic of China (PRC) has made major progress since the advent of reform, clearly it is still rule *by* law rather than rule of law (i.e., the rulers make and interpret the rules).

Finally, the real issue is the nature of the trend. The newly industrialized countries (NICs) and other such developmental dictatorships conceived of themselves as temporary expedients necessitated by crisis circumstances, to be lifted afterward. Upon the advent of "reform and opening," for many years, the world viewed Chinese market socialism analogously, as a trend toward increasing market liberalization. But in the light of his strong defense of socialism, there has been considerable uncertainty about this since the rise of Xi Jinping. This also begs the question of the relation between economics and politics; for economic liberalization, Western development theorists tend to assume, entails political liberalization. The CCP leadership however resolved after Tiananmen to sever any linkage between economics and

[3]Cf. Douglas Fuller (2016). *Paper Tigers, Hidden Dragons: Firms and the Political Economy of China's Technological Development* (New York: Oxford University Press).

politics in order to preserve the Leninist political structure while permitting economic change to continue to evolve. The private economy could continue to thrive on market rules because growth was useful to the state — it provided revenue, domestic legitimacy and international status. Meanwhile politics would remain a firm structural bedrock of stability, true to canonical texts, staffed now by young and well-educated technocrats who understood how to run the economic machine without getting tainted. Eventually, Western observers tended to infer, the continuing superior performance of the private sector would impel commensurate political changes toward greater pluralism, if not necessarily liberal democracy.

This hopeful chain of logic legitimated Western political leaderships' economic opening to a system which until then had been thought to be irrevocably dedicated to their destruction. It also inspired a "reform" grouping within the Chinese leadership that conceived of modernization in relatively liberalizing terms, at least in the economic arena. But the official narrative is now quite different. It is that the Chinese socialism succeeded not despite its socialist ideological superstructure but because of it; it would hence become more socialist not less and as it did, it would succeed all the more. Although the two terms are used interchangeably in the literature (including this book), my own conclusion is that the Chinese system in its current trajectory is not state capitalism but indeed an adaptive Chinese form of state socialism, with limited (and closely monitored) capitalist characteristics. But ultimately it is a theoretically inconsistent hybrid (e.g., socialism as end, capitalism as means, or socialist rhetoric, capitalist practice), its future systemic identity *in statu nascendi*.

The state-owned enterprise (SOE) has always been the core of the state or public sector, the focus of Gang Chen's perceptive analysis. China still owns approximately 150,000 SOEs, which Xi believes are the basic components of an economic system in which public ownership plays the dominant role alongside multiple forms of ownership.[4] Around 50,000 (33%) of all SOEs are owned by the central government, the remainder by local governments. The central government directly controls and manages around 102 strategic SOEs through

[4] "The Decision on Major Issues," 15 November 2013.

SASAC, of which 66 are also listed on stock exchanges domestically and/or internationally. The state-owned sector remains a vital component of China's industrial economy. The SOEs, both central and local, account for 30% of total GDP, 44% of industrial assets, and about 20% of China's urban employment. SOEs maintain a controlling position in China's stock markets — the 10 top-valued companies by market capitalization in China's Shanghai Composite Index are all state-owned.[5] Chinese corporations account for 48.1% of the capitalization of Hong Kong's stock market. In the first decade of the 21st century, after a series of reforms modeled after Western corporate best practices, profits soared. According to Paul Hubbard, China's 500 largest firms — both private and public — earned $9.2 trillion in 2013, of which only 14% was earned by privately owned companies.[6] This impressive success may be attributed largely to Zhu Rongji's sweeping SOE reforms in the late 1990s: by "grasping the big and dropping the small," he eliminated the "zombies" through privatization or mergers (some 400,000 SOEs closed and 40 million workers laid off) to the advantage of the more efficient surviving firms.

Since the global financial crisis (GFC), SOE measures of production efficiency have however fallen behind those of their private competitors. The return on equity (ROE) of SOEs is now only about half that of firms in the private sector.[7] SOEs were overleveraged,

---

[5]Scott Cendrawski (2015). "Here's what you may not know about the Chinese stock market," *Fortune*, 2 September.

[6]US–China Economic and Security Review Commission, Hearing on China's Shifting Economic Realities and Implications for the United States, written testimony of Paul Hubbard, 24 February 2016.

[7]Lin Yifu, *Jie Du*, pp. 28–30; see also "Reform of China's ailing state-owned firms is emboldening them," *The Economist*, 2017. Available at: https://www.economist.com.news.finance-and-economics/. According to the Rhodium Group, as of June 2018, the average return on assets among SOEs was 3.9%, compared with 9.9% for private firms. The latter accounted for 28% of China's industrial assets but contributed to only 18% of the total profit. Further, they racked up RMB 100 trillion (US$15 trillion) in debt by the end of 2017, equivalent to 120% of the national GDP. There are however differences among SOEs: those in the sectors monopolized by the state generally have very good profitability, while those in sectors with small entry barriers for non-SOEs generally record poor performance.

inefficient, and fostered industrial overcapacity in the sectors they dominated. Since SOEs were unable to compete with private firms in downstream industries such as consumer goods, they retreated to upstream industries that provide key intermediate input services, such as energy, telecommunications and financial services. This despite the fact that China's leading SOEs are not exactly running on an even playing field. They benefit from a medley of preferential government policies. National SOEs (*yangqi*) are large, enjoy economies of scale and favored access to essential economic inputs (land, hydrocarbons, finance, telecoms, and electricity), and exercise considerable power in markets like steel and minerals. SOEs enjoy preferential access to credit and the ability to issue publicly traded equity and debt. They are not subject to the same tax burdens as their private sector competitors. As Chen points out, this approach "on the one hand, revitalized moribund SOEs into competitive conglomerates with soaring profitability and asset scales, while on the other hand, exacerbated the long-lasting principal–agent dilemma facing SOE management and insider control problems associated with mismanagement and lack of sufficient supervision."

During the November 2013 Third Plenum of the 18th Party Congress, Xi Jinping called for broad SOE reforms, emphasizing improved SOE operational transparency and legal reforms that would subject SOEs to greater competition by opening up more industry sectors to domestic and foreign competitors and by reducing provincial and central government preferential treatment. The Third Plenum also called for "mixed ownership" economic structures, encouraging minority private investment and providing greater economic balance between private and state-owned businesses in certain industries, including equal access to factors of production, competition on a level-playing field, and equal legal protection. The problem of executive corruption and other entrepreneurial excesses was to be countered in the crackdown on corruption.

Implementation of these reforms in Xi's first term (2012–2017) — except in the anticorruption campaign, which bagged a number of "big tigers" and thousands of "flies" — has been flaccid. The regime can claim success in cutting regulations for Small and

Medium Enterprises (SMEs), for liberalizing bank interest rates and permitting some private and foreign banks, and for improving international access to Chinese capital markets. Liberalization of China's capital market failed (see Eichengreen, Chapter 9) in 2015, and the concurrent stock market turmoil convinced the leadership to cling to the public sector it could directly control. SOEs (particularly "pillar" SOEs) are the primary entities through which the CCP steers the economy towards the regime's strategic ends; market reform in these sectors would mean giving up central control and dramatically reducing the government's ability to achieve the goals identified in the 13th Five-Year Plan (FYP) and the 10-year "made in China 2025" industrial policy. There is also the issue of vested interests. SOE chief executive officers, usually appointed by the organization department of the Party's central committee, have in their heyday been more powerful (and better paid) than their governmental counterparts, resulting in "regulatory capture."

The major thrust of the second round of SOE reform at the 19th Party Congress has hence been on gaining more CCP control, not less. SOEs, Xi Jinping stressed in 2016, are under the command of the Party (*guo qi xing dang* — SOEs are surnamed Party). Xi pledged at the 19th Congress to make SOEs "stronger, better, and bigger," and turn them into "world-class, globally competitive firms." CEO executive compensation and status will be reduced, subordinating them more credibly to central bureaucrats. The role of Party Committees is to be strengthened in corporate governance. The hundred central *yangqi* are to be merged into fewer (around 40) but even larger "national champions" able to compete with multinational corporations (MNCs) in the global marketplace.[8]

As Gang Chen makes clear in his conclusion, Xi Jinping's vision of reform in the "new era" is quite distinct from the decentralizing reforms of Deng Xiaoping or even the corporate reforms of Jiang Zemin and Zhu Rongji. These are essentially Leninist reforms designed to preserve and enhance a more politically responsible set of global corporate actors. Nevertheless, the government work report in

---

[8] *China Daily* (2015). "China to Reduce Number of Central SOEs to 40," 27 April.

March 2019 did introduce the ideal of "competitive neutrality," removing some of the entitlements SOEs had hitherto enjoyed: "when it comes to access to factors of production, market access and licenses, business operations, government procurement, public biddings, and so on, enterprises under all forms of ownership will be treated on an equal footing."[9]

One bright spot on China's industrial horizon is technological innovation. China's technological revolution has spurred major innovations in the sphere of financial technology (FinTech), mobile payment systems, electric and autonomous vehicles, facial recognition, and platform computerization. China is now the world's largest producer of electric cars (new energy vehicles — NEVs), with 1.2 million passenger cars produced and sold in 2019. Whether this innovation model can outperform the Silicon Valley model based on private venture capital remains to be seen, but Kaifu Lee, who has had ample experience in both systems, is optimistic.[10] The American model may be more capital efficient, he opines, but the Chinese model of throwing a lot of capital and talent at a given project can work wonders. And over the past decade, Chinese funding for the Internet technology sector has grown twice as fast as GDP. E-commerce is expanding vigorously; the number of customers surpassed the US in 2013. And a venture capital sector arose to support it. For three of the 4 years leading up to 2014, total venture capital funding held steady at around US$3 billion. In 2014, that suddenly quadrupled to $12 billion, and then doubled again to $26 billion in 2015.[11] In 2018, Chinese startups, led by outstanding success stories like Baidu, Tencent and Alibaba (BAT), secured more than $30.9 billion in venture capital funding, surpassing for the first time the amount received by their US counterparts in the same year.

---

[9]Li Keqiang (2019). "Report on the work of the government" (2nd Session of the 13th NPC). Available at: www.gov.cn/premier/speeches/2019/03/16/content_281476565265580.htm.

[10]See Kai-fu Lee (2018). *AI Superpowers: China, Silicon Valley, and the New World Order* (New York: Houghton Mifflin Harcourt).

[11]Kai-fu Lee, *AI Superpowers*, p. 65.

A quarterly breakdown however shows that market funding peaked in mid-2018 and subsequently declined, beset not only by the constraints of the crackdown on shadow banking but the trade war and the ensuing coronavirus plague. To the extent that such businesses thrive, the government wants a piece of the action. There are more than 1,000 state-owned venture capital firms in China, controlling more than US$750 billion. For integrated circuits, China's technological Achilles' heel, a total US$150 billion in funding has already been announced. The Party now insists on taking a stake in national champions like Baidu or Tencent as well, along with a voting board seat. Although the private sector has thus far sourced most of the innovation, the high-tech effort is symbiotic, with extensive overlap of financial funding and government guidelines — and civil–military "fusion."

Historically, China's fiscal policy (taxing and spending) has been fragmented, due to the size of the country and dispersion of units, ad hoc adjustments to pell-mell growth, and the dialectic between decentralization and recentralization. In the Maoist era of command planning, capital was appropriated from the agricultural to the industrial sector via "socialist primitive accumulation" (the "scissors" whereby farm inputs were priced higher than outputs). Fixed asset investment was relatively high (about 25% of GDP) while holding consumption down. Economic activity was decentralized and there was little flow of goods and services between regions. For example, roughly 75% of the grain grown in China was consumed by the families that produced it.

Three of the most important tax reforms during the reform era were the introduction of corporate taxes in place of profit remittance in the 1980s (*li gai shui*), the implementation of direct and value-added central taxes in 1994, and the abolition of the agricultural tax in 2006. First came the introduction of a corporate tax (33%) in place of profit remittances (100% of the profits of SOEs and collectives in the Maoist era). The devolution of partial ownership to agricultural and industrial producers in the early reform era created a highly effective growth incentive but starved local governments of their main source of revenue, a problem to some extent alleviated by the comprehensive tax and fiscal reform introduced in late 1993. Hitherto,

Beijing would dicker with local governments over the share of locally collected taxes to be remitted to the center and what remained local. The reforms reclassified types of taxes and reassigned their distribution in favor of the center (hence referred to as the *fenshuizhi*, or tax assignment system).

This system solved the problems of the 1990s but sowed the seeds for those that arose in the wake of the GFC, including infrastructure over-investment, financialization of the economy, proliferation of collateralized debts based on realty, and the creation of asset bubbles. Budget system reforms and spending were not addressed at this time, leaving the politics of the budget to be sorted out by the 31 local governments (i.e., 22 provinces, 5 autonomous regions, and 4 centrally administered cities) with relatively little redistribution among them. Since joining the WTO in December 2001, China enjoyed a spectacular growth of exports: from 6.7% in 2001 to 22.4% in 2002, 34.7% in 2003, 35.3% in 2004, 27.6% in 2005, 23.9% in 2006, and 20.7% in 2007. The GFC forced immediate policy adjustments to cope with the sudden collapse of external demand. In late 2009, China thus launched a massive stimulus package, which offset falling exports with domestic infrastructure investment and staunched a recession.

But as *Kang Chen* makes clear in his insightful chapter, the bailout left in its wake a huge debt overhang. This was not mainly central government debt, as the government distributed loans rather than grants. The SOEs, with easy access to the banks, were the principal loan recipients. Local governments, with constricted access to the formal banking sector, turned to "local government financing vehicles" (LGFVs) for liquidity, giving rise to an unaccountable "shadow banking" sector. Local governments made prolific use of this resource: after increasing indebtedness by 61.92% in 2009, by June 2013 total debts of local governments had increased by RMB7.2 trillion (ca. US$1.4 trillion), forcing the Ministry of Finance (MOF) to issue bonds to cover the debts.[12] In 2017, the MOF announced that the balance of local government debt exceeded RMB16.47 trillion ($2.39 trillion), not counting LGFV loans; estimates of total debt ranged

[12]Xia, *China's Financial Crisis*, p. 12.

from RMB5 trillion ($725 billion) to RMB46 trillion ($6.67 trillion) as of 2018.[13] A March 2018 report released by the Financial Stability Board in Basel found that about 15%, or roughly US$7 trillion, of the world's non-bank loans were held in China, warning that these posed "systemic risk." Average annual loan growth increased from 11% in 1998–2003 to 20% in 2008–2012, more than double GDP growth, causing total indebtedness to rise to 235.7% of GDP by 2014.[14] Many of these loans have turned out to be non-performing. As investment rose, it thus became less efficient, as new loans were used to pay servicing costs to the old, causing the incremental capital output ratio (ICOR) to more than double since 2007, Kang Chen notes. China's total debt in proportion to the economy is now larger than Japan's when its asset bubble burst in 1991. And the greater the debt load, the less effective countercyclical monetary policy becomes.

The leadership's reaction to this challenge has been responsive but somewhat spasmodic, balanced by an insistence on maintaining a high enough growth rate to double China's 2010 GDP by 2020. For example, on the one hand, in December 2017 Xi said reducing financial risk was one of the Party's three "critical battles" over the next 3 years (the others — fighting pollution and poverty). And Liu He, speaking at the World Economic Forum in January 2018, vowed that China would bring its debt under control within 3 years. At the inaugural meeting of the newly created Central Committee on Financial and Economic Affairs (CCFEA) in March 2018, the communique announced that China was entering the second stage of the deleveraging process (after the first stage of slowing the pace of leveraged growth), and intended to "Achieve a stable and gradual decline in the macro leverage ratio." This was the first time China's top leadership

[13]Financial Crisis Inquiry Commission (2011). *The Financial Crisis Inquiry Report* (New York: Public Affairs Press).

[14]In 2011, the Chinese Academy of Social Sciences (CASS) formed a research team to assess the national debt to assets ratio, which found that from 1996 to 2014 the ratio of total debt to GDP rose from 113% to 235.7%. Lin Yifu, *Jie Du*, pp. 12–13. McKinsey Global Institute arrived at a higher estimate of US$28 trillion by mid-2014, or 282% of GDP.

had publicly mentioned the need for deleveraging at the macro level. On the other hand, the stock market roller coaster in 2015 was followed by alarming capital flight, a readjustment of the foreign exchange ratio, and a fresh outburst of credit in 2016 leading up to the 19th Congress, where Xi eliminated term limits on the presidency and restructured the leadership.

Kang Chen sees in this a persisting strain between "policy preferences" and "revealed preferences," or between rhetoric and action. He points to three examples. First, while the policy preference, as announced by Xi Jinping as early as the 18th Party Congress, has been to shift from an obsession with high GDP growth rates to a "new normal" in which the quality of growth (including environmental considerations and above all deleveraging the debt) would eclipse the obsession with growth, the revealed preference is to try to do both, hoping that growth will pull the economy out of its debt trap, as it has in the past. But the growth rate has slowly declined since 2010, burdened by the high incremental capital output ratio. Whenever growth slips below the announced annual target range, however, the "revealed preference" has been to stimulate the economy with a fresh infusion of liquidity, stimulating growth while blowing the deficit back up.

The second policy preference is to give the market a "decisive role" in the allocation of resources. The revealed preference has however been for the Party to continue to play the decisive role in the allocation of resources. Simply allowing a market to function does not make China a market economy — feudalism also had markets — only when market logic becomes the fundamental organizing principle of the economy, to which the state must also defer, can we speak of a market system. But this undermines the authority of the Party. When the chips are down, politics (i.e., the Party) is in command, in Xi's "new era" as in the old one.

The third policy preference is to delegate authority downward and let the markets do their work, but as we have already seen, Xi Jinping's revealed preference since 2012 has been to centralize power under the aegis of the Party. It is believed that tight centralization will alleviate the insubordination, policy drift, corruption, and other dysfunctions attributed to market liberalization and thereby overcome the perceived "contradiction" between an authoritarian government and a free market economy.

What impact has economic reform had on the Chinese working population? The lot of the "proletariat," as *Marc Blecher* pithily sums up in Chapter 4, "improved absolutely, declined relatively, and became more uneven." Real wages rose appreciably (13%) from 1978 to 2015, after decades of zero growth during the Maoist decades — much of this was achieved during the first decade of reform (15%), improving more slowly thereafter. Because the marginal propensity to consume (MPC) tends to decline with income (in that the poor consume a larger proportion of their income), China's tax system has been in effect regressive. The 1994 fiscal reform enhanced revenue collection substantially, especially for the central government, but did not redistribute income, because the major innovation was a flat value-added tax on consumption. Thus, government expenditure has been China's default growth engine. Since the turn of the millennium the relative share of national income allocated to consumption declined from 60% to around 47% while investment increased to nearly 50%, one of the most austere such ratios ever seen anywhere. Since 2010 consumption has gradually returned to the previous ratio, though fixed asset investment still remains relatively high at 44%.[15]

China's Gini index — a statistical measure of inequality, from 0 (completely unequal) to 1 (completely equal) — rose steeply during the reform era (from 0.2 in the 1980s to around 0.5 since 2000) and remains high after taxes (i.e., net Gini is very close to gross Gini). The welfare net collapsed in the heyday of free market reforms and the decline of the *danwei* system in the 1980s and has remained weak. The government's budgeting for health, education and welfare ranks comparatively low internationally (even among developing countries), partly because these expenditures are left to the 31 local governments. The State Council released a document in 2013 promising to reduce

[15]Tracy Chen (2007). "Why China's consumers are hottest global economic force," *Bloomberg*, 29 December. Available at: https://www.bloombergquint.com/opinion/2017/12/28/why-china-s-consumers-are-hottest-global-economic-force.

income inequality through progressive taxation, but there has not been much follow-through. Still, since 2015 there has been no further increase in the Gini and even marginal decrease. Although unemployment doubled between 1990 and 2015, there is no visible homelessness in China (in stark contrast to the much richer United States). China's working population has not benefited in proportion to investment, but it has benefited absolutely. Moreover, Blecher finds that the old gap between the labor aristocracy of SOE workers and private or foreign-invested enterprise (FIE) sector workers has flattened, though the state still seems to assume greater responsibility for the former. The November 2017 Central Economic Work Conference ranked the elimination of poverty among China's top three developmental priorities for the next 3 years, though that will be a challenge after COVID-19, China announced in 2020 it had completely eliminated "absolute poverty," defined as income below 2,300 RMB per year (about US$335 or $1 per day, well below the World Bank standard of $1.90 per day).

Agricultural reform was the first major economic reform of the reform and opening era, and it has remained a top priority for the past 16 years, as indicated by its listing as the state's annual "No. 1, Central Document" (the first policy document released in the New Year, which is widely seen as an indicator of the Chinese Government's priorities). Echoing reforms briefly introduced in the wake of the Great Leap disaster, the key reform started spontaneously (and semi-clandestinely) in famine-ridden Anhui and Sichuan provinces before being officially endorsed by Deng Xiaoping in 1980 as the Household Responsibility System. This reform, leasing land to households and gradually relaxing what they could do with it, was important not only because of its immediate impact on agricultural productivity but because it provided a blueprint for China's subsequent economic system reforms in an era of experimental "stepping from stone to stone to cross the river" [*mozhe shitou guo he*].

Jane Du shows how these reforms have been continued, sometimes based on generalization of local experiments, more often introduced from the top down. Tens of millions of farms (still mostly small, under 2.5 acres in size) now produce food to feed one-fifth of the world's population on 7% of its arable land. At the same time, farmers were permitted to establish free farmers' markets in urban areas, and some families could operate as "specialized households," producing a scarce commodity or service on a profit-making basis. This expanded to a township and village enterprise (TVE) sector that soon began contributing up to 30% of national GDP. Less than 20% of China's labor force is now engaged in agriculture — sharply lower than in 1991, when over half the Chinese labor force farmed. The number of people experiencing extreme rural poverty fell from 250 million in 1978, to under 15 million by 2007, and by 2020 the goal is to eliminate rural poverty altogether. Du's focus here is on food security, which the government has been able to achieve sustainably by focusing on staple grain production. But reform continues — current problems include the degradation of farmland with excessive chemical fertilizers, dwindling water supply, and a growing income gap between rural and urban areas, a gap which appeared to be closing in the 1980s.

Given the relative but declining gains from modernization unequally distributed, one would expect a high incidence of popular dissent in China, and indeed that has been the case, as innovatively analyzed by *Martin Dimitrov*. (A "mass incident" he defines broadly as any "planned or impromptu gathering that forms because of internal contradictions," which can include public speeches or demonstrations, physical clashes, public airings of grievances, and other group behaviors that disrupt social stability.) The most dramatic protest since the Cultural Revolution was of course centered at (but by no means limited to) Tiananmen Square in Beijing in April–May 1989. This protest was suppressed on the night of June 3–4 with a conspicuous display of violence meant to have a demonstration effect against any such future protest (*xia ji jing hou* — kill the chicken to warn the monkey).

Indeed, the lesson has been learned: The Chinese plunged into the apolitical sea of commerce after 1989 and there has been no such nation-wide political protest since. But success has only been partial. As Dimitrov shows, the annual number of protests has grown steadily since the early 1990s, though these are relatively small, apolitical, and lack any "connective tissue" to adjoining protests. Based on the first systematic analysis of a nationwide dataset of over 65,000 protests from 2013 to 2016, Dimitrov finds that protests increased from 8,700 in 1993 to 180,000 in 2010. And contrary to theoretical expectations, although the more disruptive they are the more likely the protesters are to get what they want, these protests have not generally been seriously disruptive. The main reason has to do with the highly effective way the leadership has dealt with them. First, the leadership has made "stability" a public virtue transcending all others, the leading criterion for promotion of local officials, and public disturbance the most frequently cited crime warranting incarceration or house arrest. Second, based on *principiis obsta*, a vigilant leadership quickly classifies any incipient disturbance into one of several cases and applies appropriate contraceptive measures, severely punishing only those political incidents with potential contagious impact and using stern but less harsh sanctions on localized social incidents. Dimitrov tells us much new about the pattern of protest as well — they tend to congregate just before spring festival and they occur not in the poorest areas but predominantly in the more developed and wealthy regions along the south and east coast. Although far from routinized, for a "responsive authoritarian' regime protests have become an effective informal means of (negative) feedback and communication.

While the underlying cause of the proliferating protests is the stultification of formalized avenues for the communication of popular grievances (take for example the petition, which has become basically useless in this role), the regime is sensitive to the risk of blinding itself to the buildup of festering problems. As a prophylactic, it has introduced such expedients as the open government initiative (OGI), mandating local governments to publish a variety of indicators about its performance.[16] The purpose of this and other such tools is not participatory democracy *per se*, but enhancing the central government's ability to monitor and discipline unresponsive or corrupt local-level cadres. But from a functional perspective, informal low-level,

[16]See R. Stromseth, Edmund J. Malesky, and Dimitar D. Gueorguiev (2017). *China's Governance Puzzle: Enabling Transparency and Participation in a Single-Party State* (New York, Cambridge University Press).

small-scale protest has *faute de mieux* become a regular, if unpredictable, channel of political participation in China.

The chapter by *Rou-Lan Chen* and myself calls attention to the fact that China's economic growth has since the Great Leap Forward been strong but rather choppy, gradually falling into a cycle driven and steered imperfectly from the top by the state's fixed asset investment. Growth in fixed capital formation typically peaks every 5 years. Recent peaks occurred in 1978, 1984, 1988, 1993, 2003 and 2009. The corresponding troughs were in 1981, 1986, 1989, 1997 and 2005. Most investment is carried out by SOEs or by firms that are at least partially state-owned. Most of them are under the control of local governments. As their performance evaluations are heavily based on GDP growth within their jurisdictions, local cadres have a strong incentive to promote large-scale investment projects. Moreover, they face no real bankruptcy risk; if they get into trouble, the state will bail them out.

This political economic dynamic has long been observed but never statistically demonstrated. By testing and applying a sophisticated error-correction model (ECM), we are able to demonstrate a clear empirical connection between central fiscal and economic policy and local fixed asset investment decisions, and to illuminate the political and psychological mechanism whereby this is established. Between the motives of central-level management and local cadres, there is an elective affinity: the center needs to generate growth and political support from below, and local cadres need investment capital and opportunities for upward career mobility from above.

Especially since the tax-sharing fiscal reforms of 1994 and the elimination of local taxes in 2006, there has been a large budget gap for local cadres to fill, which they typically do by borrowing and investing in projects that will impress their patrons. A cycle typically begins with a relaxation of central government credit and industrial policy. This allows local governments to push investment aggressively, both through the SOEs they control directly and by offering investment-promotion incentives to local private investors and enterprises. The resulting boom puts upward pressure on prices and may also result in shortages of key inputs such as coal and electricity. Given cadre ambition to rise and the lack of hard budget constraints, it is very easy for this to result in overheating and industrial overcapacity.

During earlier periods, a boom tended to coincide with the rise of more liberal elite groupings who tolerated intellectual "blooming and contending" in cultural as well as economic dimensions while a bust would jibe with the rise of more conservative cadre factions inclined to crack down on such "chaotic" intellectual effervescence. Once inflation has risen to a level at which it begins to threaten social stability, the central government will intervene by tightening enforcement of industrial and credit policy, resulting in a bust. Thus, the boom–bust economic cycle often coincides with an opening–closing (*fang shou*) political cultural cycle, *ceteris paribus*. However, due to the intimidating demonstration effect of the Tiananmen crackdown and the subsequent purge of radical reformers, the *fang-shou* cycle seems to have been effectively subdued, at least for the time being.

Though protests have not ended altogether, they have been downsized, depoliticized and dispersed. Investment driven boom–bust economic cycles continue, though they are less choppy and no longer entangled with elite factional disputes. Moreover, though they may also be precipitated by exogenous disturbances such as the GFC, they are more typically synchronized with the 5-year schedule of central Party conferences (N.B., beginning 1 year *after* each conference). One of the new and interesting findings of this chapter is that top-down fiscal and monetary policy guidance is increasingly counterbalanced by a resistant autonomous market momentum, which can still be overcome politically but with ever increasing difficulty.

While our model explains cyclical variation, there may also be one-off events and longer-term trends. Thus while fixed-asset investment has been unusually high since the GFC, declining gradually after 2011 (excepting 2016), the system has been burdened by very high national debt. The same cyclical dynamics apply, but the government no longer has as much fiscal ammunition to apply stimulus. This would imply a "smoothing out" somewhat of the peaks and valleys of the model on the one hand, but also a much more fragile economy if hit by financial crisis or external shock (e.g., Trump's trade war), on the other.

2. China's Place in the World

The rise of Deng Xiaoping and his "reform and opening" policy focused squarely on the economic development as the political *summum bonum*, quietly scrapping "politics in command." One of his boldest innovations was to conceive of "opening to the outside world" not as an invitation to naked capitalist exploitation (as it had been deemed in the Maoist era), but as a potentially valued contributor to China's economic growth. And indeed, as domestic economic growth took off with marketization in the early 1980s, China's opening to the outside world accelerated even more swiftly, enabling the leadership to shift from revolutionary ideology to economic performance as the prime legitimation for continued CCP dictatorship.[17] In 1978, China was ranked 32nd in the world in export volume, while by 1989, it had become the 13th largest exporter.

Although Deng's business model faltered at Tiananmen and trade and growth both plummeted, Deng's reaffirmation of reform in his 1992 "southern voyage" was highlighted by still wider opening (e.g., more generous terms for foreign investors) and an upsurge of foreign trade (particularly after China's entry into the World Trade Organization (WTO) in late 2001). Between 1978 and 1990, the average annual rate of trade expansion was above 15%, substantially above GDP growth, continuing for the next decade. In 1978, China's exports were only 2% of world market share, but by 2010, China had a world market share of 10.4% according to the WTO, and China overtook the US as the world's largest trader (in goods). In 1996, China allowed free convertibility of the RMB through the current (not the capital) account. While the economy has grown somewhat

---

[17]This opening was somewhat exaggerated in early reports, which viewed China's exports as having bounded from 20% of GDP in 2001 to nearly 40% by 2007. Nevertheless, a recent recomputation by Jonathan Anderson found that exports have indeed risen (the headline exports-to-GDP ratio has almost doubled since 2000), though the main contributor to GDP is investment, not exports. "An Old Chinese Myth," *The Economist*, 3 January 2008. Available at: https://www.economist.com/node/10429271.

less trade-dependent since the GFC, (trade dependency was 65.2% in 2006, dropping to 41.5% in 2014), exports as of 2019 still contribute around 20% of GDP.

Trade was followed, especially since 1993, by an opening to foreign direct investment (FDI). Since 1978, China has had two economies: a domestic economy dominated by SOEs, and an export economy along the eastern seaboard dominated by private and foreign-invested firms'. The opening to FDI was not uncontested, given China's national narrative of a "century of humiliation" and three decades of stress on "self-reliance." There has historically been an ambivalent relationship between foreign investors and host governments in which the former strive to maximize profits with little consideration for indigenous interests, as classically described in the Leninist model of imperialism. China has in this context been a global innovator, inviting but guiding foreign investors to contribute to domestic modernization on Chinese terms.

The regime began with four carefully isolated special economic zones (SEZs) in the southeast, adjacent to Hong Kong and Taiwan, in 1979, and these succeeded beyond expectations, creating a bandwagon effect. In the mid-1980s, 14 coastal open cities (COCs) were entitled to set up their own economic and technological development zones (ETDZs); followed in 1992–1993 by 18 additional ETDZs, a third group of 22 in 2000–2002, and finally by the open coastal belt (OCB). Initially attracted by the prospect of evading still relatively high Chinese import barriers to produce for the world's biggest potential consumer market, investors found market access restricted by various informal barriers and consequently opted to produce for export, taking advantage of a well-disciplined and relatively cheap labor force to become globally price competitive. Even so, the attractions of the legendary China market have made the PRC a leading FDI recipient since the early 1990s. In 1990, China became the world's leading destination of FDI and it has been among the top three since 2008, with total inward foreign investment of US$126 billion in 2016. But the growth rate has been choppy since the GFC. Incoming FDI growth has generally leveled off since 2011 and declined in 2016, especially from the developed economies.

Why? For its part, China has grown wary of international market vicissitudes and somewhat more selective about FDI since the GFC. Aside from the risk of political cultural contamination, China does not derive as much profit from foreign-invested firms or from participating in global value chains as it thinks it should (e.g., only about 5% of the profit for assembling Apple smartphones stays in China). China today prefers to nurture its own "national champions," particularly since Xi Jinping in 2015 introduced "Made in China 2025," a 10-year plan specifying 10 industries that China wants to compete in by 2025 and become globally dominant in during the first half of this century.[18] Xi wants these firms to be both innovative and technologically self-reliant. Therefore, China privileges those investments that fit its industrial policy and often stipulates sharing technology in joint venture agreements.

Waning Chinese interest in FDI coincides with a cooling of enthusiasm among foreign investors. Multinational investors have complained of China's slowing GDP growth rate, climbing wage rates, locally biased legal regime, and weak property rights, causing many to seek greener fields elsewhere. From the perspective of capitalist investor states, the offshoring of capital has become disadvantageous in terms of the loss of employment and technology, and some developed countries have striven to reduce both the trade deficit and the FDI that helps engender it and induce firms to "reshore." In recent years, FDI has accounted for only about 2.5% of China's gross capital formation and FIEs have supplied just 0.5% of fixed asset investment. And yet, despite the shift of focus to the development of indigenous technology, any steep decline of FDI would be viewed as

[18]The 10 industries are: Robotics, new-energy vehicles, biotechnology, aerospace, high-end shipping, advanced rail equipment, electric power equipment, new materials (such as those used in screens and solar cells), and new generation information technology and software (including integrated circuits and telecommunications devices), as well as agricultural machinery. There is also a separate development strategy for Artificial Intelligence, published in 2017; China aims to become the world's primary AI innovation center by 2030. "How 'Made in China 2025' Frames Trump's Trade Threats," *Bloomberg News*, 10 April 2018. Available at: https://www.bloomberg.com/news/articles/2018-04-10/how-made-in-china-2025-frames-trump-s-trade-threats-quicktake.

worrisome. FIEs are currently responsible for just under 50% of China's exports and more than 50% of its imports, they generate more than 20% of sales, employment, and value-added in China's industrial sector, and in some advanced areas — such as computers, autos, and chemicals — the percentages are even higher. Since 2015 China has hence been revising its regulatory framework to improve the foreign investment climate and in 2019 passed a new foreign investment law.[19] According to statistics from the Ministry of Commerce, 35,000 new foreign-invested companies were founded in 2017, an increase of 27.8% since 2016.

Since 2014, China's Outward Foreign Direct Investment (COFDI) has exceeded incoming. This was an important watershed politically, shifting China from a passive to an active role in the global economic arena, from *taoguang yanghui* to *fenfa youwei*. It has also excited questions about China's "grand strategy," for while incoming FDI (or IFDI) can change China, COFDI could change the global landscape, possibly to China's advantage. In a rare empirical investigation of China's strategic intentions, *Shaun Breslin* finds a considerable variety of views, ranging from a denial of any grand strategy at all to boldly ambitious conceptualizations. It seems that China's grand strategy is easy to describe but hard to accomplish: it is to realize the "great national rejuvenation" and the "China Dream," in the high-flown rhetoric of Xi Jinping. Like Donald Trump, Xi Jinping wants China to be great. While the nation can enthusiastically unite around this goal, there is diversity about what exactly "great" means and how best to achieve it, and there is of course a tendency to smuggle local ambitions into the grand strategy. Thus, China's strategy can be disaggregated into policy nuances accommodating provincial/regional, ministerial, or industrial interests, and advertised abroad in a way that emphasizes transnational "win–win" deals.

Although COFDI was first endorsed by the CCP leadership in the 1999 call to "go out" [*zou chuqu*], the real takeoff had to wait until environmental conditions were propitious. Beginning in 2001 with its

[19]In May 2018, the State Council announced that from June 30 foreign-invested businesses will be able to register on a central website by filling out just one form.

entrance to the WTO, China's export boom began generating what soon became the world's biggest foreign exchange surplus, capital that could not easily be used domestically without incurring inflation. So COFDI took off in the late 2000s, particularly during the GFC, ironically, though not in any strategically consistent direction. From 2002 to 2016, COFDI increased by ca. 35.8% annually, according to Breslin, rising from 25th in the world to sixth in terms of annual investment. Over half of it was however destined for Hong Kong, the British Virgin Isles and the Cayman Islands, leading to speculation that much of it was "round tripping" back to China to avoid taxes or take advantage of FDI incentives. Much of the rest at this stage was used to invest in equity stakes in energy sources, mines or other raw materials in the developing world.

Beginning around 2015, COFDI however shifted direction from the developing to the developed world. Investment in the 28 EU countries jumped from US$850 million to $36 billion, four times direct European investment in China for that year (and by the end of 2017, the cumulative stock of Chinese investment in Europe since 2000 had surpassed cumulative European investment in China). The headline reason for this was the drive to acquire advanced technology coincident with the 2015 advent of "China 2025," but other considerations also played their part, e.g., the devaluation of the RMB and the stock market gyrations prompted some to use *zou chuqu* as a cover for capital flight. Chinese authorities hence responded with a tightening of capital controls. This, plus ratcheting security concerns in the US and to a lesser extent the EU, precipitated a sharp drop in COFDI in 2017 and a still sharper drop in 2018–2019. China has, since the GFC, also increasingly resorted to economic statecraft to underscore diplomatic points, but this seems more oriented to defending national dignity than pursuit of any strategic power play. Breslin sagely concludes that if China has any political economic grand strategy, it is highly adaptable to circumstantial and temporal exigencies.

Through decades of explosive economic growth, China continued to restrict the cross-border use of the renminbi (RMB) or yuan. Prior to 2004, RMB-denominated trading was prohibited outside mainland China. In the wake of the GFC, an international financial disaster that China attributed to inept American stewardship of the international financial system, China suggested that the United States dollar be replaced by a new international currency. This proposal fell on deaf ears, so China has proceeded to internationalize the RMB. The Chinese government made that a stated policy goal in the 12th FYP (2010). A more widely used currency was conceived to accelerate the pace of reform, as *Barry Eichengreen* notes. It would also enhance China's international prestige (the "great power" factor), give it greater influence in setting prices of commodity imports from oil to iron ore, and reduce the country's vulnerability to the idiosyncratic rise and fall of the dollar. Establishing the RMB as a settlement and investment currency would be the first step, an easier process than making it an international reserve currency. Trade settlement is based on contractual arrangements allocating currency fluctuation risks and administrative costs between the parties, while investments are determined by the profitability of financial products denominated in the currency at issue. RMB trade settlements thus proliferated since 2009 in correlation with China's growing international trade and the increasing purchasing power of Chinese firms.

The first step was to free companies and individuals to hold RMB deposits in Hong Kong, still the largest center for offshore RMB deposits, followed by Singapore, Taipei, London, Frankfurt, Johannesburg, Sydney, and finally New York. Overseas RMB holders were granted access to RMB-denominated securities through the Renminbi Qualified Foreign Institutional Investors program and other cross-border trading links. The People's Bank of China struck RMB swap agreements with Russia and many other trading partners. From the beginning of 2010 to the end of 2012, total RMB deposits in Hong Kong rose from 64 billion RMB (US$10.2 billion) to 589 billion RMB and on to an all-time high of 1 trillion RMB 2 years later. The accumulation of RMB in Hong Kong came at the relative expense of deposits of US dollars, as US dollar deposits earned little to no interest, while the RMB from 2010 through to mid-2015 paid interest of a few percentage points and seemed almost guaranteed to continue appreciating against the

US dollar. By 2015, the RMB had expanded to become the fifth most used currency globally for international payments.

Then came the summer of 2015. With the RMB at an all-time high against the dollar, the People's Bank of China (PBOC), without warning, pushed the RMB down by more than 3% over three days. Why? The PBC liberalized its external accounts and domestic financial markets in concert with its attempt to convince the IMF that the RMB was freely usable. The IMF did so determine, despite China's not meeting the usual criteria, and the RMB joined the US dollar, the Euro, the yen, and the pound sterling in its special drawing rights (SDRs) basket in October 2016. But RMB liberalization proved premature and unsustainable. The PBOC's intervention precipitated capital flight of nearly a trillion RMB. In December 2017, the State Administration of Foreign Exchange (SAFE) curtailed the movement of capital abroad, and COFDI also declined. Zhou Xiaoquan retired as head of the PBOC at the 19th CCP Congress, and China's interest in currency internationalization seems to have cooled since. Offshore liquidity in Hong Kong has been reined in by Chinese authorities who want the benefits of market price discovery but prefer to avoid the accompanying volatility. Rather than herald a new era of openness for the currency, inclusion in the IMF's SDR basket marked a high point from which Beijing has slowly and quietly retreated.

Since then, capital controls remain broad and largely effective. The massive currency outflows seen after the 2015 mini-devaluation have abated, but according to the latest data from SWIFT, the global share of RMB in international payments has fallen to 1% (vs. 41% for US dollar and 39% for Euro), and more than 70% of that 1% share are transactions occurring in Hong Kong as financial intermediary. RMB reserves remain relatively low at this point compared to the US dollar and the Euro. These are projected to increase as the RMB becomes more commonly used. If the Belt and Road Initiative (BRI) really takes off, there should be opportunities ahead (although most of the projects to date are to be paid in US dollars).

Despite capital controls, financial repression and a state-owned banking system, China has made incredible progress. But a reserve currency requires a large, diverse and free capital market, and China will need more time and domestic reform to create such a market. Eichengreen concludes not that the quest for currency internationalization is over, but that its use as a Trojan horse for domestic economic reform is misconceived — that it would be better to pursue the latter first, or both in tandem.

Scott Kastner's chapter, aptly punned "purchasing power," is focused on how China translates financial power into political power. The narrative of China's foreign economic policy is bimodal: "one story emphasizes a liberalizing China that has taken world markets and economic institutions by storm, and indeed allows markets to constitute a primary actor," as Margaret Pearson observes. "The second story centers on the Chinese state as the central actor, and tells of its attempt to control the globalization process and achieve empowerment through it." The second story was less salient in the early *tao guang yang hui* period, particularly during post-Tiananmen international pariah period, as the regime prioritized domestic economic modernization and tried to appease or befriend anyone useful to that end. China was sometimes deemed a "free rider" but not a serious threat.

Beginning around 2010 when it overtook Japan, China's international economic position began to change. China had become the largest exporter and second largest economy in the world, and began demanding a commensurate position in global political and economic institutions and pushing outward to seize control of its geographic periphery. It has employed the tools of economic statecraft to exert pressure on Norway, the Philippines, Japan, and most recently Korea.

But how successful has it actually been? Kastner provides a systematic attempt to measure that impact. On the issue that China ranks its core priority, that of asserting nominal sovereignty — over Taiwan, Tibet, Xinjiang — it has been very successful indeed. All but 15 nations in a world of nearly 200 have severed diplomatic relations with Taiwan (as of 2020); only about one country in the world dares sell weapons to Taiwan, which is effectively barred not only from membership in international governmental organizations (IGO) with statehood as a prerequisite but from many of those without such a prerequisite. Xinjiang's Muslim population has been fireproofed against the liberation of adjoining central Asian nations by the advent of the Shanghai Cooperation Organization. The Dalai Lama is rarely accorded state visits anywhere anymore. In the United Nations, China has effectively defanged the UN Human Rights Commission after it approved an embarrassing December 1989 resolution recommending "clemency" to Tiananmen victims (denounced by the Chinese representative as "brutal interference" in China's internal affairs). But it could be argued that though these issues may be "core" to China, they are peripheral to other countries, which are hence apt to concede them. However, Kastner finds that on issues core to their own national interests, they are less easily persuaded by China's demands. Yet even in these cases, China has been skilled in turning the asymmetry around: focusing not on the foreign state but on the firm, which may be quite happy to drop "Taiwan" from its map in exchange for a Chinese market share. Even as China has become the most important trade partner of most countries in Asia, with a positive trade balance with most of them, political relations have run the gamut from highly favorable (Cambodia, Laos) to sharply negative (Japan, Taiwan). China's economic statecraft engenders puzzlingly diverse political outcomes.

Relations between China and the European Union (EU) were established in 1975. The EU is China's largest trading partner, and China is the EU's second largest trade partner after the United States. The Europeans and Chinese alike were excited by the prospects for cooperation upon the inauguration of "reform and opening" in the early 1980s, and EU–Chinese trade increased faster than the Chinese economy itself, tripling in 10 years from US$14.3 billion in 1985 to US$45.6 billion in 1994. Yet it has remained, in *Jonathan Holslag's* terms, "an unbalanced partnership." From China's perspective, the EU represents a tantalizing double opportunity. As a united bloc, it represents a useful counterweight to the US in the global power balance, while as a still loosely integrated federation it offers alternative avenues for markets and influence. China's attempts to mobilize Brussels against Washington have however proved frustrating, as trans-Atlantic ties are historically deep and this cradle of Western values remains committed to them. To Beijing's bitter disappointment, Brussels and Washington continue to block China's aspirations for "market economy status" as a trading entity and have upheld a weapons embargo on the sale of advanced military technology on human rights grounds ever since 1989. Attempts at coalition building with the EU have also been complicated by Russian initiatives since the Cold War to regain influence in Eastern Europe, particularly among former constituent republics of the USSR. These have created a cleavage with the EU, forcing China to take sides.

Yet, Europe's incomplete integration offers alternative avenues for cooperation through individual states or subregional sets of states, such as the Visegrad V4 (Czechia, Poland, Slovakia, Hungary) or the 17+1 group (both now meet with China on an annual basis).[20] Here China's goals are mainly economic, i.e., to procure consumers, resources, and technology.

It views the relation between federal and subregional Europe as a useful wedge issue, and has for example recently used BRI funding of infrastructure projects in Eastern Europe to block unfriendly EU moves (on the Muslim reeducation camps in Xinjiang, for example). Europe's corresponding goals are likewise mostly economic, not for technology or even resources but for reciprocal access to the potentially huge China market. On this behalf, the Europeans have been willing to invest and even to share technology. Here the European quest has been for an economically level-playing field. Hence, system differences come into play. The EU is constitutionally committed to democracy and human rights, but the two sides have implicitly agreed to shelve such concerns (i.e., consign them to a politically impotent "EU–China human rights dialogue") in the interest of pursuing cooperative economic ventures and in accord with the Westphalian taboo on interference in internal affairs. In the course of economic cooperation, these differences however tend to bubble back to the surface. China enjoys a large trade surplus with Europe (though not

[20]The 17 are: Hungary, Bulgaria, Romania, Poland, Bosnia and Herzegovina, Serbia, Croatia, Slovakia, Slovenia, Albania, Macedonia, Montenegro, Czechia, Lithuania, Latvia, Estonia, and Greece.

as large as with the US), which the Europeans attribute to a systematic repression of consumption that would be impossible under democracy and accuse Beijing of violating the "rules-based international order." European complaints have been amplified since the advent of "China 2025," China's attempt to leapfrog to global technological leadership. Political system differences underlie European complaints of a lack of reciprocity, in that China can come into European markets and buy factories, but that would never be possible for Europeans to do in China. At the same time, European invested enterprises in China complain of IPR violations, judicial bias, discriminatory prosecution, and a host of policies making it difficult for them to compete. The Chinese respond, pointing out that FIEs are treated no differently than indigenous private firms, the two systems are simply different.

Xi Jinping introduced "one belt, one road" (OBOR) later rechristened the "belt and road initiative" (BRI) in 2013 in speeches in Kazakhstan and Australia; it is his signature foreign political economic policy initiative and Beijing has since given it very generous financial support and a full-bore international publicity blitz. As *Dalton Lin* shows in his wide-ranging chapter, this visionary project functions both as a domestic program to stimulate development in China's underdeveloped interior regions and a geostrategic design to lay claim to the vast and potentially rich region on China's periphery, not necessarily by claiming territorial sovereignty (as in the South China Sea), but by establishing a dominant Chinese economic presence. To legitimize the scheme, Beijing has revived a legendary historical name dating from the Han dynasty, referring to a network of trade routes from China through Central Asia to the Occident. The current edition consists of six main corridors, mainly the land route through Central Asia (Silk Road Economic Belt) and the maritime route though southeast and south Asian waters (Maritime Silk Road) with the recent addition of a polar route through the Arctic. According to Beijing, the BRI project will impact 4.4 billion people in 65 countries with an economic output of $21 trillion — two-thirds of the world's population, 50% of its GDP, and 75% of known global energy reserves (on imports of which Chinese industrial policy is increasingly dependent).

As of August 2018, over 70 countries had signed cooperation agreements or MOUs with China on various segments of the BRI. China has also signed industrial capacity cooperation agreements with over 20 countries. According to the World Bank, China had by July 2016 already invested $51.1 billion in various BRI infrastructure megaprojects. Officials boast that there are up to 900 deals under way, worth $890 billion, such as the 3,000-km high-speed rail from Kunming to Singapore. To fund this vast project, Beijing provides several financial instruments. The China Development Bank (CDB) is capitalized at $32 billion, the Export Import Bank of China (EXIM) will take on $30 billion, and Beijing will also pump additional capital into the Agricultural Development Bank of China (ADBC), altogether totaling some $62 billion. A $46 billion fund (subsequently increased to $55 billion) will underwrite the China–Pakistan Economic Corridor (CPEC). Funding will also be provided via two new multilateral banking projects, the Asian Infrastructure Investment Bank (AIIB), to which China has committed at least $50 billion toward a projected total of $100 billion, and the BRICS bank or New Development Bank (NDB), which also aims for a $100 billion currency reserve pool. While the BRICS bank is limited to BRICS countries (Brazil, Russia, India, China and South Africa), others were invited to join AIIB and, after a year's hesitation, some 57 founding members jumped in immediately, including 12 NATO members. Beijing will not have formal veto power, but China holds a 30.34% stake in the bank and the articles of agreement require 75% support for major policy decisions.[21] All Chinese funding ultimately derives from its foreign exchange reserves, currently totaling slightly more than US$3 trillion, but China has also encouraged other countries to contribute.

As might be anticipated, such a vast scheme has raised many questions. Over 95% of the projects are awarded to Chinese firms, financed by Chinese banks with Chinese labor crews (which may then remain

---

[21] Li Su, Huang Jiangnan, and Zhao Gang (2015). *Xi Jinping jingjixue di wu hang guoce yushi da guoli* [Xi Jinping's Economics Five National Policies and Ten National Powers] (Hong Kong: Xing hui tu shu you xian gong si).

in country); and China prefers if possible to retain a long-term controlling interest in project commercial infrastructure. These are awarded through opaque bilateral negotiations, usually without competitive bidding. Chinese investments in ASEAN have tended to have relatively low spillover effects (e.g., transfer of skills or technology) on local economies compared to Japanese and South Korean investments. One of the problems China confronts is how to achieve "mutuality," as BRI clients typically receive only announcements flowing downward of Beijing's intentions. Current and proposed "exchanges" have also been largely Sinocentric ("one belt, one way"). Chinese news articles about the initiative highlight other countries' interest in learning from China. Most of China's investment in international education goes to providing scholarships for students from BRI countries to study in China, or in support of Chinese study programs abroad. The separate deals are negotiated bilaterally with "no strings attached" which is highly attractive. Interest rates seem to vary depending on the temperature of the bilateral relationship, but most of the loans to the least developed countries have been commercial. Aside from the risk of moral hazard, there is the peril of losing the new asset as collateral to unsustainable indebtedness ("one belt, one trap"), at which point the project becomes collateral to be appropriated by the lender. China has adequate capital to finance this enormous scheme, but the ability of recipient countries, many in fragile financial straits to begin with, to absorb the loans is often thin, leaving them in a "debt trap." The Hambantota port in Sri Lanka was financed by Chinese loans that could not be repaid, forcing Colombo to enter a debt for equity swap leasing the facility for 99 years (renewable). In neighboring Laos, China accounted for over 40% of Laos' public external debt as of 2015, up from 35% in 2012, pushed up by debt service payments on infrastructure and power investments like the China–Laos railway, stretching (when finished, work started in 2015) 257 miles from the Chinese border to Vientiane, 70% of it through tunnels and bridges (at a cost of over half the country's \$10.5 billion 2015 GDP). Beijing accounts for the largest proportion of foreign investment in Cambodia and about 43% of the country's total debt stock, mainly in the form of loans from the CDB to

Cambodia's government. Anecdotal evidence as well as careful econometric analysis testifies that these investments could potentially improve the economic prospects of the recipients in many cases, despite cited examples of white elephant projects unable to raise sufficient revenue to cover investment costs.[22] Some projects (in Nepal, Pakistan, Thailand, Myanmar, Hungary, Tanzania) have since been canceled or renegotiated due to recipient complaints. To be sure, although this is not an eleemosynary project, and Chinese SOEs and banks have sometimes perhaps been greedy, the recipients must also bear major responsibility for not exercising due diligence in these deals.

A third problem is growing caution on the part of over-leveraged Chinese lending institutions. The neocolonial composition of bilateral trade (raw material exports vs. manufactured imports from China) that must be expedited to pay for these investments is conducive to a "natural resource curse," trapping these economies at a primary stage of economic development. Finally, there is the issue of to what extent this massive undertaking, despite Chinese insistence that it is purely economic and developmental, will entail the extension of a network of Chinese military interests. This would be natural in the sense that some of the investments are in relatively troubled regions and have already sustained casualties: The China-contracted port on Gwadar is in Balochistan, for example, which has already seen Chinese casualties, and PLA troops have been dispatched to reinforce Pakistani forces guarding the CPEC now under construction from Gwadar to

[22] See Chien-peng Chung and Thomas J. Voon (2017). "China's Maritime Silk Road Initiative," *Asian Survey*, 57 (3), 416–449. China was the world's biggest trading nation and the leading trade partner of over 130 countries in the world (and 16 Asian countries). Between 2004 and 2013, China's overseas investments increased 13.7 times, from $45 billion to $613 billion (about 10% of global OFDI flows). In 1990, the Chinese economy constituted less than 1% of the global economy, while by 2017 that number had surpassed 16% (meanwhile the US economy dropped from 26% to 24%). In 2007, the United States' economy was four times as large as that of China; by 2012, it was but twice as large (and today, less than that). The US share of global high-tech exports has fallen from just below 20% in 1999 to barely over 5% in 2014, while China's share has risen from 3% to 26% during the same period.

Kashgar. Chinese-built ports are typically "dual use," and the Indian navy has already noticed Chinese submarines patrolling the Indian Ocean and making port calls to Hambantota.

3. Conclusions

The reform and opening period marked a major historical departure from the Maoist period, but even the reform period has seen significant changes. China is a socialist dictatorship under the rule of the CCP and means to stay that way, yet the world is constantly changing and the CCP reserves the right to interpret socialism in the light of the shifting balance of forces. What seems to be meant by "socialism" is government for (on behalf of, not by) the people — to provide a common defense, to ensure successful economic development and inspire faith in a bright future, in Xi Jinping's terms to realize "great national rejuvenation" and the "Chinese dream." In a time of domestic and international turmoil unmatched since the Cultural Revolution, even social stability, the minimal prerequisite for the transcontinental ambitions of the belt and road, has been hard to ensure. The essence of China in this "new era" is to be found only beneath its many facets, as they emerge under constantly changing circumstances. China is now bigger, more modern, more powerful, and more economically important to the rest of the world than it has been since the late 18th century, and yet it also has significant weaknesses that call into question whether the self-confident face that Xi presents is most appropriate for its current stage of development.

In their separate chapters, Gang Chen has outlined the structure and ongoing reform of the central state-owned enterprise (SOE), the cornerstone of the Party-led economy. The SOEs are declining in number but increasing in size in order more effectively to succeed in an increasingly competitive global marketplace. But the dominant organizing trend here is not market logic sweeping up from the grassroots, but the command logic of the Party's regulatory and supervisory networks descending from the Party Center. The Party must control the economy to ensure that it serves the people's interests. As a former centrally planned economy defined by its telos, the far-seeing

Party still makes plans. Yet, China lives in a capitalist world in which the market rules the global economy, and the tumultuous American market has considerable influence on the world market. The American-sponsored GFC required Chinese improvization that saved it from a single year of recession but engulfed it in public debt, which has continued to escalate faster than GDP growth. It is far from unique in this. The leadership is currently attempting to deleverage while at the same time keeping the domestic market under control and retaining a minimal 6% growth rate that will enable it to double 2010 GDP by 2020. This goal now seems likely to be postponed by at least a year, thanks to the COVID pandemic.

The status of the industrial work force in China has improved absolutely, declined relatively and become more uneven, as Marc Blecher puts it. The redistributive apparatus and social welfare net in China have suffered from the departure from Maoism, despite the absolute rise in living standards, as China's Gini index has escalated considerably. Even so, outright poverty has been reduced by several hundred million. China's revolutionary legacy survives in the form of continuing ideals of equality and political integrity. These ideals manifest themselves in increasing protests throughout the land, but these are localized, depoliticized, and small, and the regime has evolved effective non-lethal policing techniques to suppress (and sometimes accommodate) them. While China is not a liberal Western pluralist democracy, it is a managed democracy with a single national Party and a hierarchy of legislative assemblies filled by regular one-party elections, and we find the political business cycle to have become synchronized with their 5-year recurrence.

China's foreign economic policy is defined by a combination of goals, threats, and resources. Xi Jinping's goals are not just to achieve the "China dream" domestically, but include foreign policy goals unmatched in their sweep since the Mao era. Xi's goals for China include expanding China's sphere of influence to include a defensible territorial periphery or "buffer" extending into the Pacific as well as becoming the dominant power in Asia and the developing world, hence at the very least a "pole" in a multipolar world. That means becoming a leader in international economic and political institutions — both extant IGOs such as the UN and those established by the PRC. It means setting rules and standards, both economic and technical, as exemplified by China's interpretation of WTO rules, or the current fight for 5G dominance. China would prefer to do so peaceably, with minimal domestic adjustment, while cultivating a broad international network of supporters, but does not preclude the calculated use of sub-threshold force. China still feels itself faced with stubborn resistance from Japan, Taiwan, India, the faithless waywardness of the Southeast Asian or Central Asian periphery, and the annoying opposition to its rise from the unipolar hegemon, which employs the delusional "China threat" theory to enveigle smaller countries into strategic encirclement and containment. China has reconciled itself to a future of relentless struggle.

There is not yet any clear consensus on a detailed "grand strategy" outlining how China means to assemble its available resources to achieve its goals and deter its threats. However, a number of plausible repertoires have made their appearance, which the CCP leadership appears to be in the process of testing out. One is the internationalization of the Chinese currency, stealing the "exorbitant privilege" of serving as international reserve currency from a hegemon that has clearly squandered its custodial rights. This, the Chinese believe would at least shield them from the vicissitudes of an erratic US monetary policy and optimally enhance China's global prestige and financial power. Moving in this direction might however require liberalizing the capital account and floating the RMB exchange rate, exposing the Chinese financial system to the chaotic loss of control that they attribute to Western casino capitalism. Still unclear is how to secure the exorbitant privilege without exposing themselves to its risks.

Scott Kastner provides a fascinating tour through the mechanisms of transforming money into power, with which China has just begun to experiment (never having had so much money before), including consumer boycotts, informal trade barriers and sanctions, the manipulation of tourism, and export embargos. Some of these power plays seem to have been effective, but there are also instances of unintended consequences and backwash effects (e.g., the 1995–1996 Taiwan Strait missile crisis, the Sino-American trade war). An outstanding case study of political economic pressure tactics in Europe is provided in Jonathan Holslag's chapter. The economic relationship between these two giants has thrived and economic relations appear to be reasonably good. But attempts to translate economics into political influence have been frustrating on either side.

If the PRC has no coherent grand political-economic strategy as yet, surely the BRI comes close to that. It promises to bring the entire geographic periphery, including much of the global South, into the Chinese economic orbit, offering loans and investments for sorely needed infrastructure that will put clients' budgets into economic thrall to China for decades to come. And the BRI is well tailored to China's available resources: A US$3 trillion foreign exchange cache that cannot easily be used domestically, China's world class infrastructure engineering capabilities, and the overcapacity of steel and concrete manufactured during the post-GFC domestic infrastructure building spree financed by the stimulus. Finally, it will also facilitate the development of China's underdeveloped and minority populated far western regions, from Yunnan to Xinjiang. Despite some missteps due to imperfect coordination of the ambitious SOEs it has unleashed, Beijing has demonstrated the capability to adapt to straitening international conditions while maintaining forward momentum.

Part II

Domestic Political Economy

https://doi.org/10.1142/9789811226588_0002

Chapter 2

Consolidating Leninist Control of State-Owned Enterprises: China's State Capitalism 2.0

Gang Chen

eaicg@nus.edu.sg

1. Introduction

The Chinese model of state capitalism has been prominently discussed in the study of the country's meteoric economic growth in the past three decades, of which a fascinating part is the miraculous rise of a large number of state-owned conglomerates that have aggressively expanded their shares of the global market.[1] Although economic

[1]Hon Chan (2009). "Politics over markets: integrating state-owned enterprises into Chinese socialist market," *Public Administration and Development*, 29: 43–54. Peter Nolan (2001). *China and the Global Economy* (Basingstoke: Palgrave). Louis Kuijs, William Mao, and Chunlin Zhang (2005). *SOE Dividends: How Much and to Whom?* (Washington, DC: World Bank). Neil Fligstein, and Jianjun Zhang (2011). "A new agenda for research on the trajectory of Chinese capitalism," *Management and*

reforms have led to significant expansion of the private sector in China, the strategic sectors of the economy, which include oil, electricity, telecommunications, shipping, aviation, steel and machinery manufacturing, are still dominated by a number of giant state-owned enterprises (SOEs). Some 40% of China's non-agricultural GDP is estimated to come from SOEs and entities directly controlled by SOEs. Despite the Party's insistence on controlling SOEs, the delicate Party–business relationship that affects corporate governance of SOEs went through a transition in the early 2000s ("State Capitalism I") from the state-run (*guoying*) stage to a decentralization process in which the Party-state controlled majority of shareholding and granted SOE executives more autonomy in running the SOEs. During this period, many SOEs became "national champions," or leading Chinese SOEs with strong international competitiveness in strategic sectors, including power generation, coal mining, automobiles, electronics, iron and steel, machinery, chemicals, construction, aerospace and pharmaceuticals.[2] The Party still exerted influence upon them through the nomenklatura system by which general managers of large SOEs were directly appointed by the Party's Central Organization Department, but most of time, the Party held a hands-off attitude towards daily operation and management of these SOEs.

Such decentralization on the one hand revitalized moribund SOEs into competitive conglomerates with soaring profitability and asset scales, while on the other hand, it exacerbated the long-lasting principal–agent dilemma facing SOE management and fostered an insider control problem[3] associated with mismanagement and lack of

---

Organization Review, 7(1): 39–62. Gang Chen (2015). "From mercantile strategy to domestic demand stimulation: Changes in China's solar PV subsidies," *Asia Pacific Business Review*, 21(1): 96–112.

[2] Kjeld Erik Brodsgaard (2012). "Politics and business group formation in China: The party in control?" *The China Quarterly*, 211: 628.

[3] Insider control is a phenomenon whereby controlling rights in organizational enterprises are legally or actually seized by management whose interests are then strongly represented in strategic corporate decision-making. See, for example, Masahiko Aoki, and Hyung-Ki Kim (1995). *Corporate Governance in Transitional Economies: Insider Control and the Role of Banks* (Washington, DC: The World Bank).

sufficient supervision. Under Xi Jinping's rein, the Party has hence been reinforcing Leninist control over SOE operations by intensifying the Party committees' role in corporate governance, regularizing the Party's disciplinary inspections of SOEs, and enhancing the functions of the Board of Supervisors, to forestall pervasive corruption and excessive speculation. In this period (state capitalism 2), the Party has transformed its indirect control of SOEs through personnel reshuffles into a more heavy-handed approach of directly interfering in decision-making and management of SOEs on a daily basis. The slogan for the SOE reform in state capitalism 2 has been "enhancing the Party's leadership over SOEs," which may have far-reaching implications upon regulatory dilemmas, corporate governance and endogenous challenges linked to China's enormous state businesses.

The COVID-19 outbreak was precisely a case in point that convinced the Party of its grip over SOEs, which could act as a buffer against internal economic shocks and external threats during disasters and crises. Since the 1980s the Party has enabled state businesses and private sectors to be increasingly engaged in disaster management. Over the years, commercial organizations, especially those state business juggernauts in insurance, contracted construction, transportation, energy, and agricultural produce, have emerged as non-negligible interest groups that constantly impose institutional pressures upon disaster policy formulation as well as pre- and post-disaster actions.[4] The Chinese government requested SOEs, especially those large-scale SOEs controlled by the central government (*yangqi*), to take active part in relief operations during the pandemic. Under disaster relief and other emergency circumstances, SOEs have played a significant role in carrying out public policy objectives. The enterprises under Party leadership and state ownership are formally justified by the government's need to overcome market failure in a wide range of areas including public service delivery and emergency responses.

---

[4]Gang Chen (2016). *The Politics of Disaster Management in China* (New York: Palgrave Macmillan), p. 98.

2. Reforming SOEs in the Stage of State Capitalism 1.0

Many SOEs used to be important components of the centralized economic planning system, focusing on heavy-industrial development. In the early 1980s, there were about 65 ministries in charge of economic planning and development, which included eight machine-building ministries and several energy ministries like the Ministry of Electricity, Ministry of Coal Mining and Ministry of Petroleum. In the 1980s, to separate government departments from commercial corporations with an intention to increase efficiency, almost all of these industry-focused ministries were abolished and a number of SOEs were set up to take over their economic functions.

The oil production, refining and investment functions of the Ministry of Petroleum and Ministry of Chemical Industry were gradually transferred to the three national oil companies (NOCs): China National Petroleum Corporation (CNPC), China Petroleum & Chemical Corporation (Sinopec) and China National Offshore Oil Corporation (CNOOC). The State Council set up the CNOOC in 1982 to cooperate with foreign investors in the exploitation of offshore oil and gas resources and CNOOC was soon given monopoly status in offshore oil and natural gas exploration. A year later, Sinopec, a spin-off from the downstream assets (refining and marketing) of the Ministry of Petroleum and the Ministry of Chemical Industry, was established.[5] In 1988, the central government disbanded the Ministry of Petroleum and established CNPC to handle all petroleum activities in China. The heads of some of these centrally administered SOEs like CNPC, Sinopec, State Grid Corp and Shenhua Group still hold ministerial rank. The general managers of these SOEs are directly appointed by the Party's Central Organization Department, some of whom are members of

[5]Erica Downs (2008). "Business interest groups in Chinese politics: The case of the oil companies," in Cheng Li (ed.), *China's Changing Political Landscape: Prospects for Democracy* (Washington, DC: Brookings Institution Press), p. 122.

the Party's powerful Central Committee, a political club of officials at ministerial or even higher ranks.

Through the revolving door mechanism manipulated by the Party's Central Organization Department, the chief executives of giant SOEs may be transferred to serve as governor or vice governor of a province, and the process is reversible. When China's economy was further integrated into the global market upon its accession to the World Trade Organization (WTO) in 2001, the central government decided to make many of these SOEs into "national champions," or internationally competitive large corporations in strategic sectors, including power generation, coal mining, automobiles, electronics, iron and steel, machinery, chemicals, construction, aerospace and pharmaceuticals.[6]

The government provided these SOEs with massive subsidies, low-interest loans and supportive policies in the hope that Chinese companies would create global brands that could enter the more profitable segments of global production chains. With the creation of the State-owned Assets Supervision and Administration Commission of the State Council (SASAC) in 2003, the central government refined its role as the public manager of the economy to represent the interest of the government as the prime "investor" and owner of these leading SOEs. It also formally adopted the strategy of "selection and concentration," hiving off and discarding non-core businesses and building strong, competitive firms around a few national champions.[7] The government's consistent support and reform turned state-owned mammoths from the country's debt-ridden factories into profit-making machines. From 2003 to 2014, the total revenue of SOEs (excluding state-owned financial enterprises) more than quadrupled from 10,734 billion yuan to 48,064 billion yuan; total profits also surged from 495.1 billion

[6]Kjeld Erik Brodsgaard (2012). "Politics and business group formation in China: The party in control?" *The China Quarterly*, 211: 628.

[7]Joo-Youn Jung (2008). "Retreat of the state? Restructuring the Chinese central bureaucracies in the era of economic globalization," *The China Review*, 8(1): 116–117.

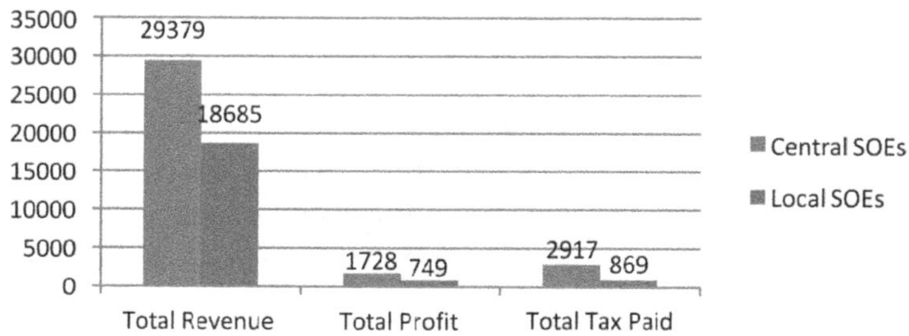

Figure 1: Revenues, profits and taxes of central and local SOEs (2014) (Billion yuan).

Source: SASAC website, "Performances of SOEs in 2014."

yuan to 2,476.5 billion yuan and tax contribution soared from 810.5 billion yuan to 3,786 billion yuan in the same period.[8]

Centrally controlled SOEs, most of which are national champions that have been favored by the central government, have an inherent edge over local SOEs in terms of scale, profit-making and tax contributions. In 2014, the total revenue, profit and tax contribution of central SOEs surpassed those of local SOEs by 57%, 131% and 236%, respectively (Figure 1).

3. Controversies over SOE Favoritism

The Chinese model of state capitalism has been prominently discussed in the study of the country's meteoric economic growth in the past two decades, of which a fascinating part is the massive policy support and subsidies of various forms conferred by the government to a wide range of state-owned industries that have aggressively expanded their shares in the global market.[9] The decade-long

[8]SASAC, "Performances of SOEs in 2014" (in Chinese), http://www.sasac.gov.cn/n86302/n326735/n326740/c1626339/content.htm, accessed 19 June 2015. Xin Li and Kjeld Erik Brodsgaard (2013). "SOE reform in China: Past present and future," *The Copenhagen Journal of Asian Studies*, 31(2): 58.

[9]See, for example, Usha Haley and George Haley (2013). *Subsidies to Chinese Industry: State Capitalism, Business Strategy, and Trade Policy* (New York: Oxford University Press) and Peter Nolan (2007). *Capitalism and Freedom: The Contradictory Character of Capitalist Globalization* (London: Anthem Press).

reform of once-moribund SOEs has successfully transformed many into globally competitive behemoths. The number of Chinese SOEs listed in the Global Fortune 500 rose from six in 2002 to 65 in 2012.[10]

However, the overexpansion of super SOEs has caused serious socioeconomic repercussions both domestically and internationally. The phrase *guojin mintui*, or "the state advances, the private sector retreats" as spawned by market proponents, best depicts the Chinese model of state capitalism, where SOEs have been competing with the domestic private sectors and foreign companies on an unequal footing. While the private sectors have difficulty accessing bank finance, SOEs have been favored by state-owned banks that often provide them with cheap credit and massive loans. The government also offers SOEs access to cheap land and undervalued natural resources.

According to a report by the Beijing-based Unirule Institute of Economics,[11] SOEs gain mostly from free use of nationally owned land and nationally owned natural resources that were extracted at very low prices, cheap loans and credit from state-owned banks and the government's fiscal subsidies. Without these policy benefits, except for the years 2006 and 2007, these Chinese SOEs were loss-makers in all the years from 2001 to 2009.

SOEs' huge profit also comes from their monopoly of certain lucrative industries that exclude the private sectors. Sectors like petrochemical, telecom, hydropower generation, railway transport and oceanic shipping are oligopolized by a few SOEs. Even for deregulated industries like shipbuilding, real estate, coal mining, automotive and food processing, SOEs are getting larger market share due to their backing from government and state-owned banks.

For example, in the past few years, the overheated property market attracted a large number of centrally administered SOEs to

---

[10] Xin Li and Kjeld Erik Brodsgaard (2013). "SOE reform in China: Past, present and future," *The Copenhagen Journal of Asian Studies*, 31(2): 59.

[11] Unirule Institute of Economics report (2011). *The Nature, Performance, and Reform of the State-owned Enterprises*. Beijing. Available at: http://www.unirule.org.cn/xiazai/2011/20110412.pdf, accessed 19 June 2015.

buy up land at record-setting prices in China. The most expensive piece of land sold at auction is called the "land king." In the second half of 2012, state-owned Poly Group, China Overseas Investment Holdings and Sinochem purchased more than 10 land kings.[12]

The government-granted monopoly or oligopoly has helped key SOEs to reap soaring after-tax profits, which remain mostly in the coffers of the SOEs rather than flowing to the public purse in the form of dividends.[13] Armed with monopolistic power and vast assets, huge SOEs which often act like "independent kingdoms"[14] have become hotbeds for bribery, embezzlement, squandering and other rent-seeking activities. Some ministerial-level heads of SOEs, including former President of Sinopec Chen Tonghai, President of China National Nuclear Corporation Kang Rixin and Vice President of China Mobile Zhang Chunjiang, had been sentenced to jail even before Xi came to power in 2012.

Top executives of SOEs are ranked similarly to civil servants, but they enjoy a different remuneration and fringe benefit package, much higher than their peers in the government departments. In addition to perks such as official cars, club and golf club memberships, senior executives of SOEs in many cases enjoy even higher incomes than senior managers in the private sectors. The chiefs of China's more

---

[12]"Controversies over the 'land kings' made by central SOEs," (in Chinese), *Huaxia Shibao*, 31 December 2012, http://weihai.house.sina.com.cn/news/2012-12-31/08341296450.shtml, accessed 22 June 2015.

[13]China once collected such dividends from SOEs before the move was halted in 1994 as part of efforts to help financially troubled firms use profits for their own growth. In 2007, China started to reconsider collecting dividends from the 150-plus state firms under the central government's direct control to finance the nation's strategic plans and for social security purposes. State energy, telecommunications and tobacco companies are now required to pay 15% of their net profit as dividends to the state, the highest rate among all major SOEs.

[14]Only the CCDI, with approval from the Politburo, has the power to investigate and detain leaders of central SOEs. Currently, there are no sufficient means to supervise government management of state-owned assets, and no report on state-owned assets is required during the annual parliamentary session of the National People's Congress for deliberation and discussion.

than 1,000 listed companies were paid an average of 448,000 yuan in 2013, while those at state-owned firms earned about 773,000 yuan.[15]

The salary package for SOE executives has been criticized for its lack of transparency and its failure to reflect the performance of executives. A State Council's regulation instituted in early 2015 serves to set this right. SOE managers will be paid based on a basic annual salary, a performance-based salary and bonus incentives.[16] According to this regulation, an SOE manager's basic salary will be two times the average salary of an enterprise's employee. The performance-based salary will be determined by the comprehensive evaluation of the manager's performance in the past year, taking into account the situation in the industry concerned and the company's revenue, profit and other factors, and not exceeding two times the basic salary. Lastly, the bonus incentives shall be no more than 30% of the managers' average salary during their tenure.[17]

The central government by 2015 owned 112 conglomerates (*yangqi*), including 277 public firms listed on the Shanghai or Shenzhen stock exchanges with a market capitalization of more than 10 trillion yuan.[18] These SOEs are administered by SASAC on behalf of the State Council. SOEs have absolute control of seven "strategic" industries: defense, power generation and distribution, petroleum and petrochemicals, telecommunications, coal, civil aviation and waterway transport.[19]

For example, in the area of exploitation of crude oil, and natural gas and downstream refining, three state-owned NOCs, namely, CNPC, Sinopec and CNOOC, are the officially authorized oligopolists, and they have reaped massive profits from China's surging oil and gas demand since the 1990s. Like their peers in other countries, the

---

[15] "China Said to Slash Senior Executive Pay at Top Banks, SOEs," *Bloomberg News*, 6 March 2015.

[16] "SOE salary reform sets an example," *China Daily*, 5 January 2015. Available at: http://www.chinadaily.com.cn/opinion/2015-01/05/content_19236352.htm, accessed 23 June 2015.

[17] *Ibid*.

[18] "China plans mergers to cut number of big state firms to 40: State media," *Reuters*, 27 April 2015.

[19] World Bank (2012). *China 2030* (Washington, DC: The World Bank), p. 105.

three Chinese NOCs have a close and interlocking relationship with the Chinese government. They fulfill important strategic and socioeconomic functions like securing the oil supply from home and abroad for the sustainable development of the national economy and stabilizing the price level of processed oil to appease domestic consumers.

Even after rounds of market-oriented reforms, China's SOEs remain powerful and politically privileged, dominating strategically important industries and commanding a disproportionate share of the country's financial and natural resources. Many of these enterprises, moreover, have grown into vested interest groups that benefit from monopoly, protectionism, state favoritism and political connections. The heads of some centrally administered SOEs even enjoy ministerial status and outrank the state administrative departments that are supposed to regulate their activities.

4. Xi Jinping's SOE Reform: State Capitalism 2.0

During the Party's Third Plenum in November 2013, Xi Jinping received a mandate to give the market a "decisive role" in allocating economic resources. The leadership endorsed a package of economic reform tasks, which included introducing more private and foreign investments into SOEs (mixed-ownership reform, or *hunhe suoyouzhi gaige*), claiming larger shares of dividends from SOEs for social welfare purposes, marketizing prices of water, natural gas, oil, electricity, transportation and telecommunications and opening up all sectors, except those prohibited or restricted by the government, to various types of market competition. The document required "decisive results" to be attained by 2020.[20]

In reality, however, little progress has been made to speed up marketization and privatization of state sectors. On the contrary, the Party's control over SOEs, especially centrally-administered SOEs, has been tightened to forge a different type of corporate governance

[20]For the full text of the reform plan of the Third Plenum, please refer to "CPC Central Committee's Decision on Some Crucial Issues about Comprehensively Deepening Reforms," *Xinhua News*, 15 November 2013.

that departs from traditional Western models. Being resentful about the Party's lax control over SOEs, Xi Jinping is trying to push China's State Capitalism into a new stage in which Leninist means of expanding Party committee's power in corporate governance and routinizing disciplinary inspections are being reinstalled in SOEs.

The 19th Party Congress in October 2017 landmarked both Xi's successful power consolidation and his drive to push China's state capitalism into the second stage featured with strengthened Party control over key SOEs. To oversee overall reform, the Third Plenum in 2013 established the Central Leading Group on Comprehensively Deepening Reforms (*zhongyang quanmian shenhua gaige lingdao xiaozu*), which was headed by Xi himself. This indicated Xi's determination to push through the SOE reform that was halted by the 2008 global financial crisis. However, the implementation of SOE reforms aimed at vested interests had been fraught with difficulties between the Third Plenum and the 19th Party Congress, a time frame when Xi was still seeking to control fragmented state sectors that had been dominated by other Party oligarchs for a long time. Reforms like the increase of SOEs' dividend rates to state coffers, or the slash in top executives' income and perks, have long been blocked by vested interests. With the strengthened Party oversight or even direct interventions in daily management, the Party leadership could take this opportunity to regain the control over state assets that had fallen into the hands of agents of those oligarchs.

The SOE reform after early 1990s gradually loosened the once-rigid Party-state's control over state firms to improve productivity and competitiveness in a gradually marketized economic context, but the Party still maintained strong influence upon SOEs mainly via the nomenklatura system through which senior SOE executives were appointed or removed by the Party's Central Organization Department, or the SASAC, which was set up in 2003 with the responsibility to supervise the preservation and increase in the value of the state-owned assets.[21] During this process of "establishing modern enterprise

[21] SASAC, "Main Functions," http://en.sasac.gov.cn/n1408028/n1408521/index.html, accessed 1 October 2017.

system in SOEs and improving corporate governance,"[22] corporate executives had more autonomy in managing corporations on a daily basis and making major decisions regarding external investment, strategic planning and setting up subsidiary companies.

Such decentralization on the one hand uplifted SOEs' competitiveness and vitality, while on the other, made the Party-state, the largest shareholder of SOEs, face the deficiency of effective supervision over these firms. The SOEs, especially those administered by the central government, experienced explosive growth since the restructure in 1990s, which caused serious socioeconomic repercussions both domestically and internationally. Compared to the private sectors that have difficulty accessing bank finance, SOEs have been favored by huge state-owned banks that often provide them with cheap credit and massive loans. The government also offered SOEs cheap land and undervalued natural resources. Despite this, the dividends offered by these SOEs to the state coffer have remained scanty. Meanwhile, the Party-state has also been facing corruption and insider control problems associated with the mismanagement and lack of insufficient supervision over these SOEs. The situation worsened when Chinese SOEs went abroad, a process that allowed them to experience changes from "hyper-strong external control" from the state to "hyper-weak external control" from the state.[23]

[22] *Ibid.*

[23] "Hyper-strong external control" refers to the situation in which the SOEs have no property rights of their own, not even being allowed to act independently as corporations. The government has full control of the fate of SOEs, including merging some loss-making SOEs with other profitable ones, changing enterprise managers and so on. "Hyper-weak external control" refers to the situation in which the insiders try to expand their power and influence throughout their management process, both mentally and in action. Because the insiders do not have, or only have a small part of, the ownership, the results have been that many have put their individual interests above anything else and try to transform the State or societal properties into their own by every possible means. Xiaokang Zhao and Wei-hua Jin (1997). "Insider control and the effects on economic systems: A critical review," in Frank A. Stowell, Ray L. Ison, Rosalind Armson, Jacky Holloway, Susan Jackson, and Steve McRobb (eds.), *Systems for Sustainability: People, Organizations, and Environments* (New York: Springer Science and Business Media), p. 389.

The SASAC, China's top watchdog over SOEs, and other regulators within the State Council like the People's Bank of China and its State Administration of Foreign Exchange (SAFE), the Ministry of Finance, China Banking Regulatory Commission, China Securities Regulatory Commission, China Insurance Regulatory Commission and the National Auditing Office, have not been able to exert efficient cross-border supervision upon the daily management of internationalized SOEs.

The State Council, China's chief administrative authority chaired by the Premier, consists of over 80 ministries, administrations and bureaus and takes charge of overall socioeconomic policy, making its supervisory role too vague and broadly-defined for the regulation over state-owned conglomerates operating overseas. Even the PBOC has difficulty in overseeing financial activities of SOEs in foreign countries, as it can only monitor the cross-border capital movement via its SAFE for the sake of anti-money laundering. Neither the State Council nor its central bank can have sufficient supervision over SOEs' overseas operation, as most of the buyout activities take place on the capital market beyond the PRC's jurisdiction. Weak oversight over daily operations of SOEs has led to horrendous corporate debt issues in China in recent years.

In Xi's state capitalism 2.0, the Party's grip over SOEs is being strengthened across the board. In addition to the existing nomenklatura system that impacts appointment of senior executives, the Party is exerting more influences upon SOEs' daily operations and major decision-makings through allowing Party committees to play a leading role in managing SOEs.[24] Previously, Party committees within SOEs were only in charge of organizing after-hours activities among Party members, and detached from board of directors that made key decisions regarding the operation and investment of SOEs. After the reform, Party committees or Party groups (*dangzu*) "would be embedded into the corporate governance structure"

[24] *Red Flag Document (hongqi Wengao)* (2017). "On strengthening the Party's leadership over SOEs" (*lun jiaqiang dang dui guoyouqiye de lingdao*), http://www.crc.chinacnr.com/culture-377.html, accessed 1 September 2017.

while the "Party construction work would be embedded into the corporate development."[25]

Xi has capitalized on public grievances against privileged cadres to launch ruthless anti-graft purges in the government, military and SOEs. The Party has strengthened control over SOEs through regularly sending disciplinary inspection teams (*xunshizu*) to SOEs. In January 2015, the Party's Central Commission for Discipline Inspection (CCDI) decided to enhance its inspection of SOEs, making combating corruption in SOEs one of its priorities for the year. In February 2015, the CCDI announced the inspection of 26 major SOEs (Table 1), including China Mobile, China Telecom, China Ocean Shipping Company (COSCO), CNPC, China National Offshore Oil Corp. (CNOOC) and China National Nuclear Corp.[26]

According to the report released by the inspection teams in June 2015, a litany of problems like embezzlement, nepotism, bribery and selling and buying of promotions were detected.[27] In the same month, the CCDI announced that another 17 SOEs would be inspected in the second half of 2015 (Table 1).

The CCDI unprecedentedly probed a large number of executives of leading centrally administered SOEs (*yangqi*) including China Huaneng Group, China State Construction Engineering Corporation, China Shipbuilding Industry Corporation, COSCO Group, Baosteel Group and Wuhan Iron and Steel Corporation. For the first time, the CCDI's website posted photos of the inspection teams notifying heads of the SOEs of the inspection results. A typical photo shows several inspectors seated on one side of a table and an enterprise's chief on the other. Activities conducted at

---

[25] *Ibid.*

[26] Shannon Tiezzi (2015). "China's state-owned companies sweat as 'Graft-Busters' converge," in *The Diplomat*, 13 February, http://thediplomat.com/2015/02/chinas-state-owned-companies-sweat-as-graft-busters-converge/, accessed 17 June 2015.

[27] The CCDI (2015). "Feedback from first-round of inspection work in 2015," (in Chinese), 16 June, http://finance.sina.com.cn/china/20150616/190022447460.shtml, accessed 17 June 2015.

Table 1: A list of SOEs inspected by the CCDI (2013–June 2015).

SOE name	Industry	Headquarters
2013		
China Grain Reserves Corp	Agriculture	Beijing
China Publishing Group Corp	Publishing	Beijing
The Export-Import Bank of China	Banking	Beijing
Three Gorges Corp	Electricity	Beijing
2014		
COFCO Group	Agriculture	Beijing
FAW Group	Automotive	Changchun
China Southern Airlines	Aviation	Guangzhou
China Petrochemical Corp	Petrochemical	Beijing
China Unicom	Telecom	Beijing
Shenhua Group	Coal	Beijing
China Huadian Corp	Electricity	Jinan
China Shipping Group	Shipping	Shanghai
China State Shipbuilding Corp	Shipbuilding	Beijing
Dongfeng Motor Company	Automotive	Wuhan
February 2015		
China Mobile	Telecom	Beijing
China Telecom	Telecom	Beijing
COSCO	Shipping	Beijing
CNPC	Petroleum	Beijing
CNOOC	Petroleum	Beijing
China National Nuclear Corp	Electricity	Beijing
State Grid Corp	Electricity	Beijing
China Datang Corp	Electricity	Beijing
Shanghai Baosteel Group	Steel	Shanghai
China Nuclear Engineering Group	Construction	Beijing
State Development and Investment Corp	Investment	Beijing
Dongfang Electric Corp	Electricity	Chengdu
China Electronics Technology Group Corp	Electronics	Beijing
China Electronics Corp	Electronics	Beijing

(*Continued*)

Table 1: (*Continued*)

SOE name	Industry	Headquarters
China Power Investment Corp	Electricity	Beijing
State Nuclear Power Technology Corp	Electricity	Beijing
Sinochem Group	Chemical	Beijing
China Minmetals Corp	Metal	Beijing
China Huaneng Group	Electricity	Beijing
China State Construction Engineering Corp	Construction	Beijing
China Southern Power Grid Company	Electricity	Guangzhou
China Shipbuilding Industry Corp	Shipbuilding	Beijing
China National Machinery Industry Corp	Machinery	Beijing
China General Technology Group	Technology	Beijing
China Guodian Corporation	Electricity	Beijing
Wuhan Iron and Steel Corp	Steel	Wuhan
June 2015		
China National Aviation Holding Company	Aviation	Beijing
China Eastern Airlines	Aviation	Beijing
China Travel Service(HK)Group Corp	Tourism	Hong Kong
China Merchants Group	Finance	Hong Kong
China Aerospace Science and Technology Corp	Aerospace	Beijing
China Aerospace Science and Industry Corp	Aerospace	Beijing
Aviation Industry Corporation of China	Defense	Beijing
China North Industries Group Corp	Defense	Beijing
China South Industries Group	Defense	Beijing
The Commercial Aircraft Corporation of China	Manufacturing	Shanghai
China Resources (Holdings) Co Ltd	Trade, Property	Hong Kong
Ansteel Group	Steel	Anshan
Aluminum Corporation of China Limited	Aluminum	Beijing
China First Heavy Industries Company	Manufacturing	Qiqihar
Harbin Electric Corp	Electricity	Harbin
China Post Group Corp	Postal Service	Beijing
China Railway Corp	Railway	Beijing

Source: Compiled by the author based on information from CCDI website.

public expense included traveling for leisure, playing golf, extravagant spending at private clubs, high-profile wedding and funeral ceremonies and gift giving as well as embezzling of public money. Some cadres involved had sought illegal profit for relatives and friends or made serious mistakes in decision-making, the CCDI said.[28]

Reforms like the increase of SOEs' dividend rates to state coffers, or the slashing of top executives' income and perks have long been blocked by vested interests. CCDI's intensive inspection of SOEs in strategic industries has allowed the leadership to roll out SOE reforms at a faster speed. In the long run, the leadership may need to further deregulate the industries dominated by SOEs to improve efficiency. The Party could gradually establish a new system of recruiting talent globally and making SOE managers accountable to their board of directors and shareholders.

As for centrally controlled SOEs, the government decided to cut the number of these conglomerates from 112 to 40 through a series of mergers.[29] The consolidation first took place in competitive industries, channeling state-owned assets to super-large enterprises to avoid cut-throat competition. SOEs are expected to contribute 30% of their profits to the state by 2020. In the meantime, the government will push forward with the marketization of interest rates and speed up the convertibility of renminbi under the capital account.

The government is expected to proceed with more SOE mergers and acquisitions as a means to improve efficiency. The two mergers of centrally administered SOEs (China CNR Corp with CSR Corp and the absorption of State Nuclear Power Technology by China Power Investment Group) and the reform template announced by the Bank of Communications to pursue mixed ownership via employee shareholding plans took effect in the first half of 2015.

---

[28] "Six large Chinese SOEs criticized for graft," *Xinhua News*, 14 June, 2015.

[29] "China plans mergers to cut number of big state firms to 40: State media," *Reuters*, 27 April 2015.

5. Conclusion

The core issue relating to Xi's reform of SOEs is how to maintain a balance between the new emerging forces of business leaders — who have benefited and continue to benefit from economic reform — and the Party-state. Many scholars take the view that economic reform in authoritarian systems is likely to lead to increased liberalization and in the long run, as new social groups demand political influence, to some form of democracy.[30] This is the so-called "King's Dilemma" which many authoritarian regimes confront.[31] However, in the Chinese case economic liberalization and decentralization have significantly slowed down due to lack of political liberalization and power recentralization at the top level. With all the authoritarian means of consolidating Party's control over SOE management, Party overseers might be able to curb corruption and force executives to be more risk-averse. Yet, unless the Party-state weans its SOEs off subsidies, cheap loans and undervalued resources and forces them to stand on their own in real market competition, these state conglomerates will remain less efficient in maximizing shareholder value for the Party-state as the major investor and owner of these SOEs.

[30] See, for example, Harry Harding (1987). *China's Second Revolution: Reform after Mao* (Washington, DC: The Brookings Institution); Joseph Fewsmith (2001). *Elite Politics in Contemporary China* (Armonk, NY: M.E. Sharpe) and Bruce Gilley (2004). *China's Democratic Future* (New York: Columbia University Press).

[31] Autocratic rulers may undermine the basis of their power by introducing reform, but they may risk the same outcome if they hesitate to embrace reform. Samuel Huntington (1970). *Political Order in Changing Societies* (New Haven: Yale University Press).

https://doi.org/10.1142/9789811226588_0003

Chapter 3

Who Hates Government Debt in China? Evidence from Revealed Preferences

Kang Chen

chenkang@nus.edu.sg

1. Introduction

The China model of economic development has been studied carefully and enthusiastically in recent years, especially after the 2008 Global Financial Crisis (GFC) which had shaken confidence in developed economies.[1]

[1]Suisheng Zhao (2010). "The China model: Can it replace the western model of modernization?" *Journal of Contemporary China*, 19(65): 419–436. Shaun Breslin (2011). "The 'China model' and the global crisis: From Friedrich list to a Chinese mode of governance?" *International Affairs*, 87(6): 1323–1343. Minglu Chen and David S.G. Goodman (2012). "The China model: One country, six authors," *Journal of Contemporary China*, 21(73): 169–185. Thomas Ambrosio (2012). "The rise of the 'China model' and 'Beijing Consensus': Evidence of authoritarian diffusion?" *Contemporary Politics*, 18(4): 381–399.

However, it is a mistake to believe that China has followed just one development model consistently throughout the last 40 years. Chen points out that there have been at least two China models which are distinctively different.[2] Under China Model I, which spanned from 1978 to the mid-1990s, the role of the market in the economy was expanding; administrative controls were removed, reduced, or decentralized; development of the private sector was enabled and facilitated; a concerted effort was made to improve living standards by meeting the huge pent up consumption demand that resulted from chronic shortages of consumer goods under the centrally planned economic system adopted by the Communist Party of China (CPC) in the pre-reform era. It is only after 1998 that China Model II, with its strong government-led investment-driven features, began to take shape. The focus of the government then shifted to monopolizing financial resources for its own investment projects. Although government investments were necessary, especially in developing fundamental infrastructure, they also created opportunities for corruption and rent-seeking activities, and some were wasted by local leaders in the effort to accrue performance appraisal for themselves. Capital inefficiency was, however, masked by the positive impact of the healthy savings built up under China Model I and China's accession to the World Trade Organization (WTO) which opened the door for millions of Chinese workers to participate in the international division of labor and for foreign investors and consumers to benefit from China's low costs of production.

China Model I produced a fairly inclusive growth. It provided millions of rural residents and urban individuals with relatively equal opportunities and equal access to those opportunities; it achieved high income growth with no significant worsening of income inequality; it lifted millions of people out of poverty.[3] China Model II,

[2]Kang Chen (2016). "Two China models and local government entrepreneurship," *China: An International Journal*, 14(3): 16–28.

[3]Yasheng Huang (2012). "How did China take off?" *Journal of Economic Perspectives*, 26(4): 147–170. Pak K. Lee (2000). "Into the trap of strengthening state capacity: China's tax-assignment reform," *The China Quarterly*, 164: 1007–1024. Chen, "Two China models and local government entrepreneurship," *China: An International Journal*, 14(3): 22.

however, was much less inclusive. Financial resources were monopolized by the government, economic growth became narrowly based, income inequality had widened, and wasteful investment projects were rampant. Ironically, while there is growing interest outside China to study and understand China Model II, the Chinese leaders themselves have decided to abandon such a model as it has become clear to them that the growth model has devastating social, environmental, economic, and political effects and is unsustainable.

The hallmark of China Model II is government investment, and its inevitable result is accumulation of local government debt which has reached an alarming level in recent years. Under the Budget Law enacted in 1994, local governments in China are not allowed to run budget deficits. However, there are two ways local governments can fund investment projects outside the budget. One is to use the proceeds generated from land sales, while the other is to borrow through local government financing vehicles (LGFVs) for building bridges and roads, as well as other city development projects. Before the GFC, China was benefiting from the export boom brought by the WTO accession. Although local government debt was growing in the early 2000s, it was still very much under control. Total local government debt was estimated at less than 6 trillion yuan (US$878 billion) in 2008, which was around 20% of China's GDP in that year. The GFC, however, changed the picture completely. Firstly, external demand weakened dramatically, and needed to be replaced by a new source of growth.

Secondly, the proceeds from land sales also were drying up because land prices were depressed at that time by unfavorable economic conditions following the GFC, land supply was increasingly constrained by the strict order from the central government to preserve farm land, and usage of funds from land sales also came under close scrutiny by the central government. Just as local government leaders were worried about lacking the means to fulfill growth targets set for them, the central government decided to use a fiscal stimulus package to respond to the GFC. This was done by allowing local governments to borrow from financial institutions to fund investment projects, which made it extremely convenient for local governments to incur debts. Soon after, the number of debt-issuing LGFVs ballooned by 3 times within 4 years to reach more than 1,800 in 2012. In addition to accelerated borrowing by LGFVs, local governments also found new ways to fund their investment projects through channels such as trust loans and wealth management products.[4]

According to China's National Audit Office (NAO), the total local government debt in June 2013, which includes both outstanding debt and implicit debt such as debt guarantees and contingent liabilities, was 17.9 trillion yuan (US$2.9 trillion). However, Bai and others point out that NAO could have significantly underestimated the size of local government debt.[5] Using the information from the WIND databank for large LGFVs, they estimated that total local government debt in June 2013 was about 39 trillion yuan (or US$6.3 trillion), more than twice the amount announced by NAO, which then grew further to 48 trillion yuan (or US$7.4 trillion) by the end of 2015, which is equivalent to 70% of China's GDP in that year.

As soon as Mr. Xi Jinping took over as President, managing local government debt was made one of the top priorities. Audit teams were sent all over China to collect data, existing debts were restructured, and local governments were ordered not to use state-owned enterprises (SOEs) and LGFVs to raise more debt. Nevertheless, China Model II proved to be resilient, as local governments found new ways to incur more debts. Auditor-General Hu Zejun reported to the National People's Congress Standing Committee in June 2017 that compared to June 2013, the balance of government debt at the end of March 2017 increased by 87%. In the same period, the government debt of western regions and some counties and districts grew by more than 100%.

---

[4]Trust products and wealth management products, which are implicitly guaranteed by local governments, are sold to retail consumers in tranches through commercial banks to fund local government investment projects. See Kang Chen and Jang-Sup Shin (2011). "The pattern of financing industrialization in China: Understanding sources of fixed investment," *Global Economic Review*, 40(2): 145–160.

[5]Chong-En Bai, Chang-tai Hsieh and Zheng (Michael) Song, "The long shadow of a fiscal expansion," *National Bureau of Economic Research Working Paper*, November 2016. Available at: nber.org/papers/w2280.

President Xi, in a speech delivered at the 5th National Financial Work Conference in July 2017, issued a stern warning to local government officials. He wanted them to put new local government debts under strict control. He also mentioned, for the first time, that local officials would be held accountable personally, for their whole lifetime, for debts incurred during their tenure of office, and investigations for such responsibilities could be retroactive. This measure, if implemented effectively, would put a stop to the common practice among local government leaders — to borrow money, generate GDP through government investment projects, then be promoted or reassigned to another location (usually in 3–4 years according to Geng *et al.*[6]) and not have to worry about debt repayment.

Premier Li Keqiang also held a State Council executive meeting in late July 2017 to discuss ways of mitigating risk of local government debts, especially hidden ones. The emphasis is on plugging up the "side doors" — government borrowings disguised under services purchased by the government, fake public–private partnerships (PPPs) with SOEs, and other forms of implicit government borrowing.

On the surface, Chinese national leaders seem to hate local government debt as it presents a serious threat to financial stability. However, it is not uncommon that policy statements are not consistent with actual practice. This chapter shows that serious contradictions actually exist when policy statements are compared with revealed preferences of policy makers. They are not only an indication on whether government debt can be successfully controlled, but also a reflection on more fundamental problems of China's political-economic system. While the policy statements reflect CPC's strong desire to enhance efficiency and efficacy through system restructuring, the revealed preferences signify its overarching objective to preserve China's centralized political system, which requires government to distribute and consume more and more resources, and to bring

---

[6]Shu Geng, Baoqing Pang, and Lingna Zhong (2016). "The political economy of term factor in China: the term of local cadres and the behavior of local governments," *China Economic Quarterly*, 15(3): 893–916.

more and more social life under its control. Chinese leaders hate government debt, but not to the extent that would make them fundamentally change the way they run the country.

The rest of this chapter is organized as follows. Section 2 discusses the policy statement of restructuring the economy under the "new normal" and the revealed preference of maintaining short-term economic growth, which at times seems more important than economic restructuring. Section 3 assesses who is playing a decisive role in allocating resources. Although the policy statement points to the market, the revealed preference indicates that the Party is playing the decisive role. Section 4 reviews the effort to transform government functions. While the policy statement is to fight against bureaucratism and formalism, and to "streamline administration and delegate power" (简政放权), the revealed preference is to recentralize control and to bureaucratize structurally, which has led to escalation of institutional costs. Section 5 explains the contradictions between the policy statements and revealed preferences by examining the three fundamental problems of China's centralized political system, i.e., lack of fiscal discipline, resistance to financial liberalization, and an unchecked rise in institutional costs. Section 6 concludes.

2. Restructuring the Economy or Maintaining Growth?

2.1. *Policy Statement 1: Restructuring the Economy Under the "New Normal"*

In 2013, within a few months of taking office, President Xi Jinping announced that China's economy is entering a "new normal" whereby the economic growth would be slower, but with higher quality and efficiency. This has been reiterated at the 19th National Party Congress held in 2017 when Xi declared that China had entered a "new era." In order to restructure the economy, a different set of performance criteria is required to mobilize local government leaders, and GDP will no longer be the basis of merit (不以GDP论英雄).

Similar views were echoed by Premier Li Keqiang, who told reporters at the press conference at the end of the 2014 session of the

People's Congress that "we are going to declare a war against our own inefficient and unsustainable model of growth and way of life."

Chinese leaders are under no illusion that such changes will be easy. On many occasions, they vowed that the government would do whatever it takes to restructure the economy, even if crippling sacrifices have to be made (壮士断腕).[7] More specifically, they talk about shutting down "zombie companies" — businesses that require government bailouts and never-ending credit support. In subsequent years, supply-side reforms, which aim to correct misallocation in production factors, were announced.

When restructuring the economy, it is necessary to accept slower economic growth in the short run. While optimists would like to argue that restructuring does not necessarily lead to economic slowdown, it is highly unlikely that the slack left by the shrinking old sectors can be sufficiently filled just in time by newly emerging sectors. Using government investment to maintain growth would only crowd out private investment and slow down restructuring. Furthermore, restructuring would entail a bigger variation in regional growth. For provinces with a concentrated share of industries at excessive capacity, a successful restructuring should see a significant slowdown in these localities. It is therefore unreasonable to require all provinces to grow at the same rate. In practice, however, political considerations prevail and administrative controls seem to be the most frequently-used tools in problem-solving.

2.2. *Revealed Preference 1: Maintaining Growth is More Important than Restructuring the Economy*

When the economy slows down, the government seems to make it the top priority to maintain growth. In 2014, eight provincial governors were summoned to Beijing to meet the Premier who reminded them that they were "duty bound to defend their territories" (守土有责) — implying that they are held accountable for maintaining economic

[7] *Xinhua Net*, 17 March 2013. Available at: http://www.xinhuanet.com/2013lh/2013-03/17/c_115053934.htm.

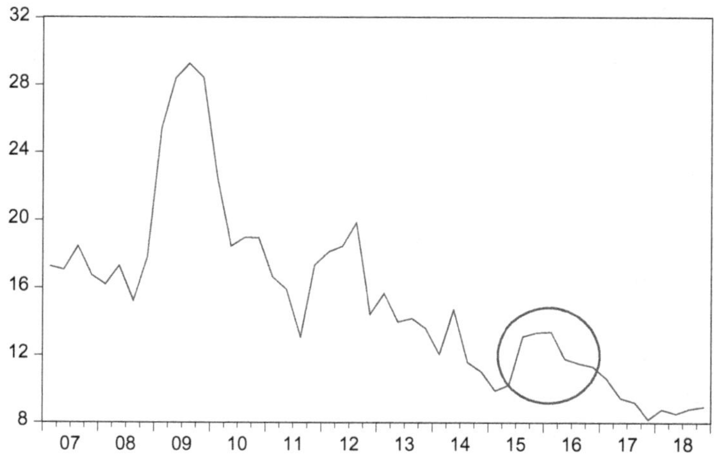

Figure 1: M2 growth rate (Q1 2007 to Q4 2018, %).
Source: CEIC Database.

growth in their provinces.[8] In 2015, a mini-stimulus was introduced. The broad money supply M2 was allowed to grow at rates above 13% for three consecutive quarters since the third quarter of 2015, which was very unusual after 2013 when the "new normal" was announced (see Figure 1).

To "defend" their territories, local governments still needed public investment to propel economic growth in their localities, which significantly slowed down the process of economic restructuring. The plan to close down loss-making "zombie companies" was resisted by local governments which, under the pressure to maintain political stability and sufficient economic growth required by the central government, kept offering "blood transfusions" to those companies.[9] In the end, only private firms were closed down, and administrative orders were used to deal with the issue of excessive capacity. For instance, in order to cut oversupply, all coal producers were asked to

[8] *Renmin Net*, 9 June 2014. Available at: http://politics.people.com.cn/n/2014/0609/c1001-25122977-2.html.

[9] Laura He (2016). "China's plan to kill zombie firms faces resistance at local level," *South China Morning Post*, 29 August.

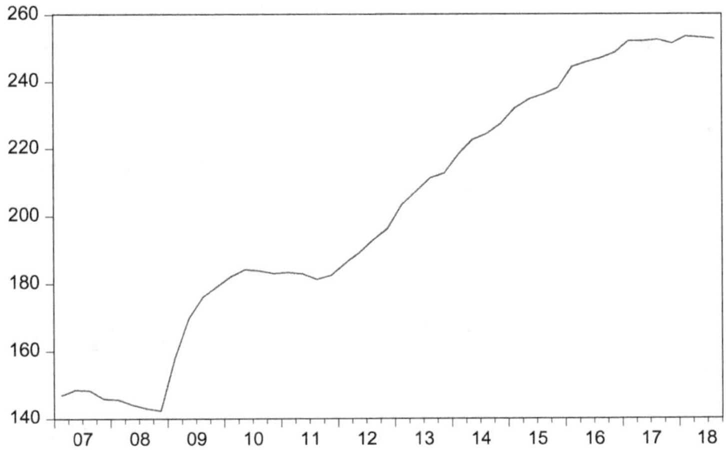

Figure 2: Credit to non-financial sector (Q1 2007 to Q3 2018, % of GDP).
Source: Bank of International Settlements, March 2019.

operate only 276 days in a year. When it resulted in a shortage of coal and prices started to shoot up, the authorities reacted by controlling prices and lifting the caps on coal output.[10] The effort to cut excessive capacity in other industries has suffered a similar fate.

Since the central government relies on local governments to deliver economic growth, and local governments can only do so through investment expansion, policies with regard to local government debt and LGFVs also have to be adjusted in relation to short-term macroeconomic conditions. In May 2015, only a few months after the Budget Law was amended to make it illegal for local governments to borrow through LGFVs, the State Council relaxed the rule and asked financial institutions to extend new loans to LGFVs to fund ongoing investment projects. This gave rise to another round of expansion of local government debt. Figure 2 shows that China's total credit to the non-financial sector increased from 142% of GDP in the last quarter of 2008 to 196% at the end of 2012, and further

[10]Ge Wu and Lu Wang (2016). "The puzzle about cutting excessive capacity," *Finance & Trade* (4).

expanded to 253% in the first quarter of 2018. The speed of credit expansion remains as fast under the "new normal" as that in the previous period which immediately followed the GFC.

It is clear from the revealed preferences that short-term problems are more urgent and should be given top priority. Local government debt can be packaged into long-term bonds, and long-term issues can wait.

3. Who is Playing the Decisive Role in Allocating Resources?

3.1. *Policy Statement 2: Let Markets Play a Decisive Role in Allocating Resources*

In 1992, CPC declared at its 14th Party Congress that the objective of economic system reform was to build a "Socialist Market Economy," which can be basically defined as an economic system that: (1) allows markets to play a fundamental role in allocating resources under macro controls of the state; (2) maintains public ownership as the principal type of ownership; and (3) creates widely shared prosperity.[11]

It is interesting to note that it was still necessary to reiterate, 20 years later, at the Third Plenum of the 18th CPC Central Committee, that "the objective of deepening economic system reform is to let markets play a decisive role in allocating resources."[12] What the market-oriented reform has done since the late 1970s is to build a reasonably well-functioning goods and services market (except for industries monopolized by the state-owned firms such as telecom, railway transportation, petroleum, power and energy). In terms of factor markets, however, the progress has been much slower. The market for labor is more advanced than the market for land, while the capital market is the least developed.

---

[11] See "Decisions by the Communist Party of China Central Committee on issues with regard to building a socialist market economic system," 14 November 1993.

[12] See "The communique of the third plenum of the 18th CPC Central Committee," 18 November 2013.

Dittmer profoundly points out that "in China there is no difference between fiscal and monetary policy or between banking and monetary policy and little difference really between the public sector and the private sector."[13] A large part of China's economic system is still stuck in the pre-reform structure, and the transition from plan to market is far from complete. The policy statement by the Third Plenum raised expectations that market-oriented reforms started in the late 1970s would be carried forward, reforms in the financial sector deepened, capital markets nurtured, and allocative inefficiencies in the system would be gradually removed. Moreover, a call to open up monopolized industries to private firms was also welcomed since competition can improve efficiency.

Indeed, the People's Bank of China (PBOC) removed the lending interest rate floor in 2013 and scrapped the deposit rate ceiling in 2015, thus interest rates appear to have been liberalized. The China Banking Regulatory Commission also began to open up the banking industry by allowing five small private banks to operate in 2014 and giving the green light to 12 more such banks in subsequent years.[14] Furthermore, the National Development and Reform Commission announced in 2014 that the private sector was encouraged to participate in development and operation of five key industrial sectors to which the entry of private firms were previously not allowed. These sectors include transportation and communication infrastructure, clean energy, oil gas pipeline network and storage, and modern coal chemical and petrochemical industrial base.

3.2. *Revealed Preference 2: The Party Should Play the Decisive Role in Allocating Resources*

Six years after the Third Plenum, the general perception is that China is moving in the opposite direction, with the Party playing the decisive role in resource allocation.

[13] Lowell Dittmer (2017). "Xi Jinping's 'new normal': *Quo Vadis*?" *Journal of Chinese Political Science*, 22: 429–446.

[14] *China Security Traders* (quanshang zhongguo), "A survival survey of new private banks," 17 June 2017.

- Interest rate liberalization turned out to be short-lived. PBOC used moral suasion to reintroduce interest floors and ceilings so as to protect profit margins of state-owned banks.[15]
- For those monopolized industries opened up to "mixed ownership," assets were priced at levels that were considered too high by private investors, and very little decision power would be shared by non-state stakeholders. As a result, few private investors were interested.[16]
- In response to the mid-2015 stock market crash, the authorities arrested those who participated in short-selling, ordered large mutual funds and pension funds to buy more stocks, and imposed a 6-month ban on large shareholders from selling stocks.
- Destocking housing inventory was one of the key supply-side structural adjustments in 2016, and many cities had unsold homes overbuilt over previous years. In order to encourage demand in the property market, city governments provided incentives to buyers, some (such as Shenyang) even offering zero down payment to buyers. Such incentives fueled another round of housing speculations, leading to runaway housing prices. The overheated property market prompted intervention from President Xi who told the Central Economic Work Conference in December 2016 that "houses are built for living in, not for speculation." In keeping with his instruction, more than 40 cities began to introduce a ban on sale of purchased properties in 2017, the duration of non-selling period varies from 2 to 10 years after obtaining the title deed. For a new property, for which it usually takes 3 years to obtain the title deed, a 2-year ban means that the buyer cannot sell the property for at least 5 years after buying it.[17]

---

[15]Yusho Cho (2016). "China takes back control of interest rates," *Nikkei Asian Review*, 24 June.

[16]KPMG China, "Puzzles about the mixed ownership reform," December 2014.

[17]"Selling ban on residential properties extended to 44 cities," *Sina News Centre*, 24 September 2017.

From what has been done in recent years by the Chinese government, it does not seem that markets are allowed to play a significant role, much less a decisive role, in allocating resources. Furthermore, President Xi Jinping, in his report at the 19th National Party Congress held in 2017, stressed that "the Party must exercise leadership over all areas of endeavor in every part of the country," and that "the leadership of the Party is the most essential attribute of socialism with Chinese characteristics, and the greatest strength of this system." Government control over factor markets, especially financial markets, is therefore going to stay and the current Chinese leadership does not seem to have any intention to change this. Small players, of course, could be allowed to enter capital markets, but major entities or "commanding heights" will be firmly controlled by the government. By keeping financial markets under control, the system has a strong capability to handle financial risks. Crashes in stock markets, bonds markets or property markets will not be allowed to develop into a financial crisis when the entire financial system is collapsing, because market transactions would be suspended by the government before it happens. Similarly, there will also be no failure of big banks, insurance companies, or financial institutions, because the troubled entities would surely be saved by the government.[18]

Maintaining financial stability this way results in enormous capital inefficiency from either inefficient use of capital or misallocation of capital among different usages. Figure 3 shows that China's Incremental Capital Output Ratio (ICOR), a simple measurement for capital efficiency, has changed rapidly from 3.0 in 2007 to 7.4 in 2016. It means that while 3 yuan worth of capital investment was needed in 2007 to generate 1 yuan of extra GDP, it required 7.4 yuan of investment to do just the same in 2016.

[18] PBOC is required by CPC to underwrite all financial clean-ups, and it has done so by extending a perpetual "put" to the entire financial system. See Carl Walter and Fraser Howie (2012). *Red Capitalism: The Fragile Financial Foundation of China's Extraordinary Rise* (Singapore: John Wiley & Sons, 2012), pp. 330–332.

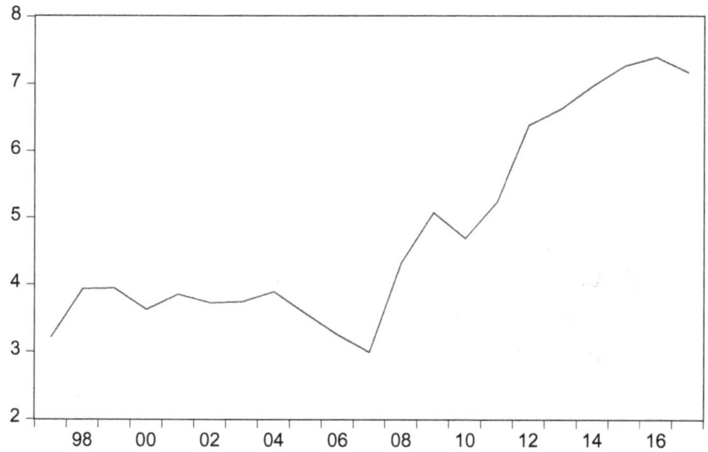

Figure 3: Incremental capital output ratio (1997–2017).

Source: CEIC Database and the author's calculation. Output is GDP at constant 2010 prices, and capital increment is Gross Fixed Capital Formation which is deflated by Fixed Asset Investment Price Index (2010 = 100).

The implications to local government debt is clear. Enormous amount of government borrowing has been wasted in many investment projects which serve to accrue performance appraisal for local leaders but do not generate acceptable economic return and social benefits. Moreover, corruption cases investigated revealed that this system of resource allocation breeds "crony capitalism," with the "princelings" and members of powerful families at the top and a multi-layered oligarchy spreading downward to different sectors and geographical regions.[19] The collusive networks make it relatively easy to embezzle public properties, usually via local government investment projects.[20]

[19]Minxin Pei (2016). *China's Crony Capitalism: The Dynamics of Regime Decay* (Cambridge: Harvard University Press).

[20]Kang Chen and Qijun Liu (2015). "Economic development and corruption in China in the shadow of rent seeking," in Roger D. Congleton and Arye L. Hillman (eds.), *Companion to the Political Economy of Rent Seeking* (Cheltenham: Edward Elgar), pp. 395–409.

4. How are Government Functions Transformed?

4.1. *Policy Statement 3: To Streamline Administration and Delegate Power*

The original objective of transforming government functions was quite ambitious. As Premier Li Keqiang put it, it was supposed to ensure that "market entities can do anything which is not prohibited by the law, and government departments must not do anything unless it is mandated by the law." The CPC also launched campaigns against bureaucratism and formalism in 2013. But as it progressed, the key emphasis shifted to reducing the scope of administrative approval. The total number of items which required approval at the central level was more than 1700 in 2013, and Premier Li set a 5-year target to reduce it by at least one third. The target had been achieved by January 2017, with 618 items being removed from approval requirement by China's central government. Moreover, many items which previously required local government approval on behalf of the central government were also removed from the approval list. Intermediary services were standardized, investment approval requirements reduced, requirement for vocational qualification permits voided, government funds and administration fees streamlined and reduced, and requirement for "non-administrative approval" permanently abolished.[21]

Another major attempt to transform government functions is to adopt "negative lists" which changes business registration from approval to filing and thus significantly reduces processing time and paperwork. The negative list for the Shanghai Free Trade Zone (SFTZ), which was first released in 2013, has been incrementally shortened, and more than 90% of foreign-invested firms within SFTZ were set up under the negative list approach. The aim is to spread outside the FTZs, but the uptake has been slow.

[21]Feng Wang (2017). "Four years of streamlining administration and delegating power: Targets achieved, but work still required to get through last mile," *21st Century Economic Report*, 16 March.

This effort has delivered some positive results: the number of new business entities registered reached more than ten thousand per day on average, and China's ranking in the World Bank's *Ease of Doing Business Index* improved from 96th place in 2013 to 46th in 2019.[22]

4.2. *Revealed Preference 3: Recentralization and Structural Bureaucratization*

The idea of streamlining administration and delegating power to lower levels of government has not been warmly embraced by central departments and local government agencies, and they have found several ways to slow down the process: (1) Being selective in delegating power. When the number of items delegated is counted, they would only give up those unimportant ones or delegate down initial steps in the process and keep at hand the ultimate approval power; (2) Creating bottlenecks at the local level by delegating work without providing additional budget and headcounts; and (3) Making no effort to synchronize delegation of power among agencies with vertical or horizontal linkages, thus nullifying its effectiveness.[23]

Moreover, while "delegating power" appears frequently in the speeches of central government leaders, recentralization actually becomes the preferred way to get things done, especially when the anticorruption campaign has removed material incentives that previously motivated local government officials. For example, the Central Commission for Discipline Inspection (CCDI) recentralized the power of appointing disciplinary heads at the local level during the anticorruption campaign, sending teams of central staff to local governments in surprise inspection tours and returning with more surprise inspections to the same locality wherever necessary. Such methods have proven to be effective in investigating corruption cases.

[22]The index improved from 61.51 to 73.64 in the same period.

[23]Xianjin Lai (2017). "Coordination problems in streamlining administration and delegating power," *Qiushi*, 27 February.

CCDI inspection teams have also been sent to central ministries and agencies, large SOEs, and universities to ensure central control.[24]

The CCDI experience was duplicated in air pollution control. Ministry of Environmental Protection (MEP) sent central inspection teams all over China to identify air pollution problems, and demanded respective local governments to address the issues. After a period of time, another inspection team from MEP would revisit the same site to check if the problem had been properly addressed. Local government leaders would be held accountable if the problem was not resolved.

One must realize that in these examples, local officials in Party discipline commissions or environmental protection bureaus are still working side by side with the inspection teams from the central government, albeit their work is considered less effective or reliable.

Whyte points out that there exist two distinct aspects of bureaucratization.[25] The first aspect — bureaucratization in *content* or *functioning* — "involves the extent to which an organization approximates the ideal-typical traits ... for example, an organization based on legal-rational authority, emphasizing formal rules and procedures and written files..." The efforts to fight bureaucratism and formalism and to streamline administration and delegate power to lower levels of government are clearly targeting this type of bureaucratization. The second aspect — bureaucratization in *form* or *structure* — "refers to a process by which more and more of social life comes to be governed by large, hierarchical, non-kinship-based organizations ... more and more the distribution and consumption of resources in society are carried out not by self-sufficient individuals and communities or through the market mechanism but are instead subject to hierarchical allocation and coordination." Recentralization and increasingly

---

[24]See Chapter 2 by Gang Chen, "Consolidating Leninist control of state-owned enterprises: China's state capitalism 2.0" in this volume for a detailed discussion about how CCDI routinized disciplinary inspections to SOEs in recent years.

[25]Martin King Whyte (1989). "Who hates bureaucracy? A Chinese puzzle," in Victor Nee and David Stark (eds.), *Remaking the Economic Institutions of Socialism: China and Eastern Europe* (Stanford: Stanford University Press, 1989), pp. 233–254.

relying on the government to allocate resources are consistent with such a process. Whyte argues that Mao Zedong, Chairman of CPC, launched a series of attacks on content bureaucratization, unleashing his impulses fully during the Cultural Revolution; he was, however, at the same time a champion of structural bureaucratization, pushing it to the fullest extent as well. The combination of structural bureaucratization with content de-bureaucratization did not work. "In the increasingly totally state-dominated China of Mao's last years the organizational problems Mao feared most, such as elite arrogance, abuses of power, pursuit of personal and family advantage, currying favor, and aversion of making decisions and taking risks, only got worse."[26] He predicted, 30 years ago, that the post-Mao reforms would only make superficial and cosmetic changes in reducing bureaucratic evils, and that China's future leaders would still be ardent but ineffective champions of the anti-bureaucratic cause. History has proved him right.

Zhou argues that the secret of China's economic miracle has been the substantial reduction of institutional costs through reform and opening.[27] Such examples in the early 1980s include abolishing collective farming, giving farmers property rights over land use, introducing product markets, allowing rural surplus labor to participate in industrial production, and accepting small private firms as a legitimate business entities. They also include opening up foreign trade and foreign investment, reforming China's foreign exchange regime and foreign trade administration, and allowing China to participate in international division of labor and benefit from its comparative advantages. However, China has not devised a mechanism to effectively check on institutional costs. From 1995 to 2012, the total wage bill increased by 8.7 times, similar to nominal GDP which grew by 8.5 times. It means the share of labor costs has not changed significantly. However, during the same period, taxes expanded by 16.7 times, non-tax fiscal revenues, 18.8 times, social security contributions,

[26]Whyte, "Who hates bureaucracy? A Chinese puzzle," pp. 240–245.

[27]Qiren Zhou (2017). *Property Rights and China's Transformation* (Beijing: Peking University Press).

28.7 times, and revenues from land sales, 64 times. Moreover, rent-seeking and corruption have been institutionalized and further increased institutional costs.

Recentralization in recent years helps to maintain conformity and guarantee policy coordination and consistency, at the cost of stifling local initiatives and creating rigidities in the system. It presents more institutional costs, including compliance costs at the local level when grassroots officials have to deal with multiple inspection teams and respond to numerous directives from many upper level governments at the same time. "Grassroots fatigue" has been used to describe the dire situation facing local officials when they are busy attending meetings, studying speeches, filling out forms, receiving inspections, accepting appraisals, and creating and maintaining evidences to show that a specific task has been performed or carried out by writing reports and taking photos or videos.[28]

5. Who Hates Local Government Debt?

When local government debt becomes a serious issue that concerns the Chinese leaders, corrective measures have been designed and implemented to address the problem. However, the revealed preferences discussed in this chapter show that controlling government debt is not a straightforward task.

China's economic reform, from its onset, has been a marriage between an authoritarian political system and a market economy, which has its inherent contradictions. On the one hand, an authoritarian system is characterized by a centralized and highly concentrated power of authority in the hands of a leader or a small elite. On the other hand, a market economy functions well only when resource allocation is decentralized and individual economic agents are free to make economic decisions. Can political centralization and economic decentralization coexist and function effectively? Many, including

[28] Enxue Wang (2017). "Grassroots fatigue: An issue that needs to be addressed urgently after the 19th Party Congress," *FT Chinese*, 8 December.

conservative Chinese leaders, were skeptical.[29] But China's rapid economic growth in the past 40 years seems to indicate that it can work fairly well in a specific period of time. Will it continue to work effectively to meet new challenges through institutional adaptations and policy adjustments? The revealed preferences show that the Chinese system has at least three fundamental problems.

5.1. *Lacking Fiscal Discipline*

Fiscal discipline is the capacity of a government to maintain smooth financial operation and long-term fiscal health. It is closely linked to fiscal capacity, i.e., the ability to extract resources, which is regarded as the most important ingredient of state capacity.[30] In a large country, fiscal capacity is related to fiscal discipline in at least three aspects. Firstly, as Sng points out, a ruler governing a large country faces severe agency problems — given the geographical size and heterogeneity of his domain, his agents are endowed with information advantages and therefore have strong incentives to extort funds from the taxpayers.[31] A wise ruler should keep taxes low to reduce bureaucratic expropriation, especially when the economy is fast expanding.[32] Secondly, institutional credibility can improve extractive capacity.[33] If the government cannot provide a policy environment with secure and well-defined property rights and reliable contract enforcement, the

---

[29]Kang Chen (1998). "Accidental freedom: Economic development experience in Post-Mao China," in K.T. Liou (ed.), *Handbook of Economic Development* (New York: Marcel Dekker), pp. 611–630.

[30]Gabriel A. Almond and G. Bingham Powell, Jr. (1966). *Comparative Politics: A Developmental Approach,* (Boston: Little, Brown and Co.). A.F.K Organski and Jacek Kugler (1980). *The War Ledger* (Chicago: Chicago University Press, 1980).

[31]Tuan-Hwee Sng (2014). "Size and dynastic decline: The principle-agent problem in late imperial China, 1700–1850," *Explorations in Economic History*, 54: 107–127.

[32]Tuan-Hwee Sng and Chiaki Moriguchi (2014). "Asia's little divergence: State capacity in China and Japan before 1850," *Journal of Economic Growth*, 19: 439–470.

[33]Lewis W. Snider (1996). *Growth, Debt, and Politics: Economic Adjustment and the Political Performance of Developing Countries* (Boulder: Westview Press).

private sector will protect its investments by withholding resources or by investing in liquid assets only.[34] Thirdly, institutional credibility cannot be developed if the central government does not impose fiscal discipline on itself by institutionalizing credible fiscal relations with local governments. This is because if fiscal burden was forced upon them by the central government, the local governments would not hesitate to violate property rights and grab from the private sector.

Shen observes that policy-making and budgeting are two separate and disjointed processes in China whereby leaders at higher level governments often initiate new policies, resulting in new expenditure responsibilities for lower-level governments.[35] Moreover, there is lack of a clear and detailed division of expenditure responsibilities among different levels of government in the Budget Law, and higher-level governments can arbitrarily shift fiscal responsibilities to lower-level governments.

This practice actually started in 1994 when the Tax Sharing System was introduced.[36] It is constantly widening the gap between local government revenue and expenditure, and there have been many discussions about reforming the central–local fiscal relations.[37] However, little progress has been made. Zhou shows that China's taxes and non-tax fiscal revenues expanded by 16.7 times and 18.8 times, respectively, from 1995 to 2012, while nominal GDP

---

[34]Aymo Brunetti and Beatrice Weder (1994). "Political credibility and economic growth in less developed countries," *Constitutional Political Economy*, 5(1): 23–43. Silvio Borner, Aymo Brunetti, and Beatrice Weder (1995). *Political Credibility and Economic Development* (Basingstoke: Macmillan Press).

[35]Wei Shen (2014). "The logic (or illogic) of China's local government debts out of control: Law, governance or other perspectives," *Hong Kong Law Journal*, 44(3): 887–916

[36]Kang Chen, Aryl L. Hillman, and Qingyang Gu (2002). "Fiscal recentralization and behavioural change of local governments: From the helping hand to the grabbing hand," *China Economic Quarterly*, 2(1): 111–130.

[37]World Bank (2002). *National Development and Sub-national Finance — A Review of Provincial Expenditures* (Beijing: Poverty Reduction and Economic Management Unit, East Asia and Pacific Region, World Bank).

grew by 8.5 times in the same period.[38] As predicted by Sng and Moriguchi,[39] corruption was rampant in China while the government was lacking in fiscal discipline.[40]

Fiscal recentralization in the mid-1990s was perhaps a response to "weak state capacity" under China Model I when both the central government's share of fiscal revenue and the share of total fiscal revenue in GDP were declining. The Chinese leaders believe that the strength of the highly centralized system is to get things done fast, and they can only do so when they face minimal constraints. Compared to governments elsewhere, the Chinese government faces much less constraints in decision-making. The absence of a lengthy budgeting process which would have slowed down decisions as it did in other countries is believed to be the key ingredient for efficacy, as is the dominant role of government in allocation of resources. When leaders in Beijing issue an order to local governments, they want their authority to be respected and their order to be carried out, regardless of its implications to local budgets. It is therefore an unattractive idea for the government to impose fiscal discipline on itself; it is also hard to imagine that the central government would want to implement any type of fiscal federalism which imposes fiscal restrictions on itself.

More specifically, *Revealed Preference 1* shows that delivering short-term economic growth is considered by the Chinese leaders as an important way to display a strong state capacity, much more so than ensuring fiscal discipline.[41] The central leaders themselves know very well how growth is generated at the local level since they were in the same position previously. As such, they cannot completely cut off funds flowing into local government investment projects. The central

---

[38] Qiren Zhou (2017). *Property Rights and China's Transformation* (Beijing: China CITIC Press).

[39] Sng and Moriguchi, "Asia's little divergence: State capacity in China and Japan before 1850."

[40] Chen and Liu, "Economic development and corruption in China in the shadow of rent seeking."

[41] *Revealed Preference 1* was discussed in Section 2.

government's behavior is perfectly anticipated by local leaders, and more debts are incurred by local governments with implicit sanction from the center.

In summary, while on the surface government debt in China appears to be a problem caused by local governments, its root cause can actually be traced to the authoritarian central government which dislikes fiscal discipline.

5.2. *Resisting Financial Liberalization*

Wade proposes a "Governing the Market" model of East Asian countries where the government is capable of allocating resources to priority sectors through a bank-based financial system which is under close government control.[42] He argues that the governments of East Asian countries have done quite well at the early stage of development since they have good knowledge of priority sectors and are able to direct resources into those sectors.

China seemed to have adopted the same strategy before the GFC when the government controlled key financial resources and used them to boost production of consumer goods in the 1980s and early 1990s, and to increase infrastructure investment in the late 1990s and early 2000s. However, investment decisions are now more difficult to make as the economy moves into a new stage of development, and the call by *Policy Statement 2* to let the market play a decisive role in allocating resources[43] reflects the realization that government investment is getting less and less efficient, and that the key to the success of supply side structural changes is financial liberalization.

However, *Revealed Preference 2* shows that the authoritarian regime is both unwilling and unable to relax its control over financial resources. On the one hand, if the market is indeed allowed to play the decisive role, more resources would be controlled by businesses or non-state entities which would then exert political influence and

---

[42]Robert Wade (1990). *Governing the Market: Economic Theory and the Role of Government in East Asian Industrialization*, (Princeton: Princeton University Press).
[43]*Policy Statement 2* and *Revealed Preference 2* were discussed in Section 3.

thus undermine the authoritarian regime. For example, well-developed financial markets would definitely impose fiscal discipline on the government. On the other hand, market instability and financial risks are something that could lead to political crisis if not handled properly, and the leaders do not have any confidence in controlling such risks if administrative methods are no longer available. Looking from these viewpoints, financial liberalization is an irreversible process and therefore regarded as undesirable.

5.3. *Escalating Institutional Costs*

As mentioned above, bringing down institutional costs is also imperative to revitalizing the real economy. This is the reason behind *Policy Statement 3* which calls for streamlining administration and delegating power.[44] However, administrative decentralization within a multilevel authoritarian system can lead to undesirable outcomes when local governments have too much discretionary power. Centrifugal forces can develop within the system and local governments can become corrupt since there is lack of checks and balances at the local levels.

Revealed Preference 3 shows that recentralization is how Chinese leaders expand state capacity. This is done through structural bureaucratization, i.e., putting more and more of social life under control of the central government. As discussed above, the process results in escalation of institutional costs for businesses and impedes economic restructuring.

In summary, Chinese leaders hate government debt, but not to the extent that would make them fundamentally change the way they run the country. While the policy statements reflect their strong desire to enhance efficiency and efficacy, the revealed preferences signify their overarching objective to preserve China's centralized political system.

6. Conclusion

This chapter discusses the contradictions between policy statements and revealed preferences. These contradictions do not show that the

[44] *Policy Statement 3* and *Revealed Preference 3* were discussed in Section 4.

Chinese government is insincere in making those policy statements. Rather, they reflect difficult challenges facing the Chinese leaders. While it is clear that the government-led investment-driven growth model is not sustainable, economic restructuring is not allowed to cause a significant drop in short-term growth rate because economic slowdown can cause political instability. Moreover, although it is hoped that market would play a bigger role in resource allocation to substantiate efficiency- and innovation-driven economic growth in the "new era," more and more resources are consumed and distributed by the government in order to ensure a strong state capacity under the centralized political system. Furthermore, even if administrative decentralization is necessary to cut bureaucratic red tape and reduce institutional costs, centralization and structural bureaucratization are comparably more important for the central leaders to ensure conformity and policy coordination within the bureaucratic hierarchy which is plagued with severe agency problems. These constrains for institutional change and policy adjustment put the theory of "authoritarian resilience" to the real test.[45]

This chapter has also illustrated that the issue of government debt cannot be studied in isolation. When fiscal discipline is lacking, a significant part of SOE borrowing (including those of LGFVs) can be used to finance off-budget fiscal spending. When key commercial banks are under government control, they can be coerced to accept government debt restructuring at unfavorable conditions.[46] Therefore,

[45]The theory of "authoritarian resilience" asserts that China's political system is able to enhance the state capacity to govern effectively through institutional adaptations and policy adjustment. Andrew J. Nathan (2003). "Authoritarian resilience," *Journal of Democracy*, 14(1): 6–17, Bruce Dickson (2005). "Populist Authoritarianism: The Future of the Chinese Communist Party," *Occasional Papers*, Carnegie Endorsement for International Peace. Erik Kjeld Brødsgaard and Yongnian Zheng (2006). "Introduction: Whither the Chinese Communist Party?" in Erik Kjeld Brødsgaard and Yongnian Zheng (eds.), *The Chinese Communist Party in Reform* (New York: Routledge).

[46]Since 2015, China's commercial banks have been asked to participate in a debt-for-bond swap program which allows local governments to exchange maturing high-cost debts with low-cost government bonds. According to Mr. Lou Jiwei, China's

government debt may change in its form and appearance. As long as the above-mentioned fundamental systemic problems are not resolved, the debt issue is expected to persist. This is because China's local governments will continue facing a soft budget constraint and be susceptible to moral hazard, while administrative centralization and structural bureaucratization will lead to further fiscal mismatch as fiscal resources concentrate at the central level and fiscal responsibilities proliferate at local levels.

Acknowledgment

The author wishes to thank Professor Lowell Dittmer and two anonymous referees for their valuable comments and suggestions.

Minister of Finance, the swap reduced the average borrowing costs from 10% to 3.5%, which is 3% lower than the minimum lending rate, http://epaper.21jingji.com/html/2015-12/23/content_28153.htm.

https://doi.org/10.1142/9789811226588_0004

Chapter

4

The Political Economy of Working Class Re-formation

Marc Blecher

mblecher@oberlin.edu

1. Introduction

In the wake of the political crisis of the Cultural Revolution, China's post-Mao leadership undertook structural reforms in order to help preserve the Party/state by refounding its legitimacy on the basis of economic growth and improved living standards.[1] The Chinese urban resident working class (i.e., those with urban household registrations), which had enjoyed employment security, basic welfare guarantees, relative equality with lower- and middle-level management, and high political and social status during the Maoist period, nonetheless had not received meaningful raises in decades. Rural migrant labor

[1]My heartfelt thanks to Lowell Dittmer, for inspiring me when he was several years my senior among the graduate students of our mentor Professor Tang Tsou, and, 50 years on, for his steadfast work and incisive analytical advice as I developed this chapter.

(i.e., farmers who came to work in urban factories, usually under contractual arrangements forged by their collectives), which sporadically supplemented the regular urban labor force, formed a lower stratum within the working class that could earn a better livelihood than farm labor but whose inferiority to urban resident workers formed the material basis of considerable radicalism in the Cultural Revolution.[2] How have the structural reforms transformed workers' livelihoods? Have they contributed to structural re-formation of the working class itself? With what implications?

2. Wages and Hours

Under structural reform, the overall economic position of China's working class improved absolutely, declined relatively, and became much more uneven. Both urban resident workers and rural migrants have experienced considerable improvements in their incomes and standards of living. Average real wages rose at an average annual rate of 8.9% between 1978 and 2017.[3] These figures include some professionals and low-level managers, so those for actual blue-collar workers were probably a bit less; but since workers comprised the vast majority of employees, the actual levels are probably not significantly lower. During the crucial early years of structural reform when industrial labor began to become commodified and subject to layoffs, 57% of workers responding to a trade union survey in 1997 said that their incomes had risen in recent years.[4]

Yet, the increases have been distributed very unevenly over time and space. Real rises in the 4%–8% range through 1999 (Figure 1) were very significant compared with the overall wage stagnation of

[2]Hong Yung Lee (1980). *The Politics of the Cultural Revolution: A Case Study* (Berkeley: University of California Press); Elizabeth Perry and Li Xun (1997). *Proletarian Power: Shanghai in the Cultural Revolution* (Boulder: Westview).

[3]Calculated from *China Statistical Yearbook 2007*, Table 5-22 and *China Statistical Yearbook 2018*, Table 4-12.

[4]全国总工会政策研究室 (All-China Federation of Trade Unions Policy Research Office) (1999). 中国职工状况调查,数据卷 (*A Survey of the Condition of Chinese Workers and Staff*) (北京: 西苑出版社), p. 1337.

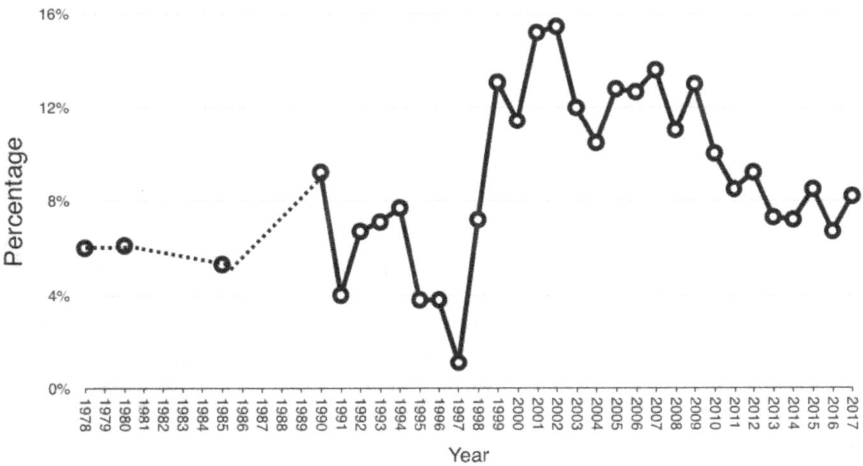

Figure 1: Average annual industrial real wage increases, 1978–2017.

Source: Calculated from *China Statistical Yearbook 2007*, Table 5-22; *China Statistical Yearbook 2014*, Table 4-11, and *China Statistical Yearbook 2018*, Table 4-11.

the Maoist decades; those in the 10%–15% range in the first decade of the new century were extraordinary. However, the rate of increase has been slowing significantly since 2009. In spatial terms (Figure 2), on the one hand, average wages in 2017 in 22 of China's 31 provinces and provincial-level municipalities clustered in a relatively narrow band between ¥55,000 and ¥72,000 per year. But on the other, five out of eight of the highest average wages were found in China's two greatest cities of Beijing and Shanghai and their environs (Tianjin [increasingly part of a conurbation with Beijing] and Zhejiang and Jiangsu [both in the Shanghai hinterland]). Guangdong, home to China's major export platforms, was another high wage case (as were the two remote provinces of Tibet and Qinghai). Yet, given Guangdong's extraordinary importance to the national and, indeed, international economies, it may at first blush seem surprising that wages there were not still higher. The answer, of course, has everything to do with the fact that so much labor in Guangdong's Pearl River Delta is sweated. The remaining case of relatively high wages was Tibet, where they are required to attract needed workers to so remote and, in many ways, culturally foreign an area. The same

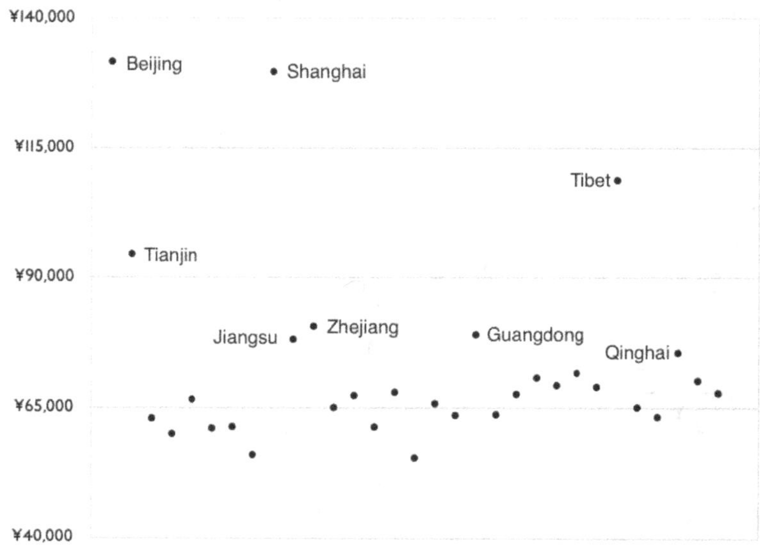

Figure 2: Average annual industrial wages by province, 2017.
Source: *China Statistical Yearbook 2018*, Table 4-11.

applies to Qinghai, where wages were slightly above the main cluster of lower-wage provinces.

As neo-liberal analysts of sweatshops have pointed out, migrants who flock to these firms do earn higher incomes than they would in the depressed villages from which they flee, where their marginal productivity and opportunities to earn any income at all are often at or near zero. That, of course, is why they do so. But as critics point out, that is a pretty low bar which can be cleared even by the generally atrocious labor conditions of Chinese sweatshops. Wages can run to as little as a few dollars a day. Often workers have not even been told what the wage is at the time they are hired, and they are never sure what to expect in their pay packets.[5] Pay has risen since the middle of the first decade of the new century due to a labor shortage produced by a confluence of ever-rising export demand and the long-term demographic effects of the one-child policy. Yet, it is also

[5] Interview, November 2002.

subject to various deductions for dormitory and hiring fees — from the factory, intermediaries, or both — as well as all manner of fines for infractions of elaborate, draconian labor rules. Then there are the fees or deposits that are charged just to get a job, which can run as high as ¥6,000.[6]

Incredibly, three-quarters of rural migrant workers have experienced arrears in payment of even these paltry wages. Already in 1997, over eleven million migrant and urban resident workers nationally were subject to wage arrears averaging ¥1,900 per worker.[7] Almost 20% of those responding to the All-China Federation of Trade Unions (ACFTU) 1997 survey reported experiencing wage arrears, and 46% of those said that they were due three months' pay or more.[8] In the late 1990s, a quarter of employed workers in Shenyang, the Liaoning provincial capital, reported wage arrears.[9] In Guangdong, 7% of workers reported wage arrears in 2009.[10] In January 2015, two protests against wage arrears running as high as ¥900,000 resulted in two deaths.[11] In 2018, 98% of protests in the construction sector, and most of those in retail, were related to wage arrears.[12]

---

[6]May Wong (ed.) (2008). *Voices From Below: China's Accession to WTO and Chinese Workers* (Hong Kong: Asia Monitor Resource Centre), p. 103.

[7]中国工会统计年鉴 (*Chinese Trade Unions Statistics Yearbook*) (1999). (北京: 中国统计出版社 [China Statistics Press]), p. 147.

[8]全国总工会政策研究室 (All-China Federation of Trade Unions Policy Research Office), 中国职工状况调查,数据卷 1997 (*1997 Survey of the Condition of Chinese Workers and Staff*), 1239.

[9]Lee, *Against the Law: Labor Protests in China's Rustbelt and Sunbelt* (Berkeley, CA: University of California Press, 2007), pp. 76–77.

[10]Cheng Zhiming, Ingrid Nielsen and Russell Smyth, "Determinants of Wage Arrears and their Implications for the Socioeconomic Wellbeing of China's Migrant Workers: Evidence from Guangdong Province," Monash University Department of Economics Discussion Paper 50/13, 2013.

[11]"Contractor's teenage daughter falls to her death in wage arrears protest," *China Labour Bulletin*, 21 January 2015, http://www.clb.org.hk/en/content/contractor%E2%80%99s-teenage-daughter-falls-her-death-wage-arrears-protest.

[12]"The State of Labour Relations in China (2018). *China Labour Bulletin*, 9 January 2019, https://clb.org.hk/content/state-labour-relations-china-2018, accessed 29 March 2019.

One effect — probably intentional — is to discourage workers from quitting when conditions become unbearable.[13]

Pushing wage levels to their lowest limit of zero, even slavery has returned. As early as 1994,

> Guangdong officials, acting on reports in the local press, uncovered a vast network of 20 stone quarries in the province where slave labour was the norm. At a quarry near the town of Qingyuan, 39 workers had been locked in sheds at night and kept under guard in the pit for up to a year with no pay. A provincial official, interviewed on local radio at the time, said that forced labour was "common across the province." In 1996 another quarry in Guangdong's Zhanjiang was found to be employing 80 workers in what was described as "a concentration camp"....
>
> In May 2000 ... 90 farmers who had been displaced from the massive Three Gorges dam project on the Yangtze River had ended up as slaves in brick factories in the northeastern city of Shenyang.[14]

In June 2007, Chinese journalists in Shanxi Province uncovered that

> ... 32 migrants had been duped into believing that they were being offered paid jobs, but once inside the brickworks in Caosheng village of Shanxi province, they were forced to work under the watch of guards and dogs for 18 hours a day. None received any money for the whole time of their enslavement, and they survived only on water and steamed rolls of bread.
>
> When a police raid freed the migrants late last month it was discovered that one man had been beaten to death with a hammer. Among the others, eight were so traumatized that they could only remember their names. All had burns on their hands and bodies from having to carry the hot bricks without protection. Their clothes had been reduced to rags, and "the grime on their bodies was so thick it could be scraped off with a knife," said the report in the *Shanxi Evening News*.[15]

[13]Interview, November 2002.

[14]Bruce Gilley (2001). "Toil and trouble," *Far Eastern Economic Review*, 16 August.

[15]Antoaneta Bezlova (2007). "Lessons from China's slavery scandal," *Asia Times*, 20 June, http://www.atimes.com/atimes/China_Business/IF20Cb02.html, accessed 10 September 2015.

Worse yet, Caosheng was not an isolated case.

> It is reported that a crackdown campaign was launched to strike 11 cities of Shanxi Province. Coal mines, brick kilns, private contractors and small-sized enterprises will be under scrutiny after media reports revealed that hundreds of children had been kidnapped and forced to work in kilns in Shanxi.[16]

In all, 550 slaves were rescued. Adding injustice to injury, the traffickers got off with a fine,[17] and it emerged that the police had been involved in the ring.[18] A subsequent investigation by the National People's Congress found "53,000 workers in Shanxi alone who were exploited in over two thousand brick kilns."[19] Four years later, slavery was still happening.

> Police have freed 30 disabled workers, used as slaves in illegal brick factories in Henan. China has failed to curb the exploitation of minors and disabled people in heavy labour, even though it announced zero tolerance and strict controls years ago.
>
> The workers, released Sept. 5 [2011], have severe learning difficulties and some cannot even form whole sentences. They were forced to work long shifts without being paid, some for more than 7 years, frequently beaten … for any disobedience and error.[20]

In 2016, over three million Chinese were estimated to be enslaved, though it's impossible to specify how many were industrial workers.[21] In 2017, students were assigned to forced labor in Foxconn factories

[16] Kang Yi, "Some Human Traffickers May Walk Away in 'Slave' Case," *China Daily*, 15 June 2007, http://www.chinadaily.com.cn/china/2007-06/15/content_895414.htm, accessed 8 September 2019.

[17] "China 'will catch slave owners'," *BBC*, June 16 2007. http://news.bbc.co.uk/go/pr/fr/-/1/hi/world/asia-pacific/6759399.stm, accessed 8 September 2019.

[18] "Officials, Police Implicated in China Slavery Ring," *Agence France Presse*, 15 June 2007.

[19] "Police Free 30 Slaves from Henan Brick Kilns," *Asianews.it*, 8 September 2011.

[20] "Police Free 30 Slaves."

[21] https://www.globalslaveryindex.org/country/china/, accessed 10 March 2018.

to gain "work experience" unrelated to their studies — not exactly slavery but certainly forced labor.[22]

Overtime in violation of China's own labor legislation has been endemic. At the turn of the century, 80% of Chinese workers put in at least ten hours daily, nearly half reported regular 7-day weeks, around a dozen died annually of overwork in Shenzhen alone, and many thousands more suffered serious, life-changing injury.[23] In 2009, 41% of workers worked overtime (much of it presumably forced), and 29% were unpaid for it.[24]

3. Unemployment and Insecurity

Even according to official statistics, which do not count workers who are "laid off" for under 3 years, unemployment nearly doubled from 1990 to 2015.[25] This was due heavily to the 1997 decision to privatize or close many state-owned enterprises. Around the turn of the century, the number of laid-off workers increased over 10-fold to 21 million (at a time when official unemployment statistics were around seven million).[26] They were entitled to receive a "basic living allowance" of ¥200–300 per month for up to 3 years. Thereafter, they were considered "unemployed" only if they registered as such with

---

[22]Yuan Yang, "Apple's iPhone X assembled by illegal student labour," https://www.ft.com/content/7cb56786-cda1-11e7-b781-794ce08b24dc, accessed 10 March 2018.

[23]*op. cit.* (see footnote 9), 163–4.

[24]Linxiang Ye, T.H. Gindling and Shi Li, "Compliance with legal minimum wages and overtime pay regulations in China," *IZA Journal of Labor & Development* (2015) 4, Article 16, page 14.

[25]Calculated from *China Statistical Yearbook 2016*, Table 4-17. The data are aggregated by province, and exclude Chongqing and Tibet, for which there were no 1990 data.

[26]Li Peilin, "中国经济社会发展的问题和趋势" ("Issues and Trends in China's Economic and Social Development"), in Xin Ru, Lu Xueyi and Li Peilin, eds., *2004年:中国社会形势分析与预测* (*2004: Analysis and Forecast of Chinese Society*). Beijing: 社会科学文献出版社 (Social Science Documentary Press), 2004; cited in David S.G. Goodman, *Class in Contemporary China* (Cambridge, UK, Polity, 2014), 132.

their local government, in which case they were expected to turn up at reemployment centers and were in theory entitled to a similarly small unemployment benefit. While those living in cities where there is ready employment for their children are often able to get by, the situation in rust belt areas has been dire since the late 1990s. In Liaoning Province, part of the Manchurian heavy industrial heartland that boomed under the Japanese occupation and then the Maoist era, employment in manufacturing dropped from 4,618,000 in 1990 to 1,447,000 by 2004,[27] and the number of workers registered as unemployed rose from 237,000 in 1990 to 462,000 in 2015.[28] In Benxi, a Liaoning city of 1.5 million in which state and collective heavy industry was the mainstay of the economy, 98% of jobs in those firms were lost between 1993 and 2002, and unemployment has run to a staggering 70%.[29] Unemployed workers in such places huddle in decrepit factory apartment blocks, often without heat, electricity, or even adequate food. Pensions that these state industry workers were promised during their Maoist heyday have often gone unpaid; four million retirees' benefits were in arrears in 2000.

Employment security has declined for all categories of workers, though some have been affected more severely than others. In the Maoist period, layoffs mainly hit rural migrants who had flocked to industrial employment in the mid-1950s boom and were then extruded back to their villages during the severe retrenchment of the Great Leap Forward. Some urban resident workers also lost their factory jobs at that time, but they were reassigned to employment in rural firms and projects, not laid off or fired. Under the structural reforms, tens of millions of urban resident workers in state and collective factories have seen their jobs disappear. Dorothy Solinger has concluded that it is impossible to arrive at a defensible figure for Chinese unemployment, a position with which China's flagship

---

[27] Lee, *Against the Law*, 74.

[28] *China Statistical Yearbook 2016*, Table 4-17.

[29] William Hurst, *The Chinese Worker After Socialism* (Cambridge: Cambridge University Press, 2009), p. 32.

People's Daily subsequently concurred[30]; but it surely also runs into the tens of millions. Unemployment is also very unevenly distributed, with peaks in the rust belts of Manchuria and in poorer inland provinces with cities dominated by now shuttered "third front" factories.[31] For example, in 2015 even the official unemployment rate in Heilongjiang Province was 40% higher than the national average.[32]

In 2007 and 2008, for the first time large numbers of rural migrants were also laid off. While starting in the early 1990s jobs for rural migrants were plentiful, especially in the construction and export sectors, the 2008 depression saw over 20 million lose their positions.[33] Unlike the urban resident laid-off of previous years and some of the urban resident unemployed, they were not entitled to any benefits whatsoever. Most went home to their villages, though they soon returned when the labor market perked up.

China's laid-off workers have faced three broad alternatives: private sector employment, self-employment, or long-term unemployment. Laid-off state and collective industry workers often lack the skills, inclinations and demographics to land work in the private sector, where youth, education, assiduity, and expectations not "tainted" by state socialist employment are prized. Self-employment can include everything from starting a business to driving a cab to peddling. The opportunities for even such petty entrepreneurship

---

[30] Dorothy Solinger, "Why We Cannot Count the 'Unemployed'," *China Quarterly* 167 (September 2001): 671–688; "城镇失业率"数字打架" 专家:会误导决策 建议废除," 人民日报, 7 April 2009, http://politics.people.com.cn/GB/1026/9084260.html.

[31] The "third front" was a program of development begun in the early 1960s to create heavy industrial plants in remote parts of inland China, partly for defensive reasons — so that an attack on the more vulnerable Manchuria would not deprive China of all such factory capacity — and partly for redistribution.

[32] Calculated from *China Statistical Yearbook 2016*, Table 4-17.

[33] "20 Million Laid-off Migrant Workers May Send China's Unemployment Rate to 10%," *China Stakes*, 6 February 2009, http://www.chinastakes.com/2009/2/20-million-laid-off-migrant-workers-may-send-chinas-unemployment-rate-to-10.html, accessed 6 June 2015.

depend, of course, on the state of the local economy, the availability of start-up capital, good information, and business acumen, all of which rarely come together. For most unemployed workers — 85% in one 1999 survey — there has been little way out, and they are forced into very early retirements on meager and rapidly shrinking "benefits" and humiliating dependence on their children.[34]

State and collective industry workers who have dodged the bullet live in constant fear of further cutbacks, especially if they work in factories in economic difficulty. They actually report that this anxiety provides an incentive to work as assiduously as possible.[35] In such firms, workers also often express the hope that a foreign investor will come along, even though they are also well-aware that in private firms, with their generally more intensive labor processes and draconian management, there is a higher risk than in state and collective ones of being fired for cause even in the absence of workforce retrenchment. Some are even willing to countenance corruption if the management is doing it to help lure an investor.[36] One worker compared the loyalty to and sense of identification with their firms that prevailed in the Maoist period to a different kind of tie today.

> People have feelings for their firm today because they cherish the opportunity to work. The workers have a sense of crisis (危机感). They are concerned that if the factory runs into trouble, it will affect them.[37]

So desperate are workers in troubled firms that in some cases they have paid more than a year's wages to employers in bribes and "fees" to keep their jobs[38] — effectively, working for free.

---

[34] Interview, 24 April 2009.

[35] Interview, 18 June 2002; Stephen E. Philion, *Workers' Democracy in China's Transition from State Socialism* (New York: Routledge, 2009), 104.

[36] Philion, *Workers' Democracy*, 103.

[37] Interview, 9 July 1996.

[38] Personal communication from Professor William Hurst.

4. Benefits

State and collective firms no longer offer urban resident workers the welfare benefits that they once did, and private employers certainly do not. Health care and education are now provided on a fee basis, and the charges can be significant. In 1993, the 20% of urban Chinese with the lowest incomes were spending 14% of their annual income on health care, and in 2003, 11%. For the second lowest quintile, the figure was 8% in both years.[39] Many workers are no longer getting necessary medical help because they cannot afford it, and many others are bankrupted when they are forced by serious illness or injury to seek care they cannot afford. In 2003, 57% of urban Chinese did not seek outpatient care when they needed it (and over a third chalked the reason up to costs), 28% did not seek inpatient care (with over half citing costs), and 35% asked for early discharge from hospital (with 53% citing costs).[40] More recent figures are hard to come by, but high health care costs for the urban poor remain a serious problem.[41]

Turning to education, in 2004–2005 the average urban household spent ¥3,522 to send one child to school. This figure amounted to almost a third of average urban total household income.[42] The percentage for workers was much higher: One migrant worker in Shenzhen earning ¥3,000/year in 2002 (ca. US$362) reported middle school

[39]Center for Health Statistics and Information of MOH, An Analysis Report of National Health Services Survey in 2003 (Beijing: China Xiehe Medical University Press, 2004), pp. 83–85; cited in Wang Shaoguang, "State Extractive Capacity, Policy Orientation, and Inequity in the Financing and Delivery of Health Care in Urban China," *Social Sciences in China*, 29,1: 75.

[40]卫生部, 第一次国家卫生服务调查, 第二次国家卫生服务调查, 第三次国家卫生服务调查, cited in Wang, "State Extractive Capacity": 81.

[41]Adam Jourdan and Ben Hirschler, "China healthcare costs forcing patients into crippling debt," *Reuters*, 9 July 2016, https://www.reuters.com/article/us-china-healthcare-debt/china-healthcare-costs-forcing-patients-into-crippling-debt-idUSKCN0ZQ03A, accessed 10 March 2018.

[42]"Survey: Education costs one-third of family income in China," *China Daily*, 22 August 2006.

fees of ¥2,000/semester.[43] In the late 1990s, when market-based school fees were developing, the value of the subsidy (in the form of discounted pricing) that some state- and collectively-owned enterprises still provided was enough for one chemical plant worker to give up much higher-paying work he had found.

> I worked there for 13 years, though I was laid off twice — once for two years and once for three. I liked being laid off, actually, since then I could take a job at an American car radio factory in the open zone as a cook, where I made a lot more money. Here in the Chemical Factory I make just ¥700/month. But when the factory called me back, I had to go. After all, I live in their housing, and they provide inexpensive schooling for my daughter.[44]

Factory-provided housing has been a significant benefit to state sector workers, despite both marketization and the deterioration of old factory-built apartment blocks. In 1988, 80% of urban housing costs were paid by public subsidy, and even in 1995 it still came to 41%. The subsidy comprised 18% of urban income in 1988, and 10% in 1995 — and, in all likelihood, much more for workers (who had relatively lower incomes).[45] Some state- and collective-sectors workers were able to live in surprisingly ample and decently maintained properties, but they were more the exception than the rule.[46]

As early as 1979, urban resident workers began to be allowed to purchase their apartments at highly subsidized prices — often 10% or 20% of their market value once a market had been established by the 1990s.[47] Many workers were happy to become homeowners at a low price, especially as rents began to climb in the 1980s under a policy designed to generate funds to help maintain the often run-down buildings. Quite a few made windfall profits as prices skyrocketed

---

[43] Interview, November 2002.

[44] Interview, 25 May 1999.

[45] Azizur Rahman Khan and Carl Riskin, *Inequality and Poverty in China in the Age of Globalization* (Oxford: Oxford University Press, 2001), 21, 35.

[46] Interview, 4 December 1995; Lee, *Against the Law*, 125.

[47] Interviews, 5 July 1996; 3 July 1996.

starting in the 1990s.[48] But the policy was not the political success that it was in Thatcher's Britain. Sales could sometimes not be completed because firms failed to ante up their required share of housing provident funds used to supply mortgages.[49] In China, workers were often forced to purchase their flats, and many found it a bad deal. "We used to pay only ¥28/month as rent. Then they made us pay ¥8,000 for the same apartment. What's the advantage to us?"[50] Moreover, what workers bought was not an unencumbered property right, but possession hemmed in by various restrictions on sub-leasing or inheritance, or was even merely a use right that remained conditional on continued employment in the firm.[51]

State factories also continued to allocate housing until 1998. But as noted above, in the 1980s and 1990s rents frequently rose to unaffordable levels, prompting a wave of non-payment.

> My factory pays me only ¥110, and rent costs ¥60 per month. How can I afford it? If I pay rent, how am I supposed to buy enough food to stay alive? I would say 80% of all tenants in this building refuse to pay rent and the Housing Bureau has stopped asking for payment. I have stopped paying rent for several years.[52]

A 1998 policy forbade any further allocations in an effort to get housing costs off enterprises' books as part of the state enterprise "reform" that was going into high gear at the time. The housing "reform" was also intended to smooth the process of layoffs by delinking employment from housing provision. It absolved the firms of the responsibility for the buildings, which then deteriorated further. In the new, partially marketized real estate environment,

---

[48] Lee, *Against the Law*, 126; Deborah Davis, "From Welfare Benefits to Capitalized Asset: The Re-commodification of Residential Space in Urban China," in Ray Forrest and James Lee, eds., *Housing and Social Change: East-West Perspectives* (New York: Routledge, 2003).

[49] Interview, 28 May 1999.

[50] Lee, *Against the Law*, 127.

[51] Interview, 7 December 2005; Lee, *Against the Law*, 126–127.

[52] Lee, *Against the Law*, 127.

government plans to develop "affordable" and "low-income" housing generally failed to produce buildings that workers could afford. So most workers remained trapped in their old and increasingly squalid quarters. Where the land under these worthless buildings was subsequently sold to real estate developers, workers generally received at best only a pittance in compensation, and usually faced no alternative but to move to remote locations that were little or no better than their previous digs. It is little wonder, then, that some state and collective sector workers have looked back wistfully on the Maoist days when their firms provided them modest but secure housing.

> Some workers pine away for the old socialist days when everyone had housing. This is especially the case for those who don't have housing, such as those who want to marry but can't because they have no place for a couple to live.[53]

For rural migrant workers, housing is a different matter altogether. Many live in crowded factory-provided dormitories and eat in factory canteens run by their employers-*cum*-landlords, who are, as Lenin put it in a different context, "skinning the ox twice."[54] Their living costs can consume most of their wages.[55] Some rent much more expensive off-site housing, for which they are meant to receive subsidies on which employers frequently renege.[56] Construction workers often have no housing at all, sleeping in the open on the work site.

Nonetheless, whether owned or rented, and whether rent is paid or not, the fact that almost all workers in China, including the

---

[53]Interview, 29 June 1996.

[54]Vladimir Lenin, *Imperialism, the Highest Stage of Capitalism*, https://www.marxists.org/archive/lenin/works/1916/imp-hsc/ch09.htm, accessed 11 March 2018).

[55]Jay Greene, "Riots, Suicides, and Other Issues in Foxconn's iPhone Factories," CNET, 25 September, 2012 (http://www.cnet.com/news/riots-suicides-and-other-issues-in-foxconns-iphone-factories/, accessed 6 June 2015).

[56]For just one example, see Wong, Chun Han, "China Factory Workers Strike Over Housing Benefits," *Wall Street Journal*, 11 March 2015, http://www.wsj.com/articles/china-factory-workers-strike-over-housing-benefits-1426054854, accessed 6 June 2015.

unemployed, have had and continue to have a place to live is highly prized and very significant. As Ching Kwan Lee has pointed out, there is little or no homelessness in the Chinese working class, even among the most destitute.[57] An apartment, no matter how dismal or remote, is a social and economic lifeline for many workers. Some who have a room they don't absolutely need rent it out to generate a bit of often sorely needed income. For others, it is a place to house grown children who are unable to get their own place in the newly marketized environment.[58] A tragic indicator of the importance of housing to Chinese workers is the fact that disputes over allocation and ownership between workers on the one hand and employers or housing authorities on the other, or even within families, are often bitter and have sometimes turned violent, including suicide.[59]

Rural migrants are also not entitled to any services or remaining benefits still provided to some urban resident workers. They have to pay 100% of their medical costs.

> It costs me three hundred *yuan* for an injection and some medicine! If we were Shenzhen locals or state-owned enterprise workers, we would not have to pay that outrageous amount. We are a pitiful lot in the city. We get no welfare from the government even though we contribute our labor.[60]

5. Conclusion: The Political Economy of Working Class Livelihoods and Incipient Homogenization

Chinese workers' compensation and material life under structural reform offer a mixed picture. While urban resident workers who have held on to factory employment have seen significant increases in real wages since the onset of the structural reforms, many among them have lost their jobs altogether and been unable to find reemployment.

---

[57] Lee, *Against the Law*, 125 *ff.*

[58] Interview, 29 June 1996; Lee, *Against the Law*, 128–129.

[59] Lee, *Against the Law*, 127 *ff.*

[60] Lee, *Against the Law*, 199.

Even the employed have lost the economic and job security to which they had become accustomed in Maoist days. That is, urban resident workers have come to experience similar levels of employment insecurity as rural migrants. The latter have toiled for very low wages that are an improvement only in comparison with the prospect of little or no income at all in their home villages. Both urban resident and rural migrant workers receive little or no benefits, and remain housed in qualitatively different but similarly squalid buildings. Finally, the percentage of state-owned enterprises in which strikes and protests occurred has risen from 4% of the total in 2014 to 12% in 2018,[61] which suggests that conditions for urban resident workers are deteriorating to levels closer to those in private firms employing rural migrants.

Overall, then, while urban resident and rural migrant workers remain divided by the household registration system and the institutional, political and legal frameworks that have grown up around it since the 1950s, in material terms the differences between them are shrinking. Kevin Lin has argued that "the distinction between migrant workers in the export sector and many workers in the state sector [is] less dichotomous than it appears."[62] Many scholars and advocates for the plight of rural migrants have argued for the abolition of the household registration (*hukou*) system, seeing it as the institutional and political basis for their subordination within the working class. But a very different and much quieter economic change has actually pushed in the opposite direction. China's structural reform is beginning to reshape the working class itself by flattening the distinction between urban resident and rural migrant workers. Instead of the latter potentially rising to the level of the former, the very opposite is starting to occur.

---

[61] Calculated from *China Labour Bulletin*, *China Strike Map*. https://maps.clb.org.hk/strikes/en, accessed 23 September 2019.

[62] Kevin Lin, "Recomposing Chinese Migrant and State-Sector Workers," in Anita Chan, ed., *Chinese Workers in Comparative Perspective* (Ithaca: ILR Press/Cornell University Press, 2015), 69.

In terms of China's macro-economy, there is a broad consensus among Western and many Chinese economists that state enterprise "reform" — involving at least partial privatization, management changes to emulate the private sector, and deregulation — is the essential next phase if the country is to continue its industrial growth. What often gets lost in such discussions is that such structural change carries a big price for urban resident Chinese workers who, for the first several decades of the structural reform, remained better off in state-owned enterprises than private ones as well as in comparison with rural migrant workers. But ongoing "reform" has begun to produce a race to the bottom that portends the homogenization of China's working class, a profound development in working class re-formation that could carry with it potentially very significant political implications.

6. Afterword: Coronavirus and Working Class Political Economy

As everywhere, coronavirus hit the poor and working class the hardest. In the first quarter of 2020, the official unemployment rate rose 19%, the largest in the history of this problematic statistic. Large firms laid off 15% of their workers, and medium and small ones 40%.[63] Workers in service industries such as hospitality, entertainment and cleaning were particularly hard hit as demand dried up. Many migrants couldn't find work for months on end, and began returning to their rural homes.[64] In early June, 2020, Premier Li Keqiang urged cities to expand street markets as a way to boost employment and economic activity — a major change for many that had been restricting them for years in favor of more formal, orderly and taxable

[63]"估测中国失业率," ("Estimating China's Unemployment Rate,"), 新财富 (*New Fortune*), 1 April 2020 (http://www.xcf.cn/article/810a9b6373f111eabf3cd4c9efcfdeca.html).

[64]Huang Chenkuang, "'The Virus is Terrifying, and So Is Being Jobless': COVID-19 has Devastated Beijing's Migrant Workers," *SupChina*, 14 April 2020 (https://supchina.com/2020/04/14/covid-19-has-devastated-beijings-migrant-workers/).

bricks-and-mortar shops. Many swung behind Li's approach with new policy incentives, though Beijing openly resisted it.[65] Many workers employed in stable manufacturing jobs have had to escape to the far more precarious gig economy.[66] Whether such temporary developments will produce lasting structural change is, of course, impossible to say.

---

[65] Jiayun Feng, "China Pins Hope on Street Vendors To Revive Economy After COVID-19," *SupChina*, 5 June 2020, (https://supchina.com/2020/06/05/china-pins-hope-on-street-vendors-to-revive-economy-after-covid-19/); Liu Zhen, "Beijing City Authorities Reject Calls to Let Roadside Stalls Return, Saying They Are 'Unsuitable' for City," *South China Morning Post*, 8 June 2020.

[66] Viola Rothschild, "Under a COVID-19 Cloud, China's Gig Economy Comes of Age," *China Brief*, 20, 10, 29 May 2020, https://jamestown.org/program/under-a-covid-19-cloud-chinas-gig-economy-comes-of-age/).

https://doi.org/10.1142/9789811226588_0005

Chapter
5

The Political Economic Context of Chinese Agriculture

Jane Du and Cheng King*
*jinch8@sysu.edu.cn

1. Introduction

The urban–rural income inequality is a significant fact in today's Chinese economy.[1] The overall Gini coefficient — the level of inequality — records show that China is a very unequal society and in a way, more "capitalist" than most capitalist countries. However, the inequality is much smaller within the respective rural and urban sectors, denoting that the main source of inequalities in Chinese society is the urban–rural difference.

[1]Naughton, Barry J. (2006). *The Chinese Economy: Transitions and Growth* (Cambridge, MA: MIT Press); Li, Shi, and Terry Sicular (2014). "The distribution of household income in China: Inequality, poverty, and policies," *The China Quarterly*, 217: 1–41; Fan, Qimiao, and Peter Nolan (eds.) (1994). *China's Economic Reforms: The Costs and Benefits of Incrementalism* (Basingstoke: Palgrave MacMillan).

In this chapter, we trace the root of Chinese urban–rural inequality to the Mao Zedong period. Collectivization inversed the outcome of land reform, and made the rural sector the source of surpluses to support urban industrialization. A well-understood economic mechanism is the price scissors maintained by the central planning economy where the rural society had to accept unfair terms of trade in order to exchange agricultural products for overpriced industrial products. In addition to inter-sectoral terms of trade, the forced plantation structure was another source of the planning system's extracted surplus from the rural. However, the impacts of Mao's legacy on the urban–rural income structure were not limited to the Mao period: Mao's collectivization not only changed the ownership structure in agricultural production, but also established a quasi-permanent firewall between urban and rural factor markets. In the post-Mao period, for a long while the planning system and the Grain Bureau remained effective and continued to deliver rural surpluses to the urban sector until its final abolishment in 2005/2006. The Grain Bureau aside, the rural sector faced three limitations or specifically, political barriers — the household registration system (*Hukou*), rural collective ownership of land capital and the rural collective's organizational rules — which restrict the rural sector's access to the labor, capital and agricultural products markets. These factors have continued to place the Chinese rural economy at an institutional disadvantage today.

2. The First Five-Year Plan and Collectivization

Almost at the same time as the establishment of the People's Republic in 1949, the Chinese Communist Party (CCP) had decided to fully embrace the Soviet Union-type of central planning economy. In the meantime, China began to confront the West and detach the Chinese economy from the international trade system, depriving itself of the opportunity to be financed by the post-war global economic system, with developed countries helming the international aid and assistance systems, and the US and Europe dominating the multilateral trade system. However, the assistance of the Union of Socialist Soviet Republics (USSR) was inadequate to propel China toward industrialization given its huge geographical and population size. Thus, the only option left for the Communist Party government was to squeeze the surpluses of the peasants and divert them from the agricultural sector to the industrial sector.[2]

Although the move had resulted in adverse conditions for peasants,[3] the Chinese agricultural sector still struggled to achieve some technical progress in the 1920s and 1930s.[4] While it was uncertain if this technical progress had fully compensated the damages to the Chinese agricultural sector caused by the Sino-Japanese War and the civil war that followed, what was certain was that the subsistence level was almost on par with average Chinese living standards,[5] leaving little room for surplus extraction. However, as the CCP's choice of the USSR style of industrialization would require the agricultural sector and peasants to foot the major cost of industrialization, the crux of the problem was in deciding on the optimal extraction level while letting the peasants play the contributor role.

Two institutional changes were introduced to convert peasants and the agricultural sector into tangible sources of surplus. The first was the State Monopoly over Procurement and Sale (*tonggou tongxiao*),[6] which abolished the whole non-state commercial networks of agricultural products, and replaced them with a state-owned distribution network from wholesalers to retailers. By doing so, the

---

[2] Ash, Robert (2006). "Squeezing the peasants: Grain extraction, food consumption and rural living standards in Mao's China," *The China Quarterly*, 188: 959–998.

[3] Ash, Robert F., Jane Du, and Cheng King (2018). "Perspectives on agricultural and grain output growth in China from the nineteenth century to the present day," in Pinilla, V. and H. Willebald (eds.), *Agricultural Development in the World Periphery: A Global Economic History Approach* (London: Palgrave MacMillan), pp. 307–333.

[4] Myers, Ramon H. (1970). *The Chinese Peasant Economy: Agricultural Development in Hopei and Shantung 1890–1949* (Cambridge: Harvard University Press).

[5] Allen Robert C., Jean-Pascal Bassino, Debin Ma, Christine Moll-Murata, and Jan Luiten van Zanden (2011). Wages, prices, and living standards in China, 1739–1925: in comparison with Europe, Japan, and India," *Economic History Review*, 64: 8–38.

[6] China's centrally planning system formally started from the First Five Year Plan (1953–1957) (*diyi ge wunian jihua*). This includes a complete monopoly over grain purchase and selling (*tonggou tongxiao*) implemented in the agriculture sector.

state had to cut off the major commercial links between peasant families and the market, thereby channeling the majority of agricultural products through the state's network and subjecting it to the state's political rent extraction; in the meantime, peasants' labor and capital were placed under stricter state control and the cost of market engagement was increased. For example, the state monopoly over cotton and cotton yarn took jobs away from peasants involved in the home-made cotton textile industry.[7]

The second was collectivization, which roped the peasant families — including their land and labor — into state-manipulated "rural cooperatives." The collectivization which was finalized by 1958 gave the CCP the institutional basis for its top-down approach to large-scale extraction. Before collectivization, the choice of what to plant and effort level were solely made by the peasants. While the cooperatives did not have enough resources to monitor peasants' effort level, they were able to decide on the varieties of crops to grow, leaving peasants with no room to devote their effort on unwanted crops.

The Chinese rural families would traditionally consume the relatively low commercial value grains, while leaving grains with high commercial value for sale to gain cash incomes. Rice and wheat are the two traditional community grains, but dry maize transactions in north China enjoyed high volume as they could be stored well enough for long-distance transportation. Thus, the plantation ratio of grain varieties was initially decided by the base of a rural farm's commercial grain sales and family's own consumption of grain.[8] Hence, rice and wheat consumption were generally frugal in rural dietary pattern across the country.

It is unclear whether such moves were simple duplications of the USSR experience, or decisions based on CCP's carefully designed strategies. The two institutional changes had dramatically altered the

[7] Xu, Jianqing (2009). "Institutional change and hand-made cotton textile industry, 1954–1965" [*Zhidu jinbu yu shougong mian fangzhi ye*, 1954–1965], *Researches in Chinese Economic History* [*Zhongguo jingji shi yanjiu*], 96(4): 66–75.

[8] Family grain consumption usually contains some potato and bean varieties with less commercial value.

role of the rural peasant (farmer) households. Some basic economic functions were taken away from rural households: the state's monopoly over procurement and sale broke up agricultural producers from the products market, and collectivization separated rural economic factors and rural family household's economic decisions.

More importantly, while collectivization could have reduced the effort level of collective farm participants, it had transferred the choice of what to plant and how to distribute agricultural output to the state.

3. The Eve of Reform

The most striking outcome of Mao's collectivization and Great Leap Forward (GLF) was Mao's Great Famine (1958–1962), a man-made catastrophe as a result of a series of defective policies. The aggregation of agricultural production under collectives (communes and brigades) critically disincentivized ordinary peasant's effort level, while the food supply could not meet the consumption need of collectives, and the over-diversion of rural labor from agricultural to steel production in the GLF greatly reduced agricultural output. Together with other institutional faults, what resulted was China's fatal shortage of rural food supply.

These immediate effects of rapid collectivization aside, the long-term and possibly more fundamental product of collectivization was the mostly ignored and changed role of the peasant class. It is almost a consensus that agricultural collectivization allowed Maoist China to use price scissors to systemically extract surplus from the rural sector to nurture the state's favored industrial sectors.[9] However, the employment of price scissors alone could not bring forth the overall recalibration of inter-sectoral relations between agricultural and industrial sectors as more elements were needed to allow the

---

[9] Ash, Robert (2006). "Squeezing the peasants: Grain extraction, food consumption and rural living standards in Mao's China," *The China Quarterly*, 188: 959–998; Lardy, Nicholas R. (1983). *Agriculture in China's Modern Economic Development* (Cambridge: Cambridge University Press); Lyons, Thomas P. (1987). *Economic Integration and Planning in Maoist China* (New York: Columbia University Press).

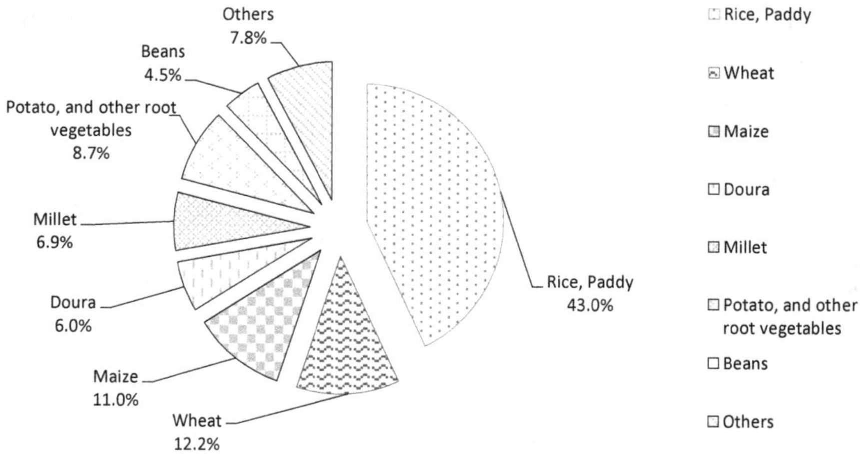

Figure 1: Structure of grain production, 1949.

Source: National Bureau of Statistics of China, *Zhongguo tongji nianjian* [*China Statistical Yearbook*]. Beijing: China Statistics Press, 1981–2018 editions; National Bureau of Statistics of China, *China Statistical Abstract 2018*, Beijing: China Statistics Press, 2018.

"squeeze" mechanism to work. Understandably, the worsening of the overall well-being of peasants during the 1952–1978 period can be attributed solely to the price scissors.

Since the collectives took over the decision right of plantations, the structures of grain varieties, and therefore, the agricultural technology frontiers of Maoist China, peasant's role in the political economy of China had been drastically altered.

The pre-collective Chinese plantation structure, as in Figure 1, which consisted of various relatively "low-value" grain kinds (45%), had been gradually transformed into a structure of collectivization. Thus, the process of collectivization was also a process of the gradual and incremental production of "high value" grains, rice and wheat.

Collectivization had rapidly shored up the share of high-value grain's sown area, from 1953's 42.6% to 1960's 46.5% (Figure 2). Even after Liu Shaoqi and Deng Xiaoping's recovery policies had permanently abolished some GLF measures, they still allowed for a temporary rise in the share of other grain's sown area. After a brief

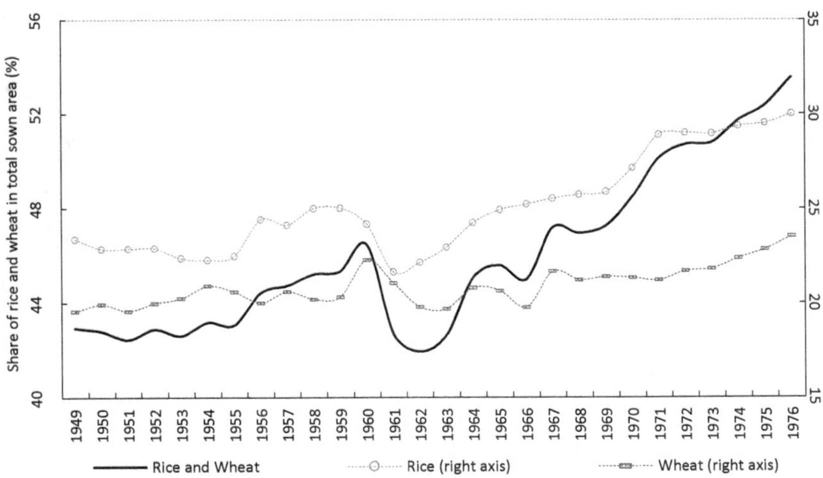

Figure 2: Share of rice and wheat in total grain sown acreage, 1949–1976.

Source: National Bureau of Statistics of China, *Zhongguo tongji nianjian* [*China Statistical Yearbook*]. Beijing: China Statistics Press, 1981–2018 editions; National Bureau of Statistics of China, *China Statistical Abstract 2018*, Beijing: China Statistics Press, 2018.

post-catastrophe (1961–1963), ease in sown area control saw a rebound of the share of rice and wheat plantation acreage to more than 45% in 1964, and then started to increase again until recent years, albeit slowly. Evidently, the long-term policy goal then was to increase the share of rice and wheat in China's agricultural production.

Although the per capita output for the pre-collectivization agricultural sector was still greater than most of the post-catastrophe years prior to 1976, the central planner's capacity to extract surplus grain — mainly rice and wheat — had been enhanced. However, this development was achieved at a price, not from the planner's pocket, but from the peasant class: the efficiency loss caused by reduced effort level, and the efficiency loss caused by regulated usage of factors — labor and land — over the government's favorable crop structures. Based on outcome (as shown in Figure 3), the 1955 per capita output of rice and wheat was recovered in 1973, but at a per capita grain output that was 70 kg lower than the 1955 output level. Most of the output losses were for coarse grains, which were previously used to feed the rural families.

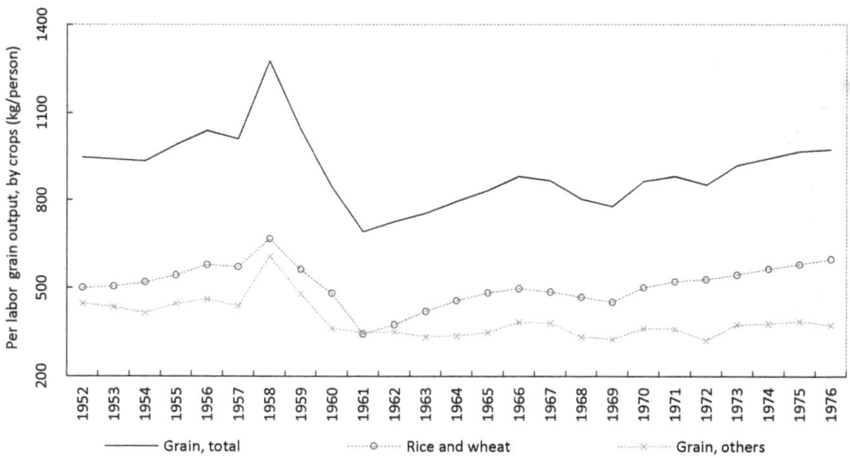

Figure 3: Per labor grain output, by crops.

Source: National Bureau of Statistics of China, *Zhongguo tongji nianjian* [*China Statistical Yearbook*]. Beijing: China Statistics Press, 1981–2018 editions; National Bureau of Statistics of China, *China Statistical Abstract 2018*. Beijing: China Statistics Press, 2018.

While the theory of China's agricultural growth during the 1979–2005 period was a "natural" result of economic development in China (e.g., the spread of Green Revolution technologies),[10] the successful application of the "dual-track system" in the design of economic institutions could not be discredited. While the de-collectivization policy did take in some liberalization elements, the strong manipulating hand of the state was still evident. A general consensus was that institutional changes, especially the de-collectivization measures, were the main driver in the surge of the agricultural economy.[11]

[10]Huang, Jikun, and Scott Rozelle (1996). "Technological change: Rediscovering the engine of productivity growth in China's rural economy," *Journal of Development Economics*, 49(2): 337–369; Li, Gucheng (2014). "The green productivity revolution of agriculture in China 1978–2008" [*Zhongguo nongye de lvse shengchanlv geming, 1978–2008*], *China Economic Quarterly* [*jingji xue (ji kan)*], 13(2): 537–558).

[11]Sun, Shengmin, and Qiang Chen (2017). "Measuring the effects of de-collectivization on China's agricultural growth: A panel instrumental approach," *China Economic Quarterly*, 16(2): 815–832).

4. The Dual-Track System

First, physical incentives were restored via the dissolution of collectives. By the later part of the 1970s, the remaining cooperative economic organizations were abolished on a gradual trial and error basis. By 1983,[12] agricultural land was once again allocated via the *de facto* household-based land ownership and according to the household's output. Even when purchase prices for agricultural products were determined by the state's procurement department, the economic gains that were directly linked to output volume and monetary income were sufficient to drive peasants to increase their effort level.

Second, peasants were once again granted decision rights in the agricultural sector. At the early stages, the state still maintained a minimum farm gate purchase quantity, but such requirement was soon eased. Peasants' plantation decisions were thus less affected by the state, and in most cases more likely based on pure economic — generally cost and benefit — considerations. As a result, driven by changes in relative demands (and therefore relative prices) the sown acreages of rice and wheat were on a declining trend, while that of soya beans and maize were on an upsurge.

Third, grain procurement generally stayed under the state's control. Although agricultural de-collectivization was a complicated history of the evolution of grain procurement system the state generally kept itself at a *pari passu* position in the control of grain distribution. To do so, the state not only monopolized grain circulation by excluding most non-state backed grain firms from farm gate procurement, it also ruled out the possibility of large-scale gray grain market via massive grain subsidies to stabilize or attain grain retail prices that were even lower for the urban sector than for the rural sector.

As a result of such institutional arrangements, the dual-track economy had formed two separate agricultural markets. At the rural

[12] Central Committee Document No. 137, *Circular on the Diligent Execution of All Operations Affecting Grain* [*Guowuyuan guanyu renzhen zuohao liangshi gongzuo de tongzhi*]. Beijing: State Council, 28 November 1982.

end, the peasant families enjoy a semi-private ownership over land, or even sell land to other peasants; at the urban end, when the mid-1990s finally saw the end of the planning system,[13] urban citizens had already enjoyed deregulated food retails for more than a decade, so much so that in the retail grain market there were very few obstacles to distort urban residents' aggregated purchasing power on agricultural products.

However, as a whole, the Chinese grain market was distorted by the state's efforts to separate economic functions from rural households and separate agricultural producers from the products market. The state's exclusive procurement power enabled it to purchase grain at a lower than equilibrium price for reselling at an even lower price in the urban sector.[14] By doing so, the state paid little for urban food subsidy — to facilitate industrialization at relatively low labor cost — by forcing the rural sector to foot most of the subsidy cost.[15,16] Thus, though the extraction level of the price scissors had been reduced, the dual-track agricultural market still delivered large-scale agricultural surpluses to the urban sector.[17] The scale of

---

[13] Before 2003, the 1993 reform was the only pilot for a complete marketization of Chinese agriculture. However, due to high inflation at the end of the 1980s and early 1990s, urban grain selling price started to soar. To stabilize urban grain selling price and food accessibility, at the end of 1993, the central government withdrew all grain purchasing and selling rights from the market, thereby calling an end to the 1993 marketization efforts.

[14] Wang, Dewen, and Jikun, Huang (2001). "An analysis of Chinese farmers' grain supply impact under the dual price system," *Economic Research Journal* [*Jingji yanjiu*], 12: 55–65.

[15] Liu, Bin, Zhaogang Zhang, and Gong Huo (2004). *China Farming, Countryside and Peasantry Issues Report* [*Zhongguo sannong wenti baogao*] (Beijing: China Development Press) [*Zhongguo fazhan chubanshe*].

[16] The price scissor also generated fiscal pressure on central finance. In the early 1990s, to alleviate fiscal pressures, the state abolished the longstanding urban grain subsidies on the one hand, while refraining from passing any substantial regulation to reform grain enterprises in order to stop fiscal leakage, on the other.

[17] Feng, Haifa, and Wei Li (1993). "Quantitative research on the accumulative funds provided by agriculture for China's industrialization" [*Woguo nongye wei gongyehua tigong zijin jilei de shuliang yanjiu*], *Economic Research Journal* [*Jingji yanjiu*] 9: 60–64.

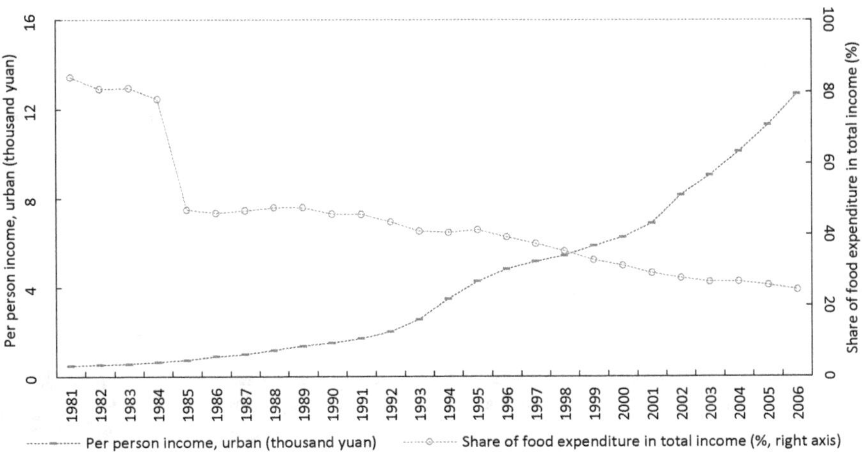

Figure 4: Urban income and share of food expenditure, 1978–2006.

Source: National Bureau of Statistics of China, *Zhongguo tongji nianjian* [*China Statistical Yearbook*]. Beijing: China Statistics Press, 1981–2018 editions; National Bureau of Statistics of China, *China Statistical Abstract 2018*. Beijing: China Statistics Press, 2018.

such surplus transfer by the late 1980s could amount to as much as 11% of agricultural value-added.[18]

The ease in the state-dominated rural to urban agricultural surplus transfer took place dramatically in the early 21st century. The speed of increasing urban income started to accelerate from the early 1990s, partly because of high inflation in the early 1990s,[19] but mainly as an outcome of rapid industrial expansion and consequential increases in urban real income (Figure 4). Accordingly, the share of per head urban food expenditure had since steadily declined, along with the decline in the importance of food price control.

---

[18]Yan Ruizhen, Daoguang Gong, Zhixiang Zhou, and Baode Bi (1990). "The status, trends and countermeasures of the price scissor between industrial and agricultural products in China" [*Zhongguo gongnongye chanpin jiage jiandaocha de xianzhuang, fazhan qushi ji duice*], *Economic Research Journal* [*Jingji yanjiu*] 2: 64–70.

[19]The 1993 and 1994 consumer price indexes, compared to that of preceding year, increased by 14.70% and 24.13%, respectively.

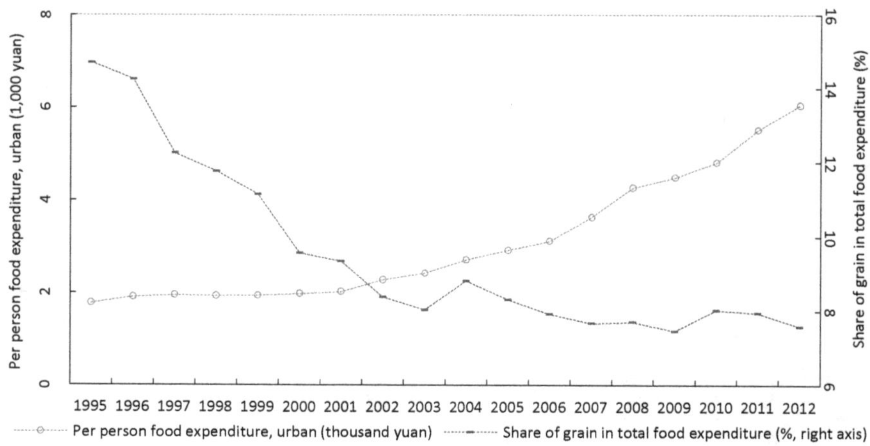

Figure 5: Share of grain expenditure in per head urban expenditure.

Source: National Bureau of Statistics of China, *Zhongguo tongji nianjian* [*China Statistical Yearbook*]. Beijing: China Statistics Press, 1981–2018 editions; National Bureau of Statistics of China, *China Statistical Abstract 2018*. Beijing: China Statistics Press, 2018.

By the early 2000s, the share of grain in China's average urban expenditure was small: in 2000, it declined for the first time to below 10%, then went further to 9% in 2002, and has since remained as such (Figure 5). Therefore, for the central government, the changes brought about by economic development had made a grain policy U-turn possible. The 2004 temporary grain shortage, caused purely by the state monopoly's over-extraction,[20] had triggered such a policy U-turn. Since 2005, the Hu Jintao and Wen Jiabao government stopped using price control to ensure cheap staple grain supply to urban consumers, and started to directly subsidize peasants.[21]

[20]Du, Jane and Cheng King (2018). "Unravelling China's food security puzzle, 1979–2008," *The China Quarterly*, 235: 804–827.

[21]Concerns over food security in China are reflected in the *Medium and Long-term Plan for National Food Security 2008–2010* (*Guojia liangshi anquan zhongchangqi guihua gangyao*, 2008–2020 nian). National Development and Reform Commission (2008). *Medium and Long-term Plan for National Food Security 2008–2020* [*Guojia liangshi anquan zhongchangqi guihua gangyao, 2008–2020 nian*] (Beijing: National Development and Reform Commission).

5. The De-regulated Agricultural Market: Peasants versus Capital

In contrast to China's rapid economic growth, the rural per head income only accounted for 37.8% of the urban sector in 2019, and the per head expenditure amounted to 47.5% of the urban sector. The reason for such a huge income gap between rural and urban sectors was the extremely low returns from agriculture. Agricultural income, especially from grain production, has been a drag to rural income growth in China.

More than two-thirds of China's total sown acreages were for grain production, and roughly about three quarters of labor inputs of the Chinese agricultural sector were devoted to grain-related works. China's total grain output expanded by around 2.2 times, while the number of workers employed by the primary industry went down by one-third. This means the nominal per capita income of crop plantation — in which grain plantation takes the majority share — in the rural sector increased 30 times. After deduction of inflation, the real per capita income in grain plantation increased by less than 5 times: the result seems at odds with China's 200 times nominal GDP growth (more than 30 times in real terms), and the almost 140 times in nominal growth of urban labor price (Figure 6).

What accounted for the low returns to agricultural labor was the cheap farm gate product prices. The farm gate purchase price for agricultural products increased — in nominal terms — about 10 times since 1978 (Figure 6). Taking in the general inflation and increases in other agricultural inputs (chemical fertilizer, seeds, pesticide and the cost of agricultural machineries), even with the increases in output, the increasing speed in income generated from agriculture is still far slower than that of the secondary and service sectors.

Farms suffered from an extremely low or no growth in profit margin. As the average nominal staple grain price had increased 4–5 times since 1990, the net profit for every 50 kg of typical staple grain sold was only CN¥27.8 (about US$4 in 2020 exchange rate) in 2011, the peak of the recent decade, which is still less than the 1995's CN¥30.8 (Figure 6). Considering that the output growth in

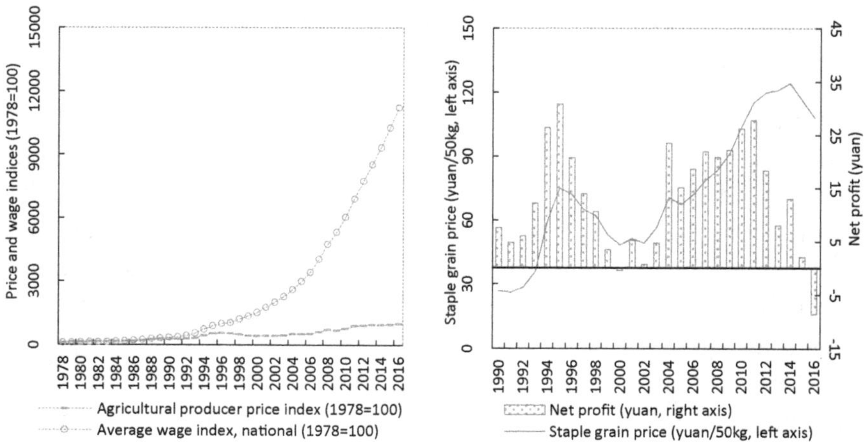

Figure 6: Grain price, profit and urban income.

Source: National Bureau of Statistics of China, *Zhongguo tongji nianjian* [*China Statistical Yearbook*]. Beijing: China Statistics Press, 1981–2018 editions; National Bureau of Statistics of China, *China Statistical Abstract 2018*. Beijing: China Statistics Press, 2018.

staple grain is slower than overall grain production, when China's grain output increased from the 1999's 508 million tons to 2019's 664 million tons, a 30.7% growth, the paddy rice output only increased from 198 million tons to 210 million tons, a 6.1% growth; and wheat growth was an edge better (114–134 million tons), albeit still below the overall grain production incremental rate. Thus, considering the fact that China's staple grain production technology has reached East Asia's technological frontiers, counting on the increase in the output to compensate losses caused by unfavorable price conditions will not work.

There are multiple causes for such an outcome. The most important factor during the first decades after grain market liberalization was the state-owned grain enterprises (grain SOEs), which were converted from previous state grain administrative branches. With three giant nationwide giant firms in operation,[22] grain SOEs joined

[22] China Oil and Foodstuffs Corporation (COFCO), China Grain Reserves Corporation (Sinograin), and Chinatex Corporation.

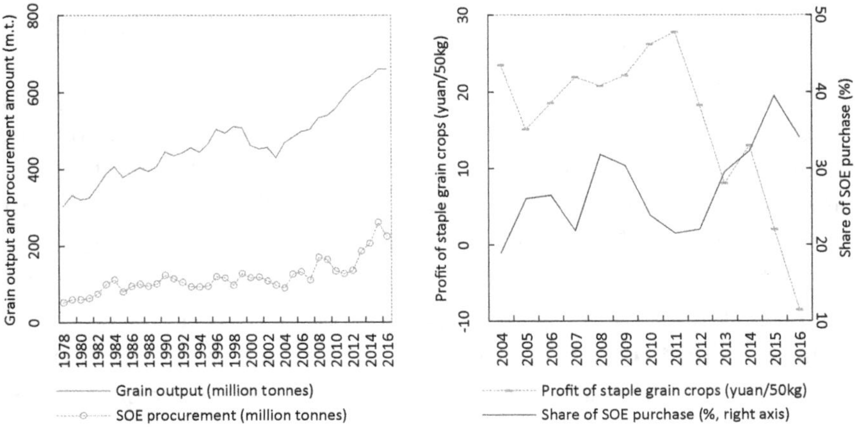

Figure 7: Farming profit and SOEs' procurement.

Source: National Bureau of Statistics of China, *Zhongguo tongji nianjian* [*China Statistical Yearbook*]. Beijing: China Statistics Press, 1981–2018 editions; National Bureau of Statistics of China, *China Statistical Abstract 2018*. Beijing: China Statistics Press, 2018.

forces in a huge network to enjoy the certain level of exclusive local monopoly power that each local grain SOE was endowed with.[23] Therefore, the ease in grain price control did not slash the share of grain SOEs in China's grain market. In contrast, the share of grain SOEs' farm gate purchase volume in China's total production not only increased after the 2005 reform, but also reached a historical peak of nearly 40% in 2015 (Figure 7) to surpass that of the State Monopoly over the Procurement and Sale period. Meanwhile, there were backdraughts in peasant grain production profit rate from purchases from grain SOEs: the more the farmers sell to grain SOEs, the less they gain from their sales (Figure 7). This phenomenon implies that there exist obvious conflicts between grain SOE's business interests and the profitability of grain farming, not to mention the possibility that grain SOEs could use their non-market measures,

[23]As local grain SOEs were converted from the Grain Bureau (the administrative department for grain distribution), they still have privileges in grain purchase and in government grain-related contract bidding.

such as political connections with government and monopoly power, to squeeze farmers' profit margins.

Other players are also at work. Since 2000, commercial capital, including Internet retail giants such as Taobao, Jingdong and Amazon, has played a key role in agricultural products sales. As of 2020, the state's protective rice purchase price is CN¥2.6/kg (the highest), and CN¥2.2/kg for wheat, while the retailing price for the respective grade of grain is at least CN¥5.0/kg. Meanwhile there is no lack of demand. The retail industry — online or offline — had enjoyed rapid expansion since 2000: for food and textiles, in most years China's consumption grew faster than the sales income of the farming sector (Figure 8). This gives rise to the question of why was the peasant still underpaid after the de-regulation when there was evidently a surge in demand from retail and distributional capitals?

6. Incomplete Rural Reform and China's Dual Economy

Since the early land reform in the 1930s, the rural sector had been segregated into landlords and ordinary peasants, turning peasants

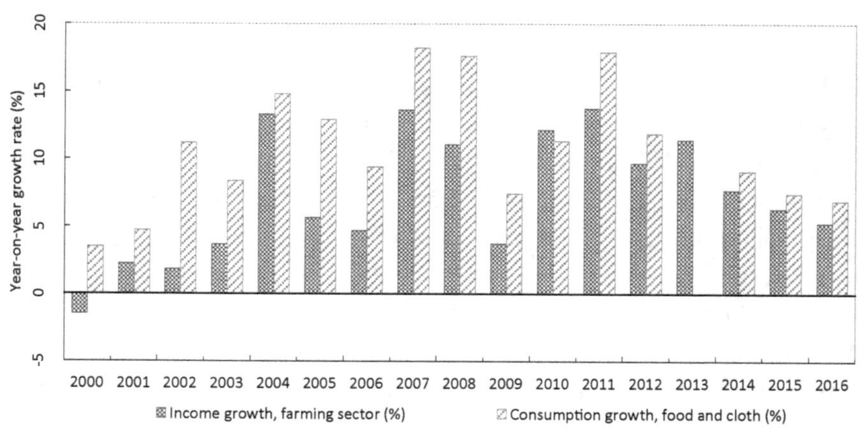

Figure 8: Growth rates for sales income and consumption, 2000–2016.

Source: National Bureau of Statistics of China, *Zhongguo tongji nianjian* [*China Statistical Yearbook*]. Beijing: China Statistics Press, 1981–2018 editions; National Bureau of Statistics of China, *China Statistical Abstract 2018*. Beijing: China Statistics Press, 2018.

into atomized individual farmers who were highly dependent on the socialist cooperative organizations. This development, along with the long-term effects of organizational changes, had a huge impact on individual peasant families' incentive levels. In general, China's commercial networks during this period were dismantled in both urban and rural sectors, and replaced with central planning.

The social and economic atomization of Chinese rural society in the 1950s was designed to incorporate the agricultural sector into a Soviet-type of central planning economy. Such an attempt was successful — despite the tragedy of GLF — in the sense that the central planning system's extraction ability from rural society had been enhanced. With central planning, the government gained control of the supply of the urban sector's staple grain, meanwhile the Chinese society has to pay for such control, in the price of rural sector's staple grain supply, and the efficiency losses of Chinese agriculture. In the name of the Soviet-type of industrialization, economic factors were reorganized according to three institutional arrangements:

(i) the central planning system arranged the usage of urban labor and capital, as well as the exchange rates between industrial goods, agricultural goods and other goods or services, and used price scissors to deliver surplus from the rural sector to prioritized sectors;
(ii) the *Hukou* system constrains both regional and urban–rural population flow to prevent voluntary labor flow;
(iii) rural cooperatives controlled both rural labor and capital (land) at the micro level, and worked as part of the State Monopoly over Procurement and Sale institutions to regulate the sales of agricultural products.

China's early 1980s rural reform removed its intra-rural control of labor inputs and returns from product sales. However, both labor and land (capital) were still moderately regulated: for labor, long-distance flows are still restricted by the *Hukou*, especially from rural to urban; for land, unless the sale is intra-local rural cooperative and within the scope of agricultural use, no rural land sales are permitted. Besides economic factors, the sales of main agricultural products were still subject to the state's compulsory purchase.

Some of the control measures were removed by the Hu-Wen government's 2005/2006 agricultural policies. However, *Hukou* and the rural cooperative are still preventing the formation of normal rural factor markets. Within the agricultural sector, the atomized land (quasi) ownership distribution, plus huge transactional costs for land ownership transfer or long-term lease, made the average farm size tiny. It is also rare to see successful cases of rural households reorganizing agricultural cooperatives — other than the collective farms — to operate agricultural business. Thus, an individual rural household has little bargaining power in the products market.

Although economic reform towards liberalization took place much later in the urban sector than in the rural sector, reform measures taken are more complete in both capital and labor market de-regulations. In particular, as the urban sector is largely the destination of labor flows, the urban labor market remains robust as long as intra-urban labor flows are less restrictive. The urban sector's access to the capital market is also more favorable than that of the rural sector. For example, as the property market in the urban sector has fewer restrictions, urban residents can easily lease as well as buy and sell properties in the market, which means a broader source of capital income than that for rural residents.

Based on the four major accounting items (operational income, salary, capital returns and transfer payments) used in the breakdown of income under Chinese statistical standards (Figure 9), the rural sector can only keep its growth pace in line with the urban sector under the "operational income" item. For all the other three income sources, there are widening gaps between the urban and rural sectors. For the labor market, capital market, and government's resident subsidy distributional channels, *Hukou* and the residuals of collectivization are all still at work to effectively exclude rural residents from superior markets or positions, which are inclusive to urban citizens only. The pure market-oriented factors — demand, supply, quality and price elements — only work fully in the product/service market, which is the source of operational income.

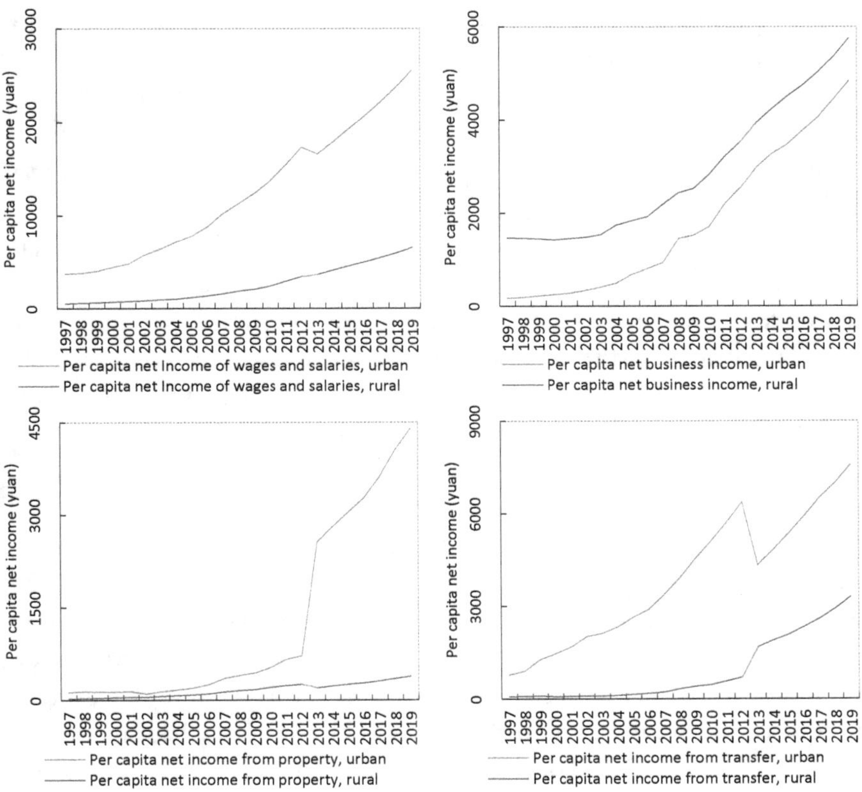

Figure 9: Major breakdowns in per capita income.

Note: Due to statistical caliber change in incomes during 2012–2013, an interrupt is inserted in this figure.

Source: National Bureau of Statistics of China, *Zhongguo tongji nianjian* [*China Statistical Yearbook*]. Beijing: China Statistics Press, 1981–2018 editions; National Bureau of Statistics of China, *China Statistical Abstract 2018*. Beijing: China Statistics Press, 2018.

7. Conclusion

While China's political propaganda may claim victory in achieving the ultimate goals of the post-1978 reform through the establishment of a fine market institution, and in attaining "common prosperity" (*gongtong fuyu*) for the people,[24] the situations on the ground are more complicated than what simple slogans have chanted.

In China's political economy, the agricultural sector and rural citizens used to be the most significant funding source of China's industrialization. The state delivered agricultural surpluses to the industrial sector via its carefully designed economic institutions, which include agricultural collectivization, household registration and compulsory state grain procurement. When such an industrialization path failed, or was proven less efficient, the state turned to grant the rural sector more economic freedom — which seemed to have worked in the economic policies of Liu Shaoqi in the early 1960s — as the starting point of the industrialization approach to stimulate energy from the bottom up.

Despite the incomplete rural reform at the early stage, this approach in general can be considered a success if reform towards creating a fine market institution is concerned. The rural population was not granted full access to the labor and capital markets throughout the post-1978 era, and even access to the agricultural product market took a rather fragmented organizational form. As a result, both the returns to agricultural production — especially grain production — and the average income of the rural sector, are significantly lower than that enjoyed by the urban sector. Thus, one side product of China's rapid economic growth since 1978 has been the widened urban–rural income gap, an elephant in the room of Chinese contemporary political economy, and the source of what Chinese Premier Li Keqiang said, the "600 million (Chinese) people with a monthly income of CN¥1000 (US$140)."[25]

Bibliography

Du, Jane, and Kent Deng (2017). "Getting food prices right: The state versus the market in reforming China, 1979–2006," *European Review of Economic History*, 21(3): 302–325.

[24] Deng Xiaoping (1993). *Selected Works of Deng Xiaoping, Volume III* (Beijing: People's Publishing House), p. 123.

[25] Zhou, Xin (2020). *Is China Rich or Poor*? Nation's Wealth Debate Muddied by Conflicting Government Data, https://www.scmp.com/economy/china-economy/article/3086678/china-rich-or-poor-nations-wealth-debate-muddied-conflicting, accessed 15 April 2020.

https://doi.org/10.1142/9789811226588_0006

Chapter 6

The Political Economy of Stability Maintenance under Xi Jinping

Martin K. Dimitrov* and Zhu Zhang

*mdimitro@tulane.edu

1. Introduction

Protests in autocracies are rare events that can lead to political instability. To illustrate this point, we need look no further than regimes in communist Europe, in the successor states of the Soviet Union, and in the Middle East that experienced long periods of relative quiescence but then collapsed as a result of a small number of protests during the Velvet Revolutions, the Color Revolutions, and Arab Spring. China appears anomalous against this background because the regime has held steady since 1989 despite the occurrence of at least one million protests. What explains this paradoxical outcome? The extensive literature on protests in China has not engaged with this question. By putting the Chinese case in a comparative perspective, our chapter generates new insights on the relationship between protests and authoritarian stability both in the case of China and more generally. We argue that protests in China are distinct from those in other autocracies in three important ways. First, the nature of the protests is different, with contention about overtly political issues being relatively rare; most protests in China are small-scale non-violent instances of "rightful resistance" involving socioeconomic demands.[1] In other autocracies, these types of grievances would be resolved through petitions, but the inadequacies of the petitioning system in China have led citizens to opt for protests. Second, the location of protests is different, with protests in the capital deliberately kept at a very low level. Third, the government shows exceptional resolve when dealing with protests, both those that are overtly political (when violent force is used) and those that focus on socioeconomic rights (when the police are typically present, though violent force is not always used). These features of contention in China, which stand in sharp contrast to the characteristics of protests in other autocracies, explain why frequent protests have not so far led to political instability in post-Tiananmen China.

We base the claims of this chapter on a variety of sources. Our discussion of destabilizing protests beyond the Chinese case is informed by newly available East European archival materials and by secondary sources in English. Our arguments about protest activity in China are based on scholarly writing in Chinese and English; on internal circulation (内部 *neibu*) materials in Chinese; and on a unique new source: a protest dataset that we created by hand coding over 65,000 instances of protests that took place between November 2013 and June 2016. The protest dataset is the most extensive source of data on protests in China that has been generated thus far. It yields information about the geographic location of the protests; the issues about which citizens protest; the tactics used by protesters; the response of the government; and the outcomes of the protests. Our dataset also sheds light on the difference between urban and rural protests in China. Although we do not have a complete catalog of all protest events, our dataset allows us to make more systematic claims

[1]On rightful resistance, see Kevin J. O'Brien and Lianjiang Li (2006). *Rightful Resistance in Rural China* (New York: Cambridge University Press).

about the nature of protest activity in China than has been possible on the basis of previously available datasets, which have contained a considerably smaller number of protests.

Our chapter makes an empirical, a methodological, and a theoretical contribution to research on protest activity in China. The empirical contribution of the chapter is to add more granularity to the notion that a protest avalanche has engulfed the country since 1989 by providing significant new information on protest incidence, protest tactics, and protest outcomes. The methodological contribution involves putting the Chinese case in comparative perspective. By identifying the key differences between protest activity in China and in other autocracies, the chapter allows us to grasp what is unique about post-Tiananmen China. The theoretical contribution of the chapter is to provide a general argument regarding the conditions under which protests can lead to instability, both in China and more generally in authoritarian regimes. This argument has specific implications about the future of China.

The chapter is organized as follows. Section 2 reviews the main theories of protest in China and identifies several lacunae in them. In particular, these theories do not systematically engage with the question of whether the ability of the Chinese regime to survive a high number of protests may reflect systematic differences between China and other autocracies in terms of the type of protests, the location of protests, and the firmness of government response to protests. This section also presents the main hypotheses that will be tested in the rest of the chapter. Section 3 provides a brief description of protest activity in post-1989 China, as revealed by the existing literature and by *neibu* sources. It also discusses politically destabilizing protests, which are largely absent from our dataset. The emphasis of this section is on the incidence and handling of political protest in China, which is contrasted with the handling of political protest in other autocracies. Section 4 describes our dataset and discusses the representativeness and validity of the data. Section 5 analyzes the patterns of protest activity revealed by the dataset, focusing in particular on the questions of where and why protests occur. Section 6 examines protest tactics, government response, and protest outcomes in cases of socioeconomic contention. This section provides the main empirical tests of our research hypotheses. It also discusses the incidence and handling of protests in the capital city. Section 7 concludes and offers some broader implications about the relationship between protest activity and regime resilience both in the case of China and in autocracies more generally.

Before we proceed further, we should discuss how this essay engages with the theme of the volume, namely China's political economy in the new era. By focusing on socioeconomic protests during Xi's first term (2013–2016), our chapter investigates how rapid economic development can produce grievances. If left unaddressed, these grievances can have potentially destabilizing effects. As growth has generated both winners and losers, stability maintenance has become a central component of the government's strategy for regime preservation. We explore these issues in more depth throughout the chapter.

2. Theories of Protest in China

The literature has not confronted the question of why protests have not led to political destabilization because it has not (with the exception of Perry 2002) examined all types of protests in China in their totality.[2] Instead, existing research has advanced separate arguments about nationalistic protests,[3] political dissent,[4] and protests about socioeconomic rights.[5] The most developed branch of the literature is

---

[2]Elizabeth J. Perry (2002). *Challenging the Mandate of Heaven: Social Protest and State Power in China* (Armonk, NY: M. E. Sharpe), esp. ix–xxxii.

[3]Jessica C. Weiss (2014). *Powerful Patriots: Nationalist Protest in China's Foreign Relations* (New York: Oxford University Press).

[4]Dingxin Zhao (2001). *The Power of Tiananmen: State-Society Relations and the 1989 Beijing Student Movement* (Chicago: University of Chicago Press); Justin Hastings (2011). "Charting the course of Uyghur unrest," *The China Quarterly*, 208: 893–912; James W. Tong (2009). *Revenge of the Forbidden City: The Suppression of the Falungong in China, 1999–2005* (New York: Oxford University Press).

[5]Thomas P. Bernstein and Xiaobo Lü (2003). *Taxation without Representation in Contemporary Rural China* (New York: Cambridge University Press); Andrew C. Mertha (2008). *China's Water Warriors: Citizen Action and Policy Change* (Ithaca,

the study of socioeconomic protests, which has focused on three specific questions and on a larger meta-question. The first question concerns protest initiation: namely, why do protests arise. The answer has been, unsurprisingly, that they result from socioeconomic grievances.[6] A more nuanced account emerges when we adopt an explicitly comparative perspective, which shows that these types of grievances would be resolved by lodging petitions in other single-party systems[7]; the low effectiveness of the petitioning system in China explains the high number of protests.[8] The second question has focused on the tactics of protesters. In particular, scholars have examined whether protest participants use peaceful or disruptive tactics.[9] The literature has concluded that protesters rely on both, but that disruptive tactics are more likely to be successful.[10] The third question has involved protest response: namely, whether the government ignores protests,

---

NY: Cornell University Press); Kevin J. O'Brien (ed.) (2008). *Popular Protest in China* (Cambridge, MA: Harvard University Press); Yongshun Cai (2010). *Collective Resistance in China: Why Popular Protests Succeed or Fail* (Stanford, CA: Stanford University Press); Xi Chen (2012). *Social Protest and Contentious Authoritarianism in China* (New York: Cambridge University Press); Yanqi Tong and Xiaohua Lei (2014). *Social Protest in Contemporary China, 2003–2010: Transitional Pains and Regime Legitimacy* (New York: Routledge); Christopher Heurlin (2016). *Responsive Authoritarianism in China: Land, Protests, and Policymaking* (New York: Cambridge University Press).

[6] Tong and Lei, *Social Protest in Contemporary China*.

[7] Martin K. Dimitrov (2014). "What the party wanted to know: citizen complaints as a 'barometer of public opinion' in Communist Bulgaria," *East European Politics and Societies and Cultures* 28(2): 271–295; Martin K. Dimitrov (2014). "Tracking public opinion under authoritarianism: the case of the Soviet Union under Brezhnev," *Russian History*, 41(3): 329–353; Martin K. Dimitrov (2019). "The functions of letters to the editor in reform-era Cuba," *Latin American Research Review*, 54(1): 1–15.

[8] Martin K. Dimitrov (2015). "Internal government assessments of the quality of governance in China," *Studies in Comparative International Development*, 50(1): 50–72.

[9] Cai, *Collective Resistance in China*; Chen, *Social Protest and Contentious Authoritarianism in China*; Heurlin, *Responsive Authoritarianism in China*.

[10] *Ibid*.

acquiesces to the demands made, or uses repression.[11] The finding has been that repression is most likely overall but that acquiescence can occur, especially when protests are forceful and when the costs of concessions are high.[12] This research has been very useful for generating some of the hypotheses that can be tested through our dataset.

The existing literature has also engaged with the meta-question of the relationship between protests and stability.[13] An argument has been developed that protests contribute to stability through three different mechanisms. The first is that they generate information about local grievances, which enables improved governance.[14] This information is so useful to the leadership that it goes as far as encouraging citizens to protest.[15] The second mechanism is that protests serve as an input institution that provides an avenue for popular participation.[16] And the third is that they enable bargained authoritarianism, which involves negotiation between the regime and citizens.[17]

Scholars of protest in other autocracies would likely view these arguments about the regime-sustaining effects of contention as

[11] See especially Cai (2018). *Collective Resistance in China*; Yao Li, *Playing by the Informal Rules: Why the Chinese Regime Remains Stable Despite Rising Protests* (New York: Cambridge University Press); and Manfred Elfstrom (2019). "Two steps forward, one step back: Chinese reactions to labor unrest," *The China Quarterly*, 240: 855–879.

[12] *Ibid.*

[13] O'Brien and Li, *Rightful Resistance in Rural China*; Cai, *Collective Resistance in China*; Chen, *Social Protest and Contentious Authoritarianism in China*; Tong and Lei, *Social Protest in Contemporary China*; Heurlin, *Responsive Authoritarianism in China*.

[14] Peter Lorentzen (2013). "Regularizing Rioting: permitting public protest in an authoritarian regime," *Quarterly Journal of Political Science*, 8(2): 127–158.

[15] *Ibid.*

[16] Andrew Nathan (2003). "Authoritarian resilience: China's changing of the guard," *Journal of Democracy*, 14(1): 6–17.

[17] Ching Kwan Lee and Yonghong Zhang (2013). "The power of instability: unraveling the microfoundations of bargained authoritarianism in China," *American Journal of Sociology*, 118(6): 1475–1508.

evidence that China is *sui generis*.[18] Protests in other autocracies have been understood as a source of weakness. This has been especially true for single-party communist regimes.[19] The divergent foci of the China-specific literature and the general literature on protests in autocracies reflect differences in both the nature of protests (which are more likely to be about socioeconomic grievances in China) and about the response to protests (which is harsher in China than elsewhere).

The central goal of this chapter is to highlight why protests in other autocracies have been a source of instability, whereas China has not experienced collapse despite a high number of protests. We argue that Chinese resilience in the face of protests reflects systematic differences between China and other autocracies in terms of the type of protests, the location of protests, and the firmness of government response to protests. Our examination of political and socioeconomic protests leads us to advance the following hypotheses, all of which focus on how the government can maintain stability in the face of protests:

H1: *Because they are potentially most destabilizing (even if they are also the rarest), political protests are managed most harshly. Repression through brute force is used.*

---

[18]Sharon Nepstad (2011). *Nonviolent Revolutions: Civil Resistance in the Late 20th Century* (New York: Oxford University Press); Guillermo Trejo (2012). *Popular Movements in Autocracies: Religion, Repression, and Indigenous Collective Action in Mexico* (New York: Cambridge University Press); Graeme B. Robertson (2011). *The Politics of Protest in Hybrid Regimes: Managing Dissent in Post-Communist Russia* (New York: Cambridge University Press); Paul Y. Chang (2015). *Protest Dialectics: State Repression and South Korea's Democracy Movement, 1970–1979* (Stanford, CA: Stanford University Press).

[19]Grzegorz Ekiert (1996). *The State Against Society: Political Crises and Their Aftermath in East Central Europe* (Princeton, NJ: Princeton University Press); Mark Beissinger (2002). *Nationalist Mobilization and the Collapse of the Soviet State* (New York: Cambridge University Press); Padraic Kenney (2002). *A Carnival of Revolution: Central Europe 1989* (Princeton, NJ: Princeton University Press).

Though consistent with theoretical expectations, this hypothesis raises an important issue of operationalization regarding which protests are political in the Chinese context. We consider protests that raise explicit demands for the protection of political rights and civil liberties to be political. By contrast, protests that are limited to socioeconomic rights are not political, even when they involve groups (such as ethnic or religious minorities) that often participate in political protests; practically, this would mean that a Mongolian protest about linguistic rights would be political, but a Mongolian protest about house demolition would not be. Because the political cases in our dataset are quite limited (involving mostly the razing of churches and removal of crosses), we evaluate H1 primarily by using *neibu* data on protests.

H2: *Socioeconomic protests in Beijing and socioeconomic protests by ethnic minorities have the potential to become a source of instability because they involve sensitive locations or groups. If such protests occur, they will be managed more harshly than protests taking place outside the capital city or not involving minorities.*

This hypothesis is derived from the existing literature, which argues that regardless of whether they are political, nationalistic, or socioeconomic,[20] protests in the capital have a higher propensity to be destabilizing both in China and in other autocracies. There is also abundant research on the hypersensitivity of the Chinese government to protests involving ethnic minorities.[21]

H3: *Socioeconomic protests that occur outside the capital and do not involve minorities are less likely to be destabilizing and will therefore receive a less brutal reaction. Nevertheless, response will be firm (police*

---

[20]Jeremy Wallace (2014). *Cities and Stability: Urbanization, Redistribution, and Regime Survival in China* (New York: Oxford University Press).

[21]Adrian Zenz and James Leibold (2017). "Chen Quanguo: the strongman behind China's securitization strategy in Tibet and Xinjiang," *China Brief*, 17(2); Hastings, "Charting the Course of Uyghur Unrest."

presence will be the modal outcome). Violent force is more likely to be used in large-scale disruptive protests and in rural protests, where there is less government accountability and the issues (such as land grabs) are more divisive.

This hypothesis is consonant with the social contract thesis, which argues that citizens in autocracies will reward the regime with quiescence if they receive guarantees of certain socioeconomic rights and will protest when the regime fails to protect these rights.[22] In the Chinese context, decentralization puts a twist on the social contract thesis, where the guarantor of socioeconomic rights is the central government and protests are directed against the local government.

Collectively, these hypotheses outline the key differences in the destabilization potential of protests in China and in other autocracies. Elsewhere, destabilization has typically resulted from political protests in the capital or from ethnic minority protests that were not suppressed.[23] When such protests occur in China, they are handled through the resolute use of brute force. However, the overwhelming majority of protests in China focus on socioeconomic matters, do not involve minorities, and take place outside the capital. Nevertheless, they also receive a firm (though not always brutal) government response.

3. Chinese Protests in Comparative Perspective

This section provides time-series data on protest activity in post-1989 China and compares the frequency of protest in China with that in other autocracies both before and after the end of the Cold War. This

---

[22] See Linda J. Cook and Martin K. Dimitrov (2017). "The social contract reconsidered: evidence from communist and state capitalist economies," *Europe-Asia Studies*, 69(1): 8–26. This argument is also consonant with O'Brien and Li, *Rightful Resistance*.

[23] Valerie Bunce (1996). *Subversive Institutions: The Design and Destruction of Socialism and the State* (New York: Cambridge University Press); Valerie J. Bunce and Sharon L. Wolchik (2011). *Defeating Authoritarian Leaders in Post-Communist Countries* (New York: Cambridge University Press).

comparison highlights the uniqueness of the Chinese case and raises the puzzle of why the regime has survived despite so many protests. One relevant conclusion that emerges from the comparison is that the most destabilizing protests in other regimes were acts of political contention that were not suppressed. In China, these types of protests are extremely rare, but they are also brutally dealt with. We discuss this issue by referencing the handful of examples of political grievances in our own dataset and by reviewing other sources of data.

3.1. *Protest Frequency in Comparative Perspective*

Although China experienced significant protest activity throughout the first four decades of communist rule, time-series data for contentious activity prior to 1989 have not become available. We can, however, document the rapid increase in the frequency of protest that occurred after 1989. Protest data have been released for 15 of the 30 years of the 1989–2018 period: 1993–2000, 2002–2006, 2008, and 2010. For these 15 years, the total number of protests is 821,100. We should bear in mind that protests did occur in the other 15 years of this period, for which no total counts of contentious events have been made available. Thus, 821,100 protests is almost certainly a significant undercount. Figure 1 presents time-series data on the number of protests between 1993 and 2010. During this period, protests increased 20-fold from 8,700 to 180,000. Our data series stops in 2010, which is the last year for which data have been made available. The aggregate data do not distinguish by type of protest, though we are fairly certain that overtly political protests have been extremely rare and that most protests have arisen in response to the violation of socioeconomic rights, such as non-payment of wages and welfare contributions, the forced demolition of housing, and land grabs.

Time-series data on protests in other autocracies are difficult to obtain. The most systematic available data are for the Soviet Union and for post-Soviet Russia. We have two different estimates of civil unrest during the pre-1989 period. One is from 1988, when the KGB produced at Gorbachev's request a list of 24 cases of protests with

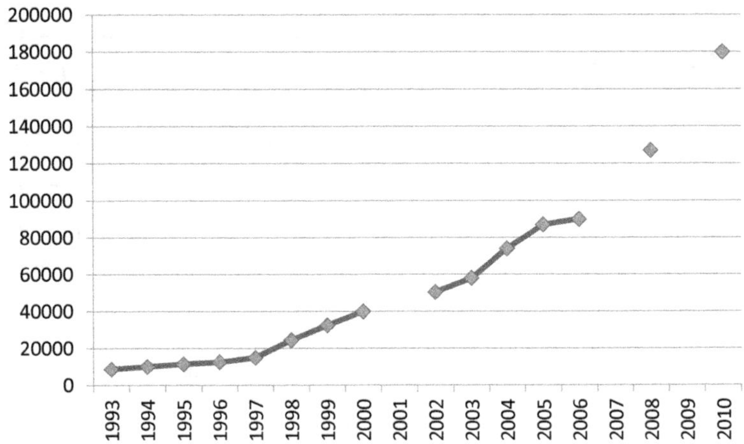

Figure 1: Protests in China, 1993–2010.

Sources: Andrew Wedeman (2011). "Enemies of the state: Mass incidents and subversion", in a Paper presented at the *Annual Meeting of the American Political Science Association*, Toronto, 3–6 September, 2009; and Sun Liping (2011). "*Shehui shixu shi dangxia de yanjun tiaozhan*", *Jingji Guancha Bao*, 25 February.

more than 300 participants that took place between 1957 and 1986.[24] The other is a National Intelligence Council count of 281 demonstrations, strikes, riots, and acts of political violence that took place between 1970 and 1982 and ranged in size from a single participant to over 10,000 protesters.[25] Although the two sources produce such different estimates of contention, both point to the fact that protest in the Soviet Union was a rare event. This began to change rapidly after 1989, when both political and socioeconomic protests became more frequent. Of all types of contention, we possess the most systematic data for strikes and other labor contentions in the Russian Federation, which are presented in Table 1. As the table makes clear, protest activity in Russia peaked in 1992, when striking had become

[24] "O massovyh besporiadok s 1957 goda," *Vestnik*, no. 6/1995, 146–154; V.A. Kozlov, *Massovye besporiadki v SSSR pri Khrushcheve i Brezhneve (1953-nachalo 1980-kh gg.)* (Novosibirsk: Sibirskii khronograf, 1999).

[25] National Intelligence Council, *Dimensions of Civil Unrest in the Soviet Union* (April 1983).

Table 1: Strikes and non-strike labor protests in Russia.

	Non-strike labor protests	Strikes	Strike participants
1990		260	99,500
1991		1,755	237,700
1992		6,273	357,600
1993		264	120,200
2000		870	30,900
2005		2,575	84,600
2008	33	60	
2009	166	106	
2010	117	88	
2011	172	91	
2012	190	95	
2013	175	102	
2014	196	97	
2015	241	168	
2016	261	158	
2017	212	122	

Sources: *Trudovye konflikty v SSSR*, 1930–1991 (Moscow: RAN, 2006), p. 409; *Rossiiskii statisticheskii ezhegodnik* (Moscow: Rosstat, 2013), p. 135; Monitoring TsSTP Trudovye protest. Available at http://trudprava.ru/expert/analytics/protestanalyt/2068, accessed on 1 April 2019.

legal and grievances about non-payment of wages were especially high. When we adjust for differences in population, protest activity per million people in Russia in 1992 is comparable to the peak of protest in China in 2010.[26] It deserves to be noted that Russia was a democracy in 1992 and that the frequency of contentious activity under Putin is lower than that observed over the past decade in China.

[26] Average protest size in China is small (15–20) protesters, producing an estimate of 2,700,000–3,600,000 participants in the 180,000 protests documented for 2010 (2,000–2,667 protesters per million people). Russia had 2,416 participants per million people in the 6,273 strikes it experienced in 1992 (see Table 1).

3.2. *System-destabilizing Protests in Comparative Perspective*

Protests were a major catalyst for regime collapse during the third wave of democratization, as well as during the Color Revolutions and Arab Spring. Typically, these protests were not aimed at highlighting electoral fraud, but at making demands for the protection of minorities and for guaranteeing basic civil rights and political liberties. Protests about electoral irregularities did occur during the Color Revolutions and in the 2011 Egyptian revolution. In the specific case of China, where no national-level competitive elections exist, an electoral revolution is impossible. This means that the odd protest about electoral irregularities may be tolerated,[27] as it has been in Russia under Putin, who is transmitting an image of accountability by allowing some electoral contention. Another type of electoral protest is a socioeconomic protest that becomes politicized; an example from the Chinese context is Wukan, where grievances about land grabs assumed a political dimension when villagers demanded a free election.[28] The Guangdong party authorities accommodated this unusual request because of the unique circumstances of the case, which were unlikely to facilitate contagion.

From China's point of view, non-electoral protests that raise political demands for minority rights (especially by Tibetans and Uighurs), religious rights (Falun Gong), or advocate for extensive political reform (Tiananmen 1989) are most dangerous. After all, it was the failure of the East European regimes to suppress such protests that led to the collapse of communist rule in 1989. These protests reflected in part socioeconomic grievances, but the solutions that the protesters demanded involved major political rather than economic concessions. One crucial feature of the European protests is that they were typically led by NGOs, ranging from churches and independent

[27] On a protest in the Guangdong village of Shishuikou aimed to prevent the reelection of corrupt cadres, see "Beijing Probes South China Fraud Protests," 9 January 2002, http://edition.cnn.com/2002/WORLD/asiapcf/east/01/09/China.protest/index.html?related, accessed 29 June 2020.

[28] Joseph Fewsmith (2013). *The Logic and Limits of Political Reform in China* (New York: Cambridge University Press), p. 12.

trade unions to historical societies (*Memorial*) and environmental organizations, which acted as vehicles of democratization.[29] For this reason, civil society groups with a political agenda are expressly forbidden in China, lest they challenge the monopoly of the party in power. This holds for religious groups (followers of Tibetan Buddhism, practitioners of Islam in Xinjiang, and those attending services at underground Christian churches), quasi-religious entities (Falun Gong), independent trade unions, and NGOs focusing on human rights. Despite such restrictions, the number of NGOs has grown exponentially since the 1980s.[30] Yet, these NGOs are only allowed to operate if they supply social services that the state cannot or will not provide; if they remain local rather than aim to establish a nationwide network; and if they refrain from voicing democratic claims.[31] In general, successful churches and NGOs have displayed a cooperative attitude with the state.[32] Although some scholars classify

[29]Ehrhart Neubert (1998). *Geschichte der Opposition in der DDR 1949-1989* (Berlin: Ch. Links); Ekiert, *The State Against Society*; Kenney, *A Carnival of Revolution*; John Darrin Tullius (1997). "Environmental groups as catalysts for political liberalization in authoritarian societies: Bulgaria and Taiwan during the 1980s," PhD Dissertation, Department of Political Science, University of Oregon; Katy Láng-Pickvance (1998). *Democracy and Environmental Movements in Eastern Europe: A Comparative Study of Hungary and Russia* (Boulder, CO: Westview Press); Barbara Jancar-Webster (1998). "Environmental Movement and Social Change in the Transition Countries," *Environmental Politics*, 7(1): 69–90; Ying-lei Charles Chang (2006). "Environmental protests and dispute resolution mechanisms in Taiwan's democratic transition," LLM Thesis, Harvard Law School.

[30]Tony Saich (2000). "Negotiating the state: the development of social organizations in China," *The China Quarterly*, 161: 121–141; Bruce Dickson (2016). *The Dictator's Dilemma: The Chinese Communist Party's Strategy for Survival* (New York: Oxford University Press), p. 125.

[31]Anthony J. Spires (2011). "Contingent symbiosis and civil society in an authoritarian state: understanding the survival of China's grassroots NGOs," *American Journal of Sociology*, 117(1): 1–45; Jennifer Y. J. Hsu (2017). *State of Exchange: Migrant NGOs and the Chinese Government* (Vancouver: UBC Press).

[32]Karrie Koesel (2014). *Religion and Authoritarianism: Cooperation, Conflict, and the Consequences* (New York: Cambridge University Press); Jessica C. Teets (2014). *Civil Society under Authoritarianism: The China Model* (New York: Cambridge University Press).

them as civil society,[33] Chinese churches and NGOs are not equivalent to the civil society groups that emerged in Eastern Europe prior to and during perestroika and challenged the legitimacy of the existing political model.[34] They work with the state, rather than against it.[35]

If they occur, political protests are met with harsh repression, as demonstrated by the cases of the 1989 protests (which spanned the area from Tibet to Beijing), by the handling of the Falun Gong movement, and by the zealous efforts to preclude "jasmine walks" after Arab Spring. Currently, ethnic protests are seen as particularly problematic. Internal (*neibu*) sources reveal that the authorities were especially concerned about the destabilizing potential of ethnic riots in the 1990s and 2000s.[36] An intensification of protest activity has occurred after the suppression of the 2008 Tibetan protests. Since then, at least 156 Tibetans have self-immolated in acts of protest.[37] In addition, Xinjiang has been rocked by violent clashes between Han Chinese and Uighurs almost every year since 2008. In the wake of Uighur minority unrest in June 2013, the Xinjiang police department issued a public notice offering awards of CN¥50,000–100,000 (about $8,300–$16,600), along with guarantees of anonymity and protection, to informants from any ethnic group (各民族群众 *ge minzu qunzhong*) who provide tips that can be used to solve cases of violent terrorism.[38] Ongoing ethnic unrest in Xinjiang since 2013 testifies to the failure of such policies. The response of the central government has been to step up repression. One technique for doing that has been

---

[33] Jessica C. Teets (2013). "Let many civil societies bloom: the rise of consultative authoritarianism in China," *The China Quarterly*, 213: 19–38.

[34] Michael Bernhard (1993). "Civil society and democratic transition in East Central Europe," *Political Science Quarterly*, 108(2): 307–326.

[35] Marie-Eve Reny (2018). *Authoritarian Containment: Public Security Bureaus and Protestant House Churches in Urban China* (New York: Oxford University Press).

[36] *Zhongguo xibu minzu diqu kongbu fanzui wenti yanjiu* (2004); *Xizang wenti dashiji 2000–2005* (2006); *Xinjiang wending gongzuo wenjian xuanbian* (1999).

[37] International Campaign for Tibet, "Self-Immolations by Tibetans," https://www.savetibet.org/resources/fact-sheets/self-immolations-by-tibetans/, accessed 29 June 2020.

[38] *Jiefang ribao*, 3 July 2013, p. 3.

the implementation of the so-called "grid-management system" (网格化管理 *wanggehua guanli*),[39] which employs sophisticated monitoring technology that enables the police and paramilitary forces in Tibet and Xinjiang to respond to social unrest extremely efficiently. Another has involved increased prosecution of political crimes: with slightly more than 1% of China's population, the Xinjiang Uighur Autonomous Region has accounted for roughly half of the individuals prosecuted for crimes of endangering state security (危害国家安全罪 *weihai guojia anquan zui*) in the 2000s and 2010s.[40] The news that has emerged from Xinjiang is that about a million Uighurs (10% of the Uighur population) are being held in re-education camps and that a 731% increase in criminal arrest rates for Uighurs took place in 2016–2017.[41] These techniques seem to be counterproductive in the long term, as they do not increase the loyalty of minority members and only exacerbate the already existing ethnic tensions. Although the situation appears calm and terrorist incidents have disappeared, there are pent up tensions among the Uighurs that can explode if a political opportunity presents itself.

Our dataset contains only 10 cases of political protests (nine in Zhejiang and one in Hebei), all involving the demolition of churches and destruction of crosses. We do not have information on whether force was used in two of these cases. It is notable that the other eight protests turned violent: in six of them, protesters were beaten up (被殴打 *bei ouda*), one resulted in an arrest, and one involved a violent confrontation (冲突激烈 *chongtu jilie*). Therefore, the limited data on political protests in our dataset are consistent with our theoretical expectations.

---

[39] Beibei Tang (2020). "Grid governance in China's urban middle-class neighborhoods," *The China Quarterly*, 221: 43–61.

[40] Hastings (2011). "Charting the Course of Uyghur Unrest." For prosecution statistics, see *Zhongguo tongji nianjian* (Beijing: Zhongguo tongji chubanshe) and http://www.duihuaresearch.org/search/label/ESS, accessed 1 April 2019.

[41] Lucas Niewenhuis (2018). "Re-education camps in China's 'no rights zone' for Muslims: What everyone needs to know," 22 August, https://supchina.com/2018/08/22/xinjiang-explainer-chinas-reeducation-camps-for-a-million-muslims/, accessed 29 June 2020.

In sum, this section finds that protests that have become destabilizing in other autocracies have been political. Although such protests may be tolerated to some extent in hybrid regimes (e.g., Russia under Putin), failure to repress them can lead to destabilization in single-party regimes (pre-1989 Eastern Europe, Taiwan under martial law, and China). This section constitutes our test of H1 that because they are potentially most destabilizing (even if they are also the rarest), political protests are managed most harshly through brute repression.

4. The Dataset

This section describes our dataset and engages with the issues of whether the data are representative and valid. The dataset consists of 65,317 cases of protests that took place in China between November 2013 and June 2016. We collected the data primarily from Lu Yuyu's online daily protest reports. Lu was a former migrant worker from Guizhou province, who began crowdsourcing information about mass incidents in China through his Twitter and Blogger accounts named "Wickedonna" in October 2012. His published archive includes text, photos and videos documenting daily incidents posted by protesters or witnesses on Weibo, Tencent QQ, Blogs, and BBSs. After searching and verifying information such as location, cause, demands, scale and police action, Lu published over 900 daily reports and categorized incidents by the nature of the protest, highlighting cases that have a higher profile (要闻*yaowen*). Our dataset is composed of 2,604 key cases (*yaowen*) and 62,713 general cases (see Table 2). In general, a much more detailed coding was possible of the key cases than the general cases, because Lu's reports were more detailed for key cases. Our data end in June 2016, when Lu was arrested for causing disturbances and could not report any new cases of protest. In August 2017, he was indicted to 4 years imprisonment for picking quarrels and stirring up trouble.[42]

[42]"China Jails Blogger, Researcher for Four Years on Public Order Charges, *Radio Free Asia*, 3 August 2017, http://www.rfa.org/english/news/china/blogger-sentence-08032017112614.html, accessed 29 June 2020.

Table 2: Key cases, general cases, and total number of cases, 2013–2016.

	2013	2014	2015	2016
Key cases	153	1,074	929	448
General cases	1,640	21,207	28,141	11,725
Total cases	1,793	22,281	29,070	12,173

Our dataset is based on detailed hand coding of the key cases and the general cases.[43] The key cases have several important features. First, they have the most informative content in terms of location, cause, demands, and police action. Key cases often involve more than 100 protesters and represent the most closely watched types of mass incidents including conflicts, strikes, protests and demonstrations. Second, the key cases are closely linked to the news highlights of Chinese domestic affairs and media reports. They include large-scale violent collective action that has attracted the attention of Chinese rights activists, including Lu Yuyu. For example, our dataset contains two protests about the Tianjin explosions in August 2015 and five nationwide demonstrations of Ezubao fraud in late 2015 and early 2016. Third, the key cases contain a range of different types of causes of protests and demands made by protesters. They also allow us to systematically analyze the inter-regional variation in protests, as well as the differences between urban and rural protests. In short, the key cases reveal important features of recent and significant mass incidents in China.

Our dataset allows us to conduct a quantitative analysis on the patterns of protests in terms of location, cause, demands, scale and

[43]Others have used machine-learning to code the Wickedonna data (Han Zhang and Jennifer Pan (2019). "CASM: A deep learning approach for identifying text and image data from social media," *Sociological Methodology*, https://doi.org/10.1177/0081175019860244 and Christian Goebel (2019). "Social unrest in China: a bird's eye view," in Teresa Wright (ed.), *Handbook of Protest and Resistance in China* (Cheltenham: Edward Elgar), pp. 27–45). Those scholars focus on questions that are different from ours. Zhang and Pan 2019 use the data to develop machine-learning algorithms that can identify protests. Goebel 2019 uses machine learning to develop a topic model for classifying the protests by type of grievance.

police actions. We have contrasting findings based on the key cases and the general cases. The general cases show that the vast majority of protests have involved small-scale non-violent collective action and have raised demands for the provision of social services and the protection of legal rights. The key cases (which are larger and more likely to involve police violence) allow us to document the factors that drive the use of force in response to protest.

Ours is the largest existing dataset of socioeconomic protest in China. It is more detailed than the China Labor Bulletin (which had 1,300 strikes and labor protests in 2014 and 2,551 in 2015),[44] Manfred Elfström's China Strikes Crowdmap (which contains information on 1,471 strikes that took place between January 2003 and December 2012),[45] Yongshun Cai's dataset (266 cases of collective resistance and 44 large-scale cases of protest that took place between 1993 and 2007),[46] Xi Chen's collective petitioning event catalog (902 cases from Hunan from the 1990s),[47] Andrew Wedeman's dataset of 4,167 collective action incidents that took place between 1990 and 2012,[48] Tong and Lei's 548 large-scale social protests that occurred between 2003 and 2010, and Li Yao's dataset of 1,418 protests in 2001–2012. The dataset contains information on multiple types of contention and is equivalent to about 10% of all protests that took place on an annual basis in China in 2014–2015.[49]

Are the data representative and valid? We carefully hand-coded the data and cross-checked the information contained in Lu Yuyu's reports to the extent possible, so we believe that our dataset is a valid representation of protest activity. The biggest concern with regard to

---

[44] http://www.clb.org.hk/

[45] https://chinastrikes.crowdmap.com/; see also Elfstrom (2019).

[46] Cai, *Collective Resistance in China*.

[47] Chen, *Social Protest and Contentious Authoritarianism in China*.

[48] Andrew Wedeman (2016). "Not in my backyard: middle class protests in contemporary China," in Leslie L. Marsh and Hongmei Li (eds.), *The Middle Class in Emerging Societies: Consumers, Lifestyles, and Markets* (New York: Routledge), pp. 200–222.

[49] We assume that the number of protests in 2014–2015 was higher than in 2010, when 180,000 protests were reported.

representativeness is that the data were crowdsourced (r-squared = 0.88 for total number of protests regressed on the number of Internet users in 2014 in a bivariate regression; t = 14.82). This suggests that reporting is heavily dependent on Internet penetration, which compromises representativeness. In addition, representativeness may be threatened by the fact that citizens are more likely to report protests in which something happens (especially violence) than protest with non-violent outcomes. We are also mindful of the absence of overtly political protests (with the exception of church protests in Zhejiang and Hebei, discussed in Section 3), which suggests that individuals may be unwilling to report political protests. At the same time, our dataset has reports about protests in sensitive locations (Beijing) and by sensitive groups (ethnic minorities), which mitigates concerns about self-censorship to a certain extent.

Another problem is that the data are incomplete. Although Lu Yuyu searched for information on a daily basis, it was difficult to gather complete data for each case since information on social media was highly censored and subject to prompt deletion by the Chinese government. Therefore, there are some missing data in terms of scale and government response in our dataset, especially for the general cases. In the end, we were not able to make a determination for most general cases whether violence was used, protesters were arrested, or negotiation was successful. Although key cases typically indicated the presence of the police, occasionally our data did not allow us to distinguish between different actions including guarding, dispersion, crackdown, arrest or confrontation. Despite these limitations, we strived to accurately document in as many cases as possible how protests were handled.

These shortcomings of the dataset in terms of representativeness notwithstanding, we are confident that this is the most comprehensive existing dataset on protests in China and that it allows us to assess the drivers and the outcomes of socioeconomic protest activity more systematically than other datasets. Stability maintenance (*weiwen*) is a top priority for the central government. The next two sections provide rich empirical details on how this work has been executed in practice.

5. The Patterns of Protest Activity

This section discusses the patterns of protest activity revealed by the dataset, focusing in particular on the questions of when, where, and why protests occur.

The dataset shows that the peak and trough of protests is related to China's cultural practices and general economic activities. According to our statistics, the highest number of protests occurs in the month before the Spring Festival, when migrant workers and investors protest over unpaid wages and investment fraud, respectively. Perhaps unsurprisingly, the lowest number of protests occurs during the Spring Festival itself, when workers return home and government offices are closed (see Figure 2). The number of protests is more evenly distributed in other months. Also, the causes of protest are related to different seasons and social activities. For example, many protests in May and June are linked to school graduation and enrollment and those in winter are focused on year-end issues such as living demands, especially heating, wages, return on investment, etc. In terms of days, the peak of protest activities occurs on Monday and

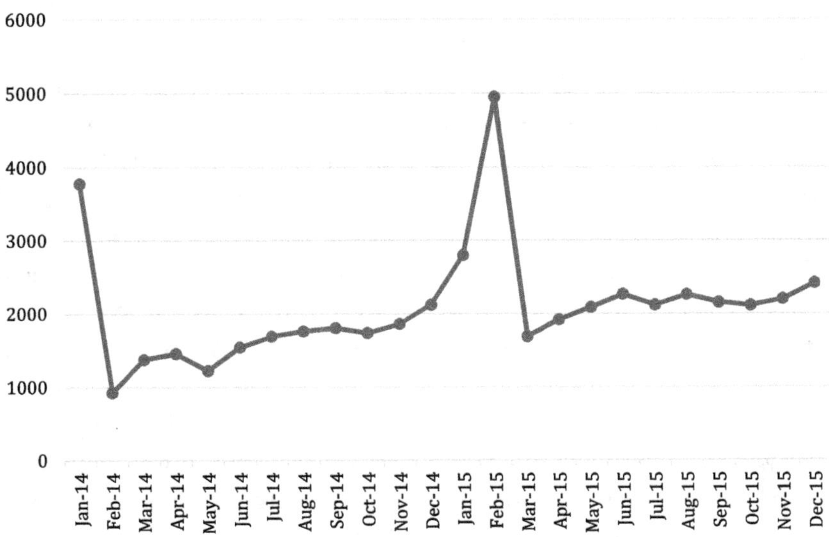

Figure 2: Total number of protests (2014 and 2015 total cases).

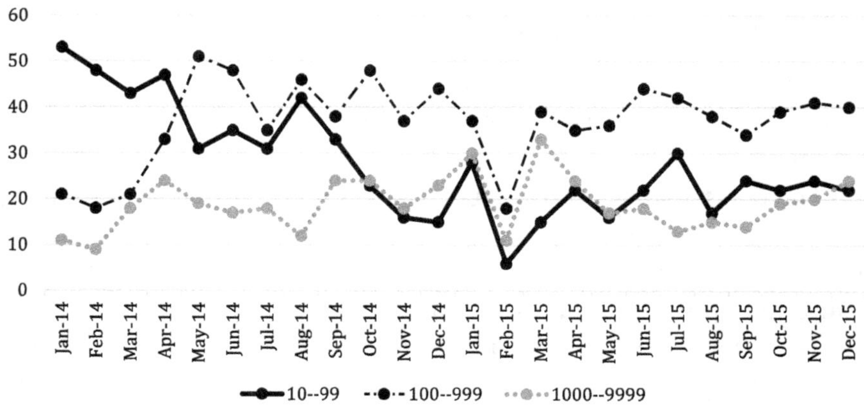

Figure 3: Scale of protests (2014 and 2015 key cases).

Friday. Perhaps unsurprisingly, fewer events happen during the weekend, as most government buildings and factories are closed.

In terms of scale, we divided protests into three categories: 10–99 participants for small-scale; 100–999 participants for medium-scale and 1,000–9,999 participants for large-scale (see Figure 3). More than half of the protests were small-scale and medium-scale. We expect that the proportion of small-scale protests would be significantly larger among the general cases than among the key cases presented in what follows, but we were unable to code the general cases for size of protest due to missing data. Scale matters because it is a critical variable for police action. In general, the smaller the scale of the protest, the lesser the repression. However, police action is also affected by the tactics, levels of violence, and location of the protests, as will be discussed in Section 6.

The dataset allows us to make some observations regarding how government response and the use of police force impact the length of protests. In general, the 2014 and 2015 key cases show that most of the events were only half-day or one-day activities and only 4.73% of them lasted more than one day. When they continued for longer than a day, the scale and level of violence of protests escalated. Both government non-responses and unjust police repression result in long-term protests. Some longer protests were continuous events, which occur sporadically but continuously throughout a month or during a year; some cases lasted for more than 1 or 2 years. These continuous events often began with grievances such as environmental pollution and then were quelled by the local government's expedient use of force. However, the grievances persisted and led to repeated and escalated protests later. Sometimes, these contentious episodes also involved new requests for the release of protesters from prior events or asking government officials to issue a clearer response. Therefore, government response and the use of police force have an impact on the duration of the protests.

The dataset also reveals that the distribution of protests across provinces in China varies considerably. As Figure 4 shows, some provinces like Guangdong, Henan, and Jiangsu experienced much higher

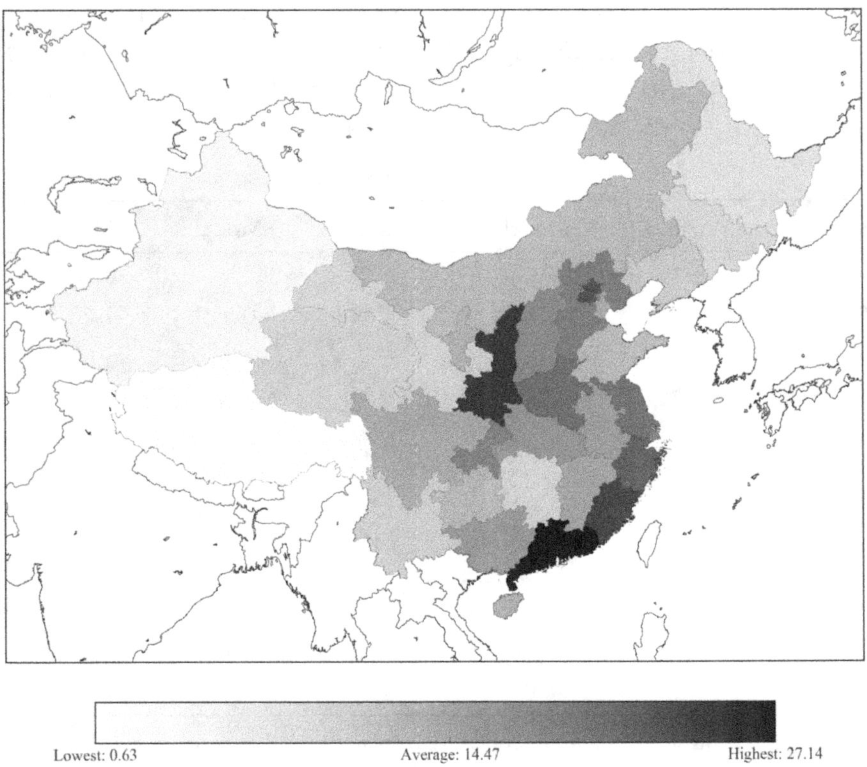

Figure 4: Total number of protests per million people by province (2014).

frequencies of protest activities than others in 2014 (see Figure 4). The geographical distribution shows that the outbreak of protests is likely to be related to the degree of local economic development. The southern regions with higher economic development experienced more problems and conflicts often easily resulting in mass incidents. In particular, the policies of local governments gave rise to grievances shaped by social and economic conditions that vary across provinces. This should not be surprising. The issues that generate the grievances behind protests emerge from patterns of change in the local political economy, especially the spread of industrial growth beyond the coastal regions, which generates conflicts over land, environmental protection, and disputes over economic interests (利益纠纷 *liyi jiufen*). This is also confirmed by the OLS regression models presented in Table 3.

Finally, an important pattern of protests in terms of location is the significant difference between rural and urban contention within the same province. According to our dataset, 70.84% of the key cases in 2014 and 2015 occurred in cities and 29.16% in rural areas

Table 3: OLS models of protests.

Independent Variable	Model 1	Model 2	Model 3	Model 4
Urbanization (%)	0.23	0.21	0.17	0.13
Unemployment (%)	-2.91	-2.38	-0.89	-1.26
Government Expenditures	-4.6e-10	—	—	—
Corruption Complaints pmp	—	0.0001	—	—
Administration Response Cases pmp	—	—	0.0009	—
Environmental Complaints pmp	—	—	—	0.00009
Constant	16.68	6.73	5.65	8.18
R-squared	0.48	0.42	0.37	0.45

Notes: DV = protests per million people; 31 provinces; 21,203 protests in 2014. The total number of general cases for 2014 is 21,207. However, four cases were multi-province cases, so they are excluded from these provincial-level OLS models.

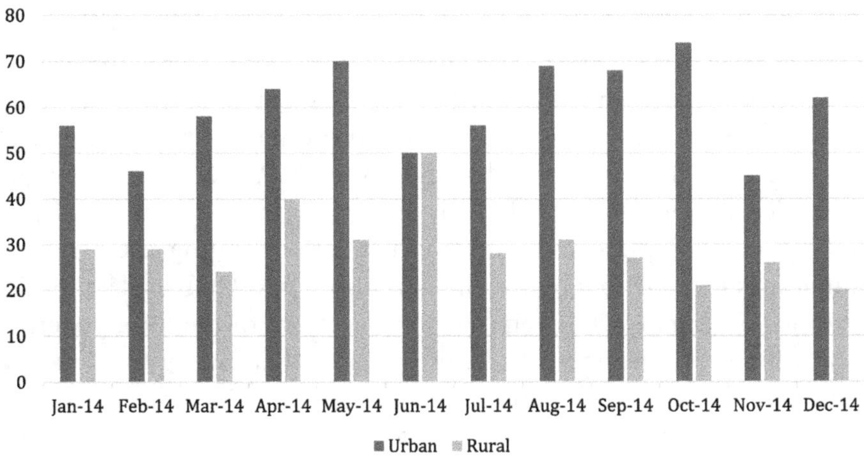

Figure 5: Number of mass incidents by location (urban–rural) in 2014 (key cases).

(see Figure 5). In cities, the main problems were strikes, wages, unequal treatment in foreign-funded enterprises, investment fraud, medical malpractice, school enrollment and environmental issues. Notably, most protests in the cities were more orderly, well-organized, and peaceful (did not involve trouble making). Some protesters used legal means such as being accompanied by a lawyer or preparing a letter of appeal. Meanwhile, the local government and police were more experienced in dealing with strikes and protests in the cities. In rural areas, however, most protests were caused by land seizures, demolitions, and local government corruption. The protests were correspondingly less orderly and more violent. The local government often relied on harsh repression and even retaliatory behavior. Also, gangs and thugs were sometimes hired by local governments to deal with land seizures and to control the protests.[50]

Compared to the protests that engulfed China in 1989, the goal of recent protests has been to obtain personal and immediate relief for specific grievances. It is clear that the participants in these contentious

[50]This is consistent with Lynette Ong (2018). "'Thugs for Hire': Subcontracting of state coercion and state capacity in China," *Perspectives on Politics*, 16(3): 680–695.

episodes are seeking neither democratization nor a change in the political structure. Instead, the drivers of protest activity are grievances that result from the actions of government officials or companies. It is important to note that most protesters do not target the central government or the leadership of the CCP, even when they go to petition in Beijing. Instead, many protesters refer to central policies or CCP leaders' speeches to justify their actions during the protest. Sometimes those who join acts of contention hold CCP leaders' photographs or slogans while remonstrating in front of the local government buildings. They need to focus on issues that can capture a large and politically significant constituency. The motivation of protests is a key variable that determines the types of tactics, the government response, the level of police force, and the outcome of the protest, as we will discuss in the next section.

6. Tactics, Government Response and Outcomes of Protests

This section addresses our H2 and H3 by evaluating government response both in sensitive cases of contention involving minorities and protests in Beijing, as well as in less-sensitive socioeconomic protests. Although Chinese citizens are not legally allowed to engage in organized collective action to express their grievances and demands, popular contention consistently arises nationwide in large numbers. Our dataset reveals that these protests exhibit some standard tactics. In turn, this makes government response to protests predictable. As noted above, different types of tactics, government response, level of police repression, and outcomes of the protest are influenced largely by protesters' motivation. These variables interact and reinforce each other during the protest activities.

In the first place, the tactics used by protesters reflect their specific grievances. As Table 4 shows, protest tactics can be classified into four major categories including physical conflict, workers' strike, legal rights defense, and demonstration. In the complete dataset, demonstration is the most common tactic, accounting for 46.27% in 2014 and 50.91% in 2015. We further divide "demonstration" into six

Table 4: Protest issues and main tactics used (2014 key cases).

					Demonstration					
	Total no.	Physical conflicts	Workers' strike	Legal rights defense	Parade	Rally	Petition	Street blocking	Sit-in	Shopkeepers' strike
Land Seizures & Demolition	212	150 (70.75%)	—	3 (1.42%)	4 (1.89%)	19 (8.96%)	1 (0.47%)	35 (16.51%)	—	—
Wages	212	7 (3.3%)	182 (85.85%)	4 (1.89%)	2 (0.94%)	10 (4.71%)	—	1 (0.47%)	6 (2.83%)	—
Unemployment	61	3 (4.92%)	—	9 (14.75%)	18 (29.51%)	27 (44.26%)	1 (1.64%)	2 (3.28%)	1 (1.64%)	—
Education Resources	38	1 (2.63%)	—	5 (13.16%)	8 (21.05%)	21 (55.265%)	1 (2.63%)	—	2 (5.26%)	—
Policies	63	—	36 (57.14%)	7 (11.11%)	1 (1.59%)	12 (19.04%)	1 (1.59%)	—	1 (1.59%)	5 (7.94%)
Living Conditions	37	—	17 (45.95%)	—	1 (2.7%)	6 (16.22%)	1 (2.7%)	7 (18.92%)	5 (13.51%)	—
Property Management	48	6 (12.5%)	—	3 (6.25%)	—	11 (22.92%)	—	12 (25%)	—	16 (33.33%)
Environment	90	3 (3.33%)	—	—	31 (34.44%)	53 (58.89%)	—	—	3 (3.33%)	—
Investment & Contract	93	11 (11.82%)	—	18 (19.36%)	6 (6.5%)	51 (54.84%)	1 (1.08%)	2 (2.15%)	4 (4.3%)	—
Accident Handling	46	1 (2.17%)	—	1 (2.17%)	5 (10.87%)	38 (82.61%)	—	1 (2.17%)	—	—
Illegal Taxis	36	6 (16.67%)	27 (75%)	—	—	—	—	3 (8.33%)	—	—
Corruption	70	38 (54.29%)	—	—	5 (7.14%)	24 (34.29%)	—	—	3 (4.29%)	—
Chengguan	36	30 (83.33%)	—	—	1 (2.78%)	5 (13.89%)	—	—	—	—
Others	32	9 (28.12%)	—	—	—	23 (71.88%)	—	—	—	—
Total	1074	265	262	50	82	300	6	63	25	21

sub-categories including parade (march), rally, petition, street blocking, sit-in, and shopkeepers' strike. When protest activities escalate in the absence of government response or harsh repression, multiple tactics are used in the same event. Continuous events also involve the use of multiple tactics. In the early period of the event, protesters typically rely on relatively modest means such as petitions and sit-in strikes. Later, they use street blocking, highway blocking and physical conflicts as forms of escalation aiming to ensure a better government response or attract greater attention from society.

In most cases, protesters exhibited a clear main tactic during the event. The tactic of physical conflict generally refers to a fierce body collision and violent behavior during the incident. It is common in the case of land seizures and demolitions since both sides (usually government and landowners) trigger the incident with fierce confrontation. In rural areas, peasants use farm tools, bricks and knives to arm themselves against demolition teams. When mass incidents are caused by land seizures and demolitions, the government will use severe coercive means including harsh repression and large-scale arrests. In such cases, protesters are preparing for a fight rather than expecting an opportunity for bargaining. As Table 4 indicates, 70.75% of protests about land seizures and demolitions resulted in body collisions and conflicts. In general, when protests are caused by problematic government policies, conflicts are the dominant tactic.

The second most commonly used tactic is a strike, here specifically referring to workers' strike. As Table 4 indicates, strikes were mainly used during protests over wages, policies, living conditions, and illegal taxes. Since strikes are directed against factories, companies, and schools, they usually begin with a refusal to work organized by a body of employees, aiming to gain a concession from their employer. Therefore, these activities are relatively moderate and usually limited to the outside perimeter of the compound of the institution. Government involvement and the use of force by the police are rarely observed, unless the strikes escalate to a demonstration, like a parade or a sit-in strike in front of government buildings.

Another relatively moderate protest tactic is using legal means including contracts, investment agreements and policies to defend individuals who have suffered a grievance like personal injury, a land dispute, medical malpractice, investment fraud, or another civil dispute. As Table 4 indicates, using legal rights defense is a common strategy when grievances are related to investment, housing contracts, or compensation. Those who protest have often entered into fraudulent contracts and agreements, thus legitimating their demands for justice. They exhibit documents during the protests, carrying agreements or contracts with them and presenting them to the local governmental officials.

We can calculate the frequency of six subtypes of demonstration tactics among the key cases in our dataset: rallies, parades (marches), petitions, street blocking, sit-ins and shopkeepers' strikes.

(1) Among these six tactics, organizing a rally is the most commonly used, accounting for 60.36% of demonstrations among the key cases in 2014. This can be explained by the fact that the requirements for a rally are relatively simple. Often, protesters gather together in an open public place, typically a town square, a stadium, or a park. They use slogans, posters and clamor to present their views and specific grievances. They also use speakers, horns, music players, and sometimes wear ethnic costumes to attract greater attention.

(2) Compared to rallies, parades (marches) are an upgraded type of group demonstration. Parades are considered a trouble-making tactic. It is hard to control parades because they move from one place to another. While slogans and posters are hand carried, transportation vehicles (bikes, private cars and pickup trucks) are also sometimes used in parades. In some cases, protesters also carry victims and even corpses while marching.

(3) Another trouble-making tactic is street and highway blocking. This causes much more trouble than other forms of demonstration, as it affects public traffic and social order to a great extent. It is also more intense, as participants in the demonstration have to use tools and weapons including bricks, trees and sticks to defend themselves.

(4) Sit-in participants often make a row or a circle in front of local government buildings like city hall or the courthouse. They also

hold pictures, posters, and slogans during the demonstration. In some cases, they prefer to organize overnight sit-ins. During the protest, they also kneel, beg, scream and engage in hunger strikes to attract the attention of government officials.

(5) Petitioners often leave their hometown or city in search of higher-level governmental institutions. This increases the mobility of the demonstration. Both sit-ins and petition demonstrations often target certain local government policies or government action in previous protests.

(6) In contrast to workers' strikes, shopkeepers' strikes are a unique method used by small business owners to express their views about certain economic policies, property management, and rights defense. A common tactic is to close their shops or to suspend the operation of a market, which results in public discontent.

As Table 4 reveals, different types of grievances result in different tactics. Protest participants strategically use tactics that help them better express their specific grievances. More important, they use tactics that will have the most direct and immediate impact on decision-makers. For example, workers' strikes produce the most effective results in factories. In turn, petitioning a higher-level government has the largest impact on local government.

Despite the use of various tactics, the intentions of most protesters are basically the same: namely, to attract government attention, response, and help. Therefore, ideally, government response is the key to solving the problem. However, the data reveal that there are often two types of response from the government towards the protests: positive and negative. The positive response includes negotiation and consultation to demobilize the protest. The negative involves using police force to repress, restore order and disperse the masses. Among the 2014 key cases, negotiation and persuasion account for only 1.05%, while the demonstration of force including police alert (戒备 *jiebei*), using the police to disperse protests (驱散 *qusan*), arresting protesters (抓捕 *zhuabu*) and confrontation (对抗 *duikang*) accounts for 75.17%. Figure 6 indicates that the most frequently used measure

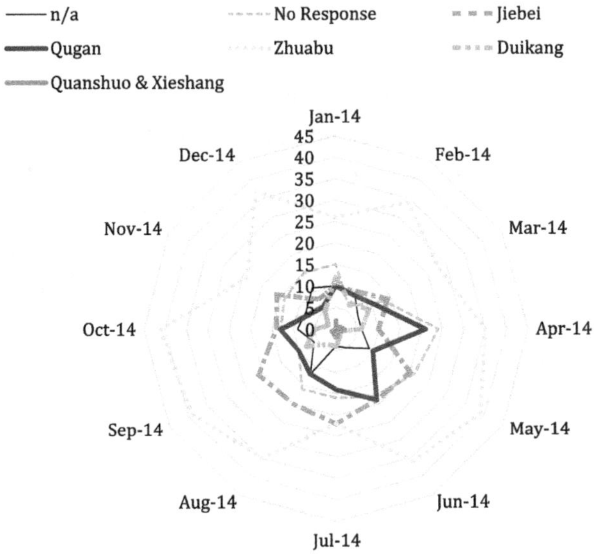

Figure 6: Types of government response to protests (2014 key cases).

by the Chinese government is repression, especially using police force to disperse and arrest protesters.

More importantly, our data reveal that government officials tend not to appear at the scene or respond to protesters' demands face to face, especially when the protest is directly against the government. While participants demand a dialogue (要求对话 *yaoqiu duihua*) or a meeting with high-ranking officials, most cases end with no response or with the police dispersing the protest. Only a few cases involve officials allowing protest representatives to enter the government building and have a meeting. In most of the key cases in 2014 and 2015, there was no direct response by officials. Instead, the police were quickly dispatched for stability maintenance (*weiwen*). Thus, the discussion of government response will focus on police action. We believe that police action not only reveals government response, but also indicates the degree of tolerance towards different forms of protest activities.

The intensity of force used by the police can be divided into four levels: police alert, dispersion of protesters, arrest of protesters, and confrontation with protesters. Police alert (*jiebei*) means the police would be present once the protest occurs but will not make direct contact with the demonstrators. Normally, police officers quickly arrive at the scene to observe, remain alert, and report to the government at any time. They generally do not take any measures against the demonstrators but do ensure that the procession will not be expanded further. For larger-scale protests, especially in cities, the police often encircle the demonstrators and make sure that the number of participants and the scope of activities remain limited. This type of police action is commonly observed during rallies, sit-in strikes, and petitions. Along with non-police action by other government agents, it can be considered a moderate show of force signaling the conditional tolerance of the government towards peaceful and non-trouble-making demonstrations.

Nevertheless, the proportion of *jiebei* and non-police action is relatively small compared with firmer actions such as dispersing, beating, arrest, and confrontation. In the case of *qusan*, the police use batons to beat the demonstrators in order to intimidate them to leave immediately. During large and intense protest activities, the police take harsh actions to arrest demonstrators, even if the protesters' demands are legitimate. In the case of *duikang*, the police use batons, shields and water guns to repress the protesters. Firm police action is often taken during trouble-making demonstrations such as parades (marches), street blocking, and violent physical conflicts. They also resolutely deal with the use of mobile phones for video recording and taking photographs, often confiscating such equipment during conflicts. This type of protest often ends with arrest actions and people injured. According to our dataset, at least 14,250 people were arrested during protests in 2015 (this includes both those arrested in key-case protests and in general-case protests).

As in other authoritarian polities, China's stability maintenance (*weiwen*) has relied heavily on the coercive apparatus.[51] However, the sheer use of brute force is not a routine practice, except for sensitive

---

[51]It is frequently asserted that the size and the rate of increase of the *weiwen* budget are bigger than those of the defense budget. However, no sufficiently detailed statistics on either the *weiwen* or the defense budget have been released.

socioeconomic protests, such as high-profile protests in Beijing (all of our 19 key cases in 2014–2015) and socioeconomic protests by minorities (16 key cases in 2014–2015). In these cases, brute force was used. For protests in Beijing, we did not have information on whether force was used in 11 cases; the other eight cases resulted in arrests. For socioeconomic protests by minorities, we do not have data on whether force was used in nine cases; the other cases resulted in either arrests (six cases) or intense conflict (one case). These findings are consistent with our H2.

Based on the 2014 and 2015 key cases in our dataset, we can say that although police response was firm, the level of police force and repression varied when dealing with different types of protests. Some of the most important determinants were location, protest object, scale, and tactics of protest activities.

Table 5 provides a logistic regression that tests the relationship of patterns of protest activities to firm action by the police. The findings are consistent with our H3. Several variables influence whether the police will use firm action. First, different types of tactics used will impact the level of police force. As the result of the regression shows, a workers' strike is less likely to receive police repression. However, trouble-making tactics often trigger harsh repression by the government. Second, firm police action is more likely when the scale of the protest is large. The larger the protest scale, the harsher the police action that takes place. Third, the police are more brutal in rural areas than in the cities. In rural areas, when it comes to land seizures and house demolition, the demolition team, police, *chengguan* (城管), toughs and local gangs often join up and suppress the protest harshly together. Fourth, if protesters target the government directly, firm police action is more likely to take place since the demonstration often occurs in front of government buildings. In some cases, local governments engage in more severe repression when they believe that their actions or policies have the support of the higher-level government.

In short, the main purpose of using police force is to control the situation and demobilize the protest. Therefore, the police are particularly careful to adopt a strategy such that no further conflicts will occur. The use of police as main government response is to ensure that

Table 5: Level of police repression and patterns of protests in China (2014 and 2015 key cases; total cases = 2,003).

	2014	2015	2014–2015
Tactics of Strike	–0.993 (0.266)***	–1.453 (0.32)***	–1.085 (0.198)***
Tactics of Legal Rights Defense	0.772 (0.298)***	0.496 (0.317)	0.701 (0.215)***
Tactics of Demonstration	0.072 (0.226)	–0.073 (0.234)	0.072 (0.16)
Location (Urban areas)	–0.104 (0.189)***	–1.002 (0.197)***	–1.027 (0.136)***
Medium-Scale (100-999)	0.782 (0.166)***	0.323 (0.186)*	0.576 (0.123)***
Large-Scale (over 1000)	1.695 (0.215)***	0.873 (0.205)***	1.236 (0.145)***
Trouble Making Tactics	0.274 (0.153)*	–0.867 (0.17)	0.166 (0.115)
Protest directly against Government	0.05 (0.15)	0.253 (0.156)	0.134 (0.108)
–	0.322 (0.242)	0.5 (0.252)**	0.38 (0.172)**
N	1,012	867	1,879
Pseudo R^2	0.1184	0.1011	0.1022

Note: Logistic regression coefficients with standard errors in parentheses (*$p < 0.10$, **$p < 0.05$, ***$p < 0.01$ two-tailed). Dependent variable is use of firm police force (1 = Firm Police Action, 0 = Soft Action including "*jiebei*, non-police and government persuasion/consultation"). Omitted variables of interest are "tactic of physical conflicts" and "small scale of protest". "Tactics of demonstration" include parade, rally, street blocking, sit-in and shopkeepers' strike.

Table 6: Types of government response (2014 key cases).

	Negotiation and persuasion (协商和劝说)	Police alert (警力戒备)	Police disperse protesters (警力驱散)	Arrest of protesters (抓捕逮捕)	Confrontation with police (对抗, 对峙)	No response (没有回应)	N/A (无数据)
2014	11 (1.02%)	184 (17.13%)	142 (13.22%)	396 (36.87%)	65 (6.05%)	181 (16.85%)	95 (8.84%)

the protest itself would remain small and would be unlikely to persist for a long time. Recourse to such repressive tactics has lowered the overall risk of political destabilization. This is also demonstrated by Table 6.

As for the aftermath of the protest, no further evidence can be provided by our dataset to show how protests end and what is the outcome of each individual case. Yet, based on the discussion of government response and police action, it could be expected that most of the protest activities end with firm action by the police. Trouble-making protesters might get arrested and detained. Depending on their grievances, they might receive further response from the authorities after the protest — however, the ringleaders may also be prosecuted. Although the government seems to rely on police force as its immediate response, the question remains whether protesters will receive government assistance to solve their problems over the long term. More importantly, how will the authorities evaluate those events and what measures will they propose to redress protesters' grievances and prevent protest from occurring again in the future due to similar problems? Those questions await further study and research.

7. Conclusion

This chapter has focused on the puzzling capacity of the Chinese regime to withstand an exceptionally high number of protests since 1989. The chapter has argued that other autocracies have collapsed when faced with a considerably smaller number of protests. We addressed this puzzle using a dataset of over 65,000 protests that took place in 2013–2016, which is supplemented with other materials. We argued that contention in China is different from that observed in other autocracies, where destabilization stemmed from political protests in the capital or by ethnic minorities that were not efficiently repressed. Chinese protests have several important features that need to be taken into account when thinking about their impact on regime stability. To begin with, protests are primarily about socioeconomic matters and overwhelmingly take place outside the capital (our dataset records 19 cases in Beijing among our key cases in 2014–2015, or less than 1% of the total number of key cases). Moreover, when China is faced with political protests, protests in Beijing, or ethnic minority protests, it responds with brutal force. Finally, our dataset shows that the response to socioeconomic contention is also firm (though not necessarily brutal), which helps prevent rapid increases in the size of protests or their horizontal geographic spread to new localities.

One final reflection concerns the impact of COVID-19 on protest activity in China. The pandemic has helped the government in terms of managing popular contention. One effect was that lockdowns precluded the opportunity for physical gathering of aggrieved citizens. Although it is possible to have protests that do not involve mass mobilization, the typical protest requires people who get together, which has been made either improbable or very difficult as a result of the social distancing measures that have been widely imposed throughout the country. Second, fear of getting infected has diminished the enthusiasm of malcontents to join up with others on the streets. The third effect of COVID-19 was that it legitimated the constant surveillance of the population in the name of protecting public health. The information collected through this universal surveillance, alongside the various blacklists that have existed for some time now, can be used to produce more accurate profiles of likely protesters and thus fulfill the needs of predictive policing. Knowing that they are being observed, citizens may be less likely to coordinate and plan a protest. Overall then, the virus has helped prevent protest activity. However, it has not eliminated dissatisfaction and grievances, which may still get expressed in new ways in the future.

https://doi.org/10.1142/9789811226588_0007

Chapter 7

Chinese Political Business Cycle Enters the New Era

Rou-Lan Chen* and Lowell Dittmer

*roulanc1@gmail.com

1. Introduction

Having brought about an amazing socioeconomic transformation since the 1970s, economic reforms have done much more than merely reshape China's economic structure; they have impacted the cyclical legitimacy variance of the communist regime. On the one hand, economic growth has been utilized as a new basis for political legitimacy in China. During the 1960s and 1970s, successful economic development seemed to correlate with authoritarian political leadership throughout Northeast Asia. This relationship vanished, however, once development slowed.[1] To ensure continuing popular support, the Chinese Communist Party (CCP) leadership learned to

[1] Bhagwati, Jagdish N. (2004). *In Defense of Globalization* (New York: Oxford University Press), pp. 92–105.

manipulate fiscal policies to enhance economic growth.[2] In the period of socialist transformation and the early reform era (i.e., after the Third Plenum of the 11th CCP), to encourage fast-track growth, the CCP pursued fiscal relaxation, allowing local governments to take more financial responsibility for local revenues and expenditure. As in the 1958 Great Leap Forward, the 1970 "fiscal responsibility system," the 1980 "eating in separate kitchens," the 1984 "local investment responsibility system," and the 1994 "tax-sharing system" all had this impact. Fiscal decentralization incentivized local officials to implement expansionary fiscal policy and engage in speculative investments, accelerating short-term growth, but ultimately leading to overheated local development. Economic booms would fuel inflation, overproduction and overly optimistic political expectations. This was typically followed by macro controls to curb local investment and to restore stability. The main purpose of this chapter is to determine to what extent these political surges and retrenchments of fixed asset investments have fallen into a cyclical pattern, and whether the driver is political or economic.

In the past decade, China's growing dependency on external trade and investment has made the economy more vulnerable to global financial disturbances. China has been engulfed in the worldwide spread of financial crises, particularly the Asian Financial Crisis (1997–1998) and the Global Financial Crisis a decade later. Since 2010, economic growth has gradually decelerated. One of main policies to stimulate growth has been fiscal relaxation as a means to attract investment. However, as China's marketization deepens, the government has been losing its ability to control the aggregate economy by manipulating fiscal policies.[3] According to the general equilibrium theory, competitive markets have an internal dynamic to

[2] Hu, Angang (1994). "Zhongguo zhengce zhouqi yu jingji zhouqi," *Chinese Social Sciences Quarterly*, 8: 85–100.

[3] Dittmer, Lowell and Yu-Shan Wu (1995). "The modernization of factionalism in Chinese politics," *World Politics*, 47(4): 467–494; Tao, Yi-Feng (2006). "Political power transition and economic opportunism: Collective action and China's political business cycle," *Issues & Studies*, 45(3): 77–102.

counteract exogenous shocks and maintain long-term equilibrium.[4] The observed business cycle responds increasingly to market volatility, not to fiscal policy manipulation. As China moves to a new stage of economic development, marketization may be expected to render fiscal policy less effective as a political tool. Can manipulations of fiscal policy still contribute to the political business cycles (PBC), and if so what is the duration of the cycle? This is the second set of dynamics this chapter sets out to explore.

In related studies about political business cycles, a set of economic indicators such as GDP, money supply, unemployment rate, taxation, and inflation have been used to explore the empirical relationships between policy manipulation and macroeconomic conditions.[5] However, unlike PBC models in electoral democracies, which generally assume an election-year cycle, an investigation of political business cycles in China must consider at least two features. First, there is no effective universal suffrage in China. Therefore, pre-election manipulation on the part of the Communist government is not done to gain support from ordinary voters. Instead, the Communist Party grants the authority to select nominees to the Central Committee, or the "selectorate." Local officials comprise the largest block in the selectorate, and it is necessary for them to generate patron–client ties.[6] After China's Party reforms, local officials still account for 30.24% of the central committee membership. Performance legitimacy has long

---

[4] Arrow, K.J. and G. Debreu (1954). "Existence of an equilibrium for a competitive economy," *Econometrica*, 22(3): 265–290; McKenzie, Lionel W. (1959). "On the existence of general equilibrium for a competitive economy," *Econometrica*, 27(1): 54–71.

[5] Alesina, Alberto, Gerald D. Cohen and Nouriel Roubini (1993). "Electoral business cycle in industrial democracies," *European Journal of Political Economy*, 9: 1–23; Ben-Porath, Y. (1975). "The years of plenty and the years of famine: A political business cycle," *Kyklos*, 28(2): 400–103; Grier, Kevin (1989). "On the existence of a political monetary cycle," *American Journal Political Journal*, 33(2): 376–389; Maccallum, Bennett (1978). "The political business cycle: An empirical test," *Southern Economic Journal*, 42: 504–515; Nordhaus, William (1975). "The political business cycle," *The Review of Economic Studies*, 42(2): 169–190.

[6] Shirk, Susan L. (1993). *The Political Logic of Economic Reform in China* (Berkeley: University of California Press), p. 4.

been deemed a crucial source of legitimacy for authoritarian regimes.[7] When there is an economic downturn that undermines the legitimacy of the CCP, it is important for the incumbents that people — and local officials in particular — can foresee a prospective economic upturn in the future. Local officials in China are essentially careerist. The *Nomenklatura* assures central appointments of local and provincial officials. Assessment and recruitment of local officials still largely relies on their performance in promoting local economic development.[8] For local officials, low GDP growth rates, meaning decreases in local investment, damages their promotion prospects. The formation of a Chinese PBC can therefore be expected to be the logical result of performance incentives for both central leaders and local officials.

Thus, when testing PBC theory in China, we focus on the economic indicators that are politically relevant at key moments. The four components of GDP growth are personal consumption, investment, government spending, and net exports. Trade and investment have been two critical components for China's growth model. In the study, we focus on investment in fixed assets (FAI) because it is the most efficient tool for local officials to maximize local revenues. During the period preceding convention of the National People's Congress (NPC), local cadres are motivated to boost economic growth because official positions are formally appointed at NPC. Hence, the effect of state policy on FAI is presumed to peak during an NPC year. Afterwards, stability maintenance (weiwen) becomes the foremost task to consolidate power. In response to the overheated economy apt to result from political stimulation, the central leadership engages in reducing money supply, resulting in a sharp

---

[7] Huntington, Samuel (1991). *The Third Wave: Democratization in the Late 20th Century* (Norman: University of Oklahoma Press), p. 2.

[8] Lu, Yi-Xun, and Ji Lin (2006). "*Zhong guo jing ji zhou qi de te dia hong guan diao kong gai jin si lu*," in Liu Shucheng and Zhu Bian (eds.), *Zhongguo Jing Ji Hou Qi Yan Jiu Bao Gao* (Beijing: She Hui Ke Xue Wen Xian), pp. 51–52; Guo, Gang (2009). "China's local political budget cycle," *American Journal of Political Science*, 53(3): 621–632.

retrenchment of FAI growth. The subsequent downswing continues until the short-term effect is diminished to some degree. Thus, the full PBC consists of: (a) (political) expansionary budget stimulus, (b) accelerated economic growth, (c) overheated economy, (d) economic retrenchment (and political suppression if necessary), and finally (e) economic slowdown or recession.

The methodology we employ to analyze China's PBC is rooted in the fact that growth in FAI can be decomposed into short-term fluctuations and long-run movements. External shocks, including technological, fiscal shocks or policy changes, are regarded as the main forces driving business fluctuations.[9] On the other hand, the market has a strong inertial propensity to pull back short-term deviations to equilibrium in the longer term. Based on this dynamic, the error correction model (ECM) is applied to explore these two movements and to observe how the long-run effects adjust short-term fluctuations. Since short-term movements are seen as deviations from the long-term equilibrium, we regard them as the irregular or cyclical portion.[10] Hence, by examining the dynamics of these transitory movements which are caused by expansionary budget at local levels and monetary tightening by the state, we can further test the existence of a Chinese investment-driven PBC.

In short, the objectives of this chapter are to find: (1) what evidence exists to prove the existence of state manipulation that can mitigate the political business cycle; (2) how lasting are the effects of a temporary shock of the state's fiscal policies to mitigate the political business cycle (i.e., what is the duration of the PBC) and what political mechanisms cause its peaks and troughs; and (3) can China's market momentum offset the effect of political manipulation of fiscal policies? This chapter first briefly reviews the fairly extensive political

---

[9] Rebelo, Sergio (2005). "Real business cycle: Past, present, and future," *Scandinavian Journal of Economics*, 107(2): 217–238.

[10] Beveridge Stephen and Charles Nelson (1981). "A new approach to decomposition of economic time series into permanent and transitory components with particular attentions to measurement of the business cycle," *Journal of Monetary Economics*, 7: 151–174.

science literature on the PBC. The second half of the chapter specifies the ECM and uses it to test for the short-term effect, the long-run effect, and their interacting effect on creating a political business cycle of FAI in China. In the final section, the chapter discusses how likely it is that the FAI cycle would expand during fiscal reforms, during NPC years, or fluctuate with external financial crises such as the GFC

2. Classic Work on Political Business Cycles

On the empirical side, there has been extensive work on PBC models to specify the political determinants of business cycles. The most profound research concerns the "election-year cycle." These writers assert that government stimulates the economy as an election approaches and stabilizes it immediately after the election.[11] As a result, business cycle peaks tend to be synchronized with the timing of national elections. To elaborate, this "election-year cycle" thesis is based on the assumptions of opportunist and rational models. The former states that since electors vote in response to the economic performance before the election, politicians will stimulate aggregate demand (by manipulating fiscal policy) before elections to create fast growth.[12] The rational model basically agrees that winning chances can be increased by pumping up economic growth before elections, but it denies the underlying assumption of the opportunist model that voters are voting retrospectively. According to the rational model, the incumbent government has incentives to engage in pre-electoral manipulations of policy, because it is vital to "signal" rational voters of its competency.[13] Despite their differences, both the opportunistic and rational models are consistent with voters behaving rationally,

[11] Chowdhury, Abdur (1993). "Political surfing over Economic Waves: Parliamentary election timing in India," *American Journal of Political Science*, 37(4): 1100–1118.
[12] Nordhaus, "*The Political Business Cycle*," 169–190; Tufte, E. (1975). "Determinants of the outcomes of midterm congressional election," *American Political Science Review*, 69: 812–826.
[13] Alesina, Cohen and Roubini, "*Electoral Business Cycle in Industrial Democracies*," 5–7.

either in voting on the basis of their evaluations or on the basis of expectations about future economic outcomes.

One of the criticisms of these election-year cycle models lies in their overestimation of state capacity. The "policy ineffectiveness" school argues that incumbent politicians cannot, even if they so desire, effectively manipulate booms during the latter half of their terms. Attempts by the authorities to manufacture election-time prosperity will be anticipated by private consumers and firms, negating real effects.[14] In this argument, the state's policy manipulation alone cannot affect real economic variables such as GDP, unemployment, and inflation. Similarly, critics have pointed out that election-year cycle models ignore long-term structural constraints. The "institutional perspective" considers that to assess the effects of pre-election manipulation, it is necessary to examine the institutions that restrain the latitude for policy manipulation and maintain market stability. In his paper, Beck disagrees that there is a clear business cycle that peaks before elections in the United States.[15] According to him, even if presidents transfer payments before elections, which can produce electoral effects, it may not precipitate important macroeconomic consequences. Since presidents share the authority of fiscal policy with Congress, it is difficult to see a single fiscal policy manipulated by presidents creating a 4-year PBC. Similarly, presidents are insufficiently powerful to force the Federal Reserve, which is independent from the control of the executive branch, to work actively for elections. Thus, it is reasonable to assume the non-existence of political monetary cycles. The failure to look at institutional capabilities leads to the failure to look at policy effects generated by that institution.

With respect to the Chinese PBC, the Dittmer–Wu project pivoted on the typical PBC assumption that the funding driving the economy is correlated with political events.[16] In 1995, they established a

[14] Sargent, T. and N. Wallace (1976). "Rational expectations and the theory of economic policy," *Journal of Monetary Economics*, 2(1): 161–183.

[15] Beck, Nathaniel (1987). "Elections and the fed: Is there a political monetary cycle?" *American Journal of Political Science*, 31: 194–216.

[16] Dittmer and Wu, "The Modernization," 467–494.

relationship between major FAI influxes and GDP booms. They also found that the economic cycle divided relative factional winners from losers: the boom phase coincided with the rise of the pro-growth radical reform faction (e.g., Hu Yaobang, Zhao Ziyang), while the resulting inflation and more importantly the rise of popular protest movements contributed to the rise of the more conservative faction (the planning apparatus and the military-security establishment), which would impose tight budgets and a constrained money supply, resulting in a top-down economic bust. Guo used a different angle to analyze the existence of a local PBC in China. Chinese local leaders strategically accelerate government spending at crucial moments during their tenure, specifically when their chances of promotion in the following year are the highest. The Chinese cadre responsibility system coupled with incomplete information and retrospective economic accountability create incentives for local officials to produce political budget cycles to signal competence to Party committees at upper levels.[17]

Many studies find significant differences in the Chinese PBC after 2000. There is still an economic business cycle, but much less evidence of either autonomous mass movements or elite factional rivalry over fiscal policy. China's economic cycle has become more responsive to the political rhythms of formal political institutions, rather than changes in informal politics.[18] Since 1993, the CCP gradually implemented banking and taxation reforms, and promoted the introduction of private funds to state-owned enterprises. As reforms proceed, the state loses the capacity for expansion and the pattern of Chinese PBC changes.[19] The massive decline of the government's extractive capacity greatly enfeebles its ability to exercise macro control.[20]

[17] Guo, "China's local political budget cycle," 622–624.

[18] Dittmer, Lowell and Yu-Shan Wu (2006). "Leadership coalitions and economic transformation in reform China: Revisiting the political business cycle," in Lowell Dittmer and Guoli Liu (eds.), *China's Deep Reform: Domestic Politics in Transition* (Lanham, MD: Rowman & Littlefield), pp. 49–80.

[19] Imai, Hiroyuki (2007). "Explaining China's business cycles," *The Developing Economies*, 34(2): 154–185.

[20] Wang, Xiaohu (Shawn) and Angang Hu (2001). *The Chinese Economy in Crisis: State Capacity and Tax Reform* (New York: M.E. Sharpe).

As Chinese leaders have needed to manipulate macroeconomic policies to bolster their political popularity, they have increasingly relied on market instruments rather than plan measures to achieve their goals. As China's economy has rapidly integrated with the global capitalist system, international factors have played an increasingly important role in determining China's domestic monetary environment.[21]

However, the legitimacy of the CCP is performance-based, creating a strong incentive to find new ways to stimulate it.[22] Research indicates that the movements of the RMB to USD central parity rate before the recent three CCP Congresses are impossible to explain as resulting from normal random variation. The analysis of the Monte Carlo simulation shows that one week before the CCP Congresses, the RMB had been excessively depreciated. That signals China's export advantage and its ability to sustain a high growth rate in the future. The excessively depreciated RMB indicates that the CCP can still manipulate monetary policies to strengthen its economic legitimacy at critical moments.

3. The Institutional Context of China's PBC and Testable Hypotheses

In light of the theoretical debate over PBC models, this chapter mainly draws upon arguments from the institutional perspective to explain Chinese cyclical economic fluctuations. As noted earlier, when analyzing PBC models, we must first understand the imposed institutional structure that constrains politicians' incentives, strategies, and abilities. China, as a special case of a reforming socialist economy, offers a different institutional design from that of the election-year cycle.

In studies of the Chinese business cycle, there are two unique institutional features that deserve special attention. First, when assessing

[21] Tao, "Political power transition," pp. 81–85.

[22] Yang, Yijia (2018). "Have the Chinese financial markets been manipulated before the CPC National Congresses?" PhD Diss., Scripps College.

economic fluctuation in China, we cannot ignore financial decentralization in the reform process. Whenever local officials are endowed with more redistribution power, it tends to encourage investment drives by local authorities through budgetary expenditure.[23] The share of local projects has dramatically risen since implementation of the tax-sharing system in 1994, which shifts the local tax base to value-added taxes, which are closely associated with local infrastructure investment. When the economy becomes overheated, it may lead to inflation or unemployment and spill over into social unrest. For the past few decades, the Chinese leadership has been obsessed with maintaining both growth and stability. Politically, central leaders have taken stability seriously and repeatedly launched "Strike Hard" to promote stability and put local authorities in charge of maintaining stability at every administrative level.[24] "Stability preservation" (weiwen) has become the top "performance" criterion, exceeding even local GDP growth. However, local sources of stability management take many forms, mainly political.[25] Therefore, when the economy overheats to a breaking point, the central government must adopt macro-control policies to counter inflation and other symptoms of overheating. The economy then eventually returns to equilibrium. Based on our findings, we propose our first hypothesis: it is the interplay of local fiscal expansion and recession that generates the business cycle of FAI in China.

Second, in China, the *Nomenklatura* system assures central control over the appointment of local and provincial officials. GDP growth is a key criterion for promotion to higher levels. In response,

[23] Fan, Gang (1993). *Gong You Zhi Hong Guan Jing Ji Li Lund a Gang* (Shanghai: San Lian Shu Dian), p. 670; Loo, Becky P.Y., and Sin Yin Chow (2006). "China's 1994 tax-sharing reforms: One system, differential impact," *Asian Survey*, 46(2): 215–237.

[24] Yang, Dali L. (2017). "China's troubled quest for order: Leadership, organization and the contradictions of the stability maintenance regime," *Journal of Contemporary China*, 26(103): 35–53; Doyon, Jérôme (2014). "Local governments under pressure: The commodification of stability maintenance," *China Perspectives*, 80–82.

[25] Banney, Jonathan (2016). "Weiwen at the grassroots: China's stability maintenance apparatus as a means of conflict resolution," *Journal of Contemporary China*, 25(99): 389–405.

for local cadres, it is vital that the central leadership assembled at NPC sees increasing GDP growth. Hence, the local government tends to increase investments when NPCs are assembled. Since the 1990s, maintaining stability has become a crucial factor for job appraisal and promotions.[26] Hence, our second hypothesis is to test whether increases in FAI are synchronized with the NPC, leading to Chinese PBC peaks during NPC years.

Following closely the second hypothesis, we then investigate whether policy manipulation continues to work effectively. There is a growing consensus in the academic community concerned with the PBC in China that cyclic fluctuations have become less volatile since the 1990s. It is generally believed that as marketization is ongoing, the proportion of the Chinese economy under direct state control has been shrinking, thereby reducing the impact of the state budget, which is the ultimate political driver of the investment cycle. This concern leads to the third hypothesis, which explores the competition between the state and the market. Specifically, we posit that during financial crises, fiscal policy can still function effectively as a political tool to sustain economic growth.

4. Error-Correction Model

4.1. *Model Specification*

In the following model, FAI serves as an indicator for macroeconomic variables. Due to data constraints, we simply selected annual FAI in China from 1953 to 2017. Such a time span highlights China's economic transition from a planned economy to a market economy. In empirical work, there is extensive research on PBC models, yet little research has been conducted on the interaction between short-term policy fluctuations and the long-term impact of these two effects. To be specific, by examining the interaction between local government expenditure and aggregate FAI, this model tests whether the short-term policy mechanisms can bring about PBCs in China.

[26] Yang, "China's troubled quest for order," 38.

If a fiscal policy effect does exist, this model goes on to explore how long it can be sustained as marketization intensifies. Furthermore, if the state can still influence the FAI cycle as market liberalization expands, we can estimate the extent to which the NPC and the global financial crisis cause its peaks and troughs. In order to investigate short-term effects, long-term effects, and their interactions, hypotheses are tested by using the cointegration methodology and by estimating an error-correction model (ECM). The suggested ECM is written as

$$\Delta \Upsilon_t = \beta_0 + \beta_1 \Delta X_{t-1} + \beta_2 \Delta W_t + \beta_3 \Delta \Upsilon_{t-1} + \beta_4(\Upsilon_{t-1} - \Phi \Upsilon_{t-2} - \theta X_{t-2} - \gamma W_{t-1}) + \beta_5 D + \beta_6 Z_{94} + \beta_7 Z_{98} + \beta_8 Z_{09} + \varepsilon_t, \quad (1)$$

where Δ as usual denotes the first difference; Υ_t is the investment in fixed assets; X_t is the ratio of budget expenditure by the local government; W_t is the M1 which is the sum of currency in circulation and overnight deposits; $\Upsilon_{t-1} - \Phi \Upsilon_{t-2} - \theta X_{t-2} - \gamma W_{t-1}$ represents the ECM; D represents the year of NPC; Z_{94} represents a year after the tax-sharing reform; Z_{98} represents a year after the Asian financial crisis; Z_{09} represents a year after Supreme mortgage crisis; ε_t is white noise.

Specifically, in Equation (1), the coefficient β_1 indicates that expenditure by the local government has a temporary (short-term) effect on investment in fixed assets. B_2 is used to test whether the central leadership can manipulate the quantity of monetary circulation to counterweigh the short-term effect of expansionary budgeting. β_3 contains information about the AR (1) process. Substantively, since FAI may be affected by its lagged values as well, this proposed model incorporates these possibilities. The coefficient β_4 measures the speed at which FAI returns back to its long-term equilibrium (also known as the error correction mechanism).[27] It tells us what proportion of disequilibrium in FAI caused by temporary expenditure effects

[27] Beck, Nathaniel (1992). "Comparing dynamic specifications: The case of presidential approval," *Political Analysis*, 3: 51–87; Engle, Robert and Granger, C.W.J. (1987). "Co-integration and error correction representation, estimation, and testing," *Econometrica*, 55(2): 251–276.

in the current period is discounted in the next period. In sum, the ECM allows both temporary changes of budget expenditure and long-term (market) equilibrium to affect FAI. Eventually, short-term effects will be adjusted by the error correction mechanism to an unnoticeable degree. β_5 can signify the importance of the NPC in stimulating the PBC. B_6 is used to measure the effects of fiscal policy changes after 1994. Specifically, it tests for whether financial decentralization can generate economic and political incentives to push local investment. B_7 and B_8 are designed to test for whether during the 1997 Asian financial crisis and the 2008 global financial crisis the CCP can still effectively manipulate fiscal policies to stimulate sustainable economic growth by increasing EAI pretesting of the ECM.

Before applying the ECM, it is crucial to examine whether its assumptions are satisfied. It is common practice in macroeconomics to decompose economic variables into a secular component and a cyclical component. The secular component is viewed as being determined by capital accumulation, market expansion, technological improvement, and other growth factors. The cyclical component, on the other hand, is assumed to be transitory with short-term factors as primary causes. Since cyclical fluctuations are assumed to dissipate over time, any permanent (non-stationary) trend in the economic series is attributed to the secular component.[28] The belief that the deviation from the permanent trend occurs because of the oscillatory motions of the business cycle leads to practices of detrending non-stationary data by using the linear regression model or differentiating non-stationary data by taking the first difference. If the residuals or remainders obtained from detrending or differencing are stationary, they are assumed to be the source of the cyclical component.[29]

The methodology for measuring the cyclical movements proposed in this chapter is based on the fact that the time series that exhibits

[28] Beveridge and Nelson "A new approach," 153–158.

[29] Nelson, Charles and Charles Plosser (1982). "Trends and random walk in macroeconomic time series: Some evidence and implications," *Journal of Monetary Economics*, 10: 139–162.

non-stationarity can be decomposed into a stationary component and a trend component. As noted earlier, the FAI series is an I(1) process; hence, after we take the first difference of the FAI series (i.e., $\Delta \Upsilon_t$), the cyclic decomposition can be done. In what follows, we can further examine the pattern of the political business cycle by identifying its peaks and troughs (some may have apparent patterns, while others may not). By the assumptions of the ECM, first of all, $\Delta \Upsilon_t$ should be stationary, that is, the left-hand side of the equation must be an $I(0)$ process. For (1) to be sensible and balancing, the right-hand side must be $I(0)$, too. That means, given ε_t is stationary, series of ΔX_{t-1}, ΔW_t and $\Delta \Upsilon_{t-1}$ should be stationary. In addition, the error correction mechanism ($\Upsilon_{t-1} - \Phi \Upsilon_{t-2} - \theta X_{t-2} - \gamma W_{t-1}$) must be stationary as well. The ECM however does not require individual Υ_{t-1}, X_{t-2}, and W_{t-1} to be stationary. As long as Υ_{t-1}, X_{t-2}, and W_{t-1} can be "cointegrated," that means, the linear combination of these three variables is the $I(0)$ process, the error correction mechanism can be expected to be stationary.

4.1.1. *Differentiating the stationary or trend stationary process*

From Figure 1, the non-decaying pattern of ACF with a large first-order autocorrelation (= 0.9) and the single large spike of PACF suggest that the FAI series (denoted as $\{\Upsilon_t\}$) might be a non-stationary process.[30] To make sure that taking the first difference of Υ_t (i.e., $\Delta \Upsilon_t$) produces a stationary process, we must test whether the $\{\Upsilon_t\}$ sequence contains a unit root. Dicky–Fuller (DF) tests are commonly used to test for the unit root. The DF test in a higher-order equation is as follows:

$$\Delta \Upsilon_t = \beta_0 + \beta_1 \Upsilon_{t-1} + \beta_2 t + \beta_3 \Delta \Upsilon_{t-1} + \varepsilon_t. \tag{2}$$

[30]The autocorrelation function (ACF) is the correlation of a variable with itself at different time lags, and the partial autocorrelation function (PACF) measures the correlation between observations of a time series after controlling for the correlation between data points at time t with those at time $t - 1$. ACFs and PACFs are frequently used to identify patterns and dynamics of a time series. In our case, estimating ACF and PAC allows us to assess how the current FAI value relates to its past series values.

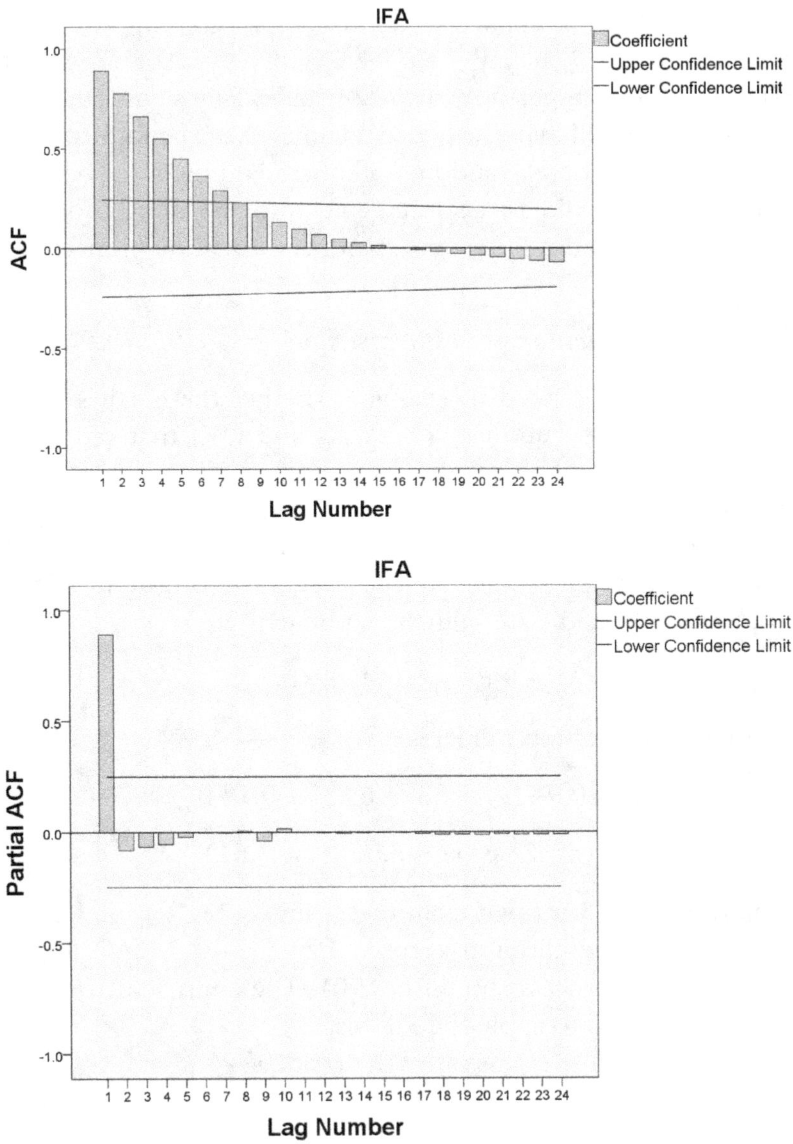

Figure 1: ACF and PACF for investment of fixed assets.

With this formulation, the augmented DF test for a unit root is carried out by testing the joint hypothesis that β_1 and β_2 equal zero. The result shows that the DF statistic = –0.8. Using the DF table, we cannot reject the null hypothesis that the $\{\Upsilon_t\}$ sequence is a random walk.

Analogous tests can be applied to test for $\Delta X_t = \beta_0 + \gamma X_{t-1} + \beta_1 \Delta X_{t-1} + \beta_2 t + \varepsilon_t$, and $\Delta W_t = \beta_0 + \beta_1 W_{t-1} + \beta_2 t + \beta_3 \Delta W_{t-1} + \varepsilon_t$. The DF statistics are –1.1 and 1.06, respectively. It is not statistically significant, so we cannot reject the null hypothesis that assumes the expenditure of local government and M1 are a random walk. Based on the tests, both $\{Y_t\}$, $\{X_t\}$ and $\{W_t\}$ are said to be integrated into the same order $I(1)$. Hence, ΔY_t, ΔX_t, and ΔY_t become stationary if first differenced.

4.1.2. *Cointegration or no cointegration*

In the next step, we need to examine whether there exists a linear combination of non-stationary $\{Y_t\}$, $\{X_t\}$ and $\{W_t\}$ that can remove the common trend of these two series and consequently make the linear combination stationary. If so, $\{Y_t\}$, $\{X_t\}$, and $\{W_t\}$ are said to be cointegrated and that also reveals long-term equilibrium (mechanisms) between these two series. The suggestive long-term relationship between FAI and state budget can be written in as

$$Y_t = \Phi Y_{t-1} + \theta X_{t-1} + \gamma W_t + e_t. \tag{3}$$

The estimated regression model is

$$Y_t = 0.94 Y_{t-1} + 5374.6 X_{t-1} + 0.14 W_t + e_t. \tag{4}$$

$$(t = 22.8)\ (t = 3.08)\ (t = 2.61)$$

The residuals e_t obtained from regressing Y_t on Y_{t-1}, X_{t-1} and W_t are estimates of equilibrium error.[31] If $\{Y_t\}$, $\{X_t\}$, and $\{X_t\}$ are cointegrated, $\{e_t\}$ process should be $I(0)$. The approach to examine stationarity of $\{e_t\}$ is to apply the DF test.

Consider the autoregression of the residuals

$$\Delta e_t = \beta_0 + \gamma e_{t-1} + \beta_1 \Delta e_{t-1} + \varepsilon_t. \tag{5}$$

The DF statistic is –3.8. If we can reject the null hypothesis that the residuals sequence has a unit root, then we can conclude that Y_t, Y_{t-1}, X_{t-1}, and W_t are cointegrated, denoted as CI(1,1,1).

[31] Greene, William (2000). *Econometric Analysis* (New Jersey: Prentice-Hall Inc.), p. 18.

Substantively speaking, investment in fixed assets, the budget expenditures of local government, and M1 must have the same stochastic trend that makes them move together, forming long-term equilibrium. Based on the DF test for estimated errors, the cointegration vector [1 –0.94 –5374.6 –0.14] obtained from this regression can produce the equilibrium relationship among Y_t, Y_{t-1}, X_{t-1}, and W_t, which we may rewrite as

$$e_t = Y_t - 0.94Y_{t-1} - 5374.6X_{t-1} - 0.14W_t. \quad (6)$$

Furthermore, the same cointegration vector can be used as estimates in place of the true values for the error correction mechanism in the ECM (1), because least squares standard errors will provide consistent estimates of the true standard errors.[32] The error correction mechanism therefore can be specified as

$$\text{ECM} = Y_{t-1} - 0.94Y_{t-2} - 5374.6X_{t-2} - 0.14W_{t-1}. \quad (7)$$

4.2. *Model Estimation of ECM*

Until now, we have eliminated the stochastic trend in $\{Y_t\}$, $\{X_t\}$, and $\{W_t\}$ by computing their first differences, ΔY_t, ΔX_t, and ΔW_t. As such, the problems of applying OLS created by random walk have been avoided. Furthermore, since Y_t, Y_{t-1}, X_t, and W_t are cointegrated, the linear combination of $Y_{t-1} - 0.94Y_{t-2} - 5374.6X_{t-2} - 0.14W_{t-1}$ is stationary and can be used in the regression analysis. Hence, the first difference of $\{Y_t\}$ can be predicted using the ECM, augmented by the past values of ΔY_t, which helps reduce autocorrelations in the error terms. The suggestive ECM is as follows:

$$\Delta Y_t = \beta_0 + \beta_1 \Delta X_{t-1} + \beta_2 \Delta W_t + \beta_3 \Delta Y_{t-1} + \beta_4 (Y_{t-1} - 0.94Y_{t-2} - 5374.6X_{t-2} - 0.14W_{t-1}) + \beta_5 D + \beta_6 Z_{94} + \beta_7 Z_{98} + \beta_8 Z_{09} + \varepsilon_t, \quad (8)$$

where the term in the parenthesis is the error correction mechanism.

[32] Banerjee, Anindya, Juan J. Dolado, John W. Galbraith and David F. Henry (1993). *Co-Integration, Error Correction, and the Econometric Analysis of Non-Stationary Data* (New York: Oxford University Press), p. 151.

5. Empirical Findings and Discussions

5.1. *A Locally Led Political Business Cycle*

The results of estimating the ECM are shown in Table 1. Generally, this model is appropriately specified because by including the lagged endogenous variable ΔY_{t-1}, the autocorrelation is not present in the error term (DW = 1.9). To explain more clearly, this model can be decomposed as ΔY_{t-1} and ΔX_{t-1}, short-term effects, and as an error-correction adjustment mechanism. The latter is interpreted as an equilibrium relationship about investment in fixed assets and expenditure of local government in the long run. In Table 1, the result indicates that short-term changes in the expenditure of local governments have a significantly positive effect on investment of fixed assets. On average, a unit increase in the ratio of local expenditure to the central expenditure is significantly expected to increase the next year's FAI by about RMB632.9 billion, holding constant the lagged FAI, lagged M1 and the equilibrium mechanism, *Ceteris paribus.* This suggests that when local governments share more loadings on expenditure, they were inclined to stimulate the increase in FAI by the manipulation of state budgets.

Whenever China's economy was mired in recession, the CCP tended to implement fiscal reform to facilitate locally led development.

Table 1: The estimated ECM.

	Coefficient	Standard errors	T	$P>\|t\|$
ΔY_{t-1}	0.67	0.06	10.85	0.00
ΔX_{t-2}	6329.16	2562.68	2.47	0.02
ΔM_{t-1}	0.27	0.07	3.95	0.00
ECM	0.67	0.10	7.03	0.00
1994	1573.2	768.90	2.05	0.03
1998	4780.23	2396.37	1.99	0.05
2009	6619.28	3328.90	1.99	0.05
Constant	701.36	694.98	1.00	0.32

Notes: Observation = 62, p-value < 0.001, adjusted R_2 = 94%, DW = 1.9.

In particular, this remarkable two-track economy existing in Communist China allows local governments to take more financial responsibility for local revenues and expenditure. The profit retention mechanism, which allows local governments to retain a proportion of tax revenues, has increased incentives to invest in local construction as well. Successful economic development not only creates material incentives for local cadres, but also paves the way for political promotion. In the Great Leap Forward campaign, the race to exaggerate grain yields was evident across all local levels, because the large scale of production was a signal to "Pull Out White Flags and Erect Red Flags", which was the principal criterion for promotion. In the mid-1980s as well, the cadre responsibility system was introduced in which recruitment of local officials largely relied on the stated goal of developing the economy.[33] Local expenditure began to rise dramatically during the fiscal decentralization in 1957–1958, 1984–1985, and in the early 1990s (Figure 2). However, after 1994, the tax-sharing system and elimination of local taxation led to a huge fiscal gap for local governments, with less tax revenue and more local budget expenditure (Figure 3). The share of local expenditures skyrocketed. To reduce the budget deficit, local governments with exclusive land administration power are motivated to increase investments in fixed assets so that they can lease as much urban land as possible to private developers.[34] As evident in Table 1, FAI is estimated to have a much higher increase (by RMB1573.2 billion) post-1994 than FAI before 1994.

The locally driven economic boom comes at the cost of economic and social unrest. Under soft budget constraints, local governments were more willing to conduct aggressive investment.[35] The easy loans from banks and loose debt constraints on local governments worsened

---

[33] O'Brien, Kevin J., and Lianjiang Li (1999). "Selective policy implementation in rural China," *Comparative Politics*, 31(2): 167–186.

[34] Wan, Yuan (2017). "Are local governments maximizing land revenue? Evidence from China," *China Economic Review*, 43: 196–215.

[35] Zhang, Lian Cheng (2009). "Jing ji hou qi de te zheng yu zhonggo jing ji de fu su," in Liu Shucheng, Lian Cheng Zhang and Oing Zhang (ed.), *Zhongguo Jing Ji Zeng Zhang Yu Jing Ji Hou Qi* (Beijing: Zhongguo Jing Ji), pp. 62–65.

Figure 2: The first difference of the ratio of local expenditure and M1 growth rate.
Source: The National Bureau of Statistics of the People's Republic of China.

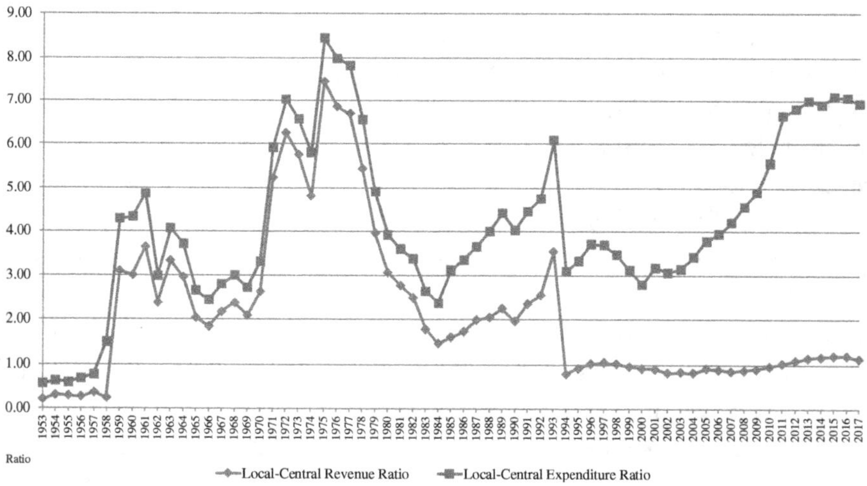

Figure 3: The ratio of Local–Central revenue and Local–Central expenditure.
Source: The National Bureau of Statistics of the People's Republic of China.

the investment fever. Without the threat of bankruptcy, local governments would engage in risky investments and neglect the externalized cost of investments. Moreover, decentralization results in transferring jurisdiction to local governments and gives them greater discretion over providing public services. Incomplete supervision of the Party reduces its ability to monitor the activities of local-level actors, thereby failing to curtail pervasive collusion from within local institutional jurisdictions.[36] The margin of power that local officials wield tends to lead to extravagance. That results in problems of inflation and local governments' high exposure to bad (unrepayable) debts.

While China benefited tremendously from overheated economic growth, the local governments are basically unconcerned with the external costs of economic development. Since maintaining stability is an absolute principle that needs to be dealt with for the CCP leadership, the central government had to adopt macro-control policies to counterweigh inflation caused by this brisk expansion of investment. In our ECM, we include M1 as a means of macro control. The results show that short-term manipulations of money supply have a significantly positive effect on investment of fixed assets with a coefficient of 0.27. This indicates that when the economy is on the cusp of overheating, the government can force the central bank to slam the brakes on currency in circulation to bring down investment effectively. From Figure 2, it appears that there is a general tendency for M1 growth rates to reflect an opposite trend to local expenditure fluctuations. When local expenditure reaches the peak of the uptrend, we can see a downtrend as M1 hits its trough. By manipulating monetary aggregates, this results in a top-down economic bust. The economic boom soon returns to equilibrium, driven by market forces. Overall, the expansion and extraction of the FAI growth has led to a *locally led political business cycle*.

5.2. *Five-year Duration of Political Business Cycle in China*

The earlier analysis indicates that FAI fluctuations are influenced by temporary increases in the local expenditure. This model also has an additional effect resulting from the error correction mechanism which can minimize the deviation of actual Υ_t from the expected equilibrium value of Υ_t. To put it in another way, the error correction mechanism $\Upsilon_t - 0.94\Upsilon_{t-1} - 5374.6X_{t-1} - 0.14W_t$ can be rewritten in the form of Υ_{t-1}

[36] Pei, M. (2014). *China's Crony Capitalism: The Dynamics of Regime Decay* (Cambridge: Harvard University Press).

$- E(\Upsilon_{t-1})$, which shows a gap between actual investment in fixed assets and the equilibrium of FAI and budget expenditure.[37] In Table 1, the coefficient of −0.67 of the EC mechanism suggests the proportion of the gap between expected equilibrium value and actual investment in fixed assets will be adjusted in the following year. In other words, FAI fluctuations are influenced by temporary increases in local expenditure and are equilibrated by long-term mechanisms. Hence, recognizing the pattern of the Chinese PBC depends upon the assessment of the interaction between these two effects.

As noted above, a temporary increase in local expenditure ratio has brought about an increase of RMB632.9 billion in the next year's FAI. But in the equilibrium level, the investment is expected to increase only by RMB537.5 billion. The short-term increase of investment is indeed about RMB95.5 billion above the equilibrium. However, budget expenditure has a long-term effect on investment in fixed assets working through the EC mechanism and the difference will be adjusted in the next year, and the remaining discrepancy will be corrected downward by a proportion of 67% for each following year. Simply put, the short-term effect of local expenditure can dissipate quickly. Suppose the Chinese government increased its local expenditure by an unusual proportion. The probable effect of this big change roughly causes a surge in FAI by RMB632.9 billion the following year. The RMB95.5 billion deviation would have been adjusted downward by the error correction mechanism at the rate of 67% per year after the second period. Therefore, in the third period, this disequilibrium is offset because ~31.8 billion of the previous year's errors were corrected this year, leading to a value that is ~31.8 billion higher than the equilibrium value (i.e., 95.5 – 95.5*(0.67) = 31.8). In the following year, this value would be adjusted again. The unusual increase in FAI would reduce by 31.8*(0.67) = 21.2 billion, remaining roughly 31.8 – 21.2 = 10.6 billion above the equilibrium value. It takes almost 5 years for the temporary increase in local

[37]From (7), $\dot{e}_{t-1} = \Upsilon_{t-1} - 0.94\Upsilon_{t-2} - 5374.6X_{t-2} - 0.14W_{t-1}$ which can be rewritten as $\Upsilon_{t-1} = 0.94\Upsilon_{t-2} + 5374.6X_{t-2} + 0.14W_{t-1} + \dot{e}_{t-1}$. Therefore, $E(\Upsilon_{t-1}) = 0.94\Upsilon_{t-2} + 5374.6X_{t-2} + 0.14W_{t-1}$.

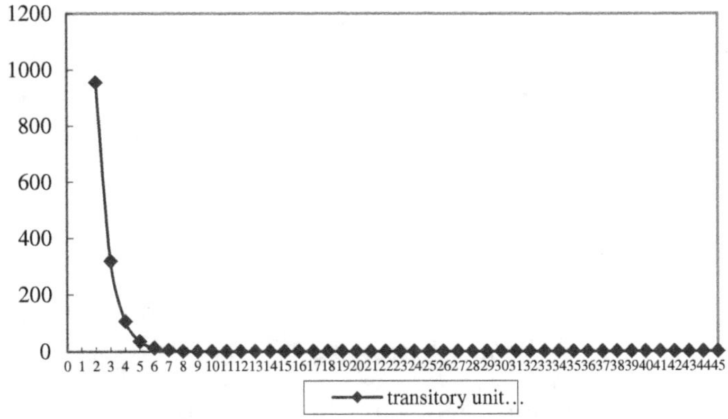

Figure 4: The temporary effect of local expenditure.

expenditure to no longer have any noticeable effect on investment. This implies that the FAI cycle is a 5-year cycle, and 5 years later, the short-term effect arrives at the trough and returns to long-term equilibrium (Figure 4). One possible explanation for this 5-year cycle, resonating with a 5-year term in office, is embedded in the political incentives of local cadres. This suggests that short-term increase in FAI is driven by the careerist concerns of myopic local officials. They tend to manipulate financial instruments to promote job advancement.

There is additional evidence to prove that the 5-year FAI cycle is due to the promotion mindset of local officials. As expected by the PBC theory, the estimated result shows a significant impact of the electoral year of the NPC on FAI. A further one-way ANOVA was conducted to test the effect of the NPC on the short-term increase in local expenditure. There was a significant effect of NPC at the $p < 0.05$ level. This indicated that the mean score for a temporary increase in local expenditure in NPC years (mean = 3.43) is significantly higher than in non-NPC years (mean = 0.42). Taken together, these results suggest that the interaction of short-term and long-term effects has led to a Chinese PBC that peaks in the years of NPC meetings. We can conclude that the Chinese PBC does exist, and it reflects the interplay of underlying political forces during changes in the central leadership. For local cadres, it is vital that the central leadership assembled at Party and national congresses sees increasing GDP growth. Hence, the local government tends to increase investment when NPCs are convened; as a result, budget stimulus and corresponding FAI growth surges correlate with NPC meetings, specifically with the 5-year cycle of Congress conventions.

5.3. *The Effectiveness of Political Business Cycles in the Era of Globalization*

With China's increasing integration into the world economy, many believe that political manipulation of economic growth might be less perceptible due to reduced state capacity, heightened by ongoing globalization. International markets may limit the effectiveness of national macroeconomic policy in the face of international competition pressures (footloose capital, regulations of international organizations, etc.). With China's integration into the world economy, it is more susceptive to international financial crises as well. China was engulfed in the 1997 Asian financial crisis and the 2008 global financial crisis. The question thus now is how effectively can China still manipulate fiscal and monetary policies which have been successful in stimulating economic growth and reining in inflation in the last four decades? From Table 1, the estimated result shows a statistically positive effect of the years 1998 and 2009 on the increase of FAI. The estimated FAI increase for 2009 of RMB661.9 billion was considerably higher than for any other annual FAI budget, controlling for lagged FAI, local budgeting and M1. The short-term FAI increase of RMB478 for 1998 also averaged generally higher than that of other years. It tells us that, despite China's deepening globalization after 2000, during an international crisis, the CCP still can effectively manipulate fiscal policies to fuel China's economic growth.

After the 1997 Asian financial crisis, China initiated a series of expansionary fiscal policies, one of which was to implement the Western China Development Program (*xibu da kaifa*) to accelerate infrastructure development and boost the region's growth. Similarly, after the 2008 economic crisis, China announced an RMB ¥4 trillion stimulus package (about US$586 billion), to inject funds into 10 sectors, including transport and other infrastructure projects. The local governments assumed fiscal responsibility in this economic stimulus plan that eventually kept China's economy in double-digit growth rates. In short, as many studies point out, Chinese government has been losing its ability to control the aggregate economy by manipulating macroeconomic policies as marketization deepens. Our analysis, however, indicates that the CCP can still effectively manipulate expansionary fiscal policies to exert large effects on FAI during crisis periods. After all, the CCP's legitimacy stems from its ability to deliver high economic growth. If economic growth disappears, so does its legitimacy.

6. Conclusion

There has been debate over PBC theories in the past 20 years. From a "rational perspective," extensive research has pointed out that all politicians have incentives to get re-elected; thus, they tend to manipulate economic policies to win elections. However, this approach has been criticized for its overestimation of the abilities of politicians. The "institutional perspective" considers that to evaluate the effects of pre-election manipulation, it is necessary to examine permanent structures that actually restrain policy manipulation and maintain market stability.

In this chapter, we take into consideration China's specific electoral and fiscal institutions to hypothesize a 5-year PBC. The ECM is applied to test how likely it is that the state can control macroeconomics by manipulating local budget expenditure. The virtue of this model is that we can test for the short-term effect of the state's expenditure change and simultaneously examine the extent to which the long-term market equilibrium can pull back the short-term deviation. The results from the estimated model are statistically significant. First, we prove that government intervention in investment in fixed assets has not been undermined or ultimately replaced by market forces. Despite ongoing marketization, Chinese local governments can still control highly mobile assets and influence aggregate FAI by local budgeting. Nevertheless, even though local expenditure may fluctuate an unusual amount at critical times and consequently produce enormous FAI growth in the following year, the negative coefficient of the ECM implies that this unusual increase will be adjusted downward to a non-obvious degree so as to maintain the equilibrium relationship between state budget and FAI in the market. The interactions between the short-term and long-term effects have led to a 5-year PBC. Second, our analysis shows that the Chinese PBC is more likely to peak at periods of fiscal reform and at the year of the NPC. This 5-year PBC pattern, which synchronizes with the 5-year term in office, suggests that the sharp increase in FAI is indeed driven by the careerist considerations of local officials.

Finally, although the state has not relinquished its authority to manipulate markets, it has changed the way it intervenes in the marketization process. Accordingly, the PBC pattern has varied with ongoing marketization. Under the planned economy, the volatile cycles were exclusively the result of excessive government intervention in the market. In the market economy, the government has made moderate interventions to bring the economic system back from the brink, thus cyclical movements have consistently become more moderate over time. When investment fever negatively affects China's robust economic growth, the central government will use macro-control tools (such as M1) to restore stability. Moreover, our study indicates that when facing external financial crisis, the CCP can still effectively manipulate expansionary fiscal policies to exert macro effects on FAI in order to maintain its legitimacy.

Part III

China in the World

https://doi.org/10.1142/9789811226588_0008

Chapter 8

China Goes Out

Shaun Breslin

Shaun.Breslin@warwick.ac.uk

1. Introduction

China's emergence as a major global economic actor in the post-Mao era, and in particular since the early 1990s, has had important consequences for the nature of the global economy. The rather phenomenal growth of Foreign Direct Investment (FDI) into China after 1993 was one of the key components of this emergence. While we should not forget that the investment strategies of foreign companies seeking to lower costs was a major driver of this change, the implementation of a range of reforms by the Chinese state to increase the attractiveness of China to foreign capital clearly played a very significant role, too. In effect, the Chinese state and transnational capital formed an informal partnership that resulted in changes to the price of a whole range of goods and commodities, where they are produced, who produces them, and in some cases, how they are produced.

The inward flow of money remains important today. China typically only trails the US in the league tables of annual FDI inflows, and has recorded record-high figures for 7 years in a row before the COVID-19 pandemic created global economic turmoil in 2020.[1] Yet, since the early 2000s, it is the money flowing out of China that has increasingly become the main area of international interest and scrutiny. Perhaps this is because massive FDI inflows have become "normal"; part and parcel of China's economic story for the best part of three decades and thus no longer particularly newsworthy. The speed of the growth of this Chinese Outward Foreign Direct Investment (COFDI) might also be enough in itself to bring attention to it. More important, however, are perceptions of how COFDI might be used to bring about broader change in the global political economy in ways that benefit China at the expense of other global actors.

Initially, the focus was on the extent to which COFDI was being used to gain access to (and possibly even ultimately control over) key resources and materials, particularly in the developing world. More recently, attention has turned to Chinese investments in more developed economies, raising questions over the long-term wisdom of allowing Chinese ownership of strategic industries; be they economically strategic or more directly related to national defence considerations. One common question cuts across both periods though. Rather than reflecting commercial logic driven by business interests, is the Chinese state driving COFDI, and using it as an instrument of "economic statecraft" to achieve nationally defined goals and ambitions?[2] If the answer is yes (as it often is), the next question is do these ambitions go beyond narrow economic goals? For example, is China utilizing the power shift that occurred during or just after the global financial crisis to develop new leadership roles or even seeking to build a new international order that reflects and supports its interests and goals?

This chapter outlines the evolution of policy and practices from 2002 to 2019. This is a time period that starts with the start of

[1] For full statistics of global comparisons, see the annual *World Investment Report* produced by UNCTAD.

[2] William Norris (2016). *Chinese Economic Statecraft: Commercial Actors, Grand Strategy and State Control* (Ithaca: Cornell University Press).

significant outflows from China, and the start of relatively full records of those outflows. As it will take a number of years before we have enough date to make sensible analyses of its long-term impact on both China and the global economy as a whole, it makes sense to stop at the onset of the pandemic. Even within this relatively short time scale, there were a number of shifts in the nature and direction of Chinese investment, which make it difficult to come to firm conclusions that will last the test of time; so even without the pandemic it would have been somewhat risky to project past trends into the future.

There are some commonalities across the changes though. The overall picture that emerges is one of both considerable residual state control and influence, but also considerable divergence and plurality of objectives and interests, too. These two apparently contradictory findings can be reconciled by making a distinction between the "overall executive discretion" of the (central) state,[3] and the agency of individual commercial and local state actors to pursue their own goals within the boundaries that this executive discretion sets. Top leaders in Beijing remain the key actors in setting overall agendas and frameworks for international economic activity at the macro level, and facilitating the internationalization of the Chinese capital and of Chinese companies. Moreover, the ability of individual economic actors to operate overseas is dependent on the state's willingness to let them do so. If these actors do not do what the state wants them to do — as was the case in 2016 and 2017 — then the state is prepared and able to step in to try to shape their behavior, or even to prevent them from operating overseas at all.

But this does not mean that the state is in day-to-day control of all that is done by Chinese companies and individuals operating overseas. Within this overall state-set framework, there is considerable scope for them to pursue their own specific agendas. This includes different parts of the state itself wanting different things. It also

[3]Luke Hurst (2011). "Comparative analysis of the determinants of China's state-owned outward direct investment in OECD and non-OECD countries," *China and World Economy*, 19(4): 79.

includes the pursuit of straightforward commercial objectives by economic actors, with even major state-owned energy companies sometimes inspired by the goal of simply making money for themselves, rather than building up strategic energy reserves for the country.[4] To be sure, as is the case in many countries, supporting nationally based companies in their attempt to make money and/or upgrade their operations is a clear state objective with the aim of not just strengthening the firm or the industry, but also strengthening the country as a whole. Behind pretty much all that the Chinese state does, there is an underpinning conception of Party interests, national interests, and the quest for power in a competitive global order. However, such "state guidance or direction with a commercial rationale"[5] should not be confused with commercial actors being directly deployed to attain grander geostrategic ends *at all times.* If the two are confused, then the danger is that action is imbued with intent, and consequences of actions are used as evidence to prove this pre-assumed intent. As a result, we can end up with only a partial picture of who is driving the growth of CODFI, and why.

2. What the Statistics Do, and Don't, Tell Us

If people are concerned about the impact of COFDI on global flows of money and resources, then one very good reason for this concern is the speed at which China has grown from being all but irrelevant to one of the major sources of global outward investment. This in itself would be enough to disrupt existing flows of goods and money, to destabilize a number of pre-existing relationships, and to focus attention on what China wants. Add to this speed and scale a more general concern that China will seek to change the nature of the

---

[4] Zhao Hongtu (2015). "The myth of China's overseas energy investment," *East Asia Forum*, 4 March, http://www.eastasiaforum.org/2015/03/04/the-myth-of-chinas-overseas-energy-investment.

[5] Deborah Brautigam and Tang Xiaoyang (2012). "Economic statecraft in China's new overseas special economic zones: Soft power, business, or resource-security?" *International Affairs*, 88(4): 800.

global order when it has the power to do so, and it is not hard to see why COFDI has become such a high-profile topic. Indeed, it is sobering to remember that the official *zou chuqu* (go out) strategy that encouraged Chinese companies to look to invest overseas was first announced as recently as 1999, formally initiated the following year, and only really gathered momentum after the 16th Party Congress in 2002. Financial flows were so limited that full national statistics from the different government agencies dealing with outward investment were only first available in 2003 (for 2002) and in many respects, it makes sense to use this as year zero in any review of the evolution of COFDI.[6]

As will be discussed in more detail shortly, there are a number of different statistical sets covering the growth of COFDI. For the sake of consistency, unless otherwise cited this chapter uses those produced by China's Ministry of Commerce (MOFCOM) as its starting point. Even using one source is not problem-free, though, as initial statistics are often subsequently re-calculated as more information comes to light. As such, it is best to treat them as indications of broad trends and the overall direction of travel rather than as precise and unchangeable facts. With this in mind, an analysis of these statistics show an annual average growth rate of 35.8% from 2002 to 2016, which resulted in the overall stock of Chinese overseas investment rising from 25th in the world in 2002 to sixth.[7] In terms of annual flows (rather than aggregated stocks), the 2016 figure of US$196 billion placed China as second only to the US as a source of outward investment (up from 26th place in 2002), accounting for 13.5% of all global outflows (compared to 0.5% in 2002).[8] After 14 years of continued annual growth, COFDI fell back rather dramatically in 2017 to

---

[6]For an assessment of COFDI before the new millennium, see Kevin Cai (1999). "Outward foreign direct investment: A novel dimension of China's integration into the regional and global economy," *China Quarterly*, 160: 856–880.
[7]NDRC (2017). "*Zhongguo Duiwai Touzi Baogao* [China Foreign Investment Report]," National Development and Reform Commission, 3–4 November, http://www.ndrc.gov.cn/gzdt/201711/W020171130400470019984.pdf.
[8]NDRC, "*Zhongguo Duiwai Touzi Baogao*," p. 3.

US$120.08 billion.[9] Depending on which figures are used, there was either a slight increase in 2018, or a further slight decline.[10] But what is clear is that even using the highest available figures, COFDI at the end of 2019 of around $100.6 billion was still some way below the 2016 high point and close to the figure for 2014.[11]

We will never know if this then would have stabilized into a consistent pattern of flows. The ebbs and flows in investment, particularly in the second half of the 2010s, make it difficult to work out what a new normality might have looked like without the pandemic. But what happened to the global economy in 2020 was anything but normal. However, even if we put these fluctuations to one side and treat the 2016 figure as something of an outlier, we can still say with some confidence that China went from being pretty much insignificant as a source of global investment flows to becoming a major actor and funder in less than a decade and a half. Whatever the exact numbers might be, this in itself is rather remarkable.

It is worth qualifying these still raw statistics with four caveats. First, despite these large numbers, the ratio of the Chinese overseas investment stock to GDP is actually relatively low by international comparison. This includes comparisons with not just those developed economies that have long been sources of global finance, but also other developing economies and rising powers as well. A figure of

---

[9]MOFCOM (2018). "MOFCOM Department of Outward Investment and Economic Cooperation Comments on China's Outward Investment Cooperation in 2017," Ministry of Commerce, 18 January, http://english.mofcom.gov.cn/article/newsrelease/policyreleasing/201801/20180102706193.shtml.

[10]MOFCOM (2019). "MOFCOM Department of Outward Investment and Economic Cooperation Comments on China's Outward Investment and Cooperation in 2018," 17 January, http://english.mofcom.gov.cn/article/newsrelease/policyreleasing/201901/20190102829745.shtml. The State Council subsequently put the figure at US$143 billion, which shows how even sticking to official Chinese statistics can lead to confusion. State Council (2019). *China and the World in the New Era*, 27 September, http://english.www.gov.cn/archive/whitepaper/201909/27/content_WS5d8d80f9c6d0bcf8c4c142ef.html.

[11]Ernst and Young, "Overview of China Outbound Investment in 2019," https://www.ey.com/cn/en/newsroom/news-releases/news-2020-ey-overview-of-china-outbound-investment-in-2019.

11.4% for China at the highest level of COFDI in 2016 compared to an overall world average of 34.6% (44.8% for developed countries, 19.8% for developing countries, and 22.6% for transition economies).[12]

Second, while outward investment surpassed inward investment in 2015, the stock of inward invested capital still exceeded the stock of overseas investment by some US$1.5 trillion.[13] The record inflows noted above prior to 2020 also subsequently turned the net value of investment flows negative again, with inward FDI exceeding COFDI in 2019 by some US$26.4 billion. This does not negate the importance of COFDI. However, it is worth reminding ourselves from time to time of the residual importance of inward FDI for the Chinese economy given some of the hyperbole that can surround discussions of outward financial flows.

The third caveat also relates to some of the ways that COFDI is sometimes discussed and reported. Although COFDI has risen quickly, it has still only been high for a relatively short period of time. What this means is that the total stock of Chinese holdings remains relatively low compared to investment from countries with much longer histories of activity. One consequence is that the focus on increases from China can give an inflated impression of just how important COFDI is in any particular economy. At the end of 2018, for example, China accounted for just 1.4% of all foreign-invested holdings in the United States, and the stock of Indian investments exceeded Chinese ones in the UK, with China 17th in a league table of all investors.[14] In Australia, despite Chinese investment growing rapidly for the best part of a decade, it still only ranked ninth in terms of total

---

[12]NDRC, "*Zhongguo Duiwai Touzi Baogao*," 9–10.

[13]Thilo Hanemann (2017). "China's rise in global M&A: Here to stay," Rhodium Group/White & Case, March 24, pp. 12–13, http://rhg.com/wp-content/uploads/2017/03/chinas-rise-in-global-ma-here-to-stay.pdf.

[14]"UK Foreign Direct Investment (2020). "Trends and Analysis: July 2019," UK Office of National Statistics, 29 July, https://www.ons.gov.uk/economy/nationalaccounts/balanceofpayments/articles/ukforeigndirectinvestmenttrendsandanalysis/july2019 and "Foreign Direct Investment (FDI): United States," US Department of Commerce, accessed 5 January 2020, https://www.selectusa.gov/servlet/servlet.FileDownload?file=015t0000000LKSn

stock of holdings with 1.8% of the total.[15] Hong Kong was fifth with 3.4%, some way behind the US (26.7%), the UK (16.4%), Belgium (9%) and Japan (6.5%).[16] Yet, discussions of the consequences of such investment in all of these countries in both the media and (some) policy circles would seem to suggest a much higher penetration and perhaps even a dependency.

Fourth, as with all statistics, and not just Chinese statistics, the raw figures do not always tell the full story, and there is a general feeling that official Chinese figures understate the real amount of money being invested by Chinese actors overseas. For example, Chinese companies do not always report earnings that they immediately reinvest overseas without first repatriating them to the Chinese parent company, so they are typically not captured by Chinese COFDI statistics.[17] They are, however, usually counted as Chinese originating investment by those who look at what is exactly been invested on the ground in recipient countries. The very extensive China Global Investment Tracker (http://www.aei.org/china-global-investment-tracker) is widely used by foreign analysts to get over the problem of reliance on Chinese statistics. While it is very useful, it does not include investments of under US$100 million, which excludes small scale investments like cross-border ones carried out predominantly by local and private actors.[18] Tan argues that Chinese statistics also often miss these small cross-border arrangements that don't need central government approval. Including these smaller investments would not have any significant impact on the aggregate picture of COFDI and overall trends, but it can have micro level consequences for specific case studies in recipient countries. As just one example, while

---

[15] DFAT, "Statistics on who invests in Australia," Australian Government Department of Foreign Affairs and Trade, May 2019, https://www.dfat.gov.au/trade/resources/investment-statistics/Pages/statistics-on-who-invests-in-australia.

[16] *Ibid.*

[17] Daniel Rosen and Thilo Hanemann (2009). "Chinas changing OFDI profile: Drivers and policy implication," *Peterson Institute Policy Brief*, No. PB09-14, June, https://piie.com/system/files/documents/pb09-14.pdf.

[18] Luo Limin, Qi Zhen and Paul Hubbard (2017). "Not looking for trouble: Chinese overseas investment by sector and ownership," *China Economic Review*, 46:144.

Mongolia claimed it had received almost US$900 million in total investment from China by 2007, official Chinese statistics captured only just over a third of this total stock.[19] The gap might not make any difference for a consideration of China's global position, but it makes a very real difference for those trying to assess the extent of Mongolian dependence on Chinese finances.

2.1. *Investment and Loans*

A further issue is how to make a distinction between investment and development assistance, as what starts as a loan can have investment-type consequences. The extensive development loans extended by the Exim Bank and China Development Bank (CDB) should be reported as portfolio investments alongside non-financial outward FDI.[20] However, these loans are often extended as part of larger development assistant packages that can include requiring recipient countries to use Chinese companies to deliver projects using Chinese sourced labor and materials.[21] These loans can also be used to "secure access by Chinese firms to natural resources" and entail part repayment in resources, resulting in some of the same consequences as COFDI.[22] Loans can also result in Chinese companies assuming ownership of projects completed with the loaned money; either through conditions attached to the original loan agreement, or through subsequent arrangements to recompense for the inability of the recipient country to repay debts to China. The best known and most repeated example is the 99-year lease on Hambantota Port in

[19]Tan Xiaomei (2013). "China's overseas investment in the energy/resources sector: Its scale, drivers, challenges and implications," *Energy Economics*, 36: 750–758.

[20]David Dollar (2014). "China as a global investor," Brookings Asia Working Group Paper, no. 4, 3 May.

[21]Kevin Gallagher and Amos Irwin (2014). "Exporting national champions: China's outward foreign direct investment finance in comparative perspective," *China and World Economy*, 22(6): 1–21.

[22]Daniel Shapiro, Carlos Vecino and Jing Li (2018). "Exploring China's state-led FDI model: Evidence from the extractive sectors in Latin America," *Asia Pacific Journal of Management*, 35(1): 12.

Sri Lanka that China Overseas Ports Holding was given in 2017 as part of a renegotiated repayment scheme for infrastructure loans from China.

While what looks like development finance can sometimes have investment-type consequences, COFDI (particularly in infrastructure projects) can have development-type consequences, too. If this blurs the divisions between different types of financial flows, the way that they are reported in the media often doesn't help either. It is not uncommon to find COFDI bundled together with loans and other development projects to create a single headline figure.[23] This can be compounded by focusing on what is announced (often with considerable fanfare and publicity) rather than what is actually spent. This is because the headline reported figure is for the overall project, with money distributed over a number of years rather than paid in one go. The overall amount is still significant, but not immediately as large and significant in the year that it is announced as can appear at first sight (or indeed, in any subsequent individual year). Moreover, there can be considerable slippage from announcement to implementation. For example, Brautigam has shown that much of what is reported as new Chinese land-based investments in Africa never actually comes to fruition at all.[24] Similarly, in 2017, Chinese investors cancelled 19 investment deals in Europe and North America, resulting in the disappearance of US$12 billion worth of previously announced financing.[25] In both cases, for those that are concerned about the rise of COFDI, the initial pronouncements helped fire the concern, with the subsequent retractions typically going unnoticed.

[23]Austin Strange *et al.* (2017). "Tracking underreported financial flows: China's development finance and the aid-conflict nexus revisited," *Journal of Conflict Resolution*, 61(5): 938.

[24]Deborah Brautigam (2015). *Will Africa Feed China?* (Oxford: Oxford University Press).

[25]Baker McKenzie (2018). "Chinese FDI squeezed in 2017 by regulatory crackdowns at home and abroad," 17 January, https://www.bakermckenzie.com/en/newsroom/2018/01/chinese-fdi-2017.

2.2. *Where Does China Invest?*

A more significant statistical problem emerges when trying to identify where COFDI actually goes. Around 65% has cumulatively gone to just three places — Hong Kong, the Cayman Islands and the British Virgin Islands. Quite simply we don't know where this money eventually ends up. Some of it is recycled as inward investment back into China to take advantage of incentives offered to foreign investors. By some calculations around a quarter of all COFDI is "round tripped" in this way.[26] Some of it will go elsewhere and potentially show up as investment from the intermediary recipient (particularly from subsidiaries in HK). Rosen and Hanemann also show how the use of specialist financial companies in Singapore and Hong Kong to arrange mergers and acquisitions (M&A) can also obscure where the money eventually goes.[27] In addition to disguising the real extent and ultimate destination of COFDI, the statistics on what sectors China invests in are also rather distorted. Because of investment in Hong Kong and the tax havens, the raw statistics in official Chinese reports show commercial and business services of various kinds (to these places) as the biggest recipient of Chinese investment. But by using China Global Investment Tracker data, in 2012 Liao and Tsui found that investments in mining and extraction were even more significant than the raw figures suggested once the Hong Kong and tax haven effects were stripped out.[28]

2.3. *Is It Still (Or Always) Too Early to Tell?*

The question of how important extraction industries really are brings us to the importance of timing. Here, there are two main

[26]Carlos Casanova, Alicia Garcia-Herrero and Xia Le (2015). "Chinese outbound foreign direct investment: How much goes where after round-tripping and offshoring?" BBVA Working Paper, no. 15/17, June, https://www.bbvaresearch.com/wp-content/uploads/2015/07/15_17_Working-Paper_ODI.pdf

[27]Rosen and Hanemann, "Chinas changing OFDI profile: Drivers and policy implication," p. 4.

[28]Wei Liao, and Kevin Tsui (2012). "China's outward direct investment: Evidence from a new micro dataset." Hong Kong Institute for Monetary Research Working Paper, no. 17, http://papers.ssrn.com/sol3/papers.cfm?abstract_id=2087385.

considerations. The first is that as China is still a relatively new actor, there is not a particularly long time-series of data available to analyze. As such, it is arguably simply too early to say anything definitive about a pattern of COFDI that stands the test of time. For example, had Liao and Tsui undertaken the exact same study just a few years later, then the importance of mining-related industries would have been somewhat lower as a result of the subsequent increase in investments in other sectors. Indeed, much of the very good literature that was produced in the mid to late 2000s has already been overtaken by events. These works remain very useful as studies of the first generation of investments, but many of their original conclusions about the nature of COFDI — where it goes and what it is trying to do — are simply not replicated by studies from about 2012 onwards.[29] Some views of Chinese intentions and actions, however, still seem to be influenced by this early pattern of investment rather than what has happened subsequently.

Second, there can be big variations from one year to the next, with what appeared to be evidence of an ineluctable trend at the time subsequently looking like a blip. The 44% jump in COFDI in 2016 over 2015 is a very good example here; not least as it was followed by a contraction of nearly 30% the following year. Moreover, it is often the case that one major deal can make a big statistical difference. For example, in 2017, ChemChina's massive US$43 billion takeover of Syngenta was enough to make the difference between a 22% year-on-year reduction of Chinese investment in Europe without the deal, and a 76% increase with it.[30] If it had been completed the year before as it was originally meant to be, then the already big increase in COFDI in 2016 would have been even bigger, and the subsequent drop off in 2017 even more severe.

[29] Of this literature, Buckey *et al.* is largely regarded as a classic example and in many respects a pathbreaker in the study of COFDI decision making. See Peter Buckley *et al.* (2007). "The determinants of Chinese outward foreign direct investment," *Journal of International Business Studies*, 38(4): 499–518.

[30] Baker McKenzie, "Chinese FDI Squeezed in 2017."

3. COFDI: Follow the Leader?

Annual fluctuations occur in investment figures for all countries. But in the Chinese case, the way that changes in the Chinese regulatory and incentive structure shape investment activity can have very dramatic effects that create new patterns almost overnight. We have already seen that the growth of substantial COFDI in the first place was initiated by the top-down decision to *zou chuqu*. Analyses of early responders to this exhortation show the importance of large state-owned enterprises (SOEs) investing in developing countries (including politically unstable ones) to access resources. Of course, other considerations played a role, too. Establishing branch offices overseas to support exports was also a characteristic of this first wave of investment.[31] Even so, the dominance of resource-based investment in these early projects looked so out of odds with typical investment patterns from other states that it created a notion of Chinese "exceptionalism."

It also generated a debate over whether Chinese firms perceived risk differently from their counterparts in other countries (particularly developed ones). The consensus was that Chinese companies did not actively seek out politically risky and unstable investment locations in preference to more stable ones, but that they were indeed less concerned about the nature of the regime of the host country than was "normally" the case.[32] In particular, SOEs seemed less bothered by political risk in host countries than investors from other countries; either because good political relationships at the highest level reduced the chances of things going wrong, or through an expectation that the Chinese state would bail them out if things went wrong (or both).[33]

---

[31] Henry Yeung and Liu Weidong (2008). "Globalizing China: The rise of Mainland firms in the global economy," *Eurasian Geography and Economics*, 49(1): 57–86.

[32] Dollar, "China as a Global Investor."

[33] Jing-Lin Duanmu (2012). "Firm heterogeneity and location choice of Chinese multinational enterprises (MNEs)," *Journal of World Business*, 47(1): 64–72.

3.1. *COFDI Regulatory Regime*

But things change — and sometimes very quickly. As investment responded to changes in state regulations and incentives, the nature of COFDI underwent a quite dramatic transformation. The regulatory regime has gone through four overlapping phases. Given the previous relatively closed nature of the Chinese economy, the starting point was simply to make COFDI possible at all. This was followed by a facilitation mode making it easier for more types of investors to do more types of things, with the third phase moving to active encouragement and promotion of specific types of investment. The fourth phase beginning in 2016 was to rethink the efficacy of ever greater opening and reintroduce some controls in what we might think of as a new "guiding" phase.

Initially, COFDI had to be approved by the National Development and Reform Commission (NDRC). This changed in two ways. First, approval was replaced by simply filing and registering projects. By 2014, only investments of over US$1 billion (as well as those in sensitive countries) had to be approved at all. Second, local governments took on more authority, and became responsible for oversight of projects under US$300 million.[34] Specific help was also introduced for those firms aiming to acquire advanced technology and knowhow, and to move up the global value chain.[35] Perhaps most fundamentally, this included in 2009 simply making it easier for companies to move money overseas; a freedom that is taken for granted in many economies, but which has been at best limited and often wholly absent for much of the period that the People's Republic of China has existed. Other supporting mechanisms for enterprises in targeted sectors included various types of subsidies and tax breaks, and help with investment insurance to mitigate risk and encourage new companies to move overseas. Given that most Chinese companies had little or no

[34] Casanova, Garcia-Herrero and Xia, "Chinese outbound foreign direct investment."

[35] Alessia Amighini, Roberta Rabellotti and Marco Sanfilippo (2013). "Do Chinese state-owned and private enterprises differ in their internationalization strategies?" *China Economic Review*, 27: 312–325.

experience of operating outside China's borders, it also entailed providing softer forms of support such as advice and training on how to operate in overseas jurisdictions.[36] It is also no coincidence that in 2016 — a year that saw a massive increase in COFDI — the Ministry of Industry and Information Technology produced a plan specifically designed to help small and medium enterprises to go overseas. The same year, MOFCOM also produced new official guidance on how such enterprises could raise their position in global production and value chains.[37]

3.2. *Becoming "Normal"?*

These reforms to the outward investment regime eventually resulted in a number of key changes in China's investment profile. First, while promoting exports had been a driver of COFDI from the beginning, this type of investment increased as Chinese companies set up affiliates overseas to help sell things. This included, for example, investing in textile production in a range of states to sell into the US and European markets and thus avoid (real or potential) trade barriers against exports from China. Second, M&A replaced brownfield (particularly energy related) investment as the main type of overseas investment. This was accompanied by a broader change in who was investing, and where the money was going; both in terms of sectors and countries.[38] While energy, resources and materials accounted for two-thirds of such M&A activity from 2005 to 2013, the above-noted regulatory changes subsequently led to many

---

[36]For details see Karl Sauvant and Michael Nolan (2015). "China's outward foreign direct investment and international investment law," *Journal of International Economic Law*, 18(4): 893–934.

[37]Ernst and Young (2017). "Sound risk management builds a solid foundation for Chinese enterprises to navigate the global landscape," *Ernst and Young China Go Abroad*, Fifth Issue, April, http://www.ey.com/Publication/vwLUAssets/ey-china-overseas-investment-report-issue-5-en/$FILE/EY-china-overseas-investment-report-issue-5-en.pdf.

[38]Hanemann, "China's Rise in Global M&A," 3–4.

companies going overseas to buy brands and technology and to establish overseas operations. Within 3 years, the share of energy, resources and materials had dropped to 20% of the total, with high-tech firms accounting for around a quarter of all acquisitions. This fed into the overall investment profile to leave leasing and commercial services and manufacturing accounting for just over half of all COFDI in 2018.[39]

This shift in sectors entailed a shift in geographic destinations, too. There was first a move to resource acquisitions in the developed world, with resource-based assets in Canada, Australia and the USA the main targets. As the scope of activity changed, this subsequently resulted in both an extension of investment activities in these countries, and a focus on other developed economies as well. As a result, "by 2015, high-income economies were capturing two-thirds of all Chinese M&A by value," with Europe emerging as the single biggest destination.[40] For around 3 years, Europe and North America emerged as the two most favored investment sites, but this didn't last long. Subsequent changes in the Chinese regulatory system combined with US–China friction and concerns about Chinese investment in other Western economies to change things again. According to the Rhodium Group's statistics, COFDI to the US fell from US$46 billion in 2016 to US$29 billion in 2017, and then not so much dropped again as collapsed to just US$4.8 billion in 2018.[41] Although investment into Europe initially seemed to be replacing money that would otherwise have gone to the US,[42] this too fell back in 2019. By the end of the decade, Chinese M&A activity in

[39]MOFCOM, "China's Outward Investment and Cooperation in 2018."

[40]Hanemann, "China's Rise in Global M&A," 4.

[41]Thilo Hanemann, Cassie Gao, and Adam Lysenko (2019). "Net negative: Chinese investment in the US in 2018," Rhodium Group, 13 January, https://rhg.com/research/chinese-investment-in-the-us-2018-recap.

[42]Ernst and Young (2018)., "How does geopolitical dynamics affect future China overseas investment?" *Ernst and Young China Go Abroad*, Eighth Issue, November, https://www.ey.com/Publication/vwLUAssets/ey-china-overseas-investment-report-issue-8-en-new/$File/ey-china-overseas-investment-report-issue-8-en.pdf, accessed 3 March 2019.

Europe and North America had fallen back to roughly the levels they had been at in 2014 and 2012, respectively, with Asia now the most popular destination.[43]

It remains, then, rather difficult to pin down patterns of investment that stand the test of time. However, this quick review of changing investment priorities does show that by the mid-2010s, the relative importance of resource-seeking investments in unstable developing states was much diminished. Subsequently, while the geographic concentration of investments shifted first to and then from Europe and North America, China's overall investment profile looked much less abnormal than it previously did. Rather than focusing on Chinese difference, by 2017, the IMF annual report was referring to the drivers of COFDI as "*the traditional desire* for new markets and technology" (emphasis added),[44] and Chalmers and Mocker were happy to conclude that the era of exceptionalism was already over.[45]

3.3. *State and Market Actors*

The number of Chinese actors engaging in overseas activities also increased. For example, while investments from the state sector were once dominated by large centrally owned SOEs, locally owned state enterprises have become ever more active overseas. Perhaps more important is the growth in non-state actors; though here it is not always easy to identify the boundaries between the state and non-state. One of the most detailed breakdowns to date of types of Chinese investors was provided by an NDRC report in 2017.[46] This showed privately owned enterprises accounted for just over a quarter of the total in 2016, with Limited Liability Companies (LLCs)

[43]Ernst and Young, "Overview of China Outbound Investment in 2019."

[44]IMF (2017). "The People's Republic Of China: Selected issues," IMF Country Report, no. 17/248, August, https://www.imf.org/~/media/Files/Publications/CR/2017/cr17248.ashx.

[45]Adam Chalmers and Susanna Mocker (2017). "The End of Exceptionalism? Explaining Chinese National Oil Companies' Overseas Investments," *RIPE* 27(1): 19–143.

[46]NDRC, *"Zhongguo Duiwai Touzi Baogao."*

providing a further 43.2%. While not counted in China as part of the state system, state enterprises often have significant or even controlling shareholdings in LLCs. In some cases, different SOEs might have minority holdings, but when added together result in the majority of shares being held by state sector actors. The only way of finding out the real situation is to look at the individual ownership structure of each individual LLC. In addition, some of the very large private investors that are identified as "National Champions" get the sort of state support for some of their overseas activities that would normally be reserved for SOEs. Huawei and the HNA are two good examples here, with the latter having a particularly busy year in 2015, supplying 10% of all COFDI.

So, what we might call the "state related sector" might be more important than the headline figures suggest. Even so, it is not insignificant that the formal state sector was surpassed as the major source of outward investment in 2015 by what official statistics call the "non-public economy", which accounted for 57.4% of COFDI in 2018. As we have already noted, individual years can see quite big changes overnight as a result of a handful of large projects. Even a single deal can make a difference when that project is as big as the deal which saw ChemChina acquire Syngenta in 2017. As a result, there are years when large central SOEs still emerge as the dominant overseas investors and this is likely to be the case in the future as well. But it is instructive that having assessed the direction of travel over a number of years, Ernst and Young concluded that small and local enterprises had become "the backbone of China's outbound investment."[47]

4. Facilitating and Controlling: Applying the Brakes

Given the argument made above about the potential pitfalls of assessing data for any single year, it might then seem strange to focus on 2017 as warranting special attention. Moreover, despite the drop in 2017, this still left COFDI at marginally higher than the 2015 total of US$118.02 billion. But even if it was the growth of investment in

[47] Ernst and Young, "Sound risk management."

2016 that was abnormal rather than the drop in 2017, the state's response to this abnormality is nevertheless illuminating and highlights a key dilemma for Chinese policy-makers; how do you liberalize the outward investment regime while at the same time maintain some control so that investors invest where the state wants them to? The explosion of investment in 2015 and 2016 was facilitated by the state's administrative and regulatory reforms. It deliberately let go of some of its previous control over who could invest and where they could invest their money. Having done this, however, it did not take long for concern to appear over the way in which this new freedom was being utilized. This included concern about the quality of some investments and about the possibility of using investment as a disguised means of capital flight. There was also some anxiety — quite rightly as it turned out — that some recipient countries might respond negatively to what was a very rapid increase of COFDI. As the then Governor of the People's Bank of China put it in March 2017:

> Some investments do not meet our industrial policy requirements for outward investment... they are not of great benefit to China and have led to complaints abroad. Therefore, we think a certain degree of policy guidance is necessary and effective.[48]

In order to rebalance the overall profile and regain some of the control that the state had previously ceded, new capital control restrictions were reintroduced in late 2016 followed in 2017 by new regulations aimed at "guiding" and regulating COFDI.[49] This guidance included revising China's sectoral discrimination policy. "Encouraged" investments included those designed to increase connectivity along the Belt and Road, to obtain high-quality equipment,

---

[48] Emily Feng (2017). "China tightens rules on states groups' foreign investments," *Financial Times*, 3 August.

[49] State Council (2017). "*Guanyu jinyibu yindao he guifan jingwai touzi fangxiang de zhidao yijian* [Guiding opinions on further guiding and regulating the orientation of overseas investment]," 4 August, http://www.gov.cn/zhengce/content/2017-08/18/content_5218665.htm.

to upgrade R&D and manufacturing capacities, to meet energy shortfalls, and to develop agricultural cooperation. Restricted investment needing approval focused on "investment in real estate, hotels, cinemas, entertainment industry and sports clubs," which had seen particularly large increases in the previous two years. It also included investment in politically sensitive or war-torn countries, those without diplomatic relations with China, and projects that either used outdated equipment or did not meet the environmental or other standards of the host country. A third list of prohibited sectors included the less than precise definition of investments that "endanger or may endanger national interests and national security," military investments, those that contravene any international laws that China is party to, pornography and gambling. That the MOFCOM report could announce that "no new projects were added in real estate, sports and entertainment areas" in 2017 suggests that some of the technically restricted sectors were in reality prohibited, too.[50] It also suggests that the policy reversal worked.

4.1. *Facilitating and Controlling: The Belt and Road*

Even though overall investment dropped in 2017, investment in the Belt and Road Initiative (BRI) countries increased by 3.5%. This suggests that a number of Chinese companies allowed themselves to be guided by the state to support its (and in this case, Xi Jinping's) preferred projects. That said, although it is growing, investment along the Belt and Road only accounted for 13% of all COFDI in 2018. As already noted, development funding from the Chinese state banks, the specialist Silk Road Fund, and the Asian Infrastructure Investment Bank can generate contracts for Chinese companies and thus have corporate investment type effects. So, the formal COFDI statistics might understate the real position. Even so, given that the BRI countries collectively account for over 60% of the world's population and around a quarter of global GDP, the overall position is perhaps less impressive than the high profile accorded to the BRI might suggest.

[50] MOFCOM, "China's Outward Investment Cooperation in 2017."

The BRI is covered in detail in this book by Dalton Lin, and so will not be dealt with in any great depth here. It is, however, worth a quick investigation into COFDI on the Belt and Road for two reasons. The first is the BRI as a case study of state guided investment. In addition to access to finance to fund Belt and Road projects and export and credit insurance for investors, the Chinese state has tried to facilitate and encourage investment in a number of ways. For example, it has signed bilateral investment and treaties with Belt and Road countries, expanded currency swaps and transnational currency settlements, and established various forms of economic development and cooperation zones to facilitate COFDI. By the end of 2018, there were 113 of these in 46 countries,[51] and they are typically lauded in MOFCOM reports as not just facilitating outward financial flows, but also making significant developmental contributions to the host country partners.

How successful these attempts have been is rather difficult to gauge as we simply do not know how much investment would have occurred in the individual countries in any case. Some of the more high-profile elements of the Belt and Road like the Pakistan Economic Corridor were agreed and signed before the BRI was even thought of. So COFDI would likely have grown in Pakistan even without any of the specific broader BRI-supporting initiatives and mechanisms. There is also evidence to suggest that the cooperation zones work best when they are building on pre-existing interactions and exchanges, and not very well when they try to establish new connections without existing relationships to build on.[52]

5. Pushback

The second reason for a quick look at the BRI is that it reminds us that investment is not just about what the investor wants. The interests of the recipients of the investment matter, too. In a number of

---

[51] Ernst and Young, "How does Geopolitical Dynamics," 5.

[52] Chen Zhangxi, "Building the Belt and Road Initiative? Practices en Route," *The Pacific Review*, 33(5): 788–812.

countries, perceptions of what the ultimate goal of the BRI might be designed to achieve has led to a partial rethink of the consequences of allowing an increased Chinese presence in host economies. The idea that China is deploying a form of neo-colonialism in Africa and other developing areas has been around for some time now. Investment, so the argument goes, is simply designed to transfer resources to China, and given that Chinese investors often use their own technology, resources, and workforces, the suggestion is that the developmental spillover or footprint into/on the wider host economy is very shallow and narrow. More recently, the idea of "debt-trap" diplomacy has entered the discussion, too — the idea that China deliberately extends loans to countries that cannot afford to pay them back in order to force them into a subordinate relationship and to take control over key resources in lieu of repayments.

Actually, the debt trap argument is to do with loans rather than investment, and gained popularity after Sri Lanka ceded control of Hambantota Port to China in 2017 after being unable to pay back loans. It's also difficult to find any concrete proof that this is a deliberate strategy rather than the consequence of bad planning and insufficient research and oversight. It may indeed be true that there is a goal to create some form of financial dependence on China, but this is not the same thing as deliberately funding projects that are destined to fail. But when it comes to perceptions and popular discourses, then pre-assumptions of Chinese intent can shape what evidence is sought, and the way that it is parsed and understood. A whole range of different interests and actions can also get lumped together to create an overall impression of what is being done for what reasons. So while COFDI is certainly not the only reason, its growth clearly has played at least some role in changing perceptions of the benefits of taking Chinese money in particular, and of the consequences of China's rise more generally.

Moreover, Chinese finance is helping change minds in other parts of the world, too. For example, for a number of years, the international environment was somewhat conducive to Chinese investment in Europe. After the financial crisis, the desire to attract investment resulted in a number of European leaders heading to China to try to strengthen commercial relations amid a form of competition to become China's best friend. This created new opportunities for Chinese investors in Europe that were not always available in other parts of the world. As just one example, while prospective investments by Huawei in both Australia and the US were blocked on political grounds, Huawei was welcomed into the UK in 2012. Ongoing financial difficulties in South, Eastern and Central Europe also created opportunities for Chinese investments there,[53] with establishment of the 16+1 process in 2012 providing a new platform for relations between China and a group of Central and Eastern European Countries. With the exception of Greece (which joined in 2019 to make it 17+1), these are all former European Communist Party states (or component parts of them) towards the western end of the Belt and Road. In all 17, Chinese finance is seen as potentially funding the sort of development projects that other European actors have been unable or unwilling to provide in the post-crisis years.

Perhaps not surprisingly, what is seen as an opportunity in Central and Eastern Europe has been perceived as a potential threat in other places. A European Parliament briefing in 2018 referred to the then still 16+1 process as a "tool for China to increase its political influence" which had already on occasions led to some Central and Eastern European states giving "priority to Chinese political interests over EU interests."[54] Moreover, the very rapid growth of investment in other parts of Europe, particular into high-tech sectors, resulted in a new debate over whether it is being used as a strategic instrument designed to increase Chinese national power at the potential future expense of others. As Thorsten Benner argues:

> There used to be a belief that Germany and China were perfectly complementary partners. Now we have realised that China has become a core competitor and that it uses investment in a very

---

[53]Nicola Casarini (2016). "When all roads lead to Beijing. Assessing China's New Silk Road and its implications for Europe," *The International Spectator*, 51(4): 95–108.
[54]Gisela Grieger (2018). "China, the 16+1 format and the EU,"' Members' Research Service, PE 625.173, 7 September, http://www.europarl.europa.eu/RegData/etudes/BRIE/2018/625173/EPRS_BRI(2018)625173_EN.pdf.

> strategic manner to copy technology and accelerate the catch-up. There is a realisation that Chinese investment has an impact on national security.[55]

The lack of reciprocity and the still relatively closed nature of some Chinese economic sectors to inward investment does not exactly help shape an impression of China as a fair and equal investment partner either. Indeed, concerns with the growth of COFDI into Europe cannot be fully separated from perceptions of the aims of the Made in China 2025 initiative, which aims to upgrade and indigenize China's technological base. In short, overseas investment — or at least some of it — is seen as being one way in which China can gain technological modernization and ultimately maybe even leadership, which might be used to enforce Chinese interests and preferences in other areas, too.

A more sceptical focus on COFDI has been more evident for longer in the US, where the use of the Committee on Foreign Investment in the United States to block proposed investment deals from China goes back as far as 1990.[56] Even so, the growth of COFDI has also resulted in an ever greater concern about Chinese intentions. The decline in COFDI in the US from US$46 billion in 2017 to just US$4.8 billion in 2018 was heavily influenced by the above-noted reintroduction of regulations in China, and efforts to reduce the level of debt. But investment screening (both actual and fears of it among investors) played at least some role in generating this sharp decrease.[57] We noted above that US$12 billion worth of previously announced deals were cancelled in 2017. Of these, Baker McKenzie calculates

[55]Cited by Tobias Buck (2018). "Germany toughens investment rules as China concerns build," *Financial Times*, 19 December, https://www.ft.com/content/568183dc-038e-11e9-99df-6183d3002ee1.

[56]The committee does not just look at investment from China, though it's fair to say that proposed Chinese investments have been a relatively important part of its work. In August 2018, a new Foreign Investment Risk Review Modernization Act came into force to update its jurisdictions and work.

[57]Hanemann, Gao, and Lysenko, "Net negative."

that US$8 billion was a result of objections from recipient countries, with only a third due to a change of mind by the Chinese investor.[58]

None of this points to China's isolation and the end of COFDI. A number of Western governments are still very committed to doing what they can to attract even more Chinese money, and investment in Belt and Road countries continues to increase. But it is important to remember that the world is not just China's to change as it sees fit. The way that others respond to China is important, too, and this response is often built around wider concerns about China's future global role and objectives that go beyond any specific focus on investment.

6. COFDI: An Economic Grand Strategy?

For some observers at least, it seems that it is not so much the case that Chinese investment leads to concerns about intentions, but rather that pre-existing concerns often shape the way these investments (and the intentions behind them) are perceived. But for others, the dramatic changes that have occurred in COFDI, particularly in the 2010s, have indeed led to some sort of rethink on what China might do and want as a Great Power.

Moreover, it is not just perceptions by the recipients that are important here. The ways that China's ambitions are being articulated and signaled from China are important, too. For example, the amount of time and money that have been spent promoting the BRI has signaled to the world China's capability and intention to operate way beyond its neighborhood backyard to bring about change in economic geographies. This signaling is supported and magnified by the way in which Xi Jinping has utilized major events at home and abroad to signal that China is now happy to accept a global leadership role and to actively seek global governance reform in some areas. In this environment, and given all else that China is doing on the global stage, it is not surprising that the actions of Chinese overseas are often viewed as being part of this effort to attain global centrality and to support

[58]Baker McKenzie, "Chinese FDI squeezed."

China's key strategic objectives. So is it correct to think of COFDI as a tool of some sort of grand Chinese economic strategy? Or one that is fundamentally different from "normal" state activity? After all, as Sauvant and Nolan argue, "virtually all developed countries (but only a few developing ones) pursue — to a larger or lesser extent — similar policies and support them through appropriate instruments."[59]

If the Chinese case is in some ways different from what happens elsewhere, then perhaps the difference is found in what such support is for. The development of Chinese enterprises and industries is not just about what is good for them, but also what is perceived to be good for China as a whole as it reinvents the basis of its economic success and the basis of its global power. There is a national goal behind it all and a conception of the need to build comprehensive national power in a competitive international order. Behind the national goal, there is also a Party goal, and a Party seeking to reinvent its legitimacy and cement its grip on political power as more traditional sources of economic growth in the post-Mao era seem to be reaching the end of their shelf-life (or at least declining in efficacy). Or perhaps the difference is found in the extent of state involvement and support compared to other countries.[60] While it has declined in relative importance, the way that investment has been used to gain control of/or access to major resources remains significant. So too is the fact that a significant amount of COFDI is supported by loans from the state banks; again particularly, (but not only) those related to energy and natural resource investments. There is also considerable state support to facilitate the upgrading of Chinese enterprises and industries to turn them into hi-tech globally competitive actors, and at least some of them into global leaders. The backing that not just state enterprises but those private investors pursuing what the state wants them to pursue as well helps create what Ramamurti and Hillemann call a "government created advantage" for Chinese

[59] Sauvant and Nolan, "China's outward foreign direct investment," 899.

[60] Rui Oliveira *et al.* (2017). "Outward foreign direct investment from emerging countries: Theoretical extension and evidence from China," *The International Trade Journal*, 31(5): 402–428.

investors that goes beyond what other governments typically offer to support their favored investors.[61]

That said, and not surprisingly, in terms of what they want to achieve, where they do it, and how much state help they get, there are significant differences between different types of investors. For example, Amighini, Rabellotti, and Sanfilippo found that private companies were much more likely to go overseas to gain technology and markets, while SOEs were more likely to seek out the things that the Chinese state thinks China needs for long-term development (such as energy and other resources).[62] Perhaps more surprisingly, there can also be big difference between the large central "National Champion" SOES, which tend to conform more to this politicized understanding of strategically (resource) driven investment, and locally owned SOEs which in general are driven by the search for commercial objectives — and most often simply profits — rather than seeking strategic gains.[63] As such, while still being very much part of the state system, their behavior is "closer in character to non-state enterprises" than to the larger, more strategic central SOEs.[64] Does this contradict the above argument that local SOEs and many LLCs have government created advantages? Not if they use these advantages to pursue commercial objectives rather than the strategic long-term goals of the central state. In short, as Buckley argues:

> The argument that in an authoritarian state 'politics trumps economics' does not however seem to be the case with an overall explanation of Chinese OFDI. Government does interfere, but this interference is differential — across ownership groups ... sectors, Provinces and types of firm.[65]

---

[61] Ravi Ramamurti and Jenny Hillemann (2018). "What is 'Chinese' about Chinese multinationals?" *Journal of International Business Studies*, 49(1): 34–48.

[62] Amighini, Rabellotti and Sanfilippo, "Do Chinese state-owned and private enterprises."

[63] Ming Hua Li, Lin Cui, Jiangyong Lu (October–November 2014). "Varieties of State Capitalism," *Journal of International Business Studies*, 45(8): 980–1004.

[64] Luo, Qi and Hubbard "Not looking for trouble," 156.

[65] Peter Buckley (2018). "Internalisation theory and outward direct investment by emerging market multinationals," *Management International Review*, 58(2): 211.

7. Conclusion

Oliveira *et al.*[66] make the simple argument that "to treat all Chinese OFDI as equal would be a mistake." What is perhaps most interesting about this statement is the need to make it at all. Why on Earth would all investment from any country let alone one as large and diverse as China be treated as a single entity in pursuit of a single goal? The fact that it is often treated this way says a lot about the way China is perceived and its ultimate objectives understood by at least some international observers. There remains a fundamental lack of trust in what China wants, and what it will do to the international order once it has the power to change it. It's fair to say that under Xi Jinping, the way that China is presenting itself to the world has not exactly undermined the idea of a centralized leadership — or even one man — in charge and in control, using whatever resources it can to bring it closer to the centrestage of world politics. COFDI is seen as one of the key power resources that it possesses. The early focus on investment in those sectors where China needed resources to continue to grow helped generate the idea of a strategic state project. Subsequently, the self-identification of Xi with projects like the Belt and Road leant credence to the idea of an attempt to use Chinese finance (though not just investment) to change political-economy geographies not just in China's own backyard, but pushing up into the backyard of others, too. The intention of upgrading the technological basis of the Chinese economy and to even gain leadership in some sectors has not gone unnoticed either, even though the specific term "Made in China 2025" has become somewhat harder to find as the Chinese leadership has responded to international criticisms of its goals. As a result, what would normally be the focus of business and management research — the investment decisions of firms — has become very firmly part and parcel of international relations and global order scholarship in the case of China.

However, the overwhelming consensus, though, of those who do look at Chinese investment decisions in detail is now that diversity is

[66]Oliveira *et al.*, "Outward foreign direct investment from emerging countries," 423.

the order of the day. In looking at what Chinese investors do, and trying to explain why, it is important (though very difficult at times) to try and distinguish between different actors and interests, and different levels of action and intention. Quite simply, not all activities undertaken by Chinese economic actors overseas are part of a clearly coordinated state strategy designed to achieve state objectives (as opposed, for example, to the state supporting companies as they try and attain their own commercial objectives). Sometimes SOEs are acting on behalf of the state, undertaking projects that Norris argues wouldn't be pursued by private economic actors just seeking market access and profits.[67] But sometimes they are not.

The state has considerable regulatory and distributive tools that it can and does utilize to try and channel overseas investment; and with some success. But just as the fact that the state could and did intervene to prevent unwelcomed investment projects in 2017 suggests an active and vigilant state, the fact that it had to intervene in this way shows that it is not all-powerful and all controlling on a day-to-day basis. The state creates opportunities and possibilities, but the easier it makes it for a range of actors to act relatively freely (be that at home or overseas), the less able it is to ensure that these actors respond in the ways that the state wants them to. As with the reform of the economy more general in the post-Mao era, there is a tension between the desire to benefit from unleashing initiative and economic freedoms on the one hand, and the desire to control the way that these new freedoms are used on the other hand.

Although, as we have noted, the overall Chinese stock of investment in other leading economies remains relatively small, the speed at which it has grown is one of the reasons that there has been a rethink about the consequences of China's rise in some places. This includes the emergence of much greater concern in a number of countries where there had previously been a stress on the opportunities that China's growth presented. Of course, it is not the only source of changed perceptions and changed thinking, but the growth of

[67] Norris, *Chinese Economic Statecraft.*

COFDI has certainly been a major factor in not just changing China's global economic profile, but how it is understood as well.

Where there is concern, it is predicated on a fundamental lack of trust in Chinese intentions, and the suspicion that investment is part of a broader economic strategy designed to give China an advantage in a competitive global order. This perception is often predicated on two other understandings. First, that over two decades of engagement with the capitalist global economy has not brought about the change in China that proponents of the liberal logic of engaging China had expected (or at least hoped for). Second, that gaining a competitive advantage is not just an end in itself, but a key tool that will be used to bring about further and more fundamental change in the global order.

This lack of trust had been increasing before the coronavirus began to spread to become a global crisis. But it's fair to say that in a number of Western states (and some non-Western ones as well), the pandemic led to a new light being shone on the wisdom (or not) of having strong economic linkages with China. While much of the focus was on the consequences of China occupying key roles in the supply chain of so many goods and commodities, these concerns spilt over into other areas of economic interactions, too. In the words of the UK Foreign Secretary while he was deputizing for the ill Prime Minister, there could be no return to "business as usual" with China after the crisis,[68] with discussing the implications of allowing Chinese ownership of key economic assets very much back on the agenda.

So, one of the impacts of the virus might be a reduction in opportunities for Chinese investors as investing screening increases. With a number of countries facing economic problems as part of the collateral economic damage of the pandemic and seeking to re-negotiate existing financial obligations with China, another scenario is that the appetite for investment along the Belt and Road might decline, too; both the appetite from others to seek Chinese investment, and the

[68] Recordings of Raab's comments are available from a number of sources, including, https://www.independent.co.uk/news/uk/politics/coronavirus-uk-china-dominic-raab-huawei-business-a9469351.html

appetite of investors to take on more projects that might not generate expected returns. Shifting investment priorities to domestic projects has also been touted as an important means of dealing with the domestic economic impact of the pandemic.[69]

That said, just as the global financial crisis resulted in a number of economic assets in crisis hit states becoming available at knock down prices, so too might the pandemic result in exciting investment opportunities for those who still have money. When it comes to the political economy of COFDI, the political always looms at least as large as the economic, and it is unlikely that the political will become any less significant anytime soon. The dilemma for a number of policy-makers could well be whether the potential perceived negative consequences of accepting Chinese investment are a price worth paying given the more immediate economic consequences of not taking it. In the first instance at least, the European Commission decided that it wasn't (a price worth paying), with regulations on state support for European companies eased to allow them to resist being purchased by non-European state-backed companies; with China very much identified as being a likely source of such activity.[70] Whether this commitment can outlast a prolonged global economic downturn remains to be seen.

Acknowledgments

Research for this chapter was supported by Leverhulme Major Research Fellowship Grant No. MRF-2016-103, "China Risen? What is Global Power (and in what ways does China have it)".

[69] *People's Daily* (2020). "*Kuoda neixu bixu wajue guonei shichang qianli* [Expansion of domestic demand must tap domestic market potential]," *People's Daily*, Commentary, 12 April, http://paper.people.com.cn/rmrb/html/2020-04/12/nw.D110000renmrb_20200412_4-01.htm.

[70] Javier Espinoza (2020). "Vestager urges stakebuilding to block Chinese takeovers," *Financial Times*, 12 April, https://www.ft.com/content/e14f24c7-e47a-4c22-8cf3-f629da62b0a7.

https://doi.org/10.1142/9789811226588_0009

Chapter 9

Role of the External Sector in Financial Reform: Renminbi Internationalization and the SDR Basket

Barry Eichengreen* and Guangtao Xia

*eichengr@berkeley.edu

1. Introduction

On 1 October, 2016, China's currency, the renminbi, was added to the basket making up Special Drawing Rights, the asset issued by the International Monetary Fund to supplement the international reserves of its member countries and which the governments of those members are required to accept in settlement of payments with one another. The event was hailed as historic, especially in China. It was said to symbolize the country's emergence as a force to be reckoned with in the global monetary and financial system. It was viewed as a step in modernizing the international system to better match 21st century realities, notably the emergence of China as an economic and financial power. It was seen as indicative of the progress that had been made in modernizing China's financial system and fostering use of its currency for cross-border transactions. It was indicative of China's growing influence on the global stage, concluding as it did a multi-year effort in which Chinese officials had campaigned for the addition of their national currency to a basket that previously was the exclusive preserve of a handful of advanced countries (the United States, United Kingdom, Japan, and the members of the euro area). As the People's Bank of China put it, "[The currency's] inclusion into the SDR is a milestone in the internationalization of the renminbi, and is an affirmation of the success of China's economic development and results of the reform and opening up of the financial sector."[1]

Others of more skeptical bent argued that the importance of the event was exaggerated. The SDR was of limited utility. It served mainly as an accounting unit for the financial transactions of the IMF itself. The unit was not widely used in commercial or official transactions, and there was no apparent demand by investors for the creation of SDR-denominated assets. Including the renminbi in the SDR basket did not automatically create a demand on the part of private investors to hold the currency.[2] Nor did adding the renminbi to the

[1]As quoted in Reuters, "China's Yuan Joins Elite Club of IMF Reserve Currencies," *Reuters*, 30 September 2016, https://www.reuters.com/article/us-china-currency-imf-idUSKCN1212WC.

[2]Some argued that adding the renminbi to the SDR basket would encourage other investors to hold the currency as a way of tracking its movement or hedging their exposure to it. See Sharon Chen (2015). "Asian central banks welcome yuan's IMF reserve-basket inclusion," *Bloomberg*, 30 November, https://www.bloomberg.com/news/articles/2015-12-01/asian-central-banks-welcome-yuan-s-imf-reserve-basket-inclusion. But there are few exposures to hedge insofar as there are little private tradings and few open positions in SDRs. As one currency trader (cited by Adinolfi) put it, "it's not like the SDR is the MSCI world index, where if a company is included, a bunch of portfolio managers need to go out and buy it." Or, as one of the rating agencies put it (quoted by Allen 2015), "Fitch does not expect this [addition of the renminbi to the SDR basket] to lead to a material shift in the demand for renminbi assets globally in the short term." See Joseph Adinolfi (2015). "What you need to know about China's inclusion in IMF currency basket," *MarketWatch*, 30 November, https://www.marketwatch.com/story/what-you-need-to-know-about-chinas-inclusion-in-imf-currency-basket-2015-11-30; Katie Allen (2015). "Chinese yuan likely to

IMF's reserve unit automatically give the Chinese government additional voice and votes in the Fund. By this view, the meaning of the renminbi's addition to the SDR basket was largely symbolic. In the words of one team of researchers, the renminbi's inclusion "is important symbolically as it elevates the Chinese currency to the premier global status. It is also an acknowledgement of China's monumental economic development over the past 35 years."[3]

In this chapter, we provide a different interpretation of the motives behind China's SDR campaign. Our argument is that the campaign to add the renminbi to the SDR basket was more than simply a vanity project; it was a strategy used by the champions of financial liberalization in China itself to force the pace of reform. Reaching agreement with the IMF on adding the renminbi to the basket required a judgment by the Fund that the currency was "freely usable" for cross-border transactions. Free usability, in IMF-speak, meant that the SDR claims of Fund members could be freely converted into the underlying currency, in this case the renminbi, and that the currency could then be freely used in cross-border payments.

Satisfying the free usability requirement presupposed some relaxation of China's regulatory controls on international capital flows, which limited the ability of importers, exporters and investors to use the currency in cross-border payments.[4] In turn, ensuring that the larger volume of cross-border capital flows pursuant on capital account liberalization was consistent with financial stability required additional domestic reforms to strengthen the financial sector.

---

be added to IMF special basket of currencies," *The Guardian*, 29 November, sec. Business, https://www.theguardian.com/business/2015/nov/29/chinese-yuan-imf-special-basket-of-currencies-us-dollar; Allen, "Yuan likely to be added."

[3]The quote is by "a BMI Research team," cited in Elena Holodny (2016). "China's yuan officially joins the SDR," *Business Insider*, 3 October, https://www.businessinsider.com/chinese-yuan-officially-joins-the-imfs-sdr-2016-10. See also the second half of the statement by the PBOC itself, heralding the IMF's decision, in the first paragraph of this paper.

[4]Relaxation is not necessarily synonymous with elimination; see the further discussion that follows.

Thus, there was a straight line from expansion of the SDR basket to pressure for Chinese financial liberalization and reform. The lure of qualifying for inclusion in the SDR basket was thus a source of "reverse pressure" for internal reform, in much the same way that joining the World Trade Organization in 2001 was a source of pressure to move to market-economy status.[5] To put it another way, the SDR was the impatient reformers' "Trojan horse."[6] Others call it "reform by stealth."[7]

But this was a strategy with risks. History is littered with examples of countries that used external financial liberalization to create pressure for domestic reform but ultimately came to grief. The domestic reforms needed to reconcile capital account liberalization with domestic financial stability do not follow automatically or in short order. External liberalization does not always cut the ground out from under vested interests resisting reform. When resistance is intense, the liberalization of cross-border financial flows can remain out in front of reforms of domestic financial governance and regulation for an extended period. Sooner or later, the result in this case will be large and volatile capital movements with destabilizing financial consequences.

This is what resulted in 2015 toward the end of a period when China pursued ongoing progressive liberalization of its external

---

[5]See Dongmin Liu (2015). "Internationalization of China's bond market, development of offshore RMB centres and provision of global safe assets," in Domenico Lombardi and Hongying Wang (eds.), *Enter the Dragon: China in the International Financial System* (Waterloo: CIGI Press), pp. 259–288 and Andrew Sheng (2015). "Five reasons for renminbi internationalisation," *South China Morning Post*, 27 March, https://www.scmp.com/comment/insight-opinion/article/1748428/five-reasons-renminbi-internationalisation.

[6]See Gabriel Wildau and Tom Mitchell (2016). "China: Renminbi stalls on road to being a global currency," *Financial Times*, 11 December, https://www.ft.com/content/e480fd92-bc6a-11e6-8b45-b8b81dd5d080.

[7]See Yukon Huang and Clare Lynch (2012). "Does internationalizing the renminbi make sense?" *Cato Journal*, 33: 571–585, and Alistair Thornton (2012). "Anaemic ascent: Why China's currency is far from going global," *Lowy Institute Analysis*, 14 August, https://www.lowyinstitute.org/publications/anaemic-ascent-why-china-currency-far-going-global.

accounts, seeking to qualify for the IMF's determination that the renminbi was freely usable. China experienced capital outflows, reserve losses, a weakening exchange rate and financial volatility. To restore stability, regulators were forced to reverse direction, tightening restrictions on international financial transactions. By this point, the decision to add the renminbi to the SDR basket was a done deal, whatever the current state of affairs.

In contrast, full renminbi internationalization was not yet accomplished. The currency still lagged far behind the dollar as a currency used in trade invoicing, as a currency of denomination for international bonds, and as a form of central bank reserves. And with Chinese policy makers' volte-face, take-up of the renminbi as a vehicle for cross-border transactions now slowed further and, on some dimensions, went into reverse. Even today, 5-plus years after the events of 2015, the renminbi still lags far behind the dollar in terms of the value of trade settlements and the share of international payments cleared through the Society for Worldwide Financial Telecommunication (SWIFT). Evidently, earlier forecasts that the renminbi would imminently rival and even surpass the dollar as an international currency were, at best, highly premature.[8]

Chinese officials did not abandon their efforts to strengthen and reform domestic financial markets. But they no longer relied on reverse pressure from renminbi internationalization to force the pace of reform. On the contrary, they displayed a renewed recognition that external liberalization should accompany domestic reform rather than preceding and seeking to force it. The showed greater awareness that prior and concurrent financial reform was a necessary prerequisite for successful currency internationalization.[9]

[8] Ansuya Harjani (2014). "Yuan to supersede dollar as top reserve currency: Survey," *CNBC*, 27 February, https://www.cnbc.com/2014/02/26/yuan-to-supersede-dollar-as-top-reserve-currency-survey.html reports a survey of 200 institutional investors — 100 headquartered in China and 100 outside — in which 53% thought that the renminbi would surpass the dollar as the world's leading reserve currency.

[9] See for example the reports in *Reuters*, (2017). "China to push yuan internationalization, free trade: Central bank official," *Reuters*, 27 April, https://www.reuters.com/article/us-china-economy-yuan-idUSKBN17T13Y.

In the remainder of this chapter, we elaborate these points in the following order. Section 2 first reviews the literature on renminbi internationalization, focusing on the different arguments made for promoting broader international use of the currency. It describes the connections between currency internationalization and domestic financial reform and how the former, by requiring capital account liberalization, created what was seen as useful pressure for the latter. Section 3 explains how the effort to see the renminbi added to the SDR basket further ratcheted up that pressure. Section 4 describes the progress made on currency internationalization, while Section 5 then explains how the process came to grief when the requisite reforms did not follow in short order. Section 6, in concluding, describes the lessons drawn.

2. Renminbi Internationalization

Renminbi internationalization is both a spontaneous and directed phenomenon. In the 1980s and 1990s, and especially after it joined the World Trade Organization in 2001, China emerged as a major trading country. Trade, together with tourism, provided multiple channels, some loosely regulated, through which foreigners could acquire renminbi and through which the currency could circulate outside the country. In an effort to track and regularize this phenomenon, Chinese officials allowed banks in Hong Kong, starting in 2004, to accept renminbi deposits and to exchange and remit renminbi balances in small amounts. In 2007, financial institutions were permitted to issue renminbi-denominated (dim sum) bonds in Hong Kong. In 2009, large enterprises in five Chinese cities were then authorized to settle their trade related transactions in renminbi with counterparties in Hong Kong, Macau, Taiwan, and the ASEAN countries. All this led to considerable growth of renminbi balances in Hong Kong and to a proliferation of renminbi-denominated financial products. At this point, the process of renminbi internationalization can be said to have been fully underway.

In the second stage, the Chinese authorities took a number of proactive steps to further encourage use of the renminbi in trade invoicing and settlements, cross-border financial transactions, and official as well as private use, not just in Hong Kong but also in other foreign financial centers and ultimately in China itself. They sought to foster the further growth of the market that had spontaneously developed offshore in Hong Kong and, its viability having been established, to bring it onshore.[10] The pilot trade settlement scheme was extended to additional cities and provinces and then to essentially all Chinese companies, regions and foreign counterparties. The People's Bank of China designated one of the Big 4 Chinese banks as official renminbi clearing bank for a succession of foreign financial centers, easing the process of clearing and settling renminbi-based financial transactions (see Table 1). It extended renminbi swap lines to central banks on every continent, encouraging those foreign central banks and regulators to allow financial institutions under their jurisdiction to engage in renminbi-denominated transactions and take positions in assets denominated in the currency[11] (see Table 2).

To bring this business back on shore, designated offshore banks (mainly in Hong Kong) were then authorized, starting in 2010, to invest their renminbi balances in the Chinese interbank bond market. First Xinjiang and then other provinces were opened to foreign direct investment of renminbi funds. In 2014, foreign and domestic equity markets were linked by the Shanghai–Hong Kong Stock Connect, through which investors on the Shanghai and Hong Kong Stock Exchanges could trade shares on the other market using their local brokers and clearinghouses. This was then followed by the Shenzhen–Hong Kong Stock Connect and by a China–Hong Kong Bond Connect allowing investors on both sides to trade bonds on one another's interbank markets. A range of reforms were implemented in the years leading up to 2015 to relax restrictions on financial inflows

---

[10]A discussion of these steps is Barry Eichengreen and Masahiro Kawai (2015). "Editors' Introduction," *Renminbi Internationalization: Achievements, Prospects and Challenges* (Washington, DC: Brookings Institution).

[11]The concern was that the local central bank had to have renminbi on hand in order to provide it to a local institution with an uncovered renminbi position when, inter alia, the exchange rate moved against it.

Table 1: Offshore RMB clearing banks (updated to December 2019).

Location	Responsible bank	Date of establishment
Hong Kong, China	Bank of China	September 2003
Macau, China	Bank of China	September 2004
Vientiane, Laos	Industrial and Commercial Bank of China	June 2012
Taiwan, China	Bank of China	November 2012
Singapore	Industrial and Commercial Bank of China	February 2013
Phnom Penh, Cambodia	Industrial and Commercial Bank of China	March 2014
London, UK	China Construction Bank	June 2014
Frankfurt, Germany	Bank of China	June 2014
Seoul, South Korea	Bank of Communications	July 2014
Paris, France	Bank of China	September 2014
Luxembourg	Industrial and Commercial Bank of China	September 2014
Doha, Qatar	Industrial and Commercial Bank of China	November 2014
Sydney, Australia	Bank of China	November 2014
Toronto, Canada	Industrial and Commercial Bank of China	November 2014
Kuala Lumpur, Malaysia	Bank of China	January 2015
Bangkok, Thailand	Industrial and Commercial Bank of China	January 2015
Santiago, Chile	China Construction Bank	May 2015
Budapest, Hungary	Bank of China	June 2015
Johannesburg, South Africa	Bank of China	July 2015
Buenos Aires, Argentina	Industrial and Commercial Bank of China	September 2015
Lusaka, Zambia	Bank of China	September 2015
Zurich, Switzerland	China Construction Bank	November 2015
Moscow, Russia	Industrial and Commercial Bank of China	September 2016
New York, US	Bank of China	September 2016

Table 1: (*Continued*)

Location	Responsible bank	Date of establishment
New York, US	J.P. Morgan Chase Bank, N.A.	February 2018
Tokyo, Japan	Bank of China	October 2018
Tokyo, Japan	MUFG Bank	June 2019
Manila, Philippines	Bank of China	September 2019

Source: PBoC.

Table 2: Central bank swap lines with PBoC (updated to December 2019).

Bank	Date	Amount	Duration
Bank of Korea	2009.4.20	180 (billion CNY)/38 (trillion KRW)	3 years
	2011.10.26	360 (billion CNY)/64 (trillion KRW)	
	2014.10.11	360 (billion CNY)/64 (trillion KRW)	
	2017.10.11	360 (billion CNY)/64 (trillion KRW)	
Hong Kong Monetary Authority	2009.1.20	200 (billion CNY)/227 (billion HKD)	3 years
	2011.11.22	400 (billion CNY)/490 (billion HKD)	
	2014.11.22	400 (billion CNY)/505 (billion HKD)	
	2017.11.22	400 (billion CNY)/470 (billion HKD)	
Bank Negara Malaysia	2009.2.8	80 (billion CNY)/40 (billion MYR)	3 years
	2012.2.8	180 (billion CNY)/90 (billion MYR)	
	2015.4.17	180 (billion CNY)/90 (billion MYR)	
	2018.8.20	180 (billion CNY)/110 (billion MYR)	
National Bank of the Republic of Belarus	2009.3.11	20 (billion CNY)/8 (trillion BYR)	3 years
	2015.5.10	7 (billion CNY)/16 (trillion BYR)	
	2018.5.10	7 (billion CNY)/2.2 (trillion BYR)	
Bank Indonesia	2009.3.23	100 (billion CNY)/175 (trillion IDR)	3 years
	2013.10.1	100 (billion CNY)/175 (trillion IDR)	
	2018.11.16	200 (billion CNY)/440 (trillion IDR)	
Central Bank of Argentina	2009.4.2	70 (billion CNY)/38 (billion ARS)	3 years
	2014.7.18	70 (billion CNY)/90 (billion ARS)	
	2017.7.18	70 (billion CNY)/175 (billion ARS)	

(*Continued*)

Table 2: (*Continued*)

Bank	Date	Amount	Duration
Central Bank of Iceland	2010.6.9	3.5 (billion CNY)/66 (billion ISK)	3 years
	2013.9.11	3.5 (billion CNY)/66 (billion ISK)	
	2016.12.21	3.5 (billion CNY)/66 (billion ISK)	
Monetary Authority of Singapore	2010.7.23	150 (billion CNY)/30 (billion SGD)	3 years
	2013.3.7	300 (billion CNY)/60 (billion SGD)	
	2016.3.7	300 (billion CNY)/64 (billion SGD)	
	2019.5.13	300 (billion CNY)/61 (billion SGD)	
Reserve Bank of New Zealand	2011.4.18	25 (billion CNY)/5 (billion NZD)	3 years
	2014.4.25	25 (billion CNY)/5 (billion NZD)	
	2017.5.19	25 (billion CNY)/5 (billion NZD)	
Central Bank of the Republic of Uzbekistan	2011.4.19	0.7 (billion CNY)/167 (billion UZS)	3 years
Bank of Mongolia	2011.5.6	5 (billion CNY)/1 (trillion MNT)	3 years
	2012.3.20	10 (billion CNY)/2 (trillion MNT)	
	2014.8.21	15 (billion CNY)/4.5 (trillion MNT)	
	2017.7.6	15 (billion CNY)/5.4 (trillion MNT)	
National Bank of Kazakhstan	2011.6.13	7 (billion CNY)/150 (billion KZT)	3 years
	2014.12.14	7 (billion CNY)/200 (billion KZT)	
	2018.5.28	7 (billion CNY)/350 (billion KZT)	
Bank of Thailand	2011.12.22	70 (billion CNY)/320 (billion THB)	3 years
	2014.12.22	70 (billion CNY)/370 (billion THB)	
	2017.12.22	70 (billion CNY)/370 (billion THB)	
State Bank of Pakistan	2011.12.23	10 (billion CNY)/140 (billion PKR)	3 years
	2014.12.23	10 (billion CNY)/165 (billion PKR)	
	2018.5.23	20 (billion CNY)/351 (billion PKR)	
Central Bank of the United Arab Emirates	2012.1.17	35 (billion CNY)/20 (billion AED)	3 years
	2015.12.14	35 (billion CNY)/20 (billion AED)	
Central Bank of the Republic of Turkey	2012.2.21	10 (billion CNY)/3 (billion TRY)	3 years
	2015.9.26	12 (billion CNY)/5 (billion TRY)	

Table 2: (*Continued*)

Bank	Date	Amount	Duration
Reserve Bank of Australia	2012.3.22	200 (billion CNY)/30 (billion AUD)	3 years
	2015.3.30	200 (billion CNY)/40 (billion AUD)	
	2018.3.30	200 (billion CNY)/40 (billion AUD)	
National Bank of Ukraine	2012.6.26	15 (billion CNY)/19 (billion UAH)	3 years
	2015.5.15	15 (billion CNY)/54 (billion UAH)	
	2019.12.10	15 (billion CNY)/62 (billion UAH)	
Banco Central do Brasil	2013.3.26	190 (billion CNY)/60 (billion BRL)	3 years
Bank of England	2013.6.22	200 (billion CNY)/20 (billion GBP)	3 years
	2015.10.20	350 (billion CNY)/35 (billion GBP)	
	2018.10.13	350 (billion CNY)/40 (billion GBP)	
National Bank of Hungary	2013.9.9	10 (billion CNY)/375 (billion HUF)	3 years
	2016.9.12	10 (billion CNY)/416 (billion HUF)	
Bank of Albania	2013.9.12	2 (billion CNY)/35.8 (billion ALL)	3 years
	2018.4.3	2 (billion CNY)/34.1 (billion ALL)	
European Central Bank	2013.10.8	350 (billion CNY)/45 (billion EUR)	3 years
	2016.9.27	350 (billion CNY)/45 (billion EUR)	
	2019.10.25	350 (billion CNY)/45 (billion EUR)	
Swiss National Bank	2014.7.21	150 (billion CNY)/21 (billion CHF)	3 years
	2017.7.21	150 (billion CNY)/21 (billion CHF)	
Central Bank of Sri Lanka	2014.9.16	10 (billion CNY)/225 (billion LKR)	3 years
Central Bank of Russian Federation	2014.10.13	150 (billion CNY)/815 (billion RUB)	3 years
	2017.11.22	150 (billion CNY)/1325 (billion RUB)	
Qatar Central Bank	2014.11.3	35 (billion CNY)/20.8 (billion QAR)	3 years
	2017.11.2	35 (billion CNY)/20.8 (billion QAR)	
Bank of Canada	2014.11.8	200 (billion CNY)/30 (billion CAD)	3 years
	2017.11.8	200 (billion CNY)/30 (billion CAD)	
Centrale Bank van Suriname	2015.3.18	1 (billion CNY)/0.52 (billion SRD)	3 years
	2019.2.11	1 (billion CNY)/1.1 (billion SRD)	

(*Continued*)

Table 2: (*Continued*)

Bank	Date	Amount	Duration
Central Bank of Armenia	2015.3.25	1 (billion CNY)/77 (billion AMD)	3 years
South African Reserve Bank	2015.4.10	30 (billion CNY)/54 (billion ZAR)	3 years
	2018.4.11	30 (billion CNY)/54 (billion ZAR)	
Banco Central de Chile	2015.5.25	22 (billion CNY)/2.2 (trillion CLP)	3 years
	2018.5.25	22 (billion CNY)/2.2 (trillion CLP)	
National Bank of Tajikistan	2015.9.3	3 (billion CNY)/3 (billion TJS)	3 years
Bank Al-Maghrib	2016.5.11	10 (billion CNY)/15 (billion MAD)	3 years
National Bank of Serbia	2016.6.17	1.5 (billion CNY)/27 (billion RSD)	3 years
Central Bank of Egypt	2016.12.6	18 (billion CNY)/47 (billion EGP)	3 years
Central Bank of Nigeria	2018.4.27	15 (billion CNY)/720 (billion NGN)	3 years
Bank of Japan	2018.10.26	200 (billion CNY)/3400 (billion JPY)	3 years
Monetary Authority of Macao	2019.12.05	30 (billion CNY)/35 (billion MOP)	3 years
Total		**3698.7 (billion CNY)**	

Source: PBoC.

and outflows between China and the rest of the world, all with the stated goal of encouraging international use of the renminbi.

The motivations for this Chinese policy of renminbi internationalization were several and varied.[12] First, there was the convenience

[12]What follows synthesizes our own previous work on this subject (e.g., Eichengreen and Kawai, "Introduction") and that of other scholars such as Lawrence Lau (2012). "The internationalization of the renminbi," *Executive Leadership Programme*, August, Institute of Global Economics and Finance: Chinese University of Hong Kong; Yiping Huang, Daili Wang and Gang Fan (2015). "Paths to a reserve currency:

value for Chinese banks and firms of wider international use of their currency and the expectation that widening that use further would enhance their international competitiveness.[13]

Second, there was the hope that fostering wider international use of the renminbi would reduce the dependence of Chinese importers and exporters of merchandise and financial services on the dollar, the currency of a country that is China's sometime friend and whose stability is periodically cast into doubt.[14] This might have additional advantages in terms of financial stability, insofar as commodities and energy, which China imports, would no longer be priced solely in dollars, whereas a substantial share of the revenues of Chinese enterprises accrue in renminbi. In a world where commodities such as oil were also priced in renminbi, currency mismatches for those enterprises might be less, in other words.[15]

Third, there was the argument that a more symmetrical, multipolar international monetary and financial system organized around the currencies of all of the leading commercial and financial powers, and

---

Renminbi internationalization and its implications," *Renminbi Internationalization: Achievements, Prospects and Challenges* (Washington, DC: The Brookings Institution), pp. 311–348; and Yongding Yu (2015). "How far can renminbi internationalization go?" in Barry Eichengreen and Masahiro Kawai (eds.), *Renminbi Internationalization: Achievements, Prospects and Challenges* (Washington, DC: The Brookings Institution), pp. 53–85.

[13]See Huang and Lynch, "Does internationalizing make sense?" and Thornton, T. (2012). *Anaemic ascent: Why China's currency is far from going global.*

[14]See Alex He (2016). "The political logic of RMB internationalization: A unique journal to a major global currency," in Domenico Lombardi and Hongying Wang (eds.), *Enter the Dragon: China in the International Financial System* (Waterloo, Canada: Center for International Governance Innovation), pp. 41–84. This hope extended to the balance sheet of the PBOC itself, insofar as leading international currencies tend to float freely, obviating the need for the central banks that issue them to hold significant foreign reserves (in China's case, in dollars).

[15]Thus, China announced plans to address this mismatch in early 2018, allowing a renminbi-denominated oil futures contract to be traded on the Shanghai Futures Exchange. See Keith Johnson (2018). "China's bid to upend the global oil market," *Foreign Policy* (blog), 18 January, https://foreignpolicy.com/2018/01/18/chinas-bid-upend-global-oil-market-petroyuan-shanghai/.

not just the US dollar, might be more symmetrical, operate more smoothly, and not be subject to the global imbalances of the "revived Bretton Wood System."[16]

Fourth, there were arguments of prestige, that a first-class power should have a first-class international currency, just like a first-class country has a national airline and an aircraft carrier.

The fifth and, in our view, key rationale for renminbi internationalization is that facilitating international use of the currency was part and parcel with the process of domestic financial reform. Temporally, efforts to reform Chinese banking and finance intensified around the exact same time, the middle of the first decade of the 21st century, at which point the process of renminbi internationalization got underway. Both aspects involved removing restrictions and official diktat as drivers of financial outcomes, and replacing them with commercial motives and rules-based supervision and regulation. Domestically, state banks were commercialized. Trust companies and other shadow banks were permitted to expand their financial operations; capital markets were allowed to develop (more enterprises were allowed to list and additional entities were allowed to trade on the Shanghai Stock Exchange; and corporate bond markets were fostered). Internationally, restrictions on inward and outward capital movements were relaxed or removed, as described above. Both dimensions can be understood as part of an effort to move China from a centrally planned and controlled financial system to more decentralized, market-based financial arrangements.

Moreover, renminbi internationalization would heighten the urgency of domestic financial reforms and, for that reason, it could be argued, speed their implementation. Relaxing restrictions on capital-account transactions was apt to increase financial inflows and outflows. Internal controls, management practices, and supervision and regulation would have to be strengthened in order for Chinese banks to withstand the larger volume of flows. Chinese banks, facing increased competition from abroad, would have to compete for

---

[16]See Xiaochuan Zhou (2009). "Reform of the international monetary system," *Essay*, 23 March, www.bis.org/review/r090402c.pdf.

funding and make investment decisions on a commercial basis, limiting scope for the operation of the traditional system of administered credit. Statutory ceilings on lending and deposit rates would have to be removed to bring domestic interest rates into line with foreign rates on what were now more deeply integrated domestic and foreign markets. Regulation of stock and bond markets would have to be strengthened to meet international standards for transparency and market integrity, given that institutions now had the option of investing in securities at home or abroad. On the macroeconomic front, it would be necessary to move from earlier arrangements in which the renminbi was pegged to the dollar to a more flexible exchange rate regime in which currency movements were allowed to buffer the domestic economy from capital-flow surges, and in which capital-flow reversals did not threaten to exhaust the authorities' foreign reserves and destabilize the currency.

If these things were not done, the implication followed, banks would fail. Enterprises would default on their debts. Stock markets would fluctuate wildly. The authorities' exchange rate commitments would be cast into doubt. In all these ways, then, the relaxation of capital-account restrictions that was integral to the campaign for renminbi internationalization would ratchet up the pressure for domestic financial reform.

3. The Role of the SDR

It is at this point that renminbi internationalization connects up with the currency's addition to the SDR basket. To qualify for inclusion in the basket, the renminbi had to be deemed freely usable. A freely usable currency is defined in the IMF's Articles of Agreement as one that is widely used to make payments for international transactions and widely traded on the principal foreign exchange markets. In 1977, IMF staff proposed that assessment of whether a currency is freely usable for international transactions should be based on the extent to which trade in goods and services is paid for in that currency and on the volume of capital transactions denominated in that currency. It proposed further that the assessment of whether a currency is widely traded should be based on the volume of transactions, the existence of forward markets, and buy–sell spreads in the foreign exchange market.[17]

The implication was that in order for the renminbi to be added to the SDR basket, China needed not just to relax its capital controls in order to encourage use of that currency in invoicing and settling trade in goods and services and also in international financial transactions. It also needed to accelerate the domestic financial reforms that were essential concomitants of capital account liberalization.[18] Logically, this meant that qualifying the country's currency for inclusion in the SDR basket was a priority goal by those seeking to force the pace of financial reform by proceeding immediately with financial opening.

To be sure, adding the renminbi to the SDR basket was not sold to stakeholders as a tactic for forcing the pace of reform, since vested interests opposed liberalization measures, or at least their imminent implementation. Chinese banks worried that deposit-rate decontrol and foreign competition would shrink their profit margins.[19] State-owned enterprises and regional governments worried about loss of concessionary access to finance.[20] Exporters were not all enamored of

---

[17]Those criteria were then clarified and adopted by the IMF Executive Board in a decision in 2000.

[18]Note our use of the word "relax" rather than alternatives like "dismantle" or "eliminate." As footnote 4 reminds the reader, capital-account convertibility (the absence of all capital controls) has not always been a prerequisite historically for a determination of free usability.

[19]Evidence on the impact of foreign bank competition is mixed; see Yajing Dong (2013). "The impact of foreign bank entry on the performance of domestic banks: A case study based on Chinese commercial banks," Unpublished, Tilburg University and Dong Luo, Yizhe Dong, Seth Armitage and Wenxuan Hou (2015). "The impact of foreign bank penetration on the domestic banking sector: New evidence from China," *European Journal of Finance*, 21: 1–29: On the Effects of deposit-rate decontrol see Alicia Garcia-Herrero, Sergio Gavila and Daniel Santabarbara (2009). "What explains the low profitability of Chinese banks?" Bank of Spain Working Paper no. 0910 and Gabriel Wildau (2015). "Interest rate deregulation dents China bank profits," *Financial Times*, 31 October, https://www.ft.com/content/973c3294-7ed2-11e5-93c6-bba4b4b36134.

[20]See the discussion in David Steinberg (2015). "The domestic political sources of China's international financial policies," in Domenico Lombardi and Hongying Wang

the more variable exchange rate likely to accompany external financial liberalization.

Rather, it was asserted that adding the renminbi to the SDR would enhance China's stature as a global player. It would give the country a seat at the top table. It would encourage wider use of the renminbi in settlement of cross-border transactions. It would reduce the dominance of the dollar in the operation of the international monetary and financial system, and in so doing limit China's own dependence on the greenback. These arguments resonated in circles where it had long been argued that a less dollar-centric international monetary and financial system was in China's interest, among those in China who had argued for a more prominent role for the SDR, and among commentators who asserted that China should speak with a louder voice in matters of global economic and financial governance. These were arguments designed to appeal even to domestic stakeholders skeptical of the merits of rapid financial liberalization, in other words. In effect, they were designed to advance financial liberalization through the back door.

Zhou Xiaochuan, long-time governor of the People's Bank of China, was prominent in these debates. Zhou repeatedly emphasized the importance of strengthening the supervision and regulation of Chinese financial markets and institutions through the adoption of international standards. In 2009, as noted above, he authored an essay highlighting the desirability of steps to enhance the role of the SDR in the global monetary and financial system.[21] That essay did not explicitly refer to adding the renminbi to the SDR basket, although it can be seen as hinting in that direction. More generally, there were few mentions of the SDR and SDR-basket composition on the central government's website prior to 2015, as Figure 1 shows. Nor did Zhou's essay draw a link between a more prominent role for the SDR and domestic financial reforms. But in a subsequent speech posted to

(eds.), *Enter the Dragon: China in the International Financial System* (Waterloo: CIGI Press), pp. 223–257.

[21] Xiaochuan Zhou (2017). "The baseline: No systematic financial risk," 4 November. http://www.pbc.gov.cn/goutongjiaoliu/113456/113469/3410388/index.html.

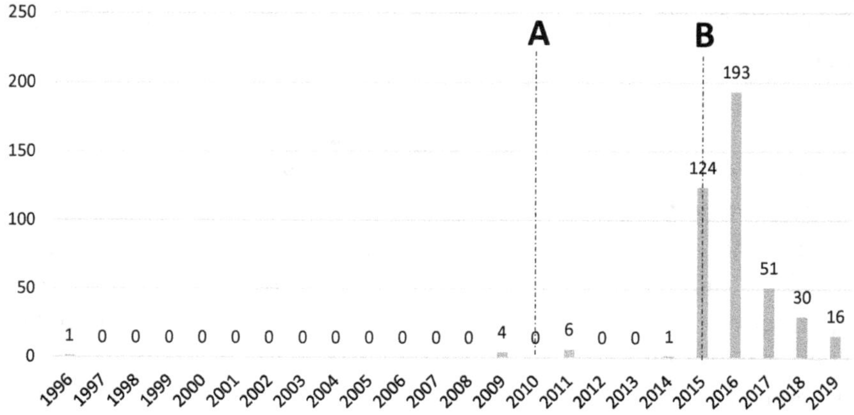

Figure 1: Number of mentions of SDR on Chinese central government website (per year, 1996–2019).

Notes:

A: 2010 Review for SDR's basket composition, which aroused official discussion in China.

B: 2015 Review for SDR's basket composition.

Sources: Central Government of the People's Republic of China website (www.gov.cn) and authors' calculations.

the PBOC website, these links appear explicitly.[22] To limit systemic financial risks, Zhou begins, it is essential to "accelerate financial sector's reform and opening up" (authors' translation). Zhou then continues "[I]nternationalization of the RMB and the two-way opening up of the financial sector have promoted the continuous improvement of the financial system."[23]

At about the same time as this speech — specifically, on the occasion of the first anniversary of the renminbi's addition to the SDR basket — the PBOC issued a Chinese-language monograph, whose title can be translated as *The Journey Towards the SDR's Inclusion of*

[22] Xiaochuan Zhou, "The baseline."

[23] Inclusion of the renminbi in the SDR basket, he observes in addition, served to strengthen China's role in international financial governance.

the Renminbi.[24] This was essentially an elaboration of Governor Zhou's previously-stated views. As the central point is put there, the addition of the renminbi to the SDR basket "can be considered as a milestone, which is not only the result of reform and openness in the past 39 years, but also an important driving force for China's further reform and opening up."

In a concurrent interview (in *Caijing* 2017 — in English, *Finance and Economics Magazine*), intended for foreign as well as domestic consumption, Zhou referred in addition to "the ratcheting effect" of SDR inclusion on domestic economic reform: "the RMB's addition to the SDR will promote China's further opening up and make it irreversible.... The renminbi is increasingly used by international organizations and in financial markets following its addition to the SDR; laws and regulations have also been revised; traders and investors are following the new rules. So it's very difficult and expensive for China to step back."[25] Not only did the goal of qualifying for the SDR intensify the pressure for domestic financial reform, in other words, but it made the latter process irreversible.

This discussion of the SDR and domestic financial reform in *Caijing* also acknowledged the existence of an alternative view, according to which the relaxation of capital account restrictions as necessary for the renminbi to be deemed freely usable should wait on prior domestic reforms. But Zhou, *Caijing's* reporters recounted, did not agree with this argument. Rather, as his views were characterized there, "he thinks that the inclusion of the RMB in the SDR means that the RMB exchange rate mechanism needs to be reformed, foreign exchange control should be gradually reduced, and the free use of RMB should be continuously improved. *And it is not the case that you have to wait until all the conditions are met before you can implement all the above reforms*" (emphasis added). Zhou concluded that

---

[24]People's Bank of China (2017). *The Journey Towards the SDR's Inclusion of the Renminbi* (Beijing: PBOC, International Division) (in Mandarin).

[25]"Zhou Xiaochuan on RMB and the SDR basket and the historic progress of the process of opening up," *Caijing*, 9 October 2017, http://yuanchuang.caijing.com.cn/2017/1009/4341116.shtml.

there was "no ideal sequence for reform, but instead opportunities should be taken as they come." The possibility of adding the renminbi to the SDR basket can be understood as one of those opportunities.

4. Progress

The first 5 years of the renminbi internationalization push, dating from Zhou's 2009 speech, saw a sharp increase in international use of China's currency. From 1% of the China's total foreign trade in the second quarter of 2010, renminbi trade settlement ballooned almost 17-fold by the mid-2013, reaching 16.5% of China's total trade[26] (see Figure 2). That explosive growth slowed subsequently, to 41% in 2014 and 10% in 2015.

Banks in Hong Kong, China had been allowed to open renminbi accounts as early as 2004, but it was only in mid-2010, when the

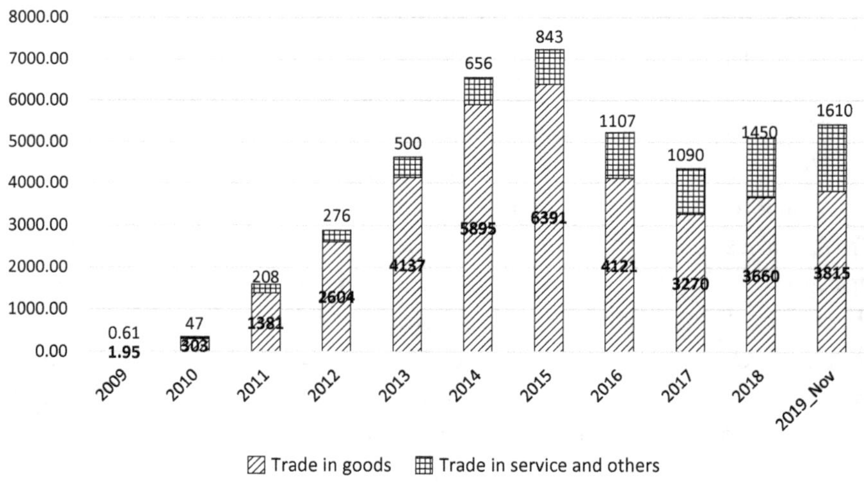

Figure 2: Renminbi trade settlement (2010–2019, billion yuan).

Note: Due to data non-availability, 2019 data only covers the first 11 months.

Source: PBoC.

[26]Admittedly, 80% of these trade settlements were with Hong Kong, however, raising some questions about the generality of use of the RMB in trade settlement with China.

renminbi settlement scheme was introduced, that renminbi deposits in Hong Kong took off. Since then, renminbi has been allowed to flow between Hong Kong and the rest of China for purposes related to trade settlement, as noted above. From some US$9.2 billion at the end of 2009 (representing 1% of total deposits in Hong Kong), renminbi deposits surged to US$47.3 billion by the end of 2010 (5.4% of total deposits), US$93 billion (9.5%) by the end of 2011, and US$96 billion (about 9%) by the end of 2012. The rate of increase slowed in 2012, but this reflected less any diminished attractiveness of the currency than investors in Hong Kong shifting away from renminbi deposits into other renminbi-denominated financial assets (Figure 3). Consistent with this interpretation, the value of renminbi deposits in Hong Kong resumed its rise subsequently, reaching US$124.6 billion, or about 11% of total deposits, at the end of October 2013.

Although the authorities continued to regulate inward and outward foreign direct investment, the controls in question were progressively relaxed. The approval process for the use of renminbi funds for outward FDI by Chinese enterprises and procedures for use of the

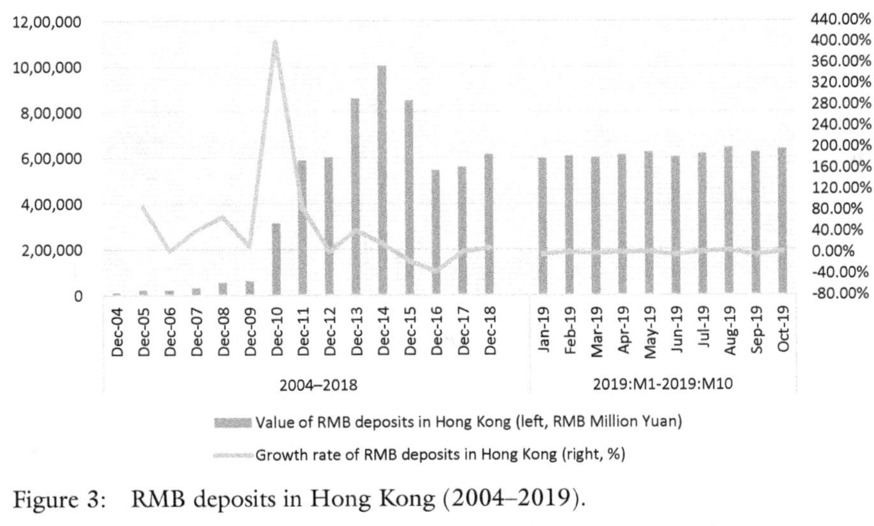

Figure 3: RMB deposits in Hong Kong (2004–2019).

Note: The data is accumulated value by the end of each given period.

Source: Hong Kong Monetary Authority.

renminbi for inward FDI were streamlined with the announcement of the Renminbi Outward Direct Investment scheme in January 2011 and creation of a Renminbi FDI scheme the following October. In 2012–2014, renminbi-denominated and settled FDI accounted for about a third of China's total FDI flows. The result was a noticeable increase in use of the renminbi for inward and outward FDI-related purposes. As Figure 4 shows, in the first part of the period, the most rapid growth of renminbi-denominated transactions was on the inbound investment side, whereas in the period's second half, the most rapid growth was on the outbound investment side.

Issuance of renminbi-denominated bonds outside China (on what is known as "the dim sum market") meanwhile rose from US$0.9 billion in 2010 to US$4.6 billion in 2011 and US$7.1 billion in 2012. Between the first quarter of 2010 and first quarter of 2015, the global share of international debt securities denominated in renminbi rose by a factor of six. Renminbi bonds were issued by financial institutions but also by other enterprises, and these placements were made by firms on the mainland, in Hong Kong and in the rest of the world alike. Figure 5 shows how the growth of the dim sum market

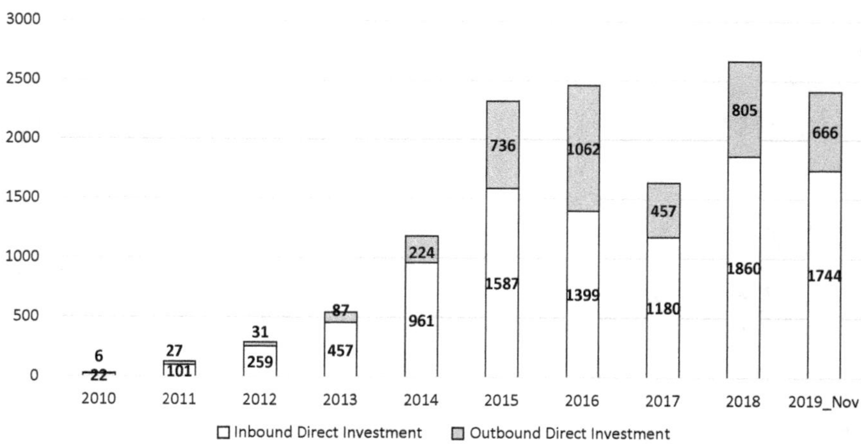

Figure 4: Renminbi-settled foreign direct investment (2010–2019, billion yuan).
Note: Due to data non-availability, 2019 data only covers the first 11 months.
Source: PBoC.

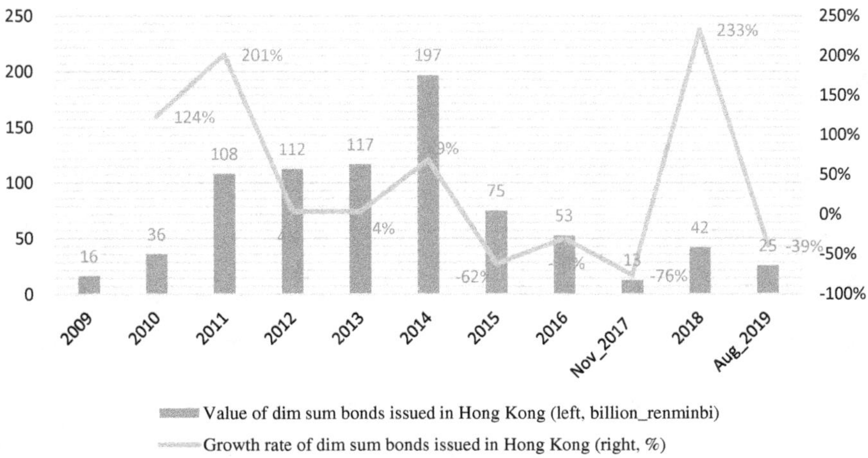

Figure 5: Dim sum bonds issued in Hong Kong (2009–2019).

Note: Due to data non-availability, 2017 data only covers the first 11 months, while that of 2019 only covers the first 8 months.

Source: Hong Kong Monetary Authority.

has been decelerating over time, as other avenues for renminbi-denominated bond issuance have opened up.

The result was a very considerable expansion in the use of the renminbi in cross-border settlements. Figure 6 shows the growth since 2011 of bank-based renminbi payments as recorded by SWIFT, which can be taken as a summary measure of the use of the currency in cross-border transactions.

All this was cited as evidence of progress, although there was room for disagreement over exactly how much. The renminbi still accounted for just 2.17% of global payments at the end of 2014. Although more than 50 central banks had reportedly added the currency to their reserve portfolios by the end of that year, the renminbi's share of global reserves was still thought to be only on the order of 1%.[27]

[27]See Saikat Chatterjee (2017). "China currency claims a bigger share of reserve manager portfolios." *Reuters*, 29 October, https://www.reuters.com/article/us-china-summit-reserves-reuters-summit/china-currency-claims-a-bigger-share-of-reserve-manager-portfolios. The IMF did not at this time distinguish renminbi reserves in its COFER database.

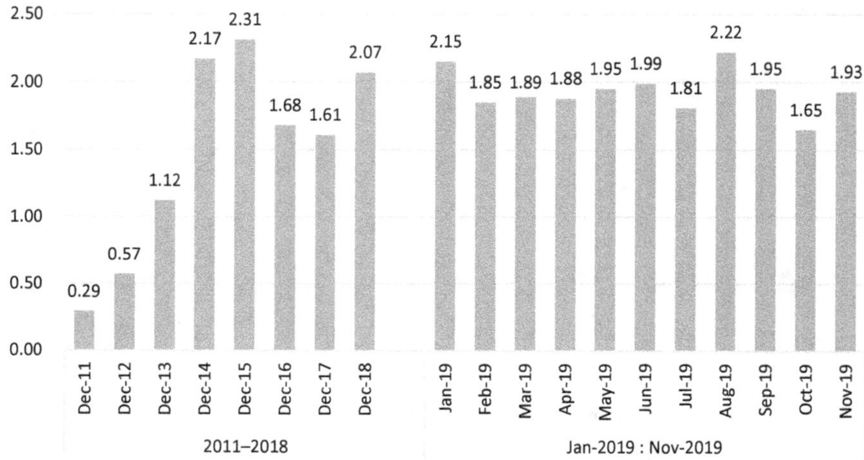

Figure 6: RMB's share as payment currency (%).

Note: Customer initiated and institutional payments. Based on value.

Source: SWIFT, updated to November 2019.

The issuance of renminbi-denominated bonds even at its peak in 2014 was still small by the standards of China's overall cross-border investment transactions. The renminbi's international use may have risen like a rocket, but the starting point some 5 years earlier had been extremely low. Still, if assessments differed, the consensus was that the rate of change was indicative of significant progress.

5. Backlash

That progress was then interrupted by instability in Chinese financial markets. The Shanghai stock exchange went on a roller coaster, rising by 150% in the year ending in June 2015 and then quickly giving back its gains. Market volatility rose relative to earlier years, with share valuations falling by as much as 10% in a day (see Figure 7). This volatility continued into early 2016. The country experienced persistent capital outflows, and the PBOC was forced to intervene to support the exchange rate, expending a cumulative $1 trillion of reserves in 2015–2016, fully a quarter of the reserves with which it entered the period (see Figure 8).

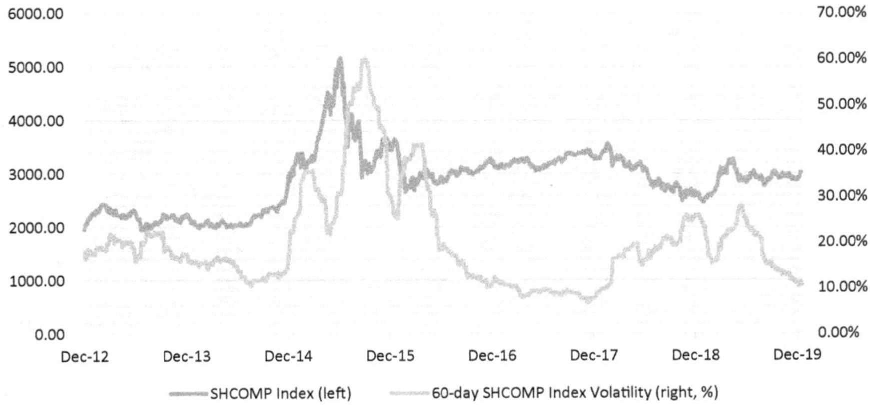

Figure 7: China's stock prices and volatility (2012/12/01–2019/12/19).
Source: Bloomberg.

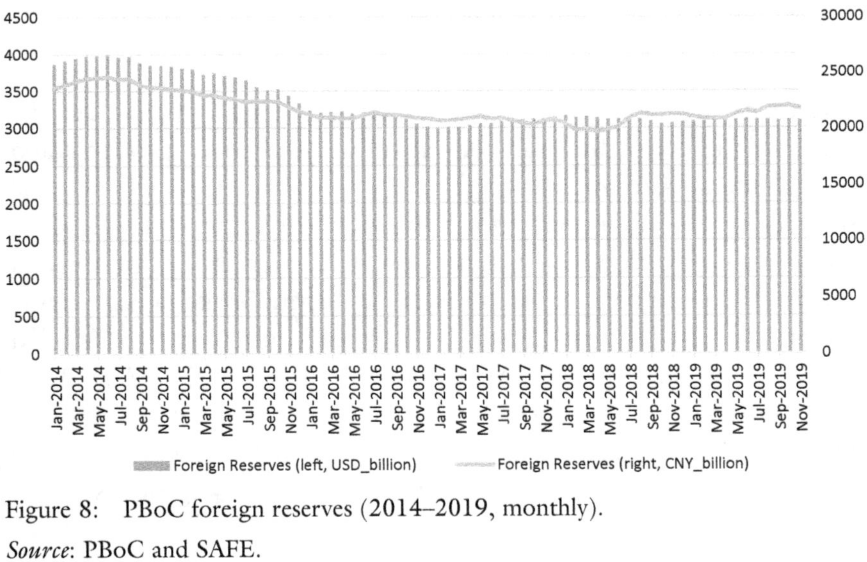

Figure 8: PBoC foreign reserves (2014–2019, monthly).
Source: PBoC and SAFE.

Was this turbulence connected to the external financial liberalization undertaken in preceding years? The gyrations of the stock market had multiple causes, to be sure, not all of which were related to external financial liberalization. The authorities had pumped large amounts of liquidity into the financial system in an effort to keep GDP growth

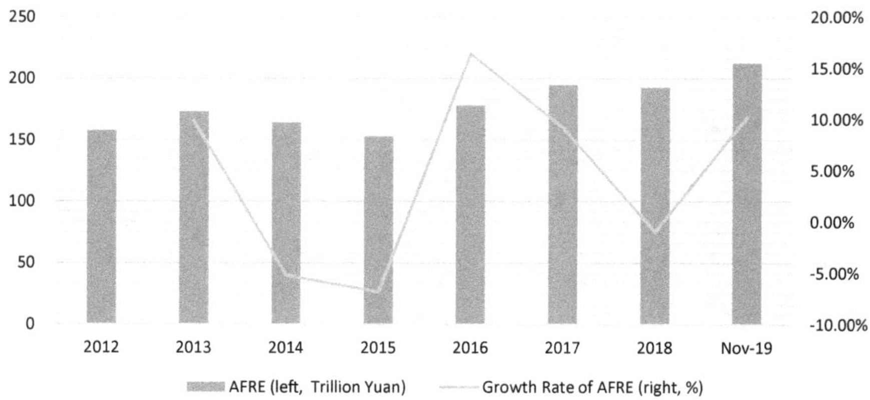

Figure 9: Total social financing (AFRE).

Note: AFRE means aggregate financing to the real economy. Due to data non-availability, 2019 data only covers the first 11 months.

Source: PBoC.

close to its official 7% target (see Figure 9). This liquidity had the predictable effect of fueling speculative investments in property and financial markets. Efforts to then clamp down on excesses in the real estate sector caused property prices in second-tier cities to fall, leading investors to plow their savings into the stock market. Politicians and regulators encouraged retail investors to open brokerage accounts and participate in the market using borrowed money in pursuit of Xi Jinping's "Chinese dream." When worries then developed in 2015 that Chinese economic growth was slowing, the market went into reverse. As prices began to fall, investors who had purchased shares on margin were forced to liquidate their positions, causing prices to fall further.

So, this story can be told, as in the last paragraph, without reference to international factors. That said, it can be plausibly argued that these unstable dynamics were accentuated by the external liberalization undertaken in the preceding period. So long as the market was rising, qualified foreign institutional investors could purchase shares on Chinese markets on their clients' behalf, adding to the demands of domestic investors. (For a list of these initiatives, see Table 3).

Table 3: RMB qualified foreign institutional investors.

Country (or region)	Amount (billion yuan)	Date
Hong Kong, China	20	August 2011
	50	April 2012
	200	November 2012
	230	July 2017
United Kingdom	80	October 2013
Singapore	100	October 2013
France	80	March 2014
South Korea	120	July 2014
Germany	80	July 2014
Qatar	30	November 2014
Canada	50	November 2014
Australia	50	November 2014
Switzerland	50	January 2015
Luxembourg	50	April 2015
Chile	50	May 2015
Hungary	50	June 2015
Malaysia	50	November 2015
United Arab Emirates	50	November 2015
Thailand	50	November 2015
United States	250	June 2016
Ireland	50	December 2016
Japan	200	May 2018
Netherlands	50	June 2019
Total	**1,990**	

Sources: People's Bank of China. Updated to 12/19/2019.

They could contribute to margin lending by Chinese financial institutions through their participation on the Chinese interbank bond market. Retail investors in Hong Kong could use their local brokers and clearinghouses to invest in Shenzhen and Shanghai.

Moreover, when the market tanked, foreign investors, like residents, now had the option of liquidating their domestic holdings and transferring their balances abroad. When the PBOC responded to the drop in the market by cutting interest rates, creating expectations of renminbi weakness, the incentive for capital flight was reinforced. It was strengthened further when questions were raised about whether even a central bank with $4 trillion of foreign reserves could continue to intervene at a rate of $100 billion a month to support the exchange rate — and if it couldn't, what would happen next.[28] These additional factors accentuating the crisis were all related to the prior liberalization of China's capital account.[29]

Finally, there was the reform of the exchange rate mechanism announced on August 11, 2015, designed to make the renminbi more heavily market-determined. Whereas previously the PBOC had set the midpoint for the ±2% daily trading band, it now moved to a system where the midpoint of the next day's exchange-rate trading band was based on the previous day's closing price. (Table 4 shows how this measure was related to the ongoing process of exchange rate reform.) This step was portrayed as another step in the direction of making the currency freely usable with an eye toward satisfying the prerequisites for inclusion in the SDR. But the rationale was not clearly communicated to the markets. As Figure 10 shows, the SDR issue was not heavily promoted by the authorities in August. Investors took the announcement as an indication of balance-of-payments weakness and of the difficulty the PBOC was experiencing

---

[28] China doesn't publish figures on net capital outflows, but these can be inferred from the current account balance and the change in foreign reserves (when the latter are adjusted for valuation effects); one estimate suggests that capital outflows approached $900 billion in the 10 months ending in November of 2015.

[29] In principle, it is possible to argue that had China moved even faster to eliminate restrictions on cross-border financial transactions in the earlier period, the authorities would have been forced to rein in liquidity creation earlier, owing to the threat of capital flight, and such large excesses in property and asset markets would not have been allowed to build up. We see no willingness or ability to move faster, which is precisely why the advocates of "reverse pressure" sought to apply it.

Table 4: Changes in China's exchange rate regime.

Date	Events
1 April 2011	Renminbi (RMB) foreign exchange options trading is officially launched to provide more exchange rate hedging instruments for enterprises and banks.
16 April 2012	The volatility range of RMB interbank spot exchange rate against the US dollar is enlarged from 0.5% to 1%.
16 April 2012	Enterprises and individuals are allowed to retain their foreign exchange income rather than having to sell them to authorized bank for dealing in foreign exchange.
29 May 2012	Under the authorization of the PBoC, China Foreign Exchange Trade System (CFETS) announced that China will improve the trading mode of RMB against Japanese yen in the interbank foreign exchange market and develop the direct trading of RMB against the yen.
9 April 2013	Under the authorization of the PBoC, CFETS announced that China will improve the trading mode of RMB against the Australian dollar in the interbank foreign exchange market and develop the direct trading of RMB against Australian dollar based on the market principle.
17 March 2014	The volatility range of RMB interbank spot exchange rate against US dollar was enlarged from 1% to 2%.
18 March 2014	The direct trading of RMB against New Zealand dollar is officially launched in China's interbank foreign exchange market to facilitate the formation of direct exchange rate of RMB against New Zealand dollar.
18 June 2014	Under the authorization of the PBoC, CFETS announced that the direct trading of RMB against the Great Britain pound is officially launched in China's interbank foreign exchange market.
2 July 2014	PBoC abolished the intervention to dollar's bid–ask spread of banks against customers, and allowed banks to price the dollar based on the supply and demand in the market, which aimed to make the RMB exchange rate more flexible.
29 September 2014	The direct trading of RMB against the euro is officially launched in China's interbank foreign exchange market.

(*Continued*)

Table 4: (*Continued*)

Date	Events
11 August 2015	PBoC reformed the exchange rate regime to liberalize RMB exchange rate through improving the quotation mechanism of central parity between the RMB against the USD.
30 August 2015	The IMF decided to add RMB to the SDR basket.
1 October 2016	The Chinese RMB was officially included in the SDR.
11 December 2016	CFETS released officially the CFETS RMB Index to improve the market mechanism for determining RMB exchange rate.
26 May 2017	PBoC announced that the countercyclical adjustment factor would be introduced to the mechanism for determining the central parity of RMB exchange rate, which triggered a second wave of RMB appreciation in this year.
9 January 2018	PBoC responded to *Chinese Business News* about the suspension of usage of the countercyclical adjustment factor, and announced that the countercyclical adjustment factor could be set freely by the quoting banks.
03 August 2018	Recently, due to factors such as trade frictions and changes in international exchange markets, there have been some signs of procyclical fluctuations in the foreign exchange market. In order to prevent macro financial risks, promote the stable operation of financial institutions, and strengthen macro-prudential management, the People's Bank of China decided to adjust the foreign exchange risk reserve ratio of forward sales from 0% to 20% from 6 August, 2018.
24 August 2018	Most of the middle price quotation lines have adjusted the "countercyclical factor." It is expected that the "counter-cyclic factor" will maintain a basically stable and positive effect on the RMB exchange rate at a reasonable and balanced level.

Sources: PBoC, State Administration of Foreign Exchange, CFETS, Sina Finance.

in supporting the exchange rate. The market reaction was strongly negative, and capital outflows intensified.

The Chinese authorities responded to this volatility by reaffirming that domestic financial stability and not currency internationalization was their first priority. They imposed a 20% reserve requirement on financial institutions trading foreign exchange forwards. They required

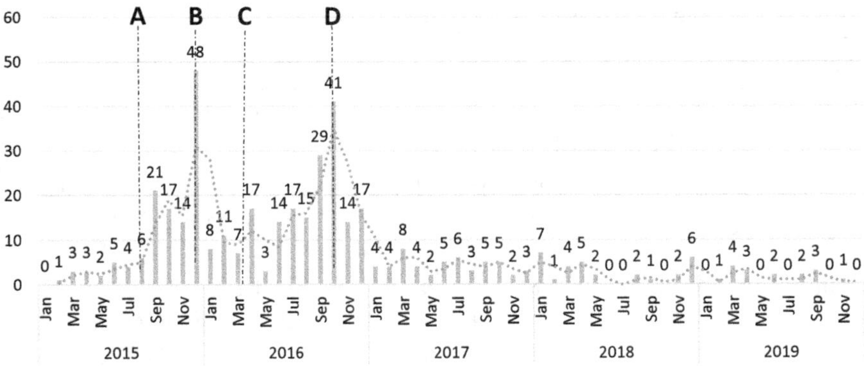

Figure 10: Number of mentions of SDR on Chinese central government website (by month, 2015–2019).

Notes:

A: 11 August, 2015, PBoC conducted the reform of exchange rate regime to liberalize RMB exchange rate.

B: 30 November, 2015: IMF decided to add RMB to the SDR basket.

C: 17 March, 2016: China's *13th Five-Year Plan* (Central Committee of the Communist Party of China 2016) was issued formally.

D: 1 October, 2016: Chinese RMB was officially included in the SDR.

Sources: Chinese Central Government website and authors' calculation.*

*The dashed line is a two-period moving average, which is used to eliminate artificial fluctuations due to, *inter alia*, delayed issuance of news articles or policy documents.

banks in Shanghai to balance renminbi outflows with inflows, whereas previously banks had been allowed to remit RMB150 overseas on behalf of their clients for every RMB100 repatriated to China. They ordered banks and financial institutions to investigate possible over-invoicing of imports. They required banks to report all cross-border cash transfers of more than RMB50,000, down from RMB200,000 previously. They cracked down on individuals using other people's quota for foreign currency purchases and on purchases by residents of insurance products in Hong Kong (see Table 5).

These measures were then supplemented in the second half of 2016 by new restrictions on large corporate investments abroad, which prohibited state-owned enterprises from devoting more than $1 billion to a single overseas real-estate transaction, and which

Table 5: Changes in China's capital control regime.

Date	Events
October 2013	Removal of commercial credits inflow and outflow restrictions (Fernández *et al.* 2016).
22 May 2014	Free Trade Account system is established at China (Shanghai) Pilot Free Trade Zone, which facilitated the cross-border finance, investment and currencies exchange.
14 July 2015	Chinese inter-bank bond markets and inter-bank foreign exchange markets are opened to foreign sovereign institutions (central Banks, international financial institutions and sovereign wealth funds) (PBoC 2015).
8 October 2015	CIPS (Phase I) goes live. Cross-Border Interbank Payment System (CIPS) offers clearing and settlement services for its participants' in cross-border RMB payments and trade.
25 January 2016	According to PBoC's new policy, foreign banks become subject to the normal required reserves policy when making renminbi deposits at their domestic agent banks, which increased required reserves. This policy aimed at suppressing the shorting in renminbi, and reverse the expectation for RMB devaluation (PBoC 2016).
1 January 2017	According to PBoC's policy, individuals are required to provide a declaration including purpose and expected time of usage when purchasing foreign currencies. This policy did not allow individuals to buy houses abroad, invest on securities or other unopened items.*
1 July 2017	PBoC adjusts the declaration standard for cash transactions from CN¥20,000 to 50,000, and requires that financial intermediaries should submit reports of block trade.**
11 October 2017	After President Trump's visit, China relaxes foreign shareholding-ratio restrictions for Chinese banks and financial asset management companies, and increases the foreign investment share in companies involved in securities, funds management, and futures.***
5 January 2018	CFETS issued the *Notice on the Arrangements for Overseas Banks to Participate in Interbank FX Market Regional Trading*, allowing qualified overseas banks to participate in interbank FX market regional trading.

Table 5: (*Continued*)

Date	Events
1 March, 2018	According to the *Sensitive Industries Catalogue for Outbound Investment* issued by the Chinese National Development and Reform Commission (2018), outbound investments in industries of weapons and military supplies, development and utilization of cross-border water resources, news media, and other previously limited industries (including real estate, hotel, film cities, entertainment firms, sports clubs and private equity companies without real business projects) will be limited and regulated from 1 March, 2018.
28 April, 2018	China Securities Regulatory Commission (CSRC) promulgated the "administrative measures on foreign-invested securities companies," allowing foreign investors to control joint-venture securities firms.
1 May, 2018	The daily quotas under both Shanghai–Hong Kong Stock Connect and Shengzhen–Hong Kong Stock Connect were expanded four times, in which the daily quota for each of the northbound trading links were adjusted to RMB 52 billion yuan from RMB 13 billion yuan, the daily quota for each of the southbound trading links were adjusted to RMB 42 billion yuan from RMB 10.5 billion yuan.
1 June, 2018	The Chinese A-share was formally included in MSCI Emerging Markets Index and Global Standard Index, which was conducive to attracting overseas investors to allocate assets on RMB share.
15 August, 2018	China Securities Regulatory Commission (CSRC) stipulates that qualified foreign natural person investors can open a-share securities accounts, starting from September 15, 2018.
31 January, 2019	Bloomberg formally confirmed the inclusion of Chinese bonds into the Bloomberg Barclays Global Composite Index from April 2019.
10 September, 2019	The State Administration of Foreign Exchange decides to remove the quota restrictions on both qualified foreign institutional investors (QFII) and renminbi qualified foreign institutional investors (RQFII).[****]

Sources: [*]http://wuhan.pbc.gov.cn/wuhan/2929354/3228579/index.html; [**]www.pbc.gov.cn/zhengwugongkai/127924/128038/128109/3226224/index.html; [***]news briefing for U.S.–China heads' meeting organized by China's Information Office of the State Council, www.gov.cn/xinwen/2017-11/10/content_5238617.htm#1; [****]http://www.safe.gov.cn/safe/2019/0910/14035.html.

scrutinized all large (greater than $10 billion) corporate acquisitions, as well as acquisitions outside the investor's core business. The State Administration of Foreign Exchange and the National Development and Reform Commission then banned certain categories of foreign investment outright while restricting others. Other financial reforms were not rolled back — the authorities continued to strengthen regulation of trust companies, shadow banks and the formal banking system — but the presumption that this process would be accompanied, even forced, by progressive liberalization of capital-account transactions was suspended for the time being.

As a result of tighter controls, the growth of international usage of the currency slowed and, along some dimensions, shifted into reverse.[30] Renminbi deposits in Hong Kong fell by 30% between their peak in December 2014 and the end of 2015.[31] Use of the currency in global bond markets was a quarter lower by the end of 2015 than at its 2014 peak. The share of China's own trade settled in renminbi shrank from 26% to 16% over the course of 2016. Whereas use of the renminbi in global payments rose strongly in 2014 and 2015, much of that increase was eliminated in the year following. SWIFT then reported a 40% drop in renminbi-denominated letters of credit in the first half of 2017. Figure 11, Standard Chartered Bank's summary index of renminbi globalization, illustrates the reversal.

Commentators continue to see fostering wider international use of the renminbi as one of the goals of Chinese economic and financial policy. They point to China's Belt and Road Initiative and its support for the Asia Infrastructure Investment Bank as additional reasons to expect use of the renminbi by other countries.[32] But they more freely

---

[30] Another factor contributing to reversal of the process was diminished expectations that the renminbi would continue to appreciate against other currencies on the back of strong Chinese economic growth.

[31] By early 2017 they were down fully 45.5% from their 2014 peak. See Hudson Lockett (2017). "HK Renminbi Deposits Fall at Record Pace in December," *Financial Times*, 26 January, https://www.ft.com/content/12e8a7b0-5f63-33e5-8a97-0c8548ab13ff.

[32] See, e.g., Solomon Teague (2017). "Renminbi payments in decline, but outlook positive, says SWIFT," *Euromoney*, 10 August, https://www.euromoney.com/article/

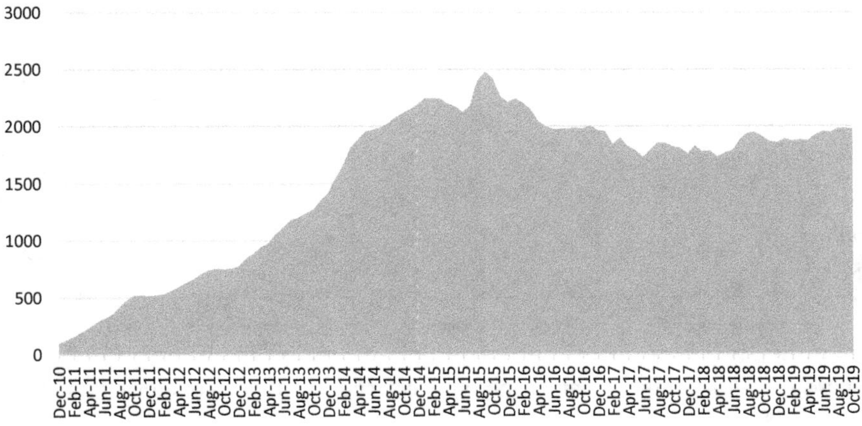

Figure 11: Standard Chartered renminbi globalization index (December 2010–October 2019).

Note: The Renminbi Globalization Index tracks four components with weights inversely proportional to their variance (onshore or CNY deposits; trade settlement and other international payments; dim sum bonds and certificates of deposit issued; and foreign exchange turnover — all from an offshore perspective and denominated in renminbi) in several countries (Hong Kong, Singapore, Taiwan, the United States, the United Kingdom, Korea, and France).

Source: Standard Chartered, updated to October 2019.

admit that the renminbi has a considerable distance to go before it qualifies as a leading international currency (a point that emerges clearly from Figure 12). They more readily acknowledge the dangers of proceeding with external liberalization in advance of domestic reform and of using currency internationalization as a lever with which to ratchet up the pressure for internal reform. Indicative of these facts, even Governor Zhou, when looking toward retirement, emphasized potential threats to domestic financial stability as a key challenge for Chinese policy makers.[33]

---

b147qq00jqmcpm/renminbi-payments-in-decline-but-outlook-positive-says-swift and SWIFT (2017). "Will the Belt and Road revitalise RMB internationalisation?" *RMB Tracker*, Special Edition, July.

[33]Again the reference is to Zhou, "The baseline."

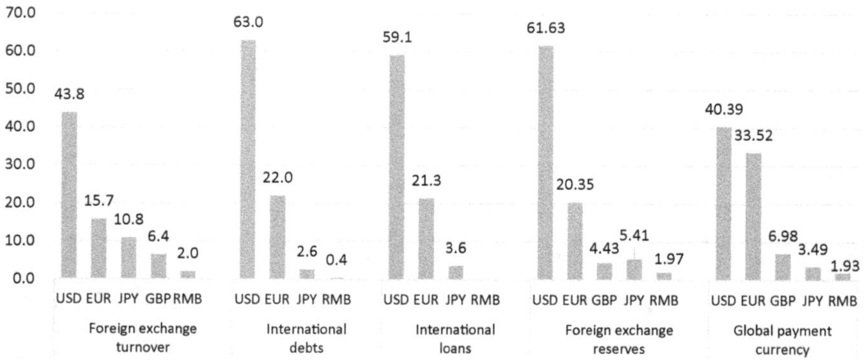

Figure 12: Role of the renminbi and other currencies in the international monetary system (%).

Notes:

1. Foreign exchange turnover data are from the BIS Triennual survey, updated to April 2016.
2. International debts and loans data are both from ECB's annual review, updated to the fourth quarter, 2016. Debts data values are narrow measure values at constant exchange rates, while loans data values are all cross-border values at constant exchange rates.
3. Foreign exchange reserves data is from IMF's COFER, representing the shares of respective currencies in the total allocated reserves, updated to the second quarter, 2019.
4. Global payment currency data is from SWIFT, representing the share of respective currency as an international payments currency, updated to November 2019.

Sources: Bank for International Settlements (BIS), European Central Bank (ECB), IMF's COFER, SWIFT.

6. Implications

Starting in 2009, Chinese officials advanced two visions for reform of the international monetary and financial system. One centered on an enhanced role for the IMF's Special Drawing Rights. The other envisaged a system in which the renminbi would play a role comparable to that of the dollar as an international unit of account, means of payment and store of value.

Are these really competing ideas, and if so does Chinese officialdom see the SDR or the renminbi as the future of the international monetary system? Do Chinese officials see addition of the renminbi to the SDR basket as a prerequisite for broadening the appeal of the latter and therefore for reforming the international monetary system in more SDR-centric directions? Or do they see recognition of the renminbi as freely usable and its addition to the SDR basket as cementing the renminbi's status as a first-class international currency and thereby advancing its international role?

The interest of Chinese officials in reform of the international monetary system is sincere, as we have shown through our review of Chinese interventions in the IMF Executive Board over more than three decades. But their consistent priority has been domestic financial development and reform. One motivation for renminbi internationalization and for attempting to satisfy the preconditions for SDR inclusion has therefore been to intensify the pressure for that domestic reform. Promoting wider international use of the renminbi presupposes relaxing controls on cross-border financial transactions, which in turn makes it more urgent to strengthen and develop domestic financial markets and institutions. Qualifying for inclusion in the SDR basket requires an IMF determination that the currency is freely usable, which similarly requires relaxing controls and makes domestic financial reforms more urgent. Thus, one strategy pursued by the promoters of domestic financial reform has been to encourage both renminbi internationalization and the pursuit of free-usability status in order to ratchet up the pressure for reform. This has come to be known as the "reverse pressure" strategy for reform.

But this strategy has risks. It may be critically important for domestic financial reform to follow external liberalization in short order, but nothing guarantees that this will be the case. Reform is complex, and influential interests resist its implementation. Fears of a growth slowdown or poorly communicated changes in the exchange rate regime may intervene before the process is complete, with destabilizing consequences. When this sequence of events unfolded in 2015–2016, the Chinese authorities responded by tightening controls and restoring a more sustainable balance between external financial liberalization and domestic financial reform.

The implication is that the case for domestic financial reform should be made on its merits, and that a pro-reform coalition must be built at home. This appears to be what is happening in China in the wake of the events of 2015–2016. At the Fifth National Conference on Finance, President Xi emphasized the importance of systemic stability and financial regulation. The words "risk" and "regulation" appear 31 and 28 times, respectively, in the report of the conference. On the sidelines of People's Congress, in October 2017, Governor Zhou issued a stark warning of risks to financial stability, warning that China faced a possible "Minsky moment."[34] In his widely noted 11 November 2017 speech, Zhou touched on renminbi internationalization and the currency's inclusion in the SDR basket, but emphasized the importance of "prevent[ing] systemic financial risks". In contrast to earlier interventions, he acknowledged that "opening up [could] induce high frequency risks."[35]

Evidently, Chinese leaders are now addressing the issue of financial stability head on, rather than hoping that, if they open the country's external accounts, the need for domestic reform will be recognized and domestic sources of resistance will be magically overcome.

Acknowledgments

We thank the Center for International Governance Innovation (CIGI) in Waterloo, Ontario, Canada, for financial support and for soliciting two careful peer reviews. Additional support for this project was provided by the Clausen Center at the University of California, Berkeley. Domenico Lombardi played an important role in the development of this project, and we thank him also for his support. This chapter draws on and reproduces in part an earlier CIGI working paper entitled "China and the SDR: Financial Liberalization through the Back Door" and an article by the same name in the *Quarterly Journal of Finance.*

[34]See Gabriel Wildau (2017). "China central bank chief warns of 'minsky moment,'" *Financial Times*, 19 October, https://www.ft.com/content/4bcb14c8-b4d2-11e7-a398-73d59db9e399.

[35]Wildau, "Central bank chief."

https://doi.org/10.1142/9789811226588_0010

Chapter 10

Purchasing Power: Exploring the Political Implications of China's Foreign Economic Ties

Scott L. Kastner
skastner@umd.edu

1. Introduction

Nearly four decades after the initiation of reform and opening, the People's Republic of China (PRC) today stands as the world's second largest economy in nominal terms, and may be the largest if purchasing power is taken into account. China's emergence as an economic giant, in turn, has dramatically increased its relevance for the global economy and the economic well-being of countries across the globe. The PRC is now the world's largest trading state, and since the early 1990s China has attracted more foreign direct investment (FDI) than any other developing country by far. In recent years, China's outbound FDI has also increased sharply, as has its foreign aid. China's massive Belt and Road Initiative (BRI) has intensified these trends, leading to large outbound flows of investment, particularly in infrastructure, across the world. Today, China stands as the largest or second largest trading partner of nearly every country in East, Central, and South Asia. China's economic footprint is increasingly global: China is now one of the largest trading partners of the United States, and is the largest or second largest trading partner of a majority of states in Africa. Even in Latin America, China trails only the United States as the region's largest trading partner.

As China's economic power grows and its economic ties to other countries deepen, does this translate into growing PRC political influence over other countries? Anecdotally, the answer often seems obvious: of course it does. Consider, for instance, the United Kingdom's recent experience with hosting the Dalai Lama. In 2012, British Prime Minister David Cameron met with the Dalai Lama in London, sparking strong protests from the Chinese government.[1] After Cameron's office defended the meeting and refused to apologize, the PRC reportedly canceled some high-level visits to the UK (including a planned trip by Wu Bangguo, a member of the Standing Committee of the Politburo), and Cameron himself was reportedly unwelcome in China in the aftermath of the meeting — leading to a cancelation of a visit planned for early 2013.[2] By late 2013, however, Cameron's approach to the Dalai Lama changed sharply. Indicating that his office had "turned a page on that issue," Cameron made amends with Beijing and agreed to distance himself from the Dalai Lama in the future.[3] In late 2013, in turn, Cameron traveled to China (along with

[1] "David Cameron's Dalai Lama Meeting Sparks Chinese Protest," *BBC News*, 16 May 2012, http://www.bbc.com/news/uk-politics-18084223.

[2] "China Cancels UK Visit over David Cameron's Meeting with Dalai Lama," *The Guardian*, 25 May 2012, https://www.theguardian.com/world/2012/may/25/china-cancels-uk-visit-dalai-lama; "China Freezes out Cameron for Meeting Dalai Lama," *The Daily Telegraph*, 7 May 2013, in *LexisNexis*.

[3] "David Cameron to Distance Britain from Dalai Lama During China Visit," *The Guardian*, 30 November 2013, https://www.theguardian.com/politics/2013/nov/30/david-cameron-distance-britain-dalai-lama-china-visit.

100 businesspeople) with the goal of expanding economic ties between the two countries.[4] The shift in policy appeared to pay off, as economic ties between the UK and China deepened in subsequent years: high profile examples of these deepening ties included a substantial Chinese investment in a new British nuclear plant,[5] and the PRC's decision to issue its first offshore sovereign bond in London in 2016.[6] When the Dalai Lama returned to the UK in 2015, Cameron pointedly refused to meet with him. When asked how he would respond to the Prime Minister's snub if given the chance, the Dalai Lama replied: "Money, money, money. That's what this is about. Where is morality?"[7]

Great Britain's approach to the Dalai Lama, moreover, is not an obvious anomaly. To the contrary, it is relatively easy to pinpoint other instances where current or (hoped for) future economic ties with China led to PRC influence over policy decisions in other countries. During the 1990s, for instance, economic retaliation appeared to have been sufficient to convince France to halt arms sales to Taiwan.[8] South Africa has denied a visa to the Dalai Lama on multiple

---

[4] "Cameron 'Turns Page' on Dalai Lama Row with China Visit," *Reuters*, 1 December 2013, http://uk.reuters.com/article/uk-britain-china-cameron-idUKBRE9AT-05G20131201.

[5] "China to Build Nuclear Reactor in Essex after Hinkley Deal Approved," *The Telegraph*, 15 September 2016, http://www.telegraph.co.uk/business/2016/09/15/china-to-build-nuclear-reactor-in-essex-after-hinkley-deal-appro/.

[6] "China Issues Its First Renminbi Sovereign Debt in London," *Financial Times*, 26 May 2016, https://www.ft.com/content/f81c777a-233e-11e6-aa98-db1e01fabc0c.

[7] "Dalai Lama Criticizes David Cameron for 'Money over Morality' Snub," *The Telegraph*, 23 September 2015, http://www.telegraph.co.uk/news/worldnews/asia/tibet/11886840/Dalai-Lama-criticises-David-Cameron-over-money-over-morality-snub.html.

[8] On PRC economic retaliation against France for its arms sales to Taiwan, see for instance: "China Threatens U.S. with Sanctions," *Chicago Tribune*, 8 January 1993, http://articles.chicagotribune.com/1993-01-08/business/9303151606_1_beijing-considers-taiwan-part-foreign-economic-relations-chinese-development-projects. On PRC response to arms sales more broadly, see Kastner, Scott L., William Reed and Ping-Kuei Chen (2013). "Mostly Bark, Little Bite? Modeling US Arms Sales to Taiwan and the Chinese Response." *Issues and Studies*, 49(3): 111–150.

occasions — including to attend a planned 2014 summit gathering for Nobel Peace Prize laureates — so as to avoid any disturbances to extensive bilateral economic ties.[9] And Norway appeared to pay a price, including lost salmon exports to China, for the Norwegian Nobel Committee's 2010 decision to award the Nobel Peace Prize to Chinese dissident Liu Xiaobo.[10] Norwegian leaders later tried to make amends by, among other things, refusing to meet with the Dalai Lama during his visit to Norway in 2014.[11] The PRC's growing economic clout, in short, often makes national leaders reluctant to adopt policies likely to anger Beijing, especially on issues that are particularly sensitive to China like Tibet and Taiwan.

Nevertheless, it is also relatively easy to find cases where extensive economic ties with China do not translate seamlessly into Chinese influence. US officials still routinely meet with the Dalai Lama, for instance, and the US continues to sell advanced weapons to Taiwan despite repeated threats of economic consequences. Just a few years ago, Taiwan appeared to be a textbook case of economic ties translating into increased PRC influence, as the Ma Ying-jeou administration embraced détente with the PRC, the country that represents both the island's biggest threat and its key economic partner. Yet, today the Taiwan case is less clear-cut in this regard. Ma's approval ratings dropped precipitously during his second term in office, and deepening cross-Strait economic cooperation appears to have helped trigger a backlash effect in Taiwan, helping to mobilize opponents of Ma's Nationalist Party. The cross-Strait détente came to a screeching halt after Tsai Ing-wen of the more China-skeptical

---

[9]"'Dalai Lama Debacle' Stirs Anger in South Africa," *New York Times*, 6 October 2014, https://sinosphere.blogs.nytimes.com/2014/10/06/dalai-lama-debacle-stirs-anger-in-south-africa/.

[10]On this case, see Fuchs, Andreas (2016). "China's Economic Diplomacy and the Politics-Trade Nexus." University of Heidelberg Department of Economics Discussion Paper Series No. 609, p. 2 and Reilly, James. (2012). "China's Unilateral Sanctions." *The Washington Quarterly*, Fall: 127–128.

[11]"Norway's Leaders Snub Dalai Lama in Deference to China," *New York Times*, 7 May 2014, https://www.nytimes.com/2014/05/08/world/europe/norways-leaders-snub-dalai-lama-in-deference-to- china.html.

Democratic Progressive Party (DPP) was elected president in 2016.[12] Economic ties with China have led to backlash in other cases as well: in Sri Lanka, for instance, extensive Chinese investments in the country eventually became a political liability for the Mahinda Rajapaksa government. During the campaign for the 2015 presidential election, Rajapaksa's political opponent decried the country's growing dependence on China as a path on which Sri Lanka "would become a colony and we would become slaves." Rajapaksa lost the election.[13]

In short, it is hard to know what to make of the anecdotal evidence that is available: does China's growing global economic presence tend to translate into growing political influence, with some notable exceptions? Or is it the examples of apparent influence that are the outliers? Unfortunately, scholarly efforts to tease out the degree to which China's foreign economic ties translate into political influence have also come to diverging conclusions. For instance, some recent quantitative studies[14] find evidence that economic dependence on China leads to political accommodation. Some qualitative studies likewise suggest that China's growing economic power is translating into increased political influence abroad — or at least the groundwork is being laid in this regard.[15] But some quantitative studies come to

[12]On the other hand, the DPP suffered heavy losses in late-2018 local elections; the Nationalist Party appears well-positioned heading into the 2020 presidential election as of the time of this writing.

[13]See Devotta, Neil (2016). "China's influence in Sri Lanka: Negotiating development, authoritarianism, and regional transformation," in Evelyn Goh (ed.), *Rising China's Influence in Developing Asia* (Oxford: Oxford University Press), pp. 129–152. Quote is on page 130.

[14]Flores-Macias, Gustavo A. and Sarah E. Kreps (2013). "The Foreign Policy Consequences of Trade: China's commercial relations with Africa and Latin America, 1992–2006," *Journal of Politics*, 75(2): 357–371; Struever, Georg (2016). {What friends are made of: Bilateral linkages and domestic drivers of foreign policy alignment with China." *Foreign Policy Analysis*, 12(2): 170–191.

[15]Chin, Gregory (2014). "China's rising monetary power," in Eric Helleiner and Jonathan Kirshner (eds.), *The Great Wall of Money: Power and Politics in China's International Monetary Relations* (Ithaca: Cornell University Press), pp. 184–212; Kirshner, Jonathan (2014). "Regional hegemony and an emerging RMB zone," in

more mixed conclusions,[16] and a number of qualitative studies are skeptical of the degree to which China's foreign economic ties translate into political influence abroad.[17]

In this chapter, I first discuss theory on why China's foreign economic ties might translate into influence abroad. I then review existing empirical evidence on the subject, focusing in particular on a handful of recent quantitative cross-national studies as a first cut. My goal is to begin unpacking why different studies come to different conclusions about the influence effects of China's external economic ties, and to point toward possible future research on the question.

2. Theory[18]

Existing international relations literature suggests at least two broad causal processes through which China's growing global economic presence could translate into increased influence over policy decisions in other countries. First, Beijing's growing economic power gives the PRC more opportunities to pursue economic statecraft, such as by threatening or imposing economic sanctions to induce policy change in other states. Second, China's economic ties can give rise to influence more indirectly by generating vested interests in other countries, who might then lobby their home governments to seek accommodating policies toward the PRC. In this section, I discuss each of these causal processes in some more detail.

Eric Helleiner and Jonathan Kirshner (eds.), *The Great Wall of Money: Power and Politics in China's International Monetary Relations* (Ithaca: Cornell University Press), pp. 213–240.

[16]Kastner, Scott L. (2016). "Buying influence? Assessing the political effects of China's international trade," *Journal of Conflict Resolution*, 60(6): 980–1007.

[17]Ross, Robert S. (2006). "Balance of power politics and the rise of China: Accommodation and balancing in East Asia." *Security Studies*, 15(3): 355–395; Drezner, Daniel W. (2009). "Bad debts: Assessing China's financial influence in great power politics," *International Security*, 34(2): 7–45; Goh, Evelyn (ed.), (2016). *Rising China's Influence in Developing Asia* (Oxford: Oxford University Press).

[18]This section draws heavily from Kastner (2016).

A large literature considers whether and when states are able to influence policy choices in other countries through the deliberate manipulation of cross-border economic ties.[19] Much of this literature focuses on coercive economic statecraft, as when states threaten or impose economic sanctions to compel or deter policy changes in other states. While a number of studies have questioned the utility of economic sanctions as a policy instrument,[20] others have responded that such studies tend to define success too narrowly.[21] Existing studies have also identified numerous factors that might condition the effectiveness of economic sanctions, including (among other factors): their comprehensiveness and the extent to which they are combined with other coercive instruments; the availability of alternative suppliers of sanctioned goods, and the extent to which such suppliers are willing to join the sanctioning regime; expectations of future conflict between the sending and the target state; and the nature of the governing coalition in the target country.[22] That sanctions may only work under certain

[19] See Baldwin (1985) for a classic discussion of different forms of economic statecraft. For applications to China, see for instance: Norris, William J. (2016). *Chinese Economic Statecraft: Commercial Actors, Grand Strategy, and State Control* (Ithaca, NY: Cornell University Press); Reilly (2012); Zhang, Ketian Vivian (2019). "Chinese non-military coercion: tactics and rationale." Brookings Institute: https://www.brookings.edu/articles/chinese-non-military-coercion-tactics-and-rationale/; Wong, Audrye (2018). "Crafting payoffs: Strategies and effectiveness of China's economic statecraft," Paper presented at the annual meeting of the American Political Science Assn, Boston (29 August); and Harrell, Peter, Elizabeth Rosenberg, and Edoardo Saravalle (2018). "China's use of coercive economic measures," (Washington DC: Center for a New American Security).

[20] Pape, Robert A. (1997). "Why economic sanctions do not work," *International Security*, 22(2): 90–136; Hufbauer, Gary Clyde, Jeffrey J. Schott, and Kimberly Ann Elliot (1985). *Economic Sanctions Reconsidered* (Washington DC: Institute for International Economics).

[21] Rowe, David M. (1999/2000). "Economic sanctions do work: economic statecraft and the oil embargo of Rhodesia," *Security Studies*, 9(1/2): 254–287; Baldwin, David A. (1985). *Economic Statecraft* (Princeton: Princeton University Press). Baldwin (1999/2000) provides a good overview of the problems inherent in assessing the effectiveness of economic sanctions.

[22] On factors that condition the efficacy of economic sanctions, see, for instance, Blanchard, Jean-Marc F. and Norrin M. Ripsman (1999/2000). "Asking the right

conditions, in turn, greatly complicates any effort to assess whether or not economic ties afford Beijing leverage in a particular case.[23]

Moreover, it can be hard to know with precision how frequently states might actually utilize economic sanctions: as Drezner[24] writes,

---

questions: when do economic sanctions work best?" *Security Studies*, 9(1/2): 219–253; Drezner (2009); Haggard, Stephan and Marcus Noland (2011). *Engaging North Korea: The Role of Economic Statecraft.* Honolulu Hawaii: East West Center Policy Studies #59; Brooks, Risa A. (2002). "Sanctions and regime type: what works, and when?" *Security Studies*, 11(4): 1–50; Solingen, Etel (2007). *Nuclear Logics: Contrasting Paths in East Asia and the Middle East* (Princeton, NJ: Princeton University Press); Kirshner, Jonathan (1997). "The microfoundations of economic sanctions," *Security Studies*, 6(3): 32–64; Rowe, David M. (2001). *Manipulating the Market: Understanding Economic Sanctions, Institutional Change, and the Political Unity of White Rhodesia* (Ann Arbor, MI: University of Michigan Press). Some studies within the trade/conflict literature have suggested, meanwhile, that the opportunity costs of trade disruption vary across different sectors (e.g., Dorussen, H. (2006). "Heterogeneous trade interests and conflict: what you trade matters," *Journal of Conflict Resolution*, 50(1), 87–107; Goenner, C.F. (2010). "From toys to warships: interdependence and the effects of disaggregated trade on militarized disputes," *Journal of Peace Research*, 47(5), 547–559; Li, Q. and Reuveny, R. (2011). "Does trade prevent or promote interstate conflict initiation?" *Journal of Peace Research*, 48(4), 437–453. Just as the pacifying effects of trade are likely to be reduced when opportunity costs of disruption are low, sanction efficacy should also be relatively low in such sectors.

[23]Some studies have begun to probe at greater lengths the specific conditions under which China is more or less likely to be able to exercise effective economic statecraft. Norris (2016) argues persuasively, for instance, that the efficacy of Chinese economic statecraft is likely to hinge on state control of a particular economic sector; presumably, this will vary across China's trading partners depending on the sectors involved in bilateral economic exchange. The finding by Davis *et al.* (2014) that poor political relations between China and a particular country are most likely to negatively affect trade in sectors that have high PRC state ownership appears consistent with Norris's argument. Drezner (2009) considers at length the conditions under which China's growing financial clout is likely to translate into political influence in other countries. Focusing in particular on PRC holdings of US treasury bonds, he argues that China's influence is likely to be curtailed to the degree that expectations of future conflict with the target are high (the target will fear that making concessions will only encourage future sanctions threats), and when the target has the capacity to retaliate (among other factors). See also Farrell *et al.* (2018) for a comparative analysis of PRC use of economic sanctions.

[24]Drezner, Daniel W. (2003). "The hidden hand of economic coercion," *International Organization*, 57: 643–659.

economic coercion is often hidden. Threats to use economic sanctions, for example, may be implicit, or may be communicated in private. The problem of implicit economic coercion appears to be especially salient in the case of China. On the one hand, as James Reilly[25] observes, "China's opposition to economic sanctions is legendary" (p. 121). China has at times blocked multilateral sanctions in the United Nations, and has been especially critical of economic sanctions adopted by countries without UN authorization.[26] On the other hand, some of the examples provided in this chapter's introduction (such as the decline in Norwegian salmon imports after the Liu Xiaobo Nobel Peace Prize) suggest that China itself engages at times in coercive — and unilateral — economic statecraft. But because the PRC has been so outspokenly critical of unilateral sanctions, when it pursues such action itself it generally does so quietly. In the Norwegian salmon case, for instance, the degree to which Norway was actually the target of sanctions was somewhat difficult to ascertain. Salmon imports from Norway declined, but this was attributed to sanitary considerations; some trade delegations were cancelled and Norwegian nationals appeared to face increased scrutiny on visa applications, but overall trade levels continued to rise.[27] Other recent high-profile cases have followed a similar pattern. In 2010, for instance, during a dispute with Tokyo over Japan's detention of a Chinese fishing boat

---

[25]Reilly, James (2012). "China's unilateral sanctions." *The Washington Quarterly*, Fall: 121–133.

[26]See Reilly (2012) for a good overview of PRC thinking on economic sanctions. On North Korea, for instance, while China has gone along with UN sanctions, it has repeatedly opposed "unilateral" sanctions on the grounds that such action will not help to resolve the nuclear issue. See, e.g., "China Tells Japan Sanctions against North Korea Won't Resolve Nuclear Issue," *Reuters*, 14 September 2016, http://www.cnbc.com/2016/09/14/china-tells-japan-sanctions-against-north-korea-wont-resolve-nuclear-issue.html.

[27]Benjamin David Backer, "Soul or Salmon: Norway's Chinese Dilemma," *The Diplomat*, 9 May 2014, http://thediplomat.com/2014/05/soul-or-salmon-norways-chinese-dilemma/; Bjørnar Sverdrup-Thygeson and Marc Lanteigne, "China and Norway: Unpacking the Deal," *The Diplomat*, 25 December 2016, http://thediplomat.com/2016/12/china-and-norway-unpacking-the-deal/; Reilly 2012.

captain, reports surfaced that Beijing was limiting the export of critical rare earth elements (REE) to Japan.[28] Reilly[29] writes (based on interviews in China) that "it appears likely that central authorities informally instructed local customs officials to delay REE exports to Japan until the dispute was resolved," and industry officials also believed that customs officials were deliberately limiting REE exports to Japan.[30] Yet, the Chinese government denied that it was limiting REE exports to Japan,[31] and some rigorous academic research questions whether the embargo actually took place.[32] Cases like the Norwegian salmon episode and the possible REE embargo suggest that it can be hard to determine if China is actually engaged in coercive economic statecraft, much less whether such statecraft is effective or not in altering target state behavior.[33]

---

[28] See, for instance, "Amid Tension, China Blocks Vital Exports to Japan," *New York Times*, 22 September 2010, http://www.nytimes.com/2010/09/23/business/global/23rare.html. REEs are used in many high-technology products, and vast majority of global REEs are mined in China.

[29] Reilly (2012, p. 129).

[30] See "Amid Tension, China Blocks Vital Exports to Japan," *op cit.*

[31] Reilly (2012, p. 129).

[32] Johnston, Alastair Iain (2013). "How new and assertive is China's new assertiveness?" *International Security*, 37(4): 7–48.

[33] Other prominent cases of apparent implicit Chinese economic coercion include a three day stoppage of oil flows to North Korea in 2003 due to what PRC officials called a "technical" issue with the pipeline, though the action was widely viewed as meant to signal dissatisfaction with perceived North Korean brinkmanship; consumer boycotts directed against Japan in 2005 and France in 2008; declining PRC tourism in Taiwan following the 2016 election of DPP candidate Tsai Ing-wen as Taiwan's president; and visa problems and cancelled shows for South Korean pop stars in the aftermath of Seoul's 2016 decision to allow deployment of the Terminal High-Altitude Area Defense system in South Korea. On these cases, see: Reilly (2012); Scobell, Andrew (2004). "China and North Korea: From comrades-in-arms to allies at arm's length," Strategic Studies Institute, March, http://www.strategicstudiesinstitute.army.mil/pdffiles/pub373.pdf; Farrell *et al.* (2018); Zhang (2019); "South Korea's 'K-Pop' Stars Caught in Crossfire of Diplomatic Spat with China," *The Telegraph*, 4 December 2016, http://www.telegraph.co.uk/news/2016/12/04/south-koreas-k-pop-stars-caught-crossfire-diplomatic-spat-china/; "China Tourists Noticeable in their Absence in Taiwan as Ties Wilt," *Reuters*, 9 September 2016, http://www.reuters.com/article/us-taiwan-china-tourism-idUSKCN11F1DO.

Economic statecraft need not involve coercion, of course. While much of the economic statecraft literature has focused on sanctions, a number of studies have considered what might be termed "engagement" policies, where a state "deliberately expands economic ties" with a target state in order to influence the target's behavior.[34] Such policies might involve a quid pro quo, where economic ties are increased in return for some policy concession, or — perhaps more commonly — may simply aim to alter the incentives of or political dynamics in the target country. For instance, referring to Hirschman's[35] classic study, Kirshner has described what he terms a "Hirschmanesque" logic, whereby economic integration helps to generate vested interests who advocate foreign policies that do not antagonize key trading partners.[36] Instances where countries have deliberately tried to generate a "Hirschmanesque" effect include the Clinton administration's engagement strategy toward China after 1994 and South Korea's Sunshine Policy toward North Korea in the late 1990s and early 2000s.[37]

---

[34] Kahler, Miles and Scott L. Kastner (2006). "Strategic uses of economic interdependence: engagement policies on the Korean Peninsula and across the Taiwan Strait," *Journal of Peace Research*, 43(5): 523–541; Drezner, D. (1999/2000). "The trouble with carrots: transaction costs, conflict expectations, and economic inducements," *Security Studies* 9: 188–218; Mastanduno, M. (2003). "The strategy of economic engagement: theory and practice," in E.D. Mansfield and B.M. Pollins (eds.), *Economic Interdependence and International Conflict: New Perspectives on an Enduring Debate* (Ann Arbor: University of Michigan Press), pp. 175–186; Davis, P. (1999). *The Art of Economic Persuasion: Positive Incentives and German Economic Diplomacy* (Ann Arbor: University of Michigan Press).

[35] Hirschman, Albert O. (1945 [1980]). *National Power and the Structure of Foreign Trade* (Berkeley: University of California Press).

[36] Kirshner, Jonathan (2008). "The consequences of China's economic rise for Sino-U.S. relations: rivalry, political conflict, and (not) war," in Ross and Zhu (eds.), *China's Ascent*; Abdelal, Rawi and Jonathan Kirshner (1999/2000). {Strategy, economic relations, and the definition of national interests," *Security Studies*, 9(1/2): 119–156.

[37] See Kastner, Scott L. and Margaret M. Pearson (2016). "Winning hearts and minds? On the sources and efficacy of economic engagement policies in US–China and China–Taiwan relations," in Steven E. Lobell and Norrin M. Ripsman (eds.), *The Political Economy of Regional Peacemaking* (Ann Arbor: University of Michigan Press), pp. 144–168; Kahler and Kastner (2006).

The PRC has also pursued this sort of economic statecraft, for instance, in its efforts to "win Taiwan hearts and minds" via increased purchases of agricultural goods after the mid-2000s.[38]

It is important to emphasize, however, that Kirshner's "Hirschmaneque" effects could arise even in the absence of economic statecraft; that is, these sorts of effects could arise naturally as one country becomes more dependent on economic ties with another country.[39] As China becomes a more important economic partner for other states, a growing coalition of economic actors in those states — such as businesses that export to China, or industries that rely on Chinese investments, or multinational corporations with operations in China — will view stable relations with China as an important goal, and will lobby against foreign policies that might antagonize China. Although it is far from guaranteed that these groups will win out in any particular case, deeper economic ties with China should increase the size and political clout of these vested interests. Scholars have identified numerous historical cases where economic exchange translated along these lines into political influence, including: Nazi Germany's interactions with Southeastern Europe[40]; United States's interactions with the Hawaiian Kingdom in the second half of the nineteenth century[41]; post-Cold War relations between Russia and other states in the former Soviet Union[42]; and British interactions with the United States prior to World War II.[43] Other studies have shown that countries dependent on trade with either superpower

[38] *Ibid.* See also: Wei, Chi-hung (2013). "China's economic offensive and Taiwan's defensive measures: cross-strait fruit trade, 2005–2008," *The China Quarterly*, 215: 641–662; and Norris (2016).

[39] See, e.g., Kirshner (2008) for a discussion of this process.

[40] See Hirschman (1945 [1980]).

[41] See Abdelal and Kirshner (1999/2000).

[42] Hancock, Kathleen J. (2006). "The semi-sovereign state: Belarus and the Russian neo-empire," *Foreign Policy Analysis*, 2(2): 117–136 and see Abdelal and Kirshner (1999/2000).

[43] In many of these cases, economic ties were deliberately deployed to generate influence effects. See Skalnes, Lars S. (1998). "Grand strategy and foreign economic policy: British grand strategy in the 1930s," *World Politics*, 50(4): 582–616.

during the Cold War tended to adopt foreign policies in line with that superpower's interests.[44] Broadly speaking, these studies suggest that countries becoming more dependent on China economically may also become more inclined to accommodate PRC interests, *ceteris paribus.*

Finally, it is worth noting that some scholars are skeptical of the ability of economic ties to translate into political influence. Many, for instance, view sanctions as relatively ineffectual, especially relating to high-stakes issues,[45] and other forms of economic statecraft face an array of challenges that make success difficult and contingent on other factors.[46] More generally, realists tend to be skeptical that economic interests will ever trump a country's core security interests. In his examination of secondary state alignment in East Asia, for instance, Ross[47] finds that economic dependence on China is neither a necessary nor sufficient condition for a country to adopt an accommodating posture toward the PRC. On the other hand, susceptibility to PRC military power is necessary and sufficient in this regard.

In sum, there are clear theoretical reasons for thinking that China's rapid economic development and growing links to the global economy could yield the PRC increasing influence over policy decisions in other countries. At the same time, however, the relationship between China's external economic ties and political influence abroad is most likely quite complicated: economic ties could give rise to increasing influence through multiple causal mechanisms, and numerous intervening variables appear to shape whether or not influence is

---

[44] Roeder, Philip G. (1985). "The ties that bind: aid, trade, and political compliance in Soviet–third world relations," *International Studies Quarterly*, 29: 191–216; Richardson, Neil R. and Charles W. Kegley, Jr. (1980). "Trade dependence and foreign policy compliance: a longitudinal analysis," *International Studies Quarterly*, 24(2): 191–222.

[45] See, e.g., Pape (1997).

[46] See, e.g., Drezner (1999/2000), Kahler and Kastner (2006) and Davis, Christina, Andreas Fuchs, and Kristina Johnson (2014). "State control and the effects of foreign relations on bilateral trade," University of Heidelberg Department of Economics Discussion Paper Series No. 609.

[47] See Ross (2006).

likely to follow economic ties in any given case. Some scholars, moreover, are doubtful that economic ties will ever translate into influence over important national security considerations. In the next section, I discuss at greater length some recent efforts to examine, empirically, whether China's foreign economic ties do indeed give rise to political influence abroad.

3. Empirics

The discussion in the previous section suggests that assessing empirically whether China's growing economic ties to other countries translate into increased PRC influence is likely to be a complicated undertaking, since the degree to which economic ties lead to PRC influence is likely contingent on other factors. That is, the key question is not if economic ties yield influence, but rather when they do (if ever). In this section, I set aside this rather sizable issue of "when," and focus more specifically on scholarship that explores simply "if" economic ties lead to increased PRC influence. As the discussion demonstrates, even studying this more basic question is plagued by serious hurdles that have left us with few clear answers — and consequently moving on to the question of "when" remains difficult and perhaps premature. To make things more manageable, I focus here on those studies that have examined this topic quantitatively, using cross-national data.

It almost goes without saying that the measuring influence is difficult. Classic studies of political influence emphasize the importance of clearly identifying scope when seeking to study whether one actor is influencing another.[48] Thus, quantitative, cross-national studies of

[48]For instance, Baldwin (1985, 20) emphasizes that "in order to make a meaningful statement about an (actual or potential) influence relationship, one must (explicitly or implicitly) specify who is influencing (or has the capacity to influence) whom (domain) with respect to what (scope)." See also: Dahl, Robert A. (1963). *Modern Political Analysis* (USA: Prentice Hall), p. 45. Dahl writes: "a statement about influence that does not clearly indicate the scope it refers to verges on the meaningless. When one hears or reads that X is highly influential, the proper question is: 'Influential with respect to what?'"

China's influence tend to conceptualize a dependent variable in more concrete terms, such as foreign policy accommodation or foreign policy convergence. That is, these studies typically focus more specifically on whether deeper economic ties with China make countries more likely to adopt policies that are consistent with Chinese preferences. Yet, measurement issues still loom large even with a more concrete conceptualization of the dependent variable as policy accommodation or convergence, especially for large-N, cross-national studies. Simply put, it is difficult to find convincing metrics of foreign policy accommodation or convergence for a large sample of countries, particularly if the research aims to explore variation both across countries and over time.

Struever[49] deals with this issue by using voting patterns in the United Nations General Assembly (UNGA) over the years 1990–2008 as a proxy, where countries that tend to vote with China are assumed to have closer foreign policy alignment. As Struever notes, a key advantage of this approach is that it provides measures for a large, cross-national sample over time. In regressions that examine the relationship between trade and alignment, Struever finds that import dependence on China is correlated with UNGA vote alignment, but export dependence and total trade dependence are not.[50] Flores-Macias and Kreps[51] also use UNGA voting patterns to capture foreign policy convergence, but they note that a key drawback to using all votes is that "there are a number of UNGA votes that are procedural in nature and not particularly important to a state's national interest." They also observe that finding convergence on UNGA votes tells us little about whether other states are converging toward China, or

---

[49]See Struever (2016).

[50]Similarity of UNGA votes is determined using a modified version of the "S" score developed by Signorino, Curtis S. and Jeffrey M. Ritter (1999). "Tau-b or Not Tau-b: Measuring the similarity of foreign policy positions," *International Studies Quarterly*, 43(1): 115–144. Note that Struever transforms the similarity score into a dichotomous variable for his empirical analyses: the trade dependence findings arise with a dependent variable that takes a value of 1 for the 25% most similar cases, and 0 otherwise.

[51]See Flores-Macias and Kreps (2013).

whether China is converging toward other countries. To deal with these problems, the authors focus more specifically on UNGA country-specific human rights resolutions. Since human rights has remained an important issue for China, and since Beijing has consistently opposed these sorts of resolutions,[52] the authors argue that a measure based only on country-specific human rights resolutions offers a more credible indicator of foreign policy convergence than a measure based on all UNGA votes. Flores-Macias and Kreps also limit their analysis to a sample of Latin American and African countries; doing so ensures that the analysis captures developing countries that lie outside China's military sphere of influence — to help address the realist concern[53] that apparent "Hirschmanesque" effects might actually arise due to military power.[54] The authors find that both trade flows and trade salience are positively (and significantly) correlated with a propensity to vote more with China on the country-specific human rights resolutions.

Some of my previous work[55] aimed to find quantitative measures that could more directly capture some level of foreign policy accommodation of Chinese interests. Even if we limit analysis to UNGA country-specific human rights resolutions, it is hard to know how much China actually lobbies or pressures other countries to vote with Beijing. If the PRC isn't lobbying in this regard, it is not entirely clear why other countries would alter their voting behavior as they become more economically dependent on China. My alternative approach has been to focus on instances where the PRC clearly lobbied other

---

[52] Foot, Rosemary and Rana Siu Inboden (2016). "China's influence on Asian states during the creation of the UN human rights council: 2005–2007," in Evelyn Goh (ed.), *Rising China's Influence in Developing Asia* (Oxford: Oxford University Press), pp. 237–255. Foot and Inboden(p. 243) note that China's opposition to country-specific human rights resolutions owes in part to its own experience with being regularly subjected to these resolutions in the aftermath of the 1989 Tiananmen Square crackdown.

[53] See Ross (2006).

[54] The time period covered by Flores-Macias and Kreps is 1992–2006.

[55] See Kastner (2016) and Kastner, Scott L. (n.d.). "China's foreign economic ties: threat or opportunity." Unpublished manuscript.

countries to take open, supportive positions on issues that directly affect important PRC interests. Briefly: after 2004, the PRC lobbied other countries to recognize China as a market economy; in 2005 Beijing encouraged countries to support China's anti-secession law relating to Taiwan; in 2007–2008 China lobbied other countries to criticize a referendum asking Taiwan voters to support UN membership; and in 2008 — in response to Western criticism — the PRC encouraged countries to express support for a PRC crackdown in Tibet. Across these measures, only recognition of market economy status was robustly correlated with trade dependence on China. Import dependence on China was correlated with support for the anti-secession law, but export dependence and overall trade dependence were not. National positions on the UN referendum and the Tibet crackdown were not related to trade dependence on China.

A third broad approach can in some sense be thought of as the flip side of accommodation, where the focus is on events or policy actions that cause frictions in relations between a particular country and the PRC. Two recent studies have examined, for instance, whether bilateral frictions affect trade with China. Though influence (or accommodation) is not the dependent variable here, studies along these lines have the potential to shed important light on the question of whether economic ties translate into influence: if frictions lead to trade reduction, it suggests in turn that countries that become trade-dependent on China have reason to be more accommodating of Chinese interests, so as to avoid trade-harming frictions. The first study, Fuchs and Klann,[56] examines whether countries hosting the Dalai Lama pay a price in terms of reduced trade with China. Dalai Lama visits, especially when accompanied by high-level political meetings, typically generate significant friction in relations with China: at a minimum, the PRC will typically issue strong condemnation of such visits. The authors find that Dalai Lama meetings with political leaders in another country do indeed lead to a temporary

[56] For a follow-up study, see Fuchs, Andreas and Nils-Hendrik Klann (2013). "Paying a visit: The Dalai Lama effect on international trade," *Journal of International Economics*, 91: 164–177 and Fuchs (2016).

reduction in exports to China, especially for machinery and transportation equipment. The second study by Davis *et al.*[57] measures frictions using events data, and likewise finds a trade-harming effect which is especially pronounced for imports controlled by state-owned enterprises.[58]

Thus, a number of studies have explored — using quantitative methodology on a cross-national sample — the relationship between a particular country's economic ties with China and the degree of that country's foreign policy convergence with/accommodation of China. Yet, the findings emerging from these studies are all over the map. Flores-Macias and Kreps,[59] using the UNGA human rights voting data, find evidence that trade leads to foreign policy convergence for developing countries in Latin America and Africa. Struever,[60] using all UNGA votes on a sample of all countries, finds that only imports from China are associated with convergence; exports and total trade are not. Fuchs and Klann[61] find evidence that crossing China by hosting the Dalai Lama has a price in terms of exports to China, which implies possible influence effects. Davis *et al.*[62] likewise find that frictions with China have negative trade consequences. Kastner,[63] using data on national responses to specific cases where China lobbied for international support, finds evidence of accommodation on the economic issue, but less so on the political issues.

---

[57] See Davis *et al.* (2014).

[58] In a separate study (Kastner, Scott L. (2015). "Dreams or reality? A preliminary exploration of the relationship between China's growing economic power and its political influence in developed countries," in Arthur S. Ding and Chih-Hsian Liou (eds.), *China Dreams: China's New Leadership and Future Impacts* (Singapore: World Scientific, pp. 57–85), I examined frictions as the dependent variable. Focusing on the willingness of developed democracies to issue statements in support of Liu Xiaobo after receiving the 2010 Noble Peace Prize (over China's strong objections), I found that trade dependence on China had no clear effect on whether or not a particular country issued a statement in support of Liu.

[59] See Flores-Macias and Kreps (2013).

[60] See Struever (2016).

[61] See Fuchs and Klann (2013).

[62] See Davis *et al.* (2014).

[63] See Kastner (2016, 2015, n.d.).

Clearly, one reason for the disparate findings emerging from these studies is that the authors are using different measures to capture foreign policy accommodation (or convergence), and it isn't obvious that these measures would be closely related to one another. Here, I don't take a strong position on the relative merits of the different measures, but rather simply note that each has advantages and disadvantages. The UNGA-based measures are useful both because they exist over a long period of time for a large sample of countries, and because they are continuous variables that vary considerably both across countries and over time. The key drawback of these measures, as noted earlier, is that they reflect votes on issues that China may only care tangentially about (if at all). In turn, it is hard to know how much they actually reflect foreign policy convergence with China, especially when all UNGA votes are used. For instance, it seems pretty straightforward to say that the fifteen or so countries that don't even recognize the PRC government (i.e., those countries still maintaining diplomatic ties with the Republic of China [ROC] government on Taiwan) are not pursuing foreign policies that converge with China's. Yet, the ROC recognizers had, on average, almost identical UNGA voting affinity to China as do the PRC recognizers in 2005.[64] I don't want to make too much of this, but it should give scholars some pause. Meanwhile, although the PRC clearly opposes most country-specific UNGA human rights resolutions, it isn't clear how actively Beijing actively pushes other countries to vote against these measures. Still, the ROC/PRC recognizer test at least provides some more confidence in this measure: PRC recognizers tend to vote with the PRC on the human rights resolutions more often than ROC recognizers, at least in 2005.[65]

The data on Dalai Lama visits utilized by Fuchs and Klann, like the UNGA measures, has the advantage of existing for a large sample

[64] In my sample, the 22 ROC recognizers (countries not even recognizing the PRC) had an average affinity ("s") score of 0.694 with China, while 162 PRC recognizers had a slightly *lower* average affinity score of 0.691.

[65] The similarity measure used by Flores-Macias and Kreps averaged 1.56 for 49 PRC recognizers, but only 1.19 for 12 ROC recognizers, in 2005.

of countries over time. Moreover, China strongly opposes (and protests) any meetings between the Dalai Lama and national leaders, which gives this indicator the added benefit of capturing something that Beijing cares about and lobbies other countries about. A key drawback of the measure, however, is that the vast majority of countries in any given year do not host the Dalai Lama. Indeed, the Dalai Lama only visited and met with government officials in 27 of the 190 countries in my sample over the years 2002–2008.[66] As such, while the measure offers a useful indicator of a willingness to take strong action that provokes tensions with Beijing, it doesn't differentiate among the vast majority of countries that don't allow Dalai Lama to visit and meet with government officials.

The data collected by Kastner have the advantage of capturing cross-national variation on issues Beijing clearly cares about and lobbies other countries over. Moreover, these data include considerable cross-national variation. For instance, out of 190 countries in my sample, 65 strongly and openly supported the anti-secession law and another 20 offered more measured support; similarly, 75 out of the 190 countries offered some level of support for PRC actions in Tibet. On the other hand, the key drawback of Kastner's indicators is that the data are only cross-sectional, and hence do not allow analysis of changes over time within countries. In short, each of the measures has advantages and disadvantages.

Given that the different measures examined here each aim to capture a similar concept (foreign policy convergence or accommodation), it is worth asking how closely the different measures actually correlate with each other. Table 1 presents a correlation matrix of several of the indicators of foreign policy accommodation/convergence with China discussed above, including:

- National response to the PRC's 2008 crackdown in Tibet (Tibet). Here, strong support for the PRC's position is coded 2, moderate support is coded 1, and no support or criticism is coded 0.[67]

[66] Fuchs and Klann (2013).
[67] From Kastner (2016).

Table 1: Correlation matrix of foreign policy accommodation/convergence measures.

	Tibet	Secession	UN Ref	Market	Dalai Lama	UNGA all	UNGA hr
Tibet	1 ($N = 190$)						
Secession	0.48 ($N = 190$)	1 ($N = 190$)					
UN ref	0.26 ($N = 190$)	0.10 ($N = 190$)	1 ($N = 190$)				
Market	0.31 ($N = 190$)	0.29 ($N = 190$)	0.30 ($N = 190$)	1 ($N = 190$)			
Dalai Lama	–0.25 ($N = 190$)	–0.22 ($N = 190$)	0.11 ($N = 190$)	–0.10 ($N = 190$)	1 ($N = 190$)		
UNGA all	0.19 (N = 190)	0.19 ($N = 190$)	0.02 ($N = 190$)	0.08 ($N = 190$)	–0.11 ($N = 190$)	1 ($N = 190$)	
UNGA hr	0.42 ($N = 61$)	0.37 ($N = 61$)	0.09 ($N = 61$)	0.08 ($N = 61$)	–0.52 ($N = 61$)	0.59 ($N = 61$)	1 ($N = 190$)

Notes: shaded boxes indicate correlation that is highly significant ($p < 0.01$). N refers to the number of countries included in each correlation; N is smaller for the UNGA hr correlations because only countries from Africa and Latin America are included here.

- National response to the PRC's 2005 anti-secession law (Secession). Here, strong support for the law is coded 2, moderate support is coded 1, and no support or criticism is coded 0.[68]
- National response to Taiwan's 2008 UN referendum (UN Ref). Here, strong criticism is coded 2, moderate criticism is coded 1, and no criticism is coded 0.[69]
- Recognition of China's status as a market economy (Market). Here, early recognition (in 2004) is coded 2, recognition between 2005 and 2008 is coded 1, and no recognition as of 2009 is coded 0.[70]
- Dalai Lama visits that included meeting with government leaders (Dalai Lama). The total number of trips the Dalai Lama took to a country in which he met with government officials over the years 2002–2008.[71]
- UNGA voting similarity, 75th percentile (UNGA all). The 25% of countries that voted most closely with China in the UNGA in 2005 are coded 1, and other countries are coded 0.[72]
- UNGA voting similarity, country-specific human rights resolutions (UNGA hr). Closeness of voting with China on UNGA country-specific human rights resolutions in the 2005 UNGA; here, I use Flores-Macias and Kreps's data, which only extends to African and Latin American countries.[73]

In the table, the correlation coefficient for each combination of measures is shown. Large positive numbers suggest a strong positive relationship between the two measures (with 1 suggesting a perfect positive relationship), and large negative numbers suggest a strong

[68] From Kastner (2016).
[69] From Kastner (n.d.).
[70] From Kastner (2016).
[71] From Fuchs and Klann (2013).
[72] Based on the measure reported on in Struever (2016). Here, I use data from Gartzke, Erik. (n.d.). "The affinity of nations: Similarity of state voting positions in the UNGA," http://erikgartzke.com/datasets.html provides on affinity, based on the "s" score.
[73] From Flores-Macias and Kreps (2013).

negative relationship (with −1 suggesting a perfect negative relationship). For instance, the table shows a correlation coefficient of 0.48 for the Secession and Tibet measures, suggesting that there was a modestly positive relationship between supporting the anti-secession law and supporting PRC policies during the 2008 crackdown in Tibet. In other words, countries that supported the PRC on the anti-secession law tended, on balance, to support PRC actions in Tibet, though the relationship between the two measures is only moderately strong. The relationship between a country's position on the UN referendum (UN ref) and the anti-secession law, on the other hand, is much weaker (0.1) and not statistically significant.

The findings from this simple correlation exercise are somewhat encouraging, but also suggest that researchers approaching the issue of PRC influence abroad quantitatively need to use caution in interpreting findings. The good news is that the measures are generally correlated with each other in expected directions. For instance, the indicators of support for the PRC on specific events like the Tibet crackdown are positively correlated with UNGA affinity to China, and negatively correlated with Dalai Lama visits. But the coefficients of correlation are only significant about 60% of the time, and in many cases we see only weak correlation. As such, how analysts measure accommodation or convergence is likely to have a large effect on the conclusions they reach; in other words, these numbers suggest that researchers exploring, quantitatively, the relationship between China's foreign economic ties and PRC political influence abroad should be cautious in interpreting their findings. Interestingly, the measure that is most consistently correlated at reasonably strong levels with the other measures is support for the 2008 crackdown in Tibet, and this measure appears to have the weakest correlation with China's external economic ties of all the different indicators.[74]

4. Moving Forward

More generally, the correlations presented in Table 1 suggest that whether China's foreign economic ties translate into influence abroad

[74]Kastner (2016).

may not be the right question. The reality that the various indicators of support for Chinese interests do not correlate closely with each other suggests that the constellation of countries that align with China varies across different issue areas. For instance, many countries that openly supported China's passage of the anti-secession law were unwilling to offer strong support for PRC actions in Tibet in 2008. A country might be willing to support China on economic issues (such as recognition of market economy status), but less willing to support China on security or human rights issues. Future research should explore this variation in more detail by unpacking the conditions under which China's foreign economic ties might or might not translate into influence abroad. That is, instead of asking whether China's foreign economic ties translate into influence abroad, scholars should consider when they do.

Meanwhile, regardless of whether economic ties do translate into influence under particular conditions, there is certainly considerable variation in the degree to which countries across the globe are willing to adopt policies that accommodate different Chinese interests; and this variation demands explanation. Future research, I believe, should ideally be framed more broadly: rather than focusing on a specific mechanism through which influence might arise (in this case, economic dependence), scholars might focus instead on variation in the willingness of different countries to accommodate Chinese interests across different issue areas. Struever's[75] work is a promising start in this direction (although it focuses solely on alignment in UNGA voting); and Ross[76] offers an interesting blueprint for how this sort of work might be done qualitatively. But it would be interesting to explore whether it is possible to identify a set of factors — such as a country's economic ties with China, its relations with the US, its domestic political institutions, etc. — that help to explain accommodation across issue areas; and whether different factors might be more or less salient depending on the issue area in question.

[75]See Struever (2016).

[76]See Ross (2006).

https://doi.org/10.1142/9789811226588_0011

Chapter 11

China's Unbalanced Economic Partnership with Europe

Jonathan Holslag
jholslag@vub.ac.be

1. Introduction

Gaining access to foreign consumers, resources, and technology: it has been one of the most important objectives of China's economic statecraft. The European Union, with its hundreds of millions of rich consumers and many technological assets, has been a key target in this regard. The Chinese government has sought to preserve its access to the European market by promising a mutually beneficial partnership. Both sides, it asserted, were to benefit from trade. Equally so, the European Union resolved on opening the Chinese market more to European investors. If a level playing field could be created, European technologically advanced firms stood to benefit. This chapter takes stock of the development of the Sino-European economic partnership since 1995. That year was important for the partnership. Relations normalized after the Tiananmen Crisis, a political dialogue was established, China applied to become a member of the World Trade Organization, and the European Union issued an important strategy paper on the future of its ties with the People's Republic. 1995 was a milestone in the maturing of the Sino-European relations.

But how are we to evaluate success in the first place? Success was often said to be the degree to which China becomes a member of the international community, replaced its inward-looking economic policies with policies of openness, and adopted the liberal conventions on trade. It was about the socialization of China, its transformation into a market economy, its maturing as a responsible stakeholder, and its integration in the world community. It was stated, for example, that the imbalances in trade between Europe and China need not cause alarm and that they were "merely a parameter for adjustment in macroeconomic policy."[1] Read: they would be temporary and disappear as China made its economy more open. That, the reasoning went, would benefit both China and the world at large. Besides this constructivist approach, there were also functional liberalist expectations. China's growth would bring more trade and quicken globalization. Trade, this line of thought implies, is good for all, as it compels countries to be more efficient and to specialize. Both China and Europe would each develop their comparative advantages. The revealed comparative advantage (RCA) approach has been applied to China and Europe several times.[2] But if scholars initially assumed that China would develop comparative advantages in the processing industry, for instance, and Europe benefit from its advantages in services and high-end industry, more recent studies found such European leadership to be less likely. Recently, emphasis has been put on the

[1]Freytag, Andreas (2008). *That Chinese Juggernaut: Should Europe Really Worry About Its Trade Deficit with China?* (Brussels: ECIPE).

[2]Li, Li, Michael Dunford, and Godfrey Yeung (2007). "International trade and industrial dynamics: Geographical and structural dimensions of Chinese and Sino-EU merchandise trade," *Applied Geography*, 32(1): 130–142; Bushra, Riaz (2016). *Convergence or Divergence from Comparative Advantage A Comparison of China and the European Union* (Brussels: European Trade Study Group).

role of foreign direct investments, not only with the supposition that investment would allow China to grow, but also that Chinese investment would be good for Europe. John Farnell and Paul Irwin Crookes, for instance, conclude that "intractable political difficulties stand in the way of a fundamental alignment of economic interest," but that there might be more opportunities for Europa in attracting Chinese capital so as to develop its infrastructure.[3]

These are relevant findings, but for this chapter, we seek a more systematic approach to evaluate how much China and Europe have been able to gain from their partnership. Therefore, it commences with identifying the objectives in policy documents and, subsequently, to open the discussion about how trade relations and specialization through trade benefit economic growth, GDP growth to be more exact. The policy objectives will be identified primarily by using official documents and statements. The European Union has been issuing policy papers regarding China throughout and even if member states often had their own ideas, Commission documents are vetted by the capitals and must thus reflect the collective interest. These Commission documents will be combined with statements from heads of states, the European Council, which assembles the member states, the European Parliament, and the European Economic and Social Committee. This should result in a valid and representative sample of sources for the European Union. As regards China, there is less discussion about the actors that promulgate policy objectives. Even though provinces have an influence on foreign policy, statements of the supreme Communist Party leadership are key, and so are the views of the State Council and the subordinate ministries. The first policy document on Europe originates from 2003, but statements have been made continuously. To assess, as the second step, the impact of trade and eventual trade specialization on the GDP of the two sides, this chapter draws from a large body of trade data. The justification of this approach will follow in the second section. Onwards, the chapter reviews changes in regard to intellectual

[3]Farnell, John and Paul Irwin Crookes (2016). *The Politics of EU–China Economic Relations: An Uneasy Partnership* (London: Palgrave), p. 316.

property and global governance. For that it uses different policy papers as well as other open sources. Finally, attention is paid to the Belt and Road Initiative (BRI, also known as One Belt One Road or OBOR). Launched in 2013, the BRI was explained by the Chinese government as an opportunity for European countries, but to what extent has the BRI helped to rebalance trade with Europe? That question is thus addressed at the end of this chapter.

2. Policy Objectives

So, what were the policy objectives that both sides identified? What comes across from the very beginning is that politics and economics were interlinked, and even if this chapter in the first place discusses the economic dimension, it remains important also to take the other into consideration. In the nineties, the relations between China and the European Union were referred to as a secondary partnership, but along the way, the two sides became more interested in transforming it into a fully-fledged strategic partnership. China had several motivations. Displeased with the unipolar world order, it took interest in advancing the prospect of a multi-polar order, with China, the European Union, Russia, and others offsetting American predominance.[4] Also important was China's pursuit to undermine the position of Taiwan. After Paris signed a deal with Taiwan to supply fighter jets, in 1992, Beijing retaliated against several French companies and demanded the closure of the French consulate in Guangzhou. Meanwhile, it concluded new billion-euro trade deals with Germany, which, after Chinese pressure, cancelled a deal to supply warships to Taiwan. German Chancellor Kohl explained his pragmatism as follows: "It is left to every country to make its own decision on China. After all, we do compete with each other on international markets. Sometimes we get the contracts, sometimes our friends do. It looks as if we have been successful this time."[5] By using its growing

[4]Yan, Xuetong (1993). 当前我国外交面临的挑战和任务 [*Challenges and Tasks Currently Facing Our Diplomacy*] (Beijing: Tsinghua University).

[5]In Kohl's China Visit, Business Comes First. *Chicago Tribune*, 17 November 1993.

domestic market as a source of bargaining power, China not only succeeded in driving a wedge between European member states, but also between Europe and the United States. Especially after the Taiwan Missile Crisis of 1995 and 1996, which led to new tensions with Washington, Beijing increased its efforts to dissuade cooperation with Taiwan. Another part of China's political agenda was to use economic coercion to deflect human rights criticism. In 1997, France, close to signing a contract for the export of passenger planes to China, backtracked from supporting a critical resolution in the UN Human Right Commission, while China stated that it would sever relations in economic and trade areas with such sponsors as Denmark and the Netherlands.[6]

So, on the one hand, China seemed to be eager to welcome Europe as a counterweight against the United States, but on the other hand, it expected Europe to remain divided enough so as to be able to shape its political agenda. This was confirmed in China's seminal policy paper on the European Union in 2003. It was seminal because it was one of the first such policy papers ever released.[7] Striking in this document is the subtle emphasis on conditionality. At first glance, the note strikes a very conciliatory tone, proposing cooperation, common prosperity, reciprocity, and respect for differences.[8] It emphasizes the importance of the European Union in a context that evolves towards more pronounced multi-polarity and globalization.[9] Yet, it also makes it very clear that access to economic opportunities comes with political requirements. "China boasts a steady economic growth, a huge market and abundant labor force," it states, which could be an opportunity for European companies. But to be given access to this market, Europe is demanded to "strictly abide by the one-China principle," to prohibit political visits and not to

---

[6] Caving in to China, *International Herald Tribune*, 14 April 1997.

[7] Ministry of Foreign Affairs (2003). *China's Policy Paper on EU* (Beijing: Ministry of Foreign Affairs).

[8] *Ibid.*, part 2.

[9] *Ibid.*, part 1.

support Taiwan's participation in international organizations.[10] Moreover, member states must "not have any contact with the Tibetan government in exile," respect that China has a different attitude towards human rights, and remove the ban on arm sales that has been in place since the Tiananmen Crisis.[11] While at the time most European counterparts were flattered by the fact that China seemed to recognize the European Union as a strategic partner, the policy thus testifies of a rather rigid conditional approach, with Beijing showing itself ready to use economic power as a means for political coercion.

Coercion was not confined to political objectives. Equally important was to use the appeal of a growing market of over one billion consumers to preserve and improve China's access to European economic assets. In the nineties, China was in the midst of a transition from policies that prioritized attracting foreign investment to build modern industries, to a policy that focused on building Chinese national champions that were to keep more of the production in Chinese hands and the promotion of exports. The search for economic security was what shaped China's economic policies. Beijing desired to develop its own national strategic industries, technologies, and outlets to the global market. From that perspective, China expected the European Union to supply technology to make its national champions more competitive, especially because the American government imposed important constraints on technology transfer. China sought access to European knowhow through innovation partnerships with governments and by demanding European companies to transfer high-tech production to China and, eventually, to share technology via joint-ventures, in exchange for access to the domestic economy. By the late nineties, the European Union had become, by far, China's main supplier of knowhow. Also important for China was to gain access to the European consumer market. In that regard, it demanded the European Union to recognize China as a market economy, to steer clear of anti-dumping measures, and to compensate

[10] *Ibid.*, part 3.1.2.

[11] *Ibid.*, part 3.2.1.

China for possible losses as a result of European enlargement.[12] Furthermore, Europe was called on to be forthcoming in the negotiations that led to China's accession to the World Trade Organization in 2001.

As the European Union was conceived primarily as an economic project, economic objectives also prevailed in its approach to China. China's growth had to benefit European growth. While expectations could differ between the member states, their shared concerns were spelled out in different policy documents of the European institutions. While China showed itself aware of the attractiveness of its large market, the European Union also highlighted that it had "much to offer" to support China's transition.[13] Three objectives were key: the promotion of the liberalization of the Chinese economy, helping China to enter the liberal global trade system, and to achieve better market access for European goods and services. The European Commission called for: the reduction of Chinese import restrictions, the limitation of industrial policy support, developing standards along the lines of international organizations, non-discrimination in government procurement, creating better investment climate, financial liberalization, and respect for intellectual property rights.[14] As China's growth came to rely heavily on exports and investment, the European Union also prodded the Chinese government to rebalance its economic model towards domestic consumption.

Europe explained its policy as constructive engagement. Contrarily to China, there was no conditionality. The motivations of Europe's approach towards China were business-driven, the agenda was liberal, and the approach was based on inducement, dialogue, and socialization. The European Commission stated that: "There are signs that the increasing exposure of all areas of Chinese life to the outside

---

[12] *Ibid.*

[13] European Commission (1995). *A Long-Term Policy for China–Europe Relations* (Brussels: European Commission), p. 5. Endorsed by the Council for General Affairs on 4 December 1995.

[14] *Ibid.* Also: European Commission (1998). *Communication: Building a Comprehensive Partnership with China* (Brussels: European Commission).

world is having a deep impact through social change and increased mutual understanding."[15] A Commissioner put it thus: "The more China is exposed to Europe's way of thinking, the more it might adopt our norms, which is good for our economy."[16]

Even if Europe's expectations were predominantly commercial, it also entertained political ambitions. As the member states became more reluctant to engage China directly on those political matters, they remained on the agenda of the European institutions. The Communication of the European Commission of 1995 identified human rights as a lasting concern. The European Parliament clearly did not think this was going far enough. Its 1995 resolution called, among others, for military transparency, the rule of law, fair treatment of ethnic minorities, and to stop support for the military junta in Myanmar.[17] The European Economic and Social Committee urged more respect for civil society organizations, labor movements, and human rights.[18]

Let us proceed with the evaluation of the degree to which both sides were able to fulfill their objectives. The focus in this chapter is, as stated, on the economic objectives. Table 1 summarizes the main goals for both sides. The rationale underpinning the economic strategy of both sides was that trade would boost GDP growth. In order to stimulate trade, the two sides prioritized market access. As much as the European Union demanded China to reduce its trade barriers, China called on the European Union to steer clear of anti-dumping measures and other trade defensive instruments. A third goal was to increase investment incomes. If foreign investors were to be treated fairly, their success would also benefit the home market. The European Union suggested China to improve market access; while China on its

[15] European Commission (1995, p. 5).

[16] Mandelson, Peter (2004). "Intervention before the European Parliament," 12 April.

[17] European Parliament (1997). *Resolution on the Commission Communication* (Brussels: European Parliament).

[18] European Economic and Social Committee (1997). "Opinion on relations between the European Union and China," *Official Journal of the European Communities*, 26 May.

Table 1: Overview of economic objectives.

	European Union	China
Trade access	Reducing import barriers	Steer clear of anti-dumping and later obtaining market economy status (MES)
Investment climate	Equal treatment foreign and domestic companies	Make European investors contribute to the strengthening of Chinese companies and later access to the European market
IPR	Respect intellectual property rights	Technology transfer
Global governance	Socialize China with liberal economic standards; WTO compliance	Selective adoption of international rules

turn also became increasingly interested in investing in the European market. Intellectual property has been a fourth area of interest. As much as Beijing sought to tap into European knowhow to modernize its economy, the European Union called for a level-playing field and respect for intellectual property rights. Finally, both sides stated that global economic governance had to be strengthened. But while Europe initially expected China to sign up to the liberal economic conventions, Beijing's ambition was chiefly to gain more influence in international organizations so as to be able to shape the conventions.

3. Trade Gains

Both Europe and China have stressed that trade is good for growth. Since 1995, China has obtained and preserved full access to the European market. The European Commission did impose some anti-dumping measures, but these were limited to less than 2% of China's total exports. Meanwhile, Chinese trade barriers lowered, especially with regards to goods. Seeking to comply with the World Trade Organization's rules, import tariffs on goods came down significantly.

Yet, many non-tariff barriers remained in place, related to government procurement and services. The policy of sterilization of the Chinese central bank, which meant that it converted foreign currency earned through export into local currency and sent the foreign currency back overseas, by buying American treasury bonds, for example, kept the currency low and meant that European imports were disadvantaged compared to Chinese exports. So, concerning trade liberalization, the gains for China were much larger: China had almost unlimited access to European consumers, while many forms of government intervention continued on the other side.

But how exactly can we measure the impact of trade on both parties' growth? The most straightforward indicator in that regard is the current account, which includes incomes from trade in goods, trade in services, and foreign investment. A positive bilateral current account implies that the direct effect of the partnership is positive. There are also indirect effects. Countries affect each other's growth via third markets. One way to examine this is to review the evolution of China's and the European Union's market share in trade in goods and services. Another way is to consider the evolution of trade with third countries in absolute terms. A third indicator is trade specialization. Trade exposes companies to competition and forces them to specialize, which could be good for productivity. In an economic relationship, however, it is important to see which party is able to specialize in high-end industries, industries, in other words, that are more productive or more efficient in adding value to inputs.

A first observation is that the direct impact of trade has been positive for China's GDP and negative for the European Union. The direct impact of bilateral trade on GDP is calculated as follows: GDP = C + I + G + (X–M), or consumption + gross investment + government purchases + the trade or current account balance. Since 1995, bilateral trade has directly contributed 2.2% to China's GDP; and cost the European Union 0.6% of its GDP. In other words: the trade partnership has been bad for European growth. The interaction in third markets also was negative for Europe. In relative terms, Europe's market share compared to China has halved since 1995. But even in absolute terms, European exports have dropped. In low-skill goods, this started in 2008; in medium-skill goods, this started in 2011; and in high-end goods, exports have been shrinking since 2013. Again, the trade partnership proved harmful for European growth.

Specialization also was mostly beneficial for China. If it was Europe's initial idea that it would go on to lead in high-tech and China would become the assembling hub of the world, the data reveal a different evolution. In Table 2, specialization is measured as follows: for about 270 kinds of goods, it is first calculated how large their share is in the total exports of China and the European Union individually. For each of the 270 categories, we then deduct the share in Europe's exports from the share of China's exports and onwards take the absolute value of this result. Finally, we add up all these results. The larger this outcome, the more the specialization. 100 means complete specialization; 0 means no specialization and thus competition. Since 1995, the resulting index has remained constant around 52% (Table 2). This means significant competition, but no increase. This confirms other recent research.[19]

Beyond this aggregate index, however, we observe a decrease of specialization between 1995 and 2017 in low-end industries, like textile, footwear, toys, and steel. This is because their share in China's total exports decreased. The decrease in complementarity in these sectors was compensated mainly by increasing complementarity in high-end sectors, mostly as a result of China's rapid gains in phones, computers, and semiconductors, and the European Union's gains in pharmaceutical goods, cars, car engines, and aircraft (Table 2). Complementarity is thus not the consequence of the European Union exporting more advanced goods. Both China and the European Union exported more advanced goods, albeit in different sectors.

This all seems to confirm the argument of liberal optimists that trade leads to specialization, but there are two instant caveats. On the one hand, specialization has come to depend on fewer sectors. Consider again the complementarity index, which has been around

---

[19]Bushra, Riaz (2016).

Table 2: Trade complementarity between China and Europe for all categories of goods and the ten categories that contributed most to complementary in 2017 indicating which side dominated the sector.

	1995	2007	2008	2009	2010	2011	2012	2013	2014	2015	2016	2017
Total complementarity	52	51.4	50	51.9	52.3	51.6	52.9	54	52.7	53	51.3	51
China: Phones and parts	0.1	2.9	2.9	3.5	3.2	3.2	3.6	3.9	4.1	4.6	4.8	5
Europe: Cars	2.8	2.7	2.5	2.1	2.7	2.9	3.1	3.1	3.3	3.5	3.4	3.3
China: Computers	0.1	4.1	3.8	4.2	4.3	3.8	3.7	3.4	3.2	2.7	2.7	2.8
Europe: Pharma	0.9	2.7	2.5	3.3	3	2.8	2.8	2.8	3	3.5	3.5	3.4
Europe: Aircraft and parts	1.3	1.1	1.1	1.4	1.3	1.1	1.3	1.4	1.6	1.9	1.9	1.9
China: Televisions and screens	0.3	0.6	0.8	1.1	1.4	1.3	1.5	2.2	1.5	1.8	1.5	1.5
Europe: Petroleum oils	0.6	1.7	2.2	1.6	1.9	2.2	2.5	2.3	2.1	1.5	1.2	1.2
China: Toys. sporting goods	1.8	1.1	1.1	1	0.8	0.8	0.8	0.7	0.7	0.9	1	1
Europe: Engines and motors	0.5	0.7	0.7	0.9	0.8	0.8	0.8	0.8	0.9	0.9	0.9	0.7
China: Furniture and parts	0	0.6	0.7	0.8	0.8	0.8	1	0.9	0.8	0.9	0.9	0.9

52%. In 1995, the 10 goods with the largest degree of specialization contributed 30% to this; in 2015, the 10 goods with the largest degree of specialization contributed 40%. On the other hand, the question arises whether complementarity in these sectors will last. Cars, especially clean cars, medicines, engines, and aircraft are all priority sectors in China's industrial policy. The increase in complementarity in medicines (a part of the "pharma" category in Table 2) and engines has already started to stagnate.

Trade complementarity becomes even more problematic for the European Union when we consider different sets of data. Consider the European Union's market share compared to China, calculated by dividing Europe's exports by the sum of Chinese and European exports. Europe's share in total exports dropped from 85% in 1995 to 48% in 2016. Strikingly, Europe's market share decreased much faster in advanced goods than in raw materials. Coincidently, its export share was 85% in both sectors in 1995, but had dropped to 41% and 68% by 2016 (Figure 1). China and not the European Union thus gained in exports of advanced goods. Liberal optimists might retort at this point that such change does not matter. For a

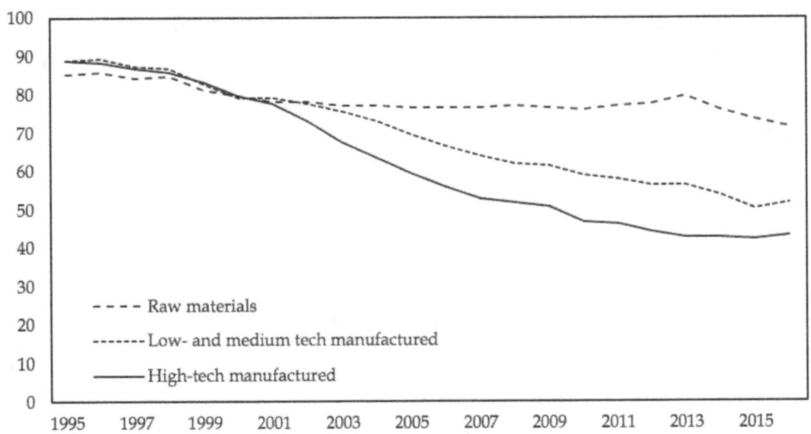

Figure 1: Market share of European exports (extra-EU) compared to Chinese exports (%).

Source: Calculations based on UNCTAD Stats.

populous country like China, it is only normal that it exports more and these relative figures might still mask that both the European Union and China gained in absolute terms.

A decreasing market share is not dramatic as long as both sides advance in absolute terms. This leads us to yet another set of data. At first glance, export data show that both parties indeed progressed. The European Union's exports increased by US$1,125 billion since 1995, China's by US$2,049 billion. So, both entities won. "Win–win," this could be called. Yet, absolute export data also reveal that the European Union's exports did not grow at all between 2008 and 2016, whereas Chinese exports expanded by about US$770 billion. After 2013, European exports even decreased 4 consecutive years. In advanced goods, European export growth has remained almost flat since 2008, whereas China's expanded by US$548 billion.

There is thus no reason to be carried away by the hope of trade specialization being beneficial to both. First, as we have seen, the complementarity index used for this chapter remains limited to about 52% and this result increasingly depends on a few industrial sectors in which China also seeks to forge ahead. Second, the European Union has lost market share in exports of advanced goods. Third, since 2008, European exports in advanced goods have also stagnated in absolute terms, and even shrank since 2013. Instead of speaking of "win–win," it is more appropriate to characterize the partnership as "stagnate-and-win."

This situation becomes more pronounced when we consider bilateral trade data. The share of advanced goods in Europe's total exports to China first increased, but since 2000 steadily dropped, from around 35% to around 25%. At the same time, the share of raw materials in its exports to China climbed. The share of high-tech in China's exports to the European Union increased from about 20% in 1995 to around 37%; while the share of exports of raw materials shrank from 16% to 6%. In bilateral trade, it is thus Europe specializing in raw materials and China specializing in advanced goods.

Optimists might retort at this point that many of China's exports are in fact produced by European companies that have invested there. To some extent, this might be true. Yet, data show that the share of so-called foreign-funded companies in Chinese exports has been declining since 2007. Between 1995 and 2007, the share of foreign-funded companies increased from 20% to 48%, but dropped again to 35% between 2007 and 2015. The share of exports produced by factories fully owned by foreign companies was only 26% in 2015. Foreign and more specifically European investment in Chinese manufacturing can thus not fully explain the surge in Chinese exports. In any case, incomes from investments in manufacturing in China transferred back to the European Union remained much smaller than the trade deficit. Between 2013 and 2006, average annual income transfers by European companies that invested in Chinese manufacturing was US$8.1 billion, on a total stock of investment of US$103 billion.

That leads us to another objective of the European Union: to secure fair treatment for European companies on the Chinese market. China's economy has opened, to be sure, but many restrictions for foreign investors remain in place. The most recent guidelines maintain many sectors as restricted or prohibited to European investors, whereas Chinese investments in Europe face almost no restrictions in the same clusters.[20] Table 3 summarizes this unbalanced situation. Besides the formal restrictions, there are many informal barriers for European companies. More than half of European companies in China claim to be treated unfavorably compared to domestic companies. More companies claim to feel less welcome compared to companies indicating that the investment climate has improved. Common complaints refer to the buy-local regulation, fiscal pressure to open important intellectual property to the Chinese government, limitations in the pharmaceutical sector, discriminatory national security legislation and discretionary enforcement of regulations.[21] In sum: progress on this issue was not satisfactory either.

---

[20]NDRC (2017). *The Catalogue of Industries for Guiding Foreign Investment* (Beijing: NDRC), 28 July.

[21]EUCCC (2017). *European Business in China: Business Confidence Survey* (Beijing: EUCCC), pp. 25–45.

Table 3: Investment regime in China and Europe.

	Chinese treatment of EU investors	EU treatment of Chinese investors
Exploration and exploitation of oil and natural gas	JV only	No restrictions, invited by Greece
Printing of publications	Minority only	No restrictions
Manufacturing of complete automobiles	Max 50%	No restrictions, acquisition of Volvo
Repair, design and manufacturing of ships	Minority only	No restrictions, activities in Greece
Aircraft design and production	Minority only	No restrictions
Production of satellite television broadcasting	Minority only	No restrictions, CCTV in multiple countries
Nuclear power stations	Minority only	No restriction, activities in UK
Construction and operation of power grids	Minority only	No restrictions, activities in Spain, Portugal, etc.
Construction and operation of network of railways	Minority only	No restriction, activities in Hungary
Construction and operation of civil airports	Minority only	No restrictions, invited by Greece
Telecommunication companies	Minority only	No restrictions, activities in most EU countries
Banks	Max 20%	No restrictions, activities in many EU countries
Insurance companies	Max 50%	No restrictions, activities in many EU countries

Source: MOFCOM and press.

A third objective has been to level the playing field in exchanging intellectual property rights (IPR). China has established new rules to enforce intellectual property rights domestically. As Chinese companies become more advanced, they too have an interest in IPR-enforcement. Yet, the bedrock of China's strategy remains independent innovation (自主创新). As the Ministry of Science and Technology put it: "China's industrialisation must complete two historical missions: to cultivate a strong independent innovation capacity and to become globally competitive with our own leading companies."[22] It calls China's dependency on foreign technology a fatal weakness and urges to avoid what it calls a technology dependence trap (技术依赖陷阱). This echoes what the State Council expressed earlier: "In key areas regarding the economy and security, core technologies cannot be bought. In the context of fierce international competition, we must therefore improve our ability for independent innovation, master core technologies in a number of areas, control key intellectual property rights and create a number of national industries that are globally competitive."[23] Key Chinese policy documents continue to refer to science and technology as an economic battlefield (经济战场) shaped by political forces.[24]

Policies resulting from these concerns remain highly ambivalent. On the one hand, there is emphasis on the importance of the market to incite competition between companies, to encourage innovation and to make efficiency gains. On the other hand, though, the State is expected to play a key role to support independent or indigenous innovation. This first of all involves financial support: through public procurement, favorable taxes, subsidies and favorable insurance rates.[25] Second, it pertains to standards: the Chinese government has to use the weight of the large domestic economy to advance global standards to chime with national industries. Third, the Chinese government has

---

[22] Ministry of Science and Technology (2007). 企业自主创新的几个政策性问题 [*Several Policy Issues for Corporate Independent Innovation*] (Beijing: MOST), Mat 31, §1.2.

[23] State Council (2006). 国家中长期科学和技术发展规划纲要 2006–2020 [*National Medium- and Long-term Science and Technology Development Plan 2006–2020*] (Beijing: State Council), § 1.1.

[24] State Council (2016). 国家创新驱动发展战略纲要印发 提出 2050 年建成世界科技创新强国, [*National Innovation-Driven Development Strategy Issued to Shape the World's Scientific and Technological Innovation by 2050*] (Beijing: State Council), 20 May.

[25] Ministry of Science and Technology (2007, 4.2).

to back companies in acquiring technology from abroad, so as to accelerate innovation. If anything characterizes China's most recent policies, it is a gradual shift from "stealing" IPR, through industrial espionage, to just buying IPR, but given the massive support of the government, there is clearly no intention of establishing a real market-based level-playing field. Chapter 3 clarifies China's most recent industrial innovation policies in more detail, but for now, we can conclude that this objective was not realized.

The fourth objective was to work together with China to strengthen global economic governance. International rules, standards and openness generally favor strong economies, but might, depending on good domestic governance, also benefit weaker economies as they open up. Europe's calculation has been that China would gain significantly by accessing European technology, capital and consumers, but that China also had to adjust to the international standards that guarantee a level-playing field for its own companies. Since the 1990s, China has become a member of almost all important international organizations. Most significant was its accession to the World Trade Organization (WTO) in 2001 and consequent commitment to liberalize trade in goods. But international economic governance, however, is about more than goods. Over 16 years after China's accession to the World Trade Organization, it appears that Europe has upheld its part of the promise, keeping its market open to China, but that China only selectively adopted the international rules that the European Union considers to be in its interest. To be sure, China has made progress, but it signs up to new rules only when it considers its economy strong enough. This approach is understandable, but for the European Union unilateral opening-up without reciprocity in terms of engagement in global rules could be harmful.

Let us consider the most important issues, starting with the General Agreement on Trade in Services (GATS). The agreement was signed in 1995, but China demanded airlines, shipping, communication, insurances, real estate and several others to be completely and partially exempted. In addition to the GATS, there is the Trade in Services Agreement (TiSA). Negotiations started in 2012 under the auspices of the World Trade Organization. China sought to join and was supported by the European Union. The United States refused to accept its application, however, fearing that China would undermine talks from inside.

Another example concerns government procurement. In 1996, the European Union ratified the Agreement on Government Procurement (GPA) under the auspices of the World Trade Organization. China was invited to join, became an observer in 2002 and waited to apply until 2007. During this period, European companies were thus not protected by international rules and they could thus not make any complaint against the privileges enjoyed by, for example, state-owned enterprises. Ever since China's formal request to join, progress has been slow, as it failed to make a proposal that also included the state-owned enterprises and generally also failed to give enough guarantees to improve market access. In 2017, the negotiations of China's accession extended into their 10th year. While progress already has been slow, China indicated that it intended to specify more exceptions. It is unclear why China needs to make any exceptions since it is basing its coverage on a positive list. In addition, the GPA requires each party to ensure that its laws, regulations and administrative procedures conform to the provisions of the Agreement. That means China needs to remove discriminating practices before its accession can be approved. Meanwhile, Chinese companies continue to benefit from unequal market access.

The European Union has also tried to engage China to sign up to the OECD framework for export credit. Export credit has been a crucial part of China's trade promotion. Chinese state banks have disbursed hundreds of billions of dollars' worth of trade credit and concessional loans, which gave an advantage to domestic exporters of goods and services, especially because China's credit was tied and it ignored rules regarding good governance. In a report, the OECD stated that environmental sustainability considerations are insufficiently considered by Chinese firms and that there is a clear lack of attention to debt sustainability in the proceedings of Chinese banks.[26]

[26]OECD Working Party on Export Credits and Credit Guarantees (2015). *Chinese Export Credit Policies and Programmes* (Paris: OECD), 16 March.

Moreover, the Chinese Exim Bank and the China Development Bank, two large state-owned banks, refused to cooperate with the OECD.

Three more initiatives in global governance could be considered. In 2014, the EU spearheaded negotiations for an agreement that removed barriers in environmental goods, the Environmental Goods Agreement (EGA). China joined the talks, but thwarted a breakthrough in 2016 by tabling additional demands and requesting very long phase-out terms for over one-third of all products on the list. Another example concerns intellectual property rights in the framework of the World Intellectual Property Organization (WIPO): European countries on average ratified 20 WIPO-administered treaties; China only 14. It has so far declined to ratify important agreements on false indications of the source of goods, on the recognition of industrial design, the protection of performers and trademark law. Finally, there is the expanded Information Technology Agreement (ITA-2). The aim of this agreement was to reduce trade barriers on more IT-solutions. China has refused many of the items proposed by the EU and the US.

The European Union has thus failed clearly to bend the economic partnership with China to its advantage. China has enjoyed over two decades of almost unlimited access to the European market, while the European Union has not delivered on four important long-term objectives: benefiting from China's economic growth through trade, obtaining fair treatment for investors, creating a level-playing field in intellectual property, and engaging China to sign up to international agreements and institutions that advance free and fair trade. The direct consequence has been a large sustained loss on the current account that has damaged European economic growth instead of benefited it. The question subsequently arises what explains Europe's acceptance of this unbalanced partnership and the absence of countermeasures, despite several complaints and critical policy documents, such as the communication of the European Commission of 2016?

4. The Belt and Road

Export credit, investment policy, global governance: all these aspects became even more relevant when China initiated the BRI in 2013.

The initial response of most member states was to give the project the benefit of the doubt, especially because many large companies and port cities were eager to join it. The first main Belt and Road governmental summit in 2017 was attended by minister-level representatives of 23 member states. When the Asia Infrastructure Investment Bank (AIIB), meant to finance some of the BRI projects, was founded, 20 member states joined it: some with the explanation that it would allow them to influence the BRI; others to benefit commercially. Slowly, however, it became clear that the BRI was largely a one-way road, with China preferring to handle projects bilaterally. Moreover, some large member states, including Germany and France, became concerned that the BRI was driving a wedge between the 28, for example by adding impetus to the 16 + 1 project, which includes several Central and Eastern European member states, or by coaxing Southern European countries into China's sphere of influence. Greece allowed COSCO Shipping to control the port of Piraeus; while a new right-populist government in Italy suggested that China's BRI funds were needed because other European countries did not invest enough.

At the time of concluding this chapter, it remained unclear to which extent Europe would change policy in response to the BRI. The European Commission did develop its own Connectivity Strategy, which sought to balance the BRI by means of European infrastructure projects, but it was not entirely clear whether the financial resources would be available and whether it would also attract the support of large European companies.[27] This was preceded already by a critical statement of the EU-ambassadors of 27 member states on the BRI.[28] Hungary refused to sign it and, overall, its repercussions for concrete policy were vague. A process was set in motion to allow member states to screen investments in strategic sectors, a measure with a clear eye

[27]European Commission (2018). *Connecting Europe and Asia: Building blocks for an EU Strategy* (Brussels: European Commission).

[28]Heide, Dana *et al.* (2018). "EU ambassadors band together against silk road," *Handelsblatt*, 17 April.

on China.[29] Several capitals put such screening procedure in place, but doubts remained about their intelligence capacity to track and monitor often complex and nebulous investment vehicles.

Then, in early 2019, came a Communication of the European Commission which called China a systemic competitor and vowed to deal with China's state capitalism more vigorously.[30] Internally, however, no consensus existed about how to proceed with it, so the execution was largely transferred to a new European Commission that was to be installed later in 2019. The association of German enterprises (BDI) issued a strong-worded paper on trade with China, with its concerns echoed by senior ministers. The French President, Emmanuel Macron, called on Europe to shake off its naivety and invited German Chancellor Angela Merkel and Commission President Juncker to assist in a part of Chinese President Xi Jinping's visit to France. Still, Mr. Juncker and Mrs. Merkel had barely left Paris when the French government announced that China would order a large number of Airbus aircraft, mostly to be built in China instead of Europe.

Hence, the BRI elicited growing distrust, but even 6 years after its initiation, it was unclear how European countries would respond and translate some intentions on paper into practice. Meanwhile, the impact of the BRI on trade became significant. Between 2013 and 2018, Chinese exports to BRI countries increased by US$75 billion; European exports to the same countries dropped by US$105 billion, despite the fact that China's low-wage advantage continued to decline throughout that period.

5. Conclusions

China and the European Union have sought to build a strategic partnership, but the policy objectives diverged from the start. Political

---

[29] Regulation (EU) 2019/452 of the European Parliament and of the Council establishing a framework for the screening of foreign direct investments into the Union, *Official Journal of the European Union,* 19 March.

[30] European Commission (2019). *EU–China: A Strategic Outlook* (Brussels: European Commission).

and economic objectives in this regard have always been interlinked and especially China has not refrained from using its economic assets to extract political concessions from Europe: often with success. It is important to consider this relation between politics and economics, yet the focus of this chapter is on the economic part of the partnership, and more specifically on the question whether bilateral trade has indeed resulted in the kind of specialization and opportunities that spurs growth. Reconstructing the policy agendas of the European Union and China, it became clear that both sides wanted economic openness, but that this too was interpreted quite differently and that China has again been much more successful than the European Union in realizing its objectives: China has managed to selectively open its economy, while it obtained almost full access to the European market.

This brought major consequences. If bilateral trade contributed to the growth of the Chinese economy, it damaged growth in the European Union. Liberal critics at this point might retort that such an observation is overly negative and testifies to zero-sum-thinking: China's growth is good for all. So, indeed, China's economy has grown, from a GDP of US$739 billion in 1995 to US$13,608 billion in 2018. This has created export opportunities for the European Union: exports to China grew from US$20 billion in 1995 to US$190 billion in 2018. Europe's economy grew much less, from US$9,600 billion to US$18,004 billion. Its GDP doubled. But despite this slower growth, Chinese exports to Europe expanded much more, from US$19 billion to US$355 billion. So, if European producers gained from the growing Chinese consumer market, they lost more of their European consumer market to Chinese producers. If the "plus" was smaller than the "minus," the final outcome remains a "minus." This deficit in trade in goods was also not compensated by the surpluses in trade in services and investment.

But how about indirect effects, Chinese growth, for example, spurring demand for European products in third markets? That was not the case either. Europe's market share dropped globally and as many of those third countries also run a deficit with China, leave alone some important raw materials producers, the effect of China on their GDP was negative and so was the indirect effect, via external demand, on Europe again negative. What about Chinese competition forcing European firms to innovate and to become more productive? That too is disputable. Many European firms have indeed been forced to invest more in innovation, but struggled to compete with their more economical or sustainable goods against much cheaper Chinese exports. So, many sectors shifted from producing whole goods, like ships built in European shipyards, to offering services, like the integration of systems of ships in Chinese shipyards, to the transfer of knowhow, like teaching Chinese shipyards to both build the ships and integrate the systems. The later activities could be considered an efficiency gain, because they lead to greater value-added per capita, but the overall impact on the economy might be negative, because even greater value-added per capita can be offset if less people are involved. The trade in both services and intellectual property also remains much smaller than the trade in goods and have therefore not offset Europe's losses in the latter cluster.

So, bilateral trade was positive for China and led to a specialization that strengthened the position of China. Europe has been unsuccessful in bending China's economic growth into an advantage for its own economy. Neither was the European Union successful in fulfilling its objectives with regard to creating a level playing field in intellectual property and investment, or to coax China deeper into the architecture of liberal economic governance. Hence, both from a functional interest-driven agenda and from a more constructivist desire to make Europe benefit from a more open and liberal Chinese economy, results are disappointing for Europe, whereas China's goal of selective opening-up, keeping pace with the strengthening of its own companies, was much more fruitful. At the time of finalizing this chapter, the tone in most European capitals towards China had toughened, with new initiatives being announced to respond to the BRI and China's growing investments in strategic sectors, but even then, 7 years after the official launching of the BRI, the extent to which they would be implemented, and redress the failure of previous policy, remained unclear.

https://doi.org/10.1142/9789811226588_0012

Chapter 12

The Political Economy of China's "Belt and Road Initiative"

Dalton Lin
dalton.lin@inta.gatech.edu

1. Introduction

China's "Belt and Road Initiative (BRI)," or "One Belt, One Road (OBOR)" project as it was initially known, is dubbed as the country's long-term national grand plan for the coming two to three decades. This chapter proposes a framework to understand the initiative's political economic objectives and to evaluate its progress. In a nutshell, the BRI is a novel combination and overseas extension of China's state capitalism model and developmental peace idea. This novel policy conception aims to help China transform its domestic economy and secure a benign international environment to continue its prosperity at home and raise its status in the world.

The Chinese government has intentionally kept the BRI's geographical scope, time frame, and plan details ambiguous to allow them maximal latitude in interpreting its success.[1] The ambiguity creates difficulties in assessing the BRI and somewhat comforts outside observers with the thought that the Chinese do not clearly understand the initiative either. However, the lack of details does not imply a lack of seriousness about it on the Chinese side. In China's 13th Five-Year Plan unveiled in March 2016, the OBOR occupies a whole chapter and is designated as the backbone project for achieving two other critical goals of the Chinese government — the development of China's west to alleviate development inequality between regions, and the construction of a new structure to deepen China's integration with the world.[2] Given that Chinese President Xi Jinping was personally involved in drafting the 13th Five-Year Plan, as well as the fact he initiated the BRI, it is easy to see how the failure to carry out the BRI might impinge on Xi's authority. As Christopher Johnson astutely contends, "it is safe to say that the Communist Party of China (CPC) Politburo assesses that failure to execute on the plan simply is not an option."[3]

The outside world's interest in understanding the BRI might have been dampened recently by China's economic slowdown, which courts doubts on China's ability to carry on with this ambitious project. However, this misses the point — the BRI is part of the

[1] So far, even in its official action plan "Vision and Actions on Jointly Building Silk Road Economic Belt and 21st-Century Maritime Silk Road (*Tuidong gongjian sichou zhilu jingjidai he 21 shiji haishang sichou zhilu de yuanjing yu xingdong*, 'Action Plan' hereafter)," China has never pinned down the exact routes for either the belt or the road. See the National Development and Reform Commission, Ministry of Foreign Affairs, and Ministry of Commerce, People's Republic of China, *Vision and Actions on Jointly Building Silk Road Economic Belt and 21st-Century Maritime Silk Road*, 28 March, 2015, http://en.ndrc.gov.cn/newsrelease/201503/t20150330_669367.html.

[2] *Zhonghua Renmin Gongheguo Guomin Jingji He Shehui Fazhan Di Shisan Ge Wunian Guihua Gangyao* [*The Thirteenth Five-Year Planning Guidelines for the National Economy and Social Development of the People's Republic of China*], 2016, http://www.gov.cn/xinwen/2016-03/17/content_5054992.htm.

[3] Christopher K. Johnson (2016). *President Xi Jinping's "Belt and Rod" Initiative: A Practical Assessment of the Chinese Communist Party's Roadmap for China's Global Resurgence* (Washington, DC: Center for Strategic and International Studies), p. 2, https://www.csis.org/analysis/president-xi-jinping%E2%80%99s-belt-and-road-initiative.

solution to the economic deceleration. Successful implementation of the BRI will help China out of the quagmire of industrial overcapacity and release resources for upgrading its economy. Meanwhile, it will provide an outlet for China's excess capital, right now still disproportionately deposited in dollar assets. In addition, carrying out the BRI will export China's wealth and expertise to recipient countries and increase Beijing's political influence, particularly over its immediate regions. Last but not least, the implementation of the BRI will give rise to a rudimentary structure of a China-centric regional (and maybe eventually international) order, where a US role is distinctively absent. By all accounts, the BRI merits a more systematic understanding.

2. BRI: The Fusion of China's Domestic and International Political Economic Models

The BRI is composed of two parts: a "Silk Road Economic Belt" that spans the Eurasia landmass from China to Europe, and a "Maritime Silk Road of the 21st Century" that leaves China's shores and passes the Indian Ocean, the Suez Canal, and the Mediterranean Sea before reaching Europe. Chinese President Xi Jinping first proposed the 'Silk Road Economic Belt' at Kazakhstan's Nazarbayev University in September 2013; a month later, he unveiled the "Maritime Silk Road" initiative in a speech to the Indonesian parliament.

The BRI was rolled out in the aftermath of the Great Recession in 2008–2012. The timing is no coincidence. Economic downturns in the advanced countries, together with significant decline in China's demographic dividend, meant China's old model of export-led growth, which was predominantly based on cheap labor, had run its course. In the wake of the Great Recession, there were no longer insatiable overseas markets to absorb goods that China was manufacturing, and continued reliance on low-skill manufacturing would mire China in the so-called middle-income trap.

Even before the Great Recession, Chinese leaders had realized the need for a new sustainable growth model that relied more on domestic consumption and innovation, instead of exports and excessive investment. The aftermath of the Great Recession pushed them to intensify efforts to transform China's economic structure. Meanwhile, the dramatic expansion of bank credit used to cushion the shock of Great Recession added to the imperative to deal with excess industrial capacity that was wasting resources and dragging down productivity.[4] On the other hand, troubles originating from the United States casted doubt on the Western model of economic modernization, which is more or less based on laissez-faire market.[5] In contrast, China weathered the crises relatively well, and this not only gave China great confidence in its own development model but also accentuated the "China model" to the developing world as an alternative path to modernity.[6]

[4] In the explanatory notes made to the Third Plenary Session of the 18th Communist Party of China (CPC) Central Committee in November 2013, Xi Jinping acknowledged that China's development is facing challenges, including that the development model is unbalanced and unsustainable, the capabilities of technological innovation remain to be enhanced, the industrial structure needs to be updated, and the rural–urban divide and income inequality remain significant. Xi proposed to overcome these issues through deepening China's economic reforms and emphasized the importance of top-level planning to ensure reforms are carried out systematically, comprehensively, and with coordination. Xi's emphasis on top-level planning reflects fixation on state capitalism, which is discussed in the following paragraphs. See Xi Jinping (2014). *The Governance of China*, Vol. I (Beijing, China: Foreign Language Press), pp. 78, 82–87.

[5] Scott Kennedy (2010). "The myth of the Beijing consensus," *Journal of Contemporary China*, 19(65): 461–477. The Great Recession specifically led to a pushback against the development model branded as the "Washington Consensus," which was popularized by the policies of US President Ronald Reagan and British Prime Minister Margret Thatcher and commonly adopted by the Bretton Woods institutions such as the IMF and the World Bank as conditions for receiving their developmental aid.

[6] The term "China model" is ill-defined though. For discussion of the "China model," see for instance Kennedy, "The myth of the Beijing consensus"; Ling Chen and Barry Naughton (201). "A dynamic china model: the co-evolution of economics and politics in China," *Journal of Contemporary China*, 26(103): 18–34. The aspect of the China model most relevant to the discussion here is what Chen and Naughton point out as the distinct feature of China's political economy: the presence of a strong intrusive government and the dominance of the political in the economy.

2.1. *China's Model of State Capitalism*

China's development model is most closely associated with the developmental state paradigm of its East Asian neighbors such as Japan, South Korea, and Taiwan. However, after its economy took off, China parted ways with these East Asian countries noticeably in its renewed emphasis on public ownership and state-owned enterprises' (SOEs) policy role. Some scholars have branded the Chinese system "state capitalism," which combines a predominantly market economy and nascent capital markets with a central role of SOEs.[7] Large Chinese SOEs created under command economy have survived the transition to market economy as Chinese political leaders needed them to buffer abrupt large-scale layoffs of workers for the sake of maintaining social stability.[8] Lately, the Chinese Party-state found that the largest among the SOEs are important tools for maintaining control of the economic commanding heights. Margaret Pearson calls these giant SOEs the "first-tier" of China's economic structure, which includes the companies in industries such as natural resources, finance, construction, electricity, and telecommunications.[9] The Party-state considers these first-tier firms as critical to China's economic and security interests and thus warranted state ownership and central control. Since the mid 2000s, the giant SOEs have been major beneficiaries of China's industrial policy and become national champions and the face of the country on the world stage due to their sheer size and resulting visibility. However, as Barry Naughton points out, they are national champions in the sense they have provided a stable supply of energy, power, transportation, communication services, and industrial materials that have enabled China's breath-taking economic growth, not that they are at the cutting edge of technological

---

[7]Barry Naughton and Kellee S. Tsai (eds.) (2015). *State Capitalism, Institutional Adaptation, and the Chinese Miracle* (New York: Cambridge University Press).

[8]The catchphrase was "grabbing the large and letting go the small [*zhuada fangxiao*]."

[9]Margaret M. Pearson (2015), "State-owned business and party-state regulation in China's modern political economy," in Barry Naughton and Kellee S. Tsai (eds.), *State Capitalism, Institutional Adaptation, and the Chinese Miracle*, pp. 31–34.

dynamism. They are also national champions in the sense that they can be commanded to work for the objectives the central government wants to achieve.[10]

In the BRI, China is extending this state capitalism *modus operandi* to its foreign economic policy. Giant SOEs controlled and managed directly by the central government, especially state-owned policy banks and contractors, are at the forefront of China's push for the BRI. On the one hand, they are enlisted to support the central government's policy initiatives in pursuit of national economic (structural transformation), energy (diversification of supplies), and security (responding to US rebalance to Asia) interests. On the other hand, their involvement acts as policy mechanisms that guide smaller SOEs as well as private firms to move their economic activities to BRI participating countries as the latter are cued by the business opportunities or financial support from those giant SOEs. It is noteworthy that China's giant construction and engineering SOEs have already shown they can be competitive internationally. Between 2000 and 2017, for instance, they won 19% of the total contract value awarded by the World Bank, more than any other country in the world. If we focus on civil works projects with unrestricted international competitive bidding only, China won 15.77% of the total World Bank contract value between 2012 and 2016, also second to none.[11] This enables China to "promise" an open bidding process for BRI projects that meet international standards while still being confident that Chinese contractors could continue their winning streak along BRI routes, finding outlets for their excess capacity to release resources at home for economic upgrading.[12]

[10]Barry Naughton (2015). "The transformation of the state sector: SASAC, the market economy, and the new national champions," in Barry Naughton and Kellee S. Tsai (eds.), *State Capitalism, Institutional Adaptation, and the Chinese Miracle*, pp. 63, 66.

[11]Calculated by the author. Data source: the World Bank's procurement contracts award summary, http://projects-beta.worldbank.org/en/projects-operations/products-and-services/brief/summary-and-detailed-borrower-procurement-reports.

[12]According to one study, though, Chinese-funded projects so far have been less transparent and less open to international participation, and as a result, 89% of

2.2. *China's Idea of Developmental Peace*

Seeking outlets for China's excess industrial capacity and capital through an international initiative, the BRI thus represents a new proactive approach in China's foreign economic policy and participation in international institutions. In the wake of the 1997 Asian Financial Crisis, China's help in establishing regional stabilizing mechanisms, such as the Chiang Mai Initiative, its ensuing charm offensive in Southeast Asian regional cooperation, and particularly its access to the World Trade Organization (WTO) intrigued commentators to debate whether a rising China would seek to (re)shape the existing international institutions to better fit its interests.[13] Earlier studies primarily found that China's international participation tended to be instrumentalist, passive, and even defensive.[14] China's embrace of multilateralism was seen as expedient to counter the emerging "China threat" theory and as opportunistic to maximize its influence in individual institutions. For example, China chose to focus on Association of Southeast Asian Nations (ASEAN) and the Shanghai Cooperation Organization (SCO) because the United States had not actively engaged in these institutions. Meanwhile, where US involvement was active, China chose to participate in large organizations such as the WTO, in which it was more difficult for the United States to dominate.[15] In its early years in the WTO, China also tended to shy

contractors participating in them are Chinese companies. Jonathan E. Hillman, "Statement before the US–China Economic and Security Review Commission for a hearing on 'China's Belt and Road Initiative: Five Years Later,'" 25 January 2018, https://www.csis.org/analysis/chinas-belt-and-road-initiative-five-years-later-0, accessed 21 May 2019.

[13]For a seminal work, see Alastair Iain Johnston (2003). "Is China a *status quo* power?" *International Security*, 27(4): 5–56; for latest discussion, see for example Scott L. Kastner, Margaret M. Pearson and Chad Rector (2016). "Invest, hold up, or accept? China in multilateral governance," *Security Studies*, 25(1): 142–179.

[14]The few exceptions typically involved issues on sovereignty and Taiwan.

[15]Hongying Wang (2000). "Multilateralism in Chinese foreign policy: the limits of socialization," *Asian Survey* 40(3): 475–491; Thomas G. Moore (2007). "Racing to integrate, or cooperating to compete? Liberal and realist interpretations of China's new multilateralism," in Guoguang Wu and Helen Landsdowne (eds.), *China Turns*

away from a central leadership and coalition-building role and behaved as a rule follower and system maintainer.[16]

A decade or so later, China's growing capability and maturity in international participation ushered in shifts in policy and postures. Take some of the aspects most relevant to the BRI, such as currency swaps and global governance, for example. On the front of international monetary relations, China began to sign a flurry of bilateral currency swap agreements (BSAs) in the aftermath of the Great Recession. Traditionally, the action was viewed only as a supply-side story: China pushed for BSAs because it had its eye on internationalizing the use of its currency, the *renminbi* (RMB). However, recent research has found that there were demand-side stories as well. BSAs helped insulate China's trading partners from international liquidity shocks resulting from a shortage of US dollars (whether for economic or political reasons) and reduce the need of currency switches via US dollars. Circumventing the need of currency conversion through the US dollar lowers the transaction costs of cross-border economic activities for China and its trading counterparts. Moreover, it reduces the political risk of some of China's partners that have bitter relations with Washington.[17] Compared to the time of the Asian Financial Crisis, China's currency policy after the Great Recession was no longer passively reacting to situations in a dollar-denominated system. Instead, it began proactively pushing for an RMB-denominated system, and because of China's large market and status as the number one trading country in the world, there were nascent demands for an RMB-denominated system as well.

to Multilateralism: Foreign Policy and Regional Security (London: Routledge), pp. 35–50; Michael Fullilove (2011). "China and the united nations: the stakeholder spectrum," *Washington Quarterly*, 34(3): 63–85.

[16]Margaret M. Pearson (2006). "China in Geneva: Lessons from China's early years in the World Trade Organization," in Alastair Iain Johnston and Robert S. Ross (eds.), *New Directions in the Study of China's Foreign Policy* (Stanford: Stanford UP), pp. 242–275.

[17]Steven Liao and Daniel McDowell (2015). "Redback rising: China's bilateral swap agreements and renminbi internationalization," *International Studies Quarterly* 59(3): 401–422; and also the author's interview with a researcher of a Chinese Foreign Ministry affiliated think tank on 7 May 2015.

Also, in the early 2010s, China was seen as making progress, albeit uneven, in its participation in global governance. China remained primarily defensive in the United Nations (UN), taking actions in the Security Council to prevent things that hurt its own and its allies' interests instead of promoting things that helped achieve its goals. Nevertheless, it became active in UN peacekeeping missions, and despite its reservation resulting from separatist issues it faced domestically, China did not outright oppose the idea of "responsibility to protect."[18] In a nutshell, even though the disconnection between China's weight and actions continued in the country's international participation in the late 2000s and early 2010s, China had become a far more active and effective player in the international system compared to what it was at the turn of the 21st century.

The BRI signifies an even more confident and capable China that is now projecting its domestic experience to propose its own concept of global governance. Chinese scholar Wang Xuejun argues that China is shifting from being a norm-complier to being a norm-maker in the international community and calls China's idea a model of "developmental peace (DP)."[19] Simply put, the DP model means peace (or stability) through development.[20] The DP model differs from the Western liberal model of political economy in that it prioritizes development (or social economic rights, such as employment) over political rights while subordinating political reforms to the emphasis on social stability. Given that the CPC has relied on delivering economic growth instead of acquiring the consent of the ruled for legitimacy, development has been key to maintain domestic stability (or peace) since Deng Xiaoping's reform and opening-up. In its practice, China internally suppresses civil society and allows no social forces independent of the CPC to exist. Externally, China emphasizes

[18]Fullilove, "China and the united nations: the stakeholder spectrum."

[19]Xuejun Wang (2017). "Developmental peace: understanding China's Africa policy in peace and security," in Chris Alden, Abiodun Alao, Zhang Chun, and Laura Barber (eds.), *China and Africa: Building Peace and Security Cooperation on the Continent* (Palgrave Macmillian), pp. 67–82.

[20]Wang, "Developmental Peace," p. 74.

absolute sovereignty to fend off perceived Western plots of regime change.[21] The practice has since pulled China out of poverty, avoided frequent large-scale domestic turmoil and instability seen in the pre-reform era, and critically, maintained the CPC in power. The DP model thus could be attractive to developing countries to China's west and south, especially those with authoritarian regimes, who share Beijing's concern about color revolutions incited by the West and need economic development to buy off constituencies and cling to power.

The BRI, therefore, represents a novel international political economic strategy that combines China's model of state capitalism and the idea of developmental peace. The infrastructure investment under BRI auspices enables China to continue and expand its development model of state capitalism beyond its borders. Beijing injects capital into BRI projects through its policy banks, and giant Chinese SOEs "win" and execute these infrastructure projects overseas. Moreover, Beijing hopes that roads, railways, power grids, industrial parks, and increased trade with China would help China's neighbors, particularly those authoritarian regimes, deliver economic growth.[22] The DP model expects that alleviating poverty and underdevelopment through economic growth can deal with the root causes of unrest and extremism in these neighboring countries, secure friendly (and often non-democratic) regimes, and stabilize China's periphery.[23] Besides, China-sponsored development will increase recipient countries' stakes in China's rise, much like domestic constituencies'

[21] Wang, "Developmental Peace," pp. 71–74.

[22] Nadáege Rolland (2017). "China's "Belt and Road Initiative": Underwhelming or game-changer?" *Washington Quarterly* 40(1): 127–142.

[23] To borrow Jessica Chen Weiss's term, China is trying to make "a world safe for (its and others') autocracy." See Jessica Chen Weiss (2019). "A world safe for autocracy? China's rise and the future of global politics," *Foreign Affairs* 98(4): 92–102. Xi Jinping puts the DP rationale succinctly as that "development holds the master key to solving all problems." See Xi Jinping (2017). *The Governance of China*, Vol. II (Beijing, China: Foreign Language Press), p. 559; "Development is the foundation of security, and security the precondition for development." Xi, *The Governance of China*, Vol. I, p. 393.

stakes in the CPC's rule.[24] From a bird's-eye view, the BRI is, therefore, China's reassuring strategy of "peaceful rise (or peaceful development)" in practice that aims to abate the "China threat" theory. In short, Beijing hopes the Chinese-led growth will contribute to a benign international environment, which will enable China to continue its domestic development and stability.[25] The BRI thus serves not only China's economic needs but also strategic interests.

As mentioned already, the DP model expects that the BRI exports could be attractive to non-democratic developing countries on China's periphery. However, the BRI has faced challenges that come from the DP model's blind spots. Chinese leaders might truly believe in the virtuous-cycle logic of the DP model. However, the BRI's primary drive is to upgrade China's economic structure and export China's excess industrial capacity and capital, which do not necessarily contribute to recipients' development and security. This is especially true when BRI investment leads primarily to importing Chinese equipment, construction materials, and workers and accumulating debts to China.[26] Research has found that China's policy banks often transferred money directly to Chinese contractors that implemented construction projects abroad.[27] Since recipient governments did not

---

[24]In Xi Jinping's words, China welcomes its Asian neighbors to "board China's train of development." Xi, *The Governance of China*, Vol. II, p. 543.

[25]Matt Ferchen (2016). "How new and crafty is China's 'new economic statecraft'?" Carnegie Endowment for International Peace Working Paper, http://carnegieendowment.org/files/How_New_and_How_Crafty_is_Chinas_New_Economic_Statecraft_CTC_Web_Version.rd2.pdf, accessed 14 May 2019. For a classical argument, see Bijian Zheng (2005). "China's peaceful rise," *Foreign Affairs* September/October 18–24. For a more recent discussion, see Barry Buzan (2014). "The logic and contradictions of 'peaceful rise/development' as China's grand strategy," *The Chinese Journal of International Politics* 7(4): 381–420.

[26]In several host countries, doubts have been raised about how much benefit they are really reaping in BRI contracts with China. For an example in Thailand, see Sasithorn Ongdee (2014). "How beneficial to Us is the railway deal with China?" *The Nation*, November 28, http://www.nationmultimedia.com/news/national/aec/30248747.

[27]Sebastian Horn, Carmen Reinhart, and Christoph Trebesch (2019). "China's overseas lending," Kiel Working Papers 2132, Kiel Institute for the World Economy, Kiel,

even receive the money, they had the minimal latitude to use the funding as they saw fit, for better or worse.

The BRI is also likely to lead to or exacerbate asymmetric economic relations between recipient countries and China and accrue political influence to the latter due to their sheer discrepancy in economic sizes. The combination of the DP model and China's state capitalism does not make the BRI an easy sell, either. Client countries heavily dependent on China for trade and indebted to Chinese policy banks or SOEs naturally conjecture that the financing and investment under BRI auspices are coordinated schemes of the Chinese state to rip them off their coveted resources. When Chinese leaders' belief in the DP model is met with unexpected local resentment or resistance, crushed expectations are likely the results for both sides. The consequences are not just hurt feelings but also real financial risks for Chinese investment. This might explain China's incentives to spearhead new multilateral institutions such as the Asian Infrastructure Investment Bank (AIIB) to control risks, manage disputes, and legitimize intervention when necessary.[28] China's push to internationalize the use of RMB and expand its security footprints overseas might also be viewed through the same prism of taking more control of risk and protection of overseas interests into its own hands.

3. State Capitalism Plus Developmental Peace in BRI Practice

The BRI's declared aim is to link China with its periphery through transportation and communications infrastructure to facilitate

---

Schleswig-Holstein, p. 9, https://www.ifw-kiel.de/publications/kiel-working-papers/chinas-overseas-lending-12820/.

[28] Gregory T. Chin (2015). "China's bold economic statecraft," *Current History* 114(773): 217–223. Horn, Reinhart, and Trebesch argue the aforementioned "closed-circle" lending, where loans to developing countries go from Chinese policy banks directly to Chinese contractors without leaving China's financial system, is another way to control the risk. See Horn, Reinhart, and Trebesch, "China's overseas lending," p. 9.

economic, monetary, political, and social exchanges.[29] More fundamentally, though, this project of infrastructure connectivity is designed to achieve a two-pronged objective with both domestic and international aims briefly mentioned above. To find evidence of the proposed state capitalism plus developmental peace framework for understanding the BRI, one needs to look into the initiative's practice.

3.1. *State Capitalism in the BRI*

Domestically, the Chinese government hopes to use the BRI implementation to provide "policy guidance" to lead China's surplus capital and excess industrial capacity into infrastructure and industrial investment in countries along BRI routes. The "policy guidance" is achieved through measures that reduce Chinese businesses' investment risk in BRI participating countries.[30] The risk facing Chinese firms involves both political and financial uncertainty. As a result, politically, Beijing uses the BRI to push for policy coordination mechanisms with participating countries and institutions of transnational economic activities, above all investment treaties, to reduce the political risk facing China's investment. Financially, Beijing seeks to alleviate Chinese businesses' financial risk by offering capital in the initial investment stage, through equity procurement by state-owned institutions such as the Silk Road Fund (SRF).[31] In the follow-on

---

[29] See "Action Plan."

[30] "Li Keqiang (2015). *Yong Zhongguo Zhuangbei he Guoji Channeng Hezuo Jieyuan Shijie* [Li Keqiang: Use Chinese Equipment and International Industrial Capacity Cooperation to Befriend the World]," *Xinhua*, 3 April, http://www.xinhuanet.com/politics/2015-04/03/c_1114869356.htm. accessed 20 May 2019.

[31] The SRF was established on 29 December 2014, with an initial capitalization of 10 billion US dollars from China's foreign exchange reserves (6.5 billion), the China Investment Corporation (1.5 billion), the China Exim Bank (1.5 billion), and the China Development Bank (0.5 billion). The China Exim Bank and the China Development Bank also make their own loans and have so far been the dominant creditors to BRI projects. See Wendy Wu and Frank Tang, (2017). "Xi's US$113b pledge 'more seed fund than credit pipeline'," *South China Morning Post*, 14 May,

investment phases, the Chinese government further facilitates financing through its policy banks, most importantly the China Development Bank and the Export–Import Bank of China, as well as newly-established international institutions, such as the Chinese-led AIIB. Such funding reduces Chinese firms' financial pressure, especially in infrastructure projects requiring a huge amount of capital and taking much longer time to see returns than other commercial investment types.

Take one of the BRI's flagship projects, the China–Pakistan Economic Corridor (CPEC), for example. After Pakistan agreed to accept SRF investment in CPEC power projects, SRF first acquired 15% equities of the China Three Gorges South Asia Investment Ltd (CTGSAIL), a subsidiary and investment arm of the state-owned China Three Gorges Corporation. Equipped with abundant capital, CTGSAIL then won the general contract to build the Karot Hydropower Project for Pakistan through a build-own-operate-transfer (BOOT) project financing model. Later, the China Machinery Engineering Corporation, a subsidiary of the state-owned China National Machinery Industry Corporation Ltd., won the construction contract with an engineering, procurement and construction (EPC) package. The project broke ground in December 2015 and is slated to complete in 2020. After completion, CTGSAIL will operate the hydropower plants for 30 years before transferring the ownership over to the Pakistan government.

The Karot Hydropower Project is a quintessential example of China's state capitalism operating overseas through the BRI. With SRF's investment, Chinese state-owned contractors (in this case, the China Three Gorges Corporation) have had a government-backed funding source to muster a large amount of capital to bid for infrastructure projects. In the follow-on stages of construction, Chinese policy banks' loans help lessen the financial pressure. In fact, with the backing of the SRF and China's policy banks, Chinese SOEs can

---

http://www.scmp.com/news/china/diplomacy-defence/article/2094311/xis-us113b-pledge-more-seed-fund-credit-pipeline.

move from offering packages of EPC to those of financing plus EPC (FEPC).[32]

Given that most developing countries face a shortage of funding to satisfy their infrastructure needs, China's state capitalism that enables the FEPC bidding package enhances Chinese SOEs' competitiveness and increases China's opportunity of exporting excess capacity and capital through overseas contracts. CTGSAIL's President bluntly stated that the company has a strong sense of mission to serve China's national strategy. The company teams up with China's hydropower design, engineering, and construction entities to participate in the international market. In CTGSAIL President's words, they "adopt 100% Chinese standards, use 100% China-made products and materials, and spur a large amount of China's superior industrial capacity to 'go out' together."[33] By building outlets for excess domestic industrial capacity, Beijing hopes that the BRI will eventually facilitate China's economic upgrading by releasing resources from industries with excess capacity and making them available for those emerging and thereby creating higher added value.[34] In Xi Jinping's words, the BRI will help transform the Chinese economy toward one that has an equal footing between "bringing in [foreign capital

---

[32]Yuewen Fu (2015). "*Cong zongchengbao xiang 'zongchengbao + tourongzi' fangxiang fazhan* [Moving from General Contract to 'General Contract + Investment and Financing']," *China Energy News*, 27 April, http://paper.people.com.cn/zgnyb/html/2015-04/27/content_1559250.htm, accessed 18 May 2019.

[33]In CTGSAIL President Shaofeng Wang's own words. See Zhimin Wang (2015). "*Mubiao: Mei 6 yi qiaodong 100 yi guoji zijin: zhongguo sanxia nanya touzi youxian gongsi wangshaofeng dongshizhang tan ziben guojihua* [Objective: Every 600 Million Spur 10 Billion International Capital: CTGSAIL President Shaofeng Wang Discussing Capital Internationalization]," *Guoji Gongcheng yu Laowu* [*International Project Contracting & Labor Service*] 7: 27–31.

[34]For example, industries that fit together into China's concept of "strategic emerging industries" are sectors that Beijing would like to offer policy preferences. See Barry Naughton (2011). "China's economic policy today: the new state activism," *Eurasian Geography and Economics*, 52(3): 324–325.

and know-how]" and "[domestic excess capital and overcapacity] going out."[35]

3.2. *The BRI and Developmental Peace*

Internationally, Beijing hopes the BRI implementation will reduce the country's reliance on US-led multilateral institutions. The timing and objectives of China's BRI are similar to Japan's past experience of turning to outward investment to deal with excess industrial capacity and foreign exchange reserves accumulated through a long period of astonishing economic growth. The key difference between China's strategy and Japan's is that the latter tried to achieve these goals within the US-led system of global governance, while the former does so without. For instance, though Japan has played a dominant role in the Asian Development Bank (ADB), the ADB was, in the first place, promulgated and endorsed by the United States, and Washington has maintained a voting power comparable with Tokyo's in the ADB.[36] In contrast, China has chosen to establish its own international development financing institutions, such as the AIIB, and the United States has opted to stay outside it.

Japan's approach had the advantage of alleviating other countries' suspicion of Tokyo's political intentions behind its wealth and tempering their incentives to obstruct Japan's efforts. However, the approach subjected Japan to the ultimate pressure of the United States. For instance, when Washington perceived Tokyo's growing economic strength as a threat, Japan was forced to sign the 1985 Plaza Accord and sharply appreciated the Japanese yen, which eventually contributed to Japan's asset bubble and trapped the country in a

---

[35] Xi Jinping (2014). "Jiakuai Tuijin Sichou Zhilu Jingjidai He 21 Shiji Haishang Sichou Zhilu Jianshe [Xi Jinping: Speeding Up the Advance of the Silk Road Economic Belt and Maritime Silk Road of the 21st Century Construction]," *Xinhua Net*, 6 November, http://news.xinhuanet.com/politics/2014-11/06/c_1113146840.htm.

[36] As of 31 December, 2016, Japan and the United States hold the same voting power in the ADB at 12.784% each. See "Members, Capital Stock, and Voting Power," *Annual Report 2016*, the Asian Development Bank.

lost decade."[37] Ronald McKinnon and Kenichi Ohno state bluntly that the yen's appreciation was seen as a political alternative to American protectionism, that is, the withdrawal of US commitment to open trade in the American-led international system.[38] In 1997, when the United States opposed Japan's proposal of an Asian Monetary Fund (AMF) due to worries that the AMF might become a regional rival to the US-led International Monetary Fund (IMF), Japan simply walked back the idea. This was despite the fact that going with the IMF structure amid the Asian Financial Crisis might not protect Japan's national interest due to Tokyo's lack of institutional leverage in the IMF.[39] US constraints were further revealed in the fact that a substitute standby financial mechanism in Asia gained Japan's back only after US objection softened sufficiently.[40]

In contrast, China has chosen to create its own structure and deal with the issues of redundancy outside the existing international governance system.[41] Beijing wants to channel its excess capital and

---

[37] "China Seeks to Learn from Mistakes of 1985 Plaza Accord," *Japan Times*, 9 September 2006, https://www.japantimes.co.jp/news/2006/09/09/business/china-seeks-to-learn-from-mistakes-of-1985-plaza-accord/#.WmoaB5M-fUI; Ronald McKinnon and Kenichi Ohno (1997). *Dollar and Yen* (Cambridge, MA: MIT Press).

[38] McKinnon and Ohno, "Dollar and Yen," p. 177.

[39] Phillip Y. Lipscy (2003). "Japan's Asian monetary fund proposal," *Stanford Journal of East Asian Affairs*, 3(1): 96. According to Lipscy, then Deputy Treasury Secretary Larry Summers called his Japanese counterpart Eisuke Sakakibara to lodge complaints and strong disapproval. Summers criticized the plan for excluding the United States and allowing autonomy outside the IMF. However, Sakakibara believed the US objection was driven by Washington's perception that "Japan was posing a challenge to American hegemony in Asia through the AMF."

[40] Michael Richardson and International Herald Tribune (1999). "Japan endorses standby fund to stabilize Southeast Asia," *New York Times*, 27 November http://www.nytimes.com/1999/11/27/news/japan-endorses-standby-fund-to-stabilize-southeast-asia.html.

[41] Evan A. Feigenbaum, in contrast, argues that China is adopting a dual strategy of becoming more active in the existing US-led system and at the same time endorsing parallel structures to hedge against the possibility that the US-led order fails to accommodate China's interests. See Evan A. Feigenbaum (2017). "China and the world: dealing with a reluctant power," *Foreign Affairs*, 96(1): 36. However, China's

industrial capacity through a new framework of international governance under the aegis of the BRI. The framework is composed of four emerging pillars. The first is a China-centric international economic integration architecture that includes China's numerous extant and planned bilateral and multilateral free trade agreements (FTAs). Examples include the upgraded versions of the China–Pakistan and China–ASEAN FTAs, as well as the Regional Comprehensive Economic Partnership (RCEP) signed in August 2020.[42] The second pillar is Chinese-led international development financing mechanisms, such as the AIIB, SRF, BRICS New Development Bank,[43] and the proposed SCO financing institutions. The third is an international monetary system where the RMB will eventually play the role as a primary reserve and trading currency in the China-centric international structure. China has concluded BSAs with various countries, including global financial centers like Britain and neighbors like Singapore and Malaysia. Beijing has also gradually expanded the global network of RMB clearing banks to promote the use of RMB in cross-border trade and investment. China's aim is to first regionalize and ultimately internationalize the use of its currency.[44]

The fourth pillar is Chinese-proposed security arrangements. China has not yet explicitly made security arrangements a part of its BRI designs. However, a security discourse is necessary, and the reason is two-fold. First, in view of the complicated security environments that the BRI faces in various countries and regions, security coordination mechanisms with participating countries are inevitable. Only with assured security could China enjoy

---

efforts to deal with its excessive capacity and capital predominantly go through its own newly established system. It is noteworthy that involvement in the US-led system is also a gateway to acquiring credibility for some of the elements of China's own structure, such as establishing people's confidence in the value of the renminbi and viability of the AIIB's loans.

[42] Countries negotiating the RCEP include the ASEAN states, Australia, China, India, Japan, South Korea, and New Zealand.

[43] "BRICS" stands for Brazil, Russia, India, China, and South Africa.

[44] Jing Li (2011). "*Renminbi guojihua: guoji fanying ji pingjia* [RMB Internationalization: International Reactions and Evaluation]," *Jingjixue dongtai* [*Economic Perspectives*] 12(6): 48–53.

reasonable returns on BRI infrastructure investments, which in turn are critical to establish the BRI's credibility (both domestically and internationally) and attract sustained engagement of other parties. Among China's various proposals for closer security cooperation, at least three — the SCO Regional Anti-Terrorist Structure (RATS), the China–ASEAN Defense Ministers' Special Meetings, and the Conference on Interaction and Confidence-Building Measures in Asia (CICA) — are situated in the regions directly relevant to the BRI.

Second, to abate other countries' suspicions about China's intention behind inventing the BRI and going without the existing international institutions, Beijing needs a security discourse to counter the threat perception of other states. Chinese leaders have long worried that such a threat perception might drive other countries to align together to abort its rise. The worries had motivated Beijing to carefully craft a slogan of "peaceful rise" that aimed to alleviate the rest of the world's concerns about China's arbitrary use of its growing power. Later, the slogan was revised to "peaceful development" because Beijing was afraid that the word "rise" might still sound too threatening.

The concept of "peaceful development" aims to make countries in the world treat China's rise as their opportunities instead of a threat. Xi Jinping contended in an internal study session of the CPC Politburo that "whether or not the peaceful development is doable depends, to a great extent, on whether we can transform the world's opportunities into China's opportunities and transform China's opportunities into the world's opportunities."[45] The BRI plays an important role in the latter task. Wang Yi, China's Foreign Minister, thus claimed that the BRI aimed to achieve common development and common prosperity along its routes and to ensure that China's economic growth provided the world with a "China opportunity."[46]

---

[45]Xi, *The Governance of China*, p. 248.

[46]Yi Wang (2014). "*Zhongguo tese daguo waijiao 2014 fengsheng shuiqi* [Major Country Diplomacy with Chinese Characteristics Gaining Traction in 2014],"

The BRI's strategic role in the concept of "peaceful development" can be inferred from Xi's explication of his "Asian security concepts" in a speech to the CICA in 2014. The "Asian security concepts" are composed of four elements — "common, comprehensive, cooperative, and sustainable" security.[47] According to Xi, common security means no country or groups of countries should pursue security at the expense of others' security, rejecting the value of traditional alliance systems. Common security also means that no one country should monopolize regional security affairs and that all countries' sovereignty, territorial integrity, and choice of political regime types (or in Xi's words, social institutions and development paths) should be respected. Cooperative security is a related concept, which emphasizes dialogues and opposes the use or the threat of force for any one country's self-interest. Both concepts are not only thinly veiled criticisms of US track records of military intervention around the world but also China's vow to live up to its words of pursuing no domination.[48]

Most relevant to the BRI are the concepts of comprehensive and sustainable security. Comprehensive security means considering and dealing with traditional and non-traditional security issues holistically. Sustainable security means, from China's perspective, development is the master key to solve all regional security issues, be they traditional or non-traditional. The concepts of comprehensive security and sustainable security combined are essentially the explication of China's developmental peace idea. With its proclaimed goals of common development and common prosperity, the BRI is thus a lever to put China's developmental peace idea into

Liaowang [*Outlook*], 31 December, http://www.gov.cn/xinwen/2014-12/31/content_2799043.htm. accessed 11 January 2020.

[47] Shuquan Tang and Hong Chang (2014). "*Xi Jinping zai yaxin fenghui zuo zhuzhi fayan* (*quanwen*) [Xi Jinping Giving Keynote Speech at CICA Summit (Full Text)]," *People's Net*, 21 May, http://world.people.com.cn/n/2014/0521/c1002-25046183.html, accessed 11 January 2020.

[48] *Ibid.*

practice, fulfill its rhetoric of peaceful development, and counter a "China threat" theory.

Opting to work outside the existing system, China bears the great risk and faces significant obstacles associated with untested new international structures. The risk includes political uncertainty in coordinating policies with participating states and evaluating political dynamics in host countries when dialogue mechanisms and area-studies expertise mostly remain to be built[49]; commercial uncertainty in securing returns when the investment is made in less institutionalized environments and financing is provided to opaque regimes; and security uncertainty in protecting investment projects in volatile foreign regions where collective security arrangements are largely absent. Besides, since money often buys influence, China has to face the suspicion of other states about its political intention and the obstruction of the United States and Russia in their traditional geopolitical turfs.[50] Though China faces steep challenges in the early stages of its efforts, the strategy is likely a result of sober calculation of tradeoffs: were the BRI to be successful, the United States will have a hard time constraining China's "peaceful rise," that is, continuing economic prosperity domestically and increasing political influence internationally.[51]

---

[49]Ferchen, "How new and crafty is China's 'new economic statecraft'?" pp. 11–12.

[50]One way that China deals with such suspicion and obstruction is to actively participate in the existing US-led system while promoting its BRI. See Feigenbaum, "China and the World: Dealing with a Reluctant Power." Feigenbaum considers this as a hedging strategy. However, this chapter takes an instrumentalist view of China's activism in the current US-led system. Participation in the existing order is a primary way for China to maintain a benign and status-quo image to alleviate others' threat perception. See Wang, "Multilateralism in Chinese Foreign Policy: The Limits of Socialization," pp. 475–491, and Allen Carlson (2006). "More than just saying no: China's evolving approach to sovereignty and intervention since Tiananmen," in Alastair Iain Johnston and Robert S. Ross (eds.), *New Directions in the Study of China's Foreign Policy* (Stanford: Stanford University Press), pp. 217–241.

[51] Xeutong Yan, dean of the Institute of Modern International Relations at Tsinghua University and an influential realist thinker in China, stated bluntly that the competition between China and the United States is about writing rules and that China needs

4. A Framework for Assessing the BRI's Progress

The BRI is a novel combination and extension of China's state capitalism paradigm and developmental peace idea overseas to achieve the two-pronged objective laid out above. To evaluate what progress has been made in the BRI, we need to look into the BRI's substantive details to understand what goals the initiative has achieved. A framework that breaks down different aspects of the BRI is therefore needed.

As mentioned earlier, because of its expansive geographical coverage and massive envisaged investment, the BRI involves significant economic, political, and security risks. The success of the project will depend on whether China can effectively manage these uncertainties. As a result, having existing bilateral or multilateral cooperative mechanisms with China and locating in proximity to the Chinese mainland are two dimensions that identify the BRI's key zones, which will be critical to the fate of the initiative.[52] The reason is straightforward. Existing mechanisms of cooperation make it easier to coordinate policies and manage risks in these places. Meanwhile, the short distance between China and these countries/regions ensures these places are within China's power projection diameter, where China has more coercive leverage to bring to bear when cooperation is not forthcoming and situations turn desperate.

Xi Jinping's instructions to Chinese officials concerning the BRI implementation vindicate the abovementioned two dimensions for identifying key BRI nodes. In the Eighth Meeting of the Central

---

to "buy" friends because it takes the support of the majority of countries to make rules. See "China Needs to 'Purchase' Friendships, Scholar Says," *Nikkei Asian Review*, 2 March 2015, https://asia.nikkei.com/NAR/Articles/China-needs-to-purchase-friendships-scholar-says, accessed 20 May 2019.

[52] This chapter considers "cooperative mechanisms" as those that require China and other participating countries to adjust their policies to achieve cooperative goals. In other words, it excludes institutions where China lacks institutional leverages or which function basically as talking shops. Examples of cooperative mechanisms include China's bilateral or multilateral FTAs, investment treaties, currency swap arrangements, the SCO, and the AIIB.

Leading Group for Financial and Economic Affairs on November 4, 2014, Xi Jinping said that the BRI should have "early harvest" programs and areas. He stressed that the BRI plan should particularly focus on implementation and follow the principles of "going from the easy to the hard, from the near to the far, from a point to a line, and from a line to an area." [53] The former two conditions are more likely to be satisfied in places close to China and having existing institutionalized cooperative mechanisms with Beijing. These places, in turn, are more likely to help achieve the latter two goals of Xi's instruction, serving as the starting points to be connected into lines and areas of the BRI.

If we group countries on the BRI's potential routes by these two dimensions, as exemplified in Table 1, SCO members, Mongolia, Pakistan, India, and the ten ASEAN countries stand out as key nodes in the early implementation of the BRI and serve as critical windows to watch its progress.

Taking a step further, we need to break down the BRI into different aspects inside each country/region to get well-defined goals and understand the risks involved. To fulfill the BRI's mission of digesting China's excess industrial capacity and capital through an international structure composed of the four pillars mentioned above, China needs to promote trade and investment liberalization and development cooperation with participating countries as it hopes that increased trade, investment, and financing will encourage their monetary integration with China. Furthermore, policy coordination and security cooperation with BRI host countries are also needed to manage risks. Therefore, using these five aspects — trade and investment liberalization, development cooperation, monetary integration, policy coordination, and security cooperation — as threads, we can examine the BRI's prospects and progress in individual countries or regions — the strengths, weaknesses, opportunities, and threats that each country's

[53] "Xi Jinping (2014). "*Jiakuai Tuijin Sichou Zhilu Jingjidai He 21 Shiji Haishang Sichou Zhilu Jianshe* [Xi Jinping: Speeding Up the Advance of the Silk Road Economic Belt and Maritime Silk Road of the 21st Century Construction]," *People's Daily*, 7 November, http://cpc.people.com.cn/n/2014/1107/c64094-25990858.html.

Table 1: Potential BRI countries by their proximity to and cooperative relations with China (examples, not complete lists).

	With bilateral/multilateral cooperation mechanisms	Without bilateral/ multilateral cooperation mechanisms
Neighboring countries	ASEAN countries, SCO members, Mongolia, Pakistan, India	Bhutan, Nepal, Afghanistan
Non-neighboring countries	Belarus, Sri Lanka, Iran, Turkey, Saudi Arabia, Qatar, Oman, United Arab Emirates	Maldives, Bangladesh, Kuwait, Bahrain

or region's internal and external circumstances bring to bear on China. Analyzing these five aspects also tells us how the BRI will impact China's overall relations with these places. In what follows, we apply this framework to one critical node of the BRI — Central Asia — to illustrate its work.

5. An Exemplary Case: The BRI and China–Central Asia Relations

Unlike relations with its East Asian neighbors, China has no historical baggage of territorial aggression against contemporary Central Asian states. Moreover, China and Central Asian countries share a common political understanding that is based, above all, on a commitment to a multipolar world (instead of US domination) and the principle of respecting an individual country's choice of domestic political systems (in lieu of the West's push for democratization). Such a common political understanding makes Central Asia an ideal region to promulgate China's DP model and abates some political headwinds against the promotion of the BRI. In addition, China worries that an unstable Central Asia would become sanctuaries of the so-called "three evil forces" of terrorism, separatism, and extremism in Xinjiang, making the region a prime place to experiment with the DP idea.

The SCO has been up and running for almost two decades, providing a ready-made framework for cooperation between China and its

Central Asian members that could be harnessed to advance the BRI. That said, the SCO's cooperation heretofore has focused predominantly on security issues (from confidence-building measures in its early days to anti-terrorism lately), while economic cooperation among member countries has made very limited progress in the past. China's economic interests in Central Asia are not significant — the volume of bilateral trade is low (US$41.7 billion in 2018),[54] and Central Asian states are lukewarm at best about receiving and using RMB in their international payments. Last but not least, Russia still harbors misgivings about the BRI's inroad into its backyard. In the following, we look into the five aspects identified in the previous section to examine in detail the BRI's prospects and progress in Central Asia.

5.1. *Economic and Trade Liberalization*

The fundamental hurdle to China's economic integration with Central Asia is the lack of an organic force for the process. The BRI hopes to integrate China's northwest (especially Xinjiang) with Central Asia, but the two regions' economies do not complement each other — both are sparsely populated, facing the shortage of financial and human capital.[55] This might be one of the reasons why China so far has no FTA with individual Central Asian countries. In fact, Kazakhstan, Kyrgyzstan, and Tajikistan all have their eye on the Russian-led Eurasian Economic Union (EEU): Kazakhstan and Kyrgyzstan are already EEU members, and Tajikistan has expressed its intent to join the entity. [56] Reflecting the fact described earlier that Chinese giant SOEs are not national champions based on cutting-edge technological dynamism, Central Asian countries consider China

---

[54]Data from the National Bureau of Statistics of China.

[55]Shu Yang (2014). "*Sichou zhi lu jingjidai de xianzhuang yu tupo* [The Current Status and Breakthroughs of the 'Silk Road Economic Belt']," in Chongyang Institute for Financial Studies of Renmin University of China (eds.), *Ouya shidai: sichou zhi lu jingjidai yanjiu lanpishu 2014–2015* [*The Eurasian Era: Blue Book of Silk Road Economic Study 2014–2015*] (Beijing: China Economic Publishing House), p. 59.

[56]Though China has signed an agreement on trade and economic cooperation with the EEU in May 2018.

less as a source of advanced technology and know-how and more as a guzzler of raw materials. In addition, their citizens worry that Chinese immigrants might flood in as a result of economic integration proposed by the BRI.[57]

China hopes the BRI would help develop its northwestern region. However, the success of the "Silk Road Economic Belt" might ironically depend on a more developed northwestern China, and this creates a difficult chicken-and-egg problem. Arguably, a more feasible short-term objective for the BRI may be to connect Central Asia with China's coastal areas through China's northwest, to help resume some of these places' historical role as transit trade hubs on the old silk road.[58] Fortunately, building connectivity is squarely one of the primary missions proclaimed for the BRI in its official "Action Plan." China has prioritized infrastructure and utilities projects in Central Asia, which are welcomed in the region and excelled by Chinese state-owned contractors.[59] Nonetheless, roads and railways eventually need harmonized regulations to really facilitate connectivity. Therefore, it is critical to watch whether China and Central Asian countries can synchronize their non-physical measures, such as their customs systems, to facilitate land transport. In addition, China will also need bilateral investment treaties (BITs) to reduce Chinese businesses' risks from Central Asian countries' unpredictable or even whimsical treatment of foreign investment. In particular, to achieve China's initial goals set

[57] Huirong Zhao (2014). "Jianshe 'sichou zhi lu jingjidai' de youli tioajian yu buli yinsu [The Opportunities of and Threats to the 'Silk Road Economic Belt' Construction]," in Li Sun and Hongwei Wu (eds.), *Zhongya guojia fazhan baogao 2014: "Sichou zhi lu jingjidai" zhuanji* [*Central Asian Development Report 2014: "Silk Road Economic Belt" Special Issue*] (Beijing: Social Sciences Academic Press), p. 242; Philippe Le Corre (2019). "Kazakhs wary of Chinese embrace as BRI gathers steam," Insights, National University of Singapore, 28 February, https://mei.nus.edu.sg/publication/insight-199-kazakhs-wary-of-chinese-embrace-as-bri-gathers-steam/, accessed 11 January 2020.

[58] Yang, "The current status and breakthroughs of the 'Silk Road Economic Belt.'"

[59] S.G. Luzyanin, V.A. Matveev, and L.N. Smirnova (2015). "Shanghai cooperation organization. Model 2014–2015," *Russian International Affairs Council* Working Paper No. 21 (2015), retrieved from Russian International Affairs Council website, http://russiancouncil.ru/common/upload/RIAC-WP-SCO-En.pdf.

for the BRI and expand the investment to "industrial capacity cooperation (i.e., exporting excess industrial capacity)," Beijing will need to ensure that Central Asian countries give considerable latitude to Chinese investments on aspects such as ownership, procurement of materials and equipment, and use of foreign labor.[60] However, this begs the question whether such projects would be perceived as truly "win–win" by locals and fulfill the vision of China's DP model.

5.2. *Monetary Integration*

China's push for monetary integration with Central Asia faces an uphill struggle. Even though China has signed currency swap agreements with Uzbekistan (2011), Kazakhstan (2011), and Tajikistan (2015) and established an RMB clearing bank in Kazakhstan in 2014, the use of the Chinese currency in Central Asia has progressed at a glacial pace. In 2012, China's RMB-settled trade volume with Central Asia was CN¥1.86 billion, or less than 1% of Central Asia's total trade.[61] In 2015, though the RMB-settled trade grew to almost 8 billion yuan, it just barely accounted for 1% of Central Asia's trade.[62] Take Kazakhstan, the dominant economy in Central Asia and China's primary trade partner in the region, as an example. In the third quarter of 2019, the volume of US dollar transactions in

[60] Lu Han (2017). "*Sichou zhi lu jingjidai zai zhongya de tuijin: chengjiu yu qianjing* [Silk Road Economic Belt's Progress in Central Asia: Achievements and Prospects]," *China International Studies*, 3: 108–124; Qi Li (2015). "*Zhongguo yu zhongya: chuangxin hezuo moshi, gongjian 'sichou zhi lu jingjidai' de diyuan zhanlue yihan yu shijian* [China and Central Asia: The Geostrategic Meaning and Practice of Innovating Cooperative Models and Co-building the 'Silk Road Economic Belt']," in Yawei Liu and Gaoliang Tian (eds.), *2015 nian "yidai yilu" gaoduan xueshu yantaohui yanjiu baogao: jiyu yu tiaozhan* [*2015 "One Belt One Road" Advanced Academic Symposium Research Report: Opportunities and Challenges*] (Xian: Xian Jiaotong University Press).

[61] Yan Gao (2014). "*Tuidong zhongya diqv kuajing renminbi yewu fazhan de sikao* [Thoughts on Promoting Cross-Border RMB Uses in Central Asia]," *Jinrong Jingji* [*Finance Economy*], 2: 30–32.

[62] Gui Cheng and Qi Wang (2016). "*Renminbi zhongya qvyuhua jingji jichu de shizheng fenxi* [An Empirical Analysis of the Economic Foundation of RMB Regionalization in Central Asia]," *Asia-Pacific Economic Review*, 5: 30–34.

Kazakhstan's foreign exchange market was 7.202 billion dollars. In comparison, the volume of transactions of RMB was equivalent to merely 0.013 billion dollars.[63] The value of yuan transactions as a percentage of dollar transactions was 0.18%, which was lower than the 0.38% achieved in the first quarter of 2017. The comparisons lay bare the still dismal demand for Chinese currency in Kazakhstan and in Central Asia. Furthermore, as of January 2019, Kazakhstan's RMB-denominated foreign debts were literally next to nothing.[64]

The fundamental reason for the slow progress on monetary integration is the deficiencies of China's financial market. China's capital account is not genuinely convertible, which means the financial market for RMB remains very shallow and does not provide enough tools for RMB holders to invest or hedge against risks. Therefore, even though for Chinese companies, using RMB might reduce their exposure to exchange rate fluctuations, for Central Asian businesses, choosing RMB instead of the dollar represents more risks and higher operational costs. As a result, Central Asia's dominant exports to China, including energy and raw materials, remain settled in US dollars. Much to Beijing's dismay, even border trade between Xinjiang and Central Asia is often settled in US cash bills to circumvent China's currency control.[65]

Through promoting the BRI, Beijing is hoping that, in addition to gradually deregulating its own capital account, the increase of China's trade, investment, and development financing in Central Asia will strengthen the region's incentives to use RMB. Meanwhile, Beijing is developing Xinjiang's Khorgas as an onshore "RMB offshore center" to overcome the issue that existing offshore centers, such as Hong Kong, are geographically too remote and thus too

[63] Calculated by the author. Data from the National Bank of Kazakhstan.

[64] Equivalent to 195 million US dollars out of a total external debt of 138,757 million, or less than 0.1%. Data from the National Bank of Kazakhstan on 4 January 2019.

[65] Dong Han and Shufen Wang (2014). "*Qianxi woguo yu zhongya guojia kuajing maoyi reminbi jiesuan fazhan huanman de wenti* [Analysis on the Issue of Slow Development in RMB-settled Cross-border Trade between the Nation and Central Asia]," *Duiwai Jingmao Shiwu* [*Practices of External Economy and Trade*], 5.

costly to be attractive to Central Asian participants.[66] In the short-run, one can argue that such efforts accompanying the BRI yield results if RMB-settled trade, investment and loans, and RMB clearing networks in Central Asia expand. However, the most significant and evident indicator might be whether the region's exports of energy and raw materials begin to be settled in the Chinese currency. China's launch of RMB-denominated crude futures in the Shanghai International Energy Exchange in 2018 is a step in this direction. The country has recently moved to pay Russian pipelines and oil with RMB and allow Russian banks to participate in the Shanghai Gold Exchange to buy RMB-denominated gold futures. The move is yet another effort to increase RMB's convertibility to promote yuan-backed transactions in oil and raw materials.[67]

5.3. *Development Cooperation*

Central Asian countries used to get loans predominantly from Russia. However, in the aftermath of the Great Recession, Russia's own liquidity crisis and a slump of the crude price depleted Moscow's own coffers and pressed Central Asian countries to turn to other creditors, including China, as alternatives. This opened up the opportunities for development cooperation between China and the region. For instance, before 2009, Kazakhstan had only about 0.1 billion dollar debts to China, but as of January 2019, the amount has grown to 11.02 billion dollars, surpassing the country's 9.30 billion debts to Russia.[68] Against this background of dwindling Russian funding and the abundant and eager Chinese alternative,

[66] Gao, "Thoughts on promoting cross-border RMB uses in Central Asia;" Han and Wang, "Analysis on the issue of slow development in RMB-settled cross-border trade between the Nation and Central Asia."
[67] Damon Evans (2017)."China Sees New World Order with Oil Benchmark Backed by Gold," *Nikkei Asian Review*, 1 September, https://asia.nikkei.com/Markets/Commodities/China-sees-new-world-order-with-oil-benchmark-backed-by-gold.
[68] However, this represents a gradual decrease in debts to China from US$13.25 in 2015 and US$15.97 in 2014. Data from the National Bank of Kazakhstan.

Kazakhstan, Kyrgyzstan, Tajikistan, and Uzbekistan all signed up to be the founding members of the AIIB.

Central Asia certainly has development needs that the BRI can help satisfy. In their 2015 gathering in Russia's Ufa, SCO members agreed to enhance their cooperation on cross-border motor and rail transportation, as well as transport infrastructure construction. Notably, they agreed to study the possibility of integrating Trans-Siberian Railway and Baikal–Amur Mainline with China's Silk Road Economic Belt.[69] The group also proclaimed their intent to seek funding from international development banks for these infrastructure investments, including a possible SCO development bank, which China has been advocating since 2010. However, the idea of an SCO development bank has so far failed to materialize, and Russia has been lukewarm toward or even passively discouraged the idea. Moscow's primary concern is that China would dominate such an organization should the voting powers be determined by the size of members' GDPs. Instead, Russia prefers the SCO to use the Russian-led Eurasian Development Bank (EDB), where Moscow enjoys veto power, as the organization's funding channel, but China is also ambivalent about joining the EDB.

Even though the BRI's proposal of building an integrated transportation system transiting through Central Asia is likely to create trade, transit revenues, and economic development for those countries, as China's DP model envisages, and the AIIB is set up to fund such investment, it is unclear how serious Central Asian countries are about embracing the initiative. For instance, the China–Kyrgyzstan–Uzbekistan railway has been in negotiation for more than a decade. In December 2013, Kyrgyzstan suddenly withdrew its initial support for a resource-for-railroad financing plan offered by China. The primary reason was Russia, which in May and December 2013 proposed a "Russia–Kazakhstan–Kyrgyzstan–Tajikistan" railway that bypassed China, and Kyrgyzstan prioritized its strategic partnership with Moscow.[70] On top of the Russian factor, Kyrgyzstan and Uzbekistan

[69]As of May 2019, no progress has been made in this regard.

[70]Li, "China and Central Asia: The Geostrategic meaning and practice of innovating cooperative models and co-building the 'Silk Road Economic Belt'," p. 50.

also had their simmering water disputes that poisoned the atmosphere of cooperation.[71] This illustrates how geopolitical uncertainty could be a primary hindrance to BRI's development cooperation in Central Asia (and beyond), which is not considered by China's DP model. News had it recently that Russia expressed interest in participating in the China–Kyrgyzstan–Uzbekistan railway "at the suggestion of the Kyrgyz side." This underlines that to lower geopolitical uncertainty and promote the BRI's development cooperation in Central Asia, Beijing will first and foremost need to find a compromise and understanding with Moscow, the incumbent patron of the region.[72]

Of course, reluctance to embrace the BRI does not mean a reluctance to embrace Chinese money. The fact that Chinese policy banks often transfer money directly to Chinese contractors instead of recipient governments means official statistics likely underestimate Central Asian countries' borrowing from China. Moreover, since most low-income countries do not report debts of public corporations outside the general government, recipient regimes might not even have a complete picture of how much their countries have borrowed from China and under what conditions.[73] A new dataset of China's overseas lending estimates that four Central Asian countries (Kyrgyzstan, Tajikistan, Turkmenistan, and Uzbekistan) are among the top fifty debtors to China by the debt to GDP ratio, ranging from nearly 10% (Uzbekistan) to more than 30% (Kyrgyzstan).[74] China's opaque lending in Central Asia's infrastructure, mining, and energy projects through its model of state capitalism thus creates significant debt sustainability issues in these countries that go against its proclaimed

---

[71] A.F. Klimenko (2016). "Collapse of enduring freedom: security in the SCO area," *Military Thought*, 25(1): 4.

[72] "Russia Wants to Participate in Creation of China-Kyrgyzstan-Uzbekistan Railway," *Azernews*, 4 March 2019, https://www.azernews.az/region/146668.html, accessed 21 May 2019.

[73] Sebastian Horn, Carmen M. Reinhart, and Christoph Trebesch (2020). "China's overseas lending and the looming developing country debt crisis," in Gabriel Felbermayr (ed.), *The World Economy after the Coronavirus Shock: Restarting Globalization?* (Kiel, Schleswig-Holstein: Kiel Institute for the World Economy), p. 36.

[74] Horn, Reinhart, and Trebesch, "China's overseas lending," p. 15.

idea of developmental peace. Moreover, Central Asia's hidden, substantial indebtedness to China is likely to court Moscow's misgivings about Beijing's intention in the region and have adverse impacts on the BRI's progress.

5.4. *Policy Coordination*

Speaking of development projects, Central Asian countries have their various initiatives, such as Kazakhstan's "Nurly Zhol (or Bright Path)," Turkmenistan's "National Strategy of Economic, Political and Cultural Development of Turkmenistan to 2020," and Tajikistan's "National Development Strategy-2030." Partly reflecting China's state capitalism paradigm that emphasizes "top-level planning," China pushes hard to have direct communication mechanisms between the BRI and these national initiatives to coordinate policies, in the hope that coordination at the top will ensure smooth implementation at the local level. In addition, political channels are expected to help mitigate investment risks resulting from Central Asia's flimsy rule of law and rampant corruption. However, progress in this regard has been limited and uneven.[75]

So far, Kazakhstan has been the model of policy coordination in Central Asia. Beijing and Astana at least twice, in 2015 and again in 2017, committed at the top-leader level to dock Nurly Zhol with the BRI, and projects with overlapping priorities, such as energy, infrastructure, and a logistic hub in Khorgos, have moved forward. On 2 September 2016, China and Kazakhstan signed a "Cooperation Plan for Docking the 'Silk Road Economic Belt' Construction and 'Nurly Zhol' New Economic Policy," making Kazakhstan the first country in the region to sign a bilateral agreement with China to dock its own development project with the BRI.[76] In contrast, Tajikistan's National

[75] Kristin Huang, "Why Chinese investors are struggling to gain a foothold in Tajikistan," *South China Morning Post*, 7 October, https://www.scmp.com/news/china/diplomacy-defence/article/2113810/why-chinese-investors-are-struggling-gain-foothold, accessed 21 May 2019.

[76] National Development and Reform Commission (2016). "*Zhonghua Renmin Gongheguo he Hasakesitan Gongheguo zhengfu guanyu 'sichou zhilu jingjidai' jianshe*

Development Strategy-2030 seeks to develop the country into a transit corridor, and its emphasis on improving transportation infrastructure to meet international standards matches well with the BRI's stress on connectivity. However, the two sides have not announced any plan to align their policy initiatives, and Chinese investors have been plagued by the murky legal and political environment in the country.[77]

It is notable that in the Ufa SCO summit in 2015, China successfully prodded Russia to agree to study a coordination mechanism between the EEU and the BRI within the SCO framework.[78] This indicated that China might hope to improve policy coordination with Central Asia through the SCO, by connecting the BRI with the SCO's plan for an integrated transportation system, while hoping that Central Asian states dock their individual initiatives with the SCO project as well. The development illustrates how an existing cooperative mechanism could potentially provide China with more options to overcome hurdles to the BRI.

5.5. *Security Cooperation*

The SCO originated from the confidence-building mechanisms established between China, Central Asian countries, and Russia in the 1990s. In recent years, the SCO's mandates have been expanded to dealing with non-traditional security threats, including drug and weapon trafficking, transnational crimes, and terrorism. The group has established

---

yu 'guangming zhilu' xin jingji zhengce duijie hezuo guihua," 17 October, http://www.ndrc.gov.cn/gzdt/201610/t20161017_822792.html; Ziguo Li (2017). "'*Yidai yilu*': *chengguo, wenti yu silu* ['One Belt, One Road': Achievements, Issues and Thoughts," *Ouya Jingji* [*Eurasia Economy*] 4: 6.

[77] Huang, "Why Chinese investors are struggling to gain a foothold in Tajikistan."

[78] In May 2018, EEU members signed a trade and economic cooperation agreement with China, which could potentially promote the relationship between the EEU and the BRI. Nevertheless, Nargis Kassenova argued the progress was shallow and mostly rhetorical and political. See Nargis Kassenova (2018). "More politics than substance: three years of Russian and Chinese economic cooperation in Central Asia," Russia Political Economy Project, Foreign Policy Research Institute, 24 October, https://www.fpri.org/article/2018/10/more-politics-than-substance-thee-years-of-russian-and-chinese-economic-cooperation-in-central-asia/, accessed 11 January 2020.

RATS in Tashkent in 2004 and organized anti-terrorism military exercises, codenamed "Peace Missions," several times since then. Chinese experts have made it blunt that China's primary interests in Central Asia lie in security, not in economy.[79] Now the need to safeguard the safety of BRI projects in the region will make expanding SCO's law-enforcement and defense cooperation even more important to China.

China has been hoping to increase the operational competence of the SCO's security cooperation mechanisms in recent years. In an SCO foreign ministers' meeting in June 2015, Chinese Foreign Minister Wang Yi called on SCO members to "take security cooperation as a priority and build the SCO into a reliable platform" for promoting regional peace, stability, and development, especially in Afghanistan.[80] The advocacy of strengthening the SCO's security component might have some sympathetic ears in Russia, whose military maintains dominant influence over their counterparts in Kazakhstan, Kyrgyzstan, and Tajikistan through doctrines, arms provision, and training.[81] For instance, Russian Foreign Minister Sergey Lavrov in the SCO foreign ministers' meeting in 2014 suggested transforming the RATS into a "Center to Counter New Challenges and Threats" to deal with, among others, drug-trafficking issues. In 2015, Russian Defense Minister Sergey Shoygu proposed at the SCO defense ministers' meeting to set up a national military advisers staff, which would recommend better uses of member states' military capabilities to protect their collective security. Following up on the proposal, Sergey Istrakov, Deputy

[79] Zhenis Kembayev (2014). "*Ruhe cong 'Shanghai hezuo zuzhi' tongwang 'sichou zhi lu jingjidai'* [How to Move Toward 'Silk Road Economic Belt' Through the 'Shanghai Cooperation Organization']," in Chongyang Institute for Financial Studies (ed.), *Ouya shidai: sichou zhi lu jingjidai yanjiu lanpishu 2014–2015* [*The Eurasian Era: Blue Book of Silk Road Economic Study 2014–2015*] (Beijing: China Economic Publishing House), p. 13.

[80] "China Urges Bigger Role for SCO in Regional Security," *Xinhua*, 4 June 2015, http://www.china.org.cn/world/2015-06/04/content_35744290.htm.

[81] Mariya Y. Omelicheva (2017). "Eurasia's CSTO and SCO: A failure to address the trafficking/terrorism nexus," *PONARS Eurasia Policy Memo* No. 455, p. 4, January 2017, http://www.ponarseurasia.org/sites/default/files/policy-memos-pdf/Pepm455_Omelicheva_Jan2017_0.pdf.

Chief of General Staff of the Russian military, suggested to put this body in the SCO Secretariat or Defense Ministers Council to coordinate member states' national armed forces, RATS, the Russian-led Collective Security Treaty Organization (CSTO), and the Commonwealth of Independent States' Antiterrorism Center through intelligence sharing and operation training.[82] However, progress so far has been limited to expressions of the need, intent, and political support of military coordination.[83] From Moscow's perspective, the membership of the SCO overlaps significantly with the CSTO, and Russia prefers the CSTO to play the primary role in Central Asia's security realm.[84] In response to the SCO's foot-dragging, China has turned to bilateral cooperation with SCO member states to safeguard its investment in the region. For example, the *Washington Post* reported that China had established barracks in Tajikistan to watch over Afghanistan's Wakhan Corridor, though Beijing had declined to acknowledge the deployment in order to avoid publicity and the resulting misgivings.[85]

Since Russia has always regarded Central Asia as its own backyard, the BRI's progress in Central Asia, from security cooperation to trade and economic integration, to a great extent depends on how much Russia will allow the CSTO and the EEU to establish institutionalized coordination with the SCO framework and then with the BRI. To China's fortune, Russia's relations with the West have deteriorated

---

[82] Klimenko, "Collapse of enduring freedom: security in the SCO area," pp. 10–11.

[83] Omelicheva, "Eurasia's CSTO and SCO: A Failure to Address the Trafficking/Terrorism Nexus," p. 3. As recent as in 2018, Chinese President Xi Jinping was still calling for deeper SCO defense cooperation. See Zhang Zunbi and Zhou Jin (2018). "president would like deeper SCO defense Cooperation," *China Daily*, 25 April, https://www.chinadaily.com.cn/a/201804/25/WS5adf923fa3105cdcf651a43a.html, accessed 11 January 2020.

[84] Reid Standish (2019). "China's Central Asian plans are unnerving Moscow," *Foreign Policy*, 23 December, https://foreignpolicy.com/2019/12/23/china-russia-central-asia-competition/, accessed 11 January 2020.

[85] Gerry Shih (2019). "In Central Asia's forbidding highlands, a quiet newcomer: Chinese troops," *Washington Post*, 18 February, https://www.washingtonpost.com/world/asia_pacific/in-central-asias-forbidding-highlands-a-quiet-newcomer-chinese-troops/2019/02/18/78d4a8d0-1e62-11e9-a759-2b8541bbbe20_story.html, accessed 11 January 2020.

sharply since 2013 in the wake of the crises in Georgia and Ukraine. To avoid total international isolation, Russia has inclined to maintain cordial relations with China. Meanwhile, China has taken several important confidence-building measures with Russia, such as recognizing the EEU's status, function, and significance as an international entity and declaring that China will respect Russia's interests in Central Asia as Beijing promotes the BRI. In the economic realm, China has signed an agreement on trade and economic cooperation with the EEU in May 2018. In the security realm, China has held a number of large-scale joint military exercises with Russia, giving both sides ample opportunities to carry out military planning and operations together. These measures help China demonstrate self-restraint in the use of its growing national strength and alleviate Russia's suspicion about China's intentions, increasing the likelihood of winning Russia's support for the BRI in Central Asia.

6. Conclusion

The BRI is China's effort to promote its political-economic model of "state capitalism plus developmental peace" overseas. However, the two elements have potential tension in BRI implementation. Excess industrial capacity and capital exported through state capitalism do not necessarily contribute to recipient countries' development, nor does the operation readily convince others of China's benign rise. How China strikes a balance when contradiction emerges — sacrificing economic and political gains for conformity to its rhetoric or vice versa — will define the nature of the BRI. The contradiction has become ever more acute amid the COVID-19 pandemic. The pandemic has wreaked havoc on the world economy and crashed commodity prices, exacerbating debt servicing problems in developing countries, many of which are BRI participants and heavily indebted to China.[86] The rest of the world is increasingly scrutinizing how Beijing handles the call for debt relief with these countries.

---

[86] Horn, Reinhart, and Trebesch, "China's overseas lending and the looming developing country debt crisis," p. 35; Horn, Reinhart, and Trebesch, "China's overseas lending," p. 17.

This chapter illustrates a framework for analyzing the progress and prospects of the BRI in individual countries or regions. However, it is legitimate to ask at last the question: how should we judge the overall success or failure of the BRI? Because China has deliberately left ambiguous the duration and scope of the BRI and emphasized that it will not pursue uniform progress across-the-board in every individual country and region, Beijing has considerable latitude to continue or terminate the project and declare its triumph. Thus, China's official rhetoric is not an objective benchmark. Nonetheless, China's original political-economic motives behind the BRI — exporting China's surplus capital and industrial capacity to help upgrade China's economic structure, through a China-centric international architecture to reduce its reliance on the US-led global governance framework while supporting friendly regimes on its periphery — provide us with objective touchstones to gauge the project's achievements. Therefore, by 2021, that is, upon the end of Xi Jinping's second term in office and the advent of the hundredth anniversary of the establishment of the CPC, if the Chinese economy could successfully export its overcapacity and move up in the global value chain and if Chinese-funded developmental efforts could establish credibility (through project performance) and help China befriend and stabilize neighboring regimes, then China can legitimately declare that the BRI has accomplished its near-term tasks.

Acknowledgment

The author thanks the Carter Center China Program, Noah Crafts, and Surya Narayanan for helpful research assistance.

Part IV

Conclusion

https://doi.org/10.1142/9789811226588_0013

Chapter 13

Where is China Going and Why?

Lowell Dittmer

The foregoing chapters provide a reasonably comprehensive overview of China's political economy as it has evolved into the global powerhouse we see today. Domestically, China has changed from a command economy led by a totalitarian movement regime pursuing dual goals of rapid development, ideological utopianism and world revolution into a still authoritarian but more pragmatic and economically sophisticated regime focused on rapid growth, international expansion and political stability. China's international posture changed from world revolution supplemented by armed class struggle to peaceably opening to the outside world, welcoming trade and investment from any who might be useful, whatever their political preference.

Although the change from Maoist China to the reform era that began in late 1978 was the most decisive one since Liberation, it was not a complete change nor was it the end of change. On the one hand, the Chinese Communist Party has remained uninterruptedly in command, with relatively little structural change in the hierarchical order from Mao's day to Xi's "new era." Though the ideology has changed more noticeably, it remains at its core essentially the same, in the view of its leaders: socialism consists of the CPC's unchallenged rule, trusting the Party to achieve a combination of revolutionary and developmental goals.

Yet, it is amazing how much China has changed without making a clear break from the past. Even as Xi Jinping hearkens back to such Maoist techniques as mass rectification and show trials and rebuts any attempt to differentiate between Mao's 30 years and the next 30, China has changed profoundly and irreversibly. No more reform through labor, no more commune-brigade-team framework or planned economy with rigid quotas, no more "three worlds." No point recapitulating all that has been said above, but let us return to two basic questions. First, what is the nature of the current Chinese political economy and where is it going? Second, how does Xi Jinping's new political economy fit into the global market?

This is the most rhetorically ambitious Chinese political economy since Mao, though it no longer aims for a future communist utopia but for a "great rejuvenation of the Chinese nation," for the development of a "fully developed, rich and powerful" country moving toward a "community of common destiny for all mankind." Ideologically, China today is also more avowedly "socialist" than at any time since Mao. What does this mean, in the absence of any visible commitment to world revolution? It means first of all a commitment to the commanding position of the Party, in the economy as well as in politics. "Government, the military, society and schools, north, south, east and west — the Party leads them all," as Xi announced in his 3 1/2-h address to the 19th Party Congress. Even at the famous Third Plenum in 2013, where Xi introduced his economic reform program and announced that the market would play a "decisive" role in the allocation of resources, he also pledged to maintain the "dominance" of the public sector. The reason for this insistence was not just to protect the structural interests of the elite. Xi had some very ambitious changes in mind, and he needed an effective and reliable organizational weapon to implement them.

Until he had command, Xi was very discreet about his political agenda. During the early stages of his career in the provinces, Xi displayed no particular preference for state enterprise, happy to promote any policies conducive to rapid growth. He served in provinces on the frontiers of market reform — Fujian, Zhejiang, Shanghai. But upon reaching the pinnacle, deeply impressed by the collapse of the Soviet Union, Xi has shown a consistent bias in favor of the most "socialist" sectors of the economy. Thus, SOEs are still favored in terms of state financing, access to resources, subsidies, taxes, and protected markets. The Party-state has also assumed greater control of the "private" sector, blurring the distinction between "public" and "private." The Party has the right to make arbitrary intrusions into the private sector and does so, by introducing Party committees, by arresting allegedly corrupt business executives, by expropriating farmland, and by forcing "mergers." In foreign policy, too, the Party boosts its "national champions" (such as Huawei). The massive BRI infrastructure-building policy introduced in 2013 and in 2018 enshrined in the Constitution was an enormous financial windfall for the state-owned sector.

This desire for tight centralized control has been manifest everywhere. Symbolically, most conspicuous was the removal of term limits for the President and Vice-President in the Constitution at the 13th National People's Congress (NPC) in March 2018. Although these are not technically Party positions, the consensual interpretation of this amendment was to enable Xi to retain his previously term-limited government position in tandem with retaining his Party and military positions indefinitely, which have no term limits. Aside from personal tenure security, this facilitates more comprehensive central control by eliminating any sunset clause.

Because it coincided with the rise of Xi and his consolidation of personal power, there has been a tendency to attribute the stagnation of market reform and the turn to central coordination to personal ambition, but that would be an oversimplification. There has always been an implicit "contradiction" between market reform and socialist ideal interests, which has continued to evolve dialectically since the outset of reform. The logic of market reform is that the consumer has discretion to choose — how simple to transpose that logic to the political arena! But this leads in the first instance not to electoral democracy but to political dissent, corruption, innovation, and other forms of local insubordination. The first public expression of this emerged in 1989 at Tiananmen, which was blamed not only on a misguided and disloyal younger generation, but on the undermining of socialism by market forces insinuated by a hostile anti-communist international conspiracy ("peaceful evolution"). After initial retrenchment following the Tiananmen shock, Deng Xiaoping revived economic reform in the face of elite resistance with his 1992 "southern voyage" [*nanxun*], arguing that the Soviet Union had collapsed not because of reform, but because reform came too late.

The Tiananmen protests and the ensuing collapse of Eurasian communism focused the minds of the CPC on the need to preserve elite control of what Lenin called the "commanding heights": the large-scale upstream SOEs. Meanwhile, political reform was reoriented away from popular participation and grassroots innovation to a focus on recentralization and administrative efficiency. On the one hand, the marketization of prices was rushed to completion (at the retail level) in the early 1990s, and after the 15th Party Congress in 1997 *de facto* privatization ("ownership reform") was permitted: urban housing was completely privatized even without a secondary private housing market, and the PLA's enormous industrial sector was shifted to civilian control. Under the slogan "grasp the big, drop the small" [*zhua da fang xiao*], the national SOEs were corporatized, merged and put on international stock markets, while medium and small SOEs were subjected to management buyouts, mergers, or forced bankruptcies. The establishment of the State-owned Assets Supervision and Administration Commission (SASAC) in 2003 established a bureaucratic interest in a collectivist vision of the future, with a competitive private sector at the bottom and bureaucratic "national champions" at the top. Thanks partly to SASAC's support, in part to weeding out poorly performing SOEs and off-loading non-performing loans to asset management corporations (AMCs), the profit margins of SOEs soared in 2003–2007. State support helped create some of the largest and most profitable corporations in the world, albeit at the price of an upsurge of industrial layoffs from "dropping the small." Chinese companies (mostly SOEs) accounted for 115 positions on the 2017 Fortune Global 500 list, up from 98 in 2016, including the second, third and fourth largest firms in the world. China could boast the world's second-biggest aluminum company, the world's fifth, sixth and 11th–biggest steel companies, and two of the world's biggest shipbuilders; it owned three oil companies, three airlines, and three telecommunication corporations, all of which enjoyed an oligopoly in domestic markets.

Meanwhile, political decentralization ("down to the provinces") was sharply curtailed. Whereas the 1983–1984 "one-down" reforms had reduced the number of cadres appointed by the central organization department by two-thirds, in 1990 the Party reverted to "two-down" and submitted new *nomenklatura* lists that increased the number of cadres on either the primary list (those directly appointed by the Party center) or the secondary list (subject to its approval). The financial apparatus and tax system were centralized, with four state commercial banks under the People's Bank of China that set interest and exchange rates. The separation of Party from government was basically halted under the new norm of "coordination" [*yiyuanhua*], and "anchoring Party leadership in the government" [*jiandang yuzheng*]. The previous emphasis on functional differentiation gave way to functional integration.

China's opening to the outside world proceeded apace: if capitalist relations of production were still a part of the primary stage of socialism, China's economic interaction with other capitalist economies was doctrinally correct and officially encouraged, leading to China's growing immersion in the global markets via trade, joint ventures, investment in China by multinational capitalist enterprises, even (after 2000) outgoing FDI. In early 1993, Zhu Rongji first allowed SOEs to list on the leading foreign stock markets, providing a new source of capital while facilitating domestic SOE reform; by 2000, China had listed hundreds of SOEs. As late as 2000, the joint venture format accounted for 50% of all FIEs, but after China's entry into the WTO, wholly-owned FIEs were permitted and by 2008 accounted for 80% of them. While SOEs remained prevalent in the north, in Guangdong and the Yangzi River delta FIEs and POEs (privately owned enterprises) predominated. Foreign investment basically created China's export sector and formed the leading edge of technological innovation, while the capital generated from foreign listings was invested back into the system [*tizhi nei*]. This integration of capitalist corporate economics and market opening into China's industrial economy also garnered favor in leading capitalist states, leading to theories of functional interdependence and system convergence.

But it also had the unanticipated effect of undermining the ideological legitimacy of the CPC. Especially, among China's youth it led to "three belief crises" [*san xin weiji*]: a crisis of faith in socialism, Marxism, and trust in the Party. "Primary stage theory" — the notion that China was still at the primary stage of socialism when certain capitalist leftovers would still be useful — succeeded the now openly conceded failure of the Cultural Revolution, and the contrast was stark: the Cultural Revolution represented extreme leftist ideals but was unsuccessful economically, while reform was economically successful but represented a step backward ideologically. While Mao Zedong brought China to the threshold of communism, now it lurched back to the primary stage of socialism. The economy boomed in the Hu Jintao years, averaging nearly 10% annual growth rate despite a 2009 downturn in the wake of the GFC, but reform was perceived to have stagnated.

Hence, during the Hu Jintao–Wen Jiabao era (2002–2012), the momentum quietly shifted from market liberalization to "socialism with Chinese characteristics." Jiang Zemin retired from the Central Military Commission in early 2005, Huang Ju had terminal cancer, and Zeng Qinghong stepped down in 2007. Zhou Xiaoquan, Zhu Rongji's principal architect of economic restructuring, came under fire from the left for rising inequality and the ideological vacuum that accompanied it. The reform bloc was thus weakened, and Hu Jintao and Wen Jiabao had different priorities. On the one hand, they did make mild efforts at political reform, stressing democracy within the Party, leading to greater ministerial discretion at the top and a minimal role for inner-Party elections. They cut agricultural taxes and introduced China's first rudimentary national social security system.

But further market reform was not encouraged.[1] The official slogan *min jin guo tui* (people forward, state recede) was reversed in popular parlance to *guo jin min tui*.[2] Zhu Rongji's enterprise reorganization (*zhuada fangxiao* — grasp the big and drop the small) was in many respects successful, culling unprofitable industries and improving the size and efficiency of the successful ones. But it also incurred fierce political criticism for unleashing a wave of unemployment among blue-collar workers and corruption among white-collar, as "management buy outs" (MBOs) gave windfall profit opportunities to cadres.[3] As Gang Chen notes above, it was on the basis of the perceived spread of unfair profiteering that the popular anti-corruption campaign took off in 2012.

Thus, the state after 2005 shifted to reforming rather than closing loss-making ("zombie") SOEs. Reform of the relatively successful SOEs consisted of encouraging them to adopt Western corporate best practices and to merge into even bigger "national champions" able to compete in the global arena. The number of SOEs actually increased under Hu and Wen.[4] Capitalizing on the apparent success of Zhu's millennial corporate reforms, the state in 2006 selected nine "strategic" sectors of the industrial economy, giving them privileged status in terms of financing and access to raw materials and shielding them

---

[1] US-China Business Council, "Economic Reform Scorecard," *China Business Review*, 7 March 2016, https://www.chinabusinessreview.com/economic-reform-scorecard/.

[2] The background of *guo jin min tui* policy, reversing the greater market orientation during the Deng years, was the 1989 Tiananmen impact, further reinforced by the instability of global markets as demonstrated by the Asian Financial Crisis (1997–1999) and still more the GFC in 2008, in both of which China seemed to survive with less damage than its more marketized neighbors.

[3] As a consequence of *guojin mintui*, the overall value-added share of SOEs in industry fell from 55% in 1998 to 34% in 2007, but the quality and profit share of surviving SOEs improved. Chen Kang (2019). "The economic role of the Chinese government: Between the centralized political system and decentralized markets," in Zheng Yongnian and Sarah Y Tong (eds.), *China's Economic Modernization and Structural Changes* (Singapore: World Scientific), p. 20.

[4] The number of SOEs declined from 191,000 in 2000 to 112,000 in 2007, but after the GFC bailout, it began to climb again: 136,000 in 2011, 147,000 in 2012, 155,000 in 2013, and 167,000 in 2015.

from market competition. SASAC announced in 2006 that SOEs would not only dominate strategic sectors but play a leading role in areas where the state was previously not expected to intervene. SOEs were the major recipients of the 2009 stimulus package, also permitted to list on global stock markets (not in order to diversify control, but to raise funding). By the early 2010s, some (e.g., China Petrochemical, State Grid Corporation of China, China National Petroleum) of these *yangqi* ranked among the largest corporations in the world.

The second, heavier blow to the narrative of economic liberalization was the global financial crisis (GFC) that began with the collapse of Lehman Brothers in 2008 and then ricocheted throughout the capitalist world. In 2009, 82 countries (accounting for 42% of the world) succumbed to economic crises. While China survived without a single quarter of recession, the impact of the crisis on China's economic locomotive was not inconsiderable — exports fell by a fourth in 2008–2009 due to the slump in external demand, and GDP growth dipped. The government responded with an RMB4 trillion stimulus package (US$586 billion), the largest such stimulus in the world proportionate to the underlying economy (the American bailout, in an economy then nearly four times as large, was ca. $700 billion). The stimulus took the form of bank loans to SOEs and local governments to build infrastructure and other public goods.

In Chinese eyes this crisis, like the Asian financial crisis of 1997–1999, raised doubts about the market model. As Wang Qishan (at that time leader of the Chinese delegation to the Sino-US strategic-economic dialogue) told his American counterpart Hank Paulson: "You were my teacher. [but] We aren't sure we should be learning from you anymore." "Political stability is a precondition for China's economic development," China's newly promoted vice premier in charge of financial and industrial policy, Liu He, wrote in 2008. "China cannot walk the path of Western-style democracy."

The GFC also reinforced the dawning Chinese appreciation of their own remarkable economic achievement. In 2007, before the crash, US (nominal) GDP was US$14.48 trillion, compared to China's $3.49 trillion; in 2014, US GDP was $16.77 trillion while

China's was $9.24 trillion. In other words, China's GDP rose from a mere 24% of US GDP to 55% in a mere 7 years. China surpassed Japan in GDP in 2010, and by 2018 was more than twice as large (China: $13,457 billion; Japan $5,071 billion, according to IMF). China's economy was now over eight times the size of Russia's, nearly five times larger than India's (4.66 times richer in nominal terms, 2.20 times in PPP, as of 2015), and more than four times larger than the combined GDP of the ten ASEAN countries. Doubling its GDP every decade, the country's share of global GDP rose from barely 1% in 1980 to 16% in 2016 (while its share of world population declined slightly, falling from 22% to 19%). The PRC's military spending, less than $10 billion in 1990, grew to more than $129.4 billion by 2014, biggest in Asia, second only to that of the United States and accounting for 9.8% of total global military expenditures. Despite Wen Jiabao's 2007 warning that China's economy looked strong on the surface, but in reality was "unstable, unbalanced, uncoordinated, and ultimately unsustainable," it was plausible to infer from such figures that the old Western order (led by the US) was in terminal decline while China's rise was inexorable. Although market reform made little headway during the Hu Jintao–Wen Jiabao decade, GDP growth averaged a record 10.4% per annum, impeded only by a financial crisis of Western origin. By 2019, China could boast more corporations in the Global 500 (129) than the US (121).

By the time of Xi Jinping's contested rise to supreme power, the popular mood was a mix of nationalist triumphalism and impatient anticipation of the next step forward. Many hoped for reform after a 10-year dearth of it, and an ambitious set of plans was indeed tabled at the Third Plenum of the 18th Congress, followed by surprisingly flaccid follow-through. The reasons have to do partly with industrial vested interests. The SOEs are huge, enjoy economies of scale and privileged access to resources (investment capital, land, fuel, telecoms, electricity), under direct jurisdiction of the Party-state, and flex monopoly or oligopoly power in their own markets on grounds of national security. SOEs are thus exempt from China's anti-monopoly law, and implementation under Xi Jinping of mixed ownership reform has in practice facilitated SOEs absorbing competing private firms.

SOEs dominate stock market listings, and can get bank loans with minimal screening, higher lines of credit, lower interest rates and fewer collateral requirements. They can issue publicly traded equity (bonds) and have privileged access to debt.

Xi would have trouble taking them on if he wanted to, but he does not. Xi's outsized ambitions for China could be realized only by mobilizing the powerful political apparatus he controlled. Xi stems from a "princeling" revolutionary family and came of age in a command economy. He was also the sent-down son of a purged cadre whose only chance of rehabilitation was becoming "redder than red." Xi thus has a more positive view of Mao and a darker view of the implications of reform than Deng. This emerged clearly in his analysis of the fall of the Soviet Union, an issue he revived immediately after his rise after two decades of public silence. The downfall came not because the system failed to reform, but because it failed to resist the forces of reaction. "Proportionally, the Soviet Communist Party had more members than we do, but nobody was man enough to stand up and resist," Xi said in an important 2013 speech.

China's approach to modernization under reform has undeniably benefited from the foregoing Western experience, but has always had its distinctive "Chinese characteristics," and in the light of China's economic rise to the top, it now became permissible to laud these publicly. In contrast to the Western model of development through free enterprise, the Chinese model emphasizes the key role played by government planning and industrial policy, communal rather than competitive interaction. Rather than deepening market reform, Xi emphasized the distinctive features of the Chinese path to modernization and began to promote it as an alternative to development models advocated by US-dominated Bretton Woods institutions that rely on private markets and a non-interventionist state. Having prevailed amid global financial collapse (China boosted its economy fourfold since 2000, while America consumed more and saved less by 45%),[5]

[5]Niall Ferguson and Moritz Schularick (2009). "*The End of Chimerica*," Working Paper, Harvard Business School, http://www.hbs.edu/faculty/Publication%20 Files/10-037.pdf, accessed 26 November 2013.

Xi concluded that the China model had demonstrated its superiority and that it must now seize this period of "strategic opportunity" to "take center stage in the world." Deng's "hide and abide" slogan disappeared from public discourse. China demanded a bigger voice in the World Bank and the International Monetary Fund (IMF) and got one; it even proposed that the US dollar be replaced as global currency by an alternative more equitable to developing nations (see Eichengreen, above). In Xi's first, tone-setting, speech in 2013 to the Politburo upon becoming Party general secretary (republished in April 2019, indicating its continued relevance), he spoke of "hostile foreign forces' fundamental purpose ... to overthrow the leadership of the CPC," of a "long-term struggle between the two social systems" in which. "[The party should] . . . ceaselessly build a socialism superior to capitalism, constantly win the initiative [over capitalism], win a superior position."

Yet, Wen Jiabao's diagnosis — that the economy was "unbalanced, unstable, uncoordinated, and unsustainable," all but ignored when uttered in March 2007 — has in hindsight proved prescient. Despite its amazing record, the China model now faces at least three roadblocks: overcapacity, indebtedness, and the middle-income trap. Overcapacity is essentially what happens when the export-led growth model China borrowed from the Asian tigers (South Korea, Taiwan, Singapore and Hong Kong) is actualized on far larger scale while popular purchasing power lags behind. Since 2014, China has produced more than half the steel in the world. In 2015, while the US steel industry lost 12,000 jobs, China exported 112 million tons of steel, more than what was produced by the US, Canada and Mexico combined. Just 10 years earlier China had been a net importer of steel, but between 2000 and 2007 subsidies to China's steel producers rose 3,800%, most coming through subsidized thermal coal, coking coal and electricity.[6] Despite years of "supply-side reform" designed to cut capacity, China raised crude steel production by 6.6%

---

[6]McMahon, *China's Great*, p. 184, quoting Usha and George Haley (2013). *Subsidies to Chinese Industry: State Capitalism, Business Strategy and Trade Policy* (New York: Oxford University Press).

in 2018 to 928.3 million metric tons, boosting China's share of global production still further, from 50.3% to 51.3%. The same sequence — high government planning priority, heavy government subsidies, resulting in overcapacity — happened within 5 years to the paper, glass, cement, electrolytic aluminium, and ship-building industries. It is also occurred in emerging industries such as polysilicon, solar cells, wind power equipment, electric vehicles and even robotics. Overcapacity wipes out competitors and gives Chinese firms a monopoly based on lowest clearing price. This is obviously problematic for China's trade partners, leading to a rash of WTO dumping cases. The ultimate risk of overcapacity is deflation and recession — not only in China but also in its trade partners.

A domestic concomitant of overcapacity stemming from the same underlying distortion is financialization (what the Chinese call *tuo shi xiang xu* — losing the real for the empty).[7] As one sector after another faced overcapacity, producing commodities it could not profitably sell, investors turn to assets that do not add to productivity but still seem sure to appreciate in value. Both overcapacity and financialization are symptoms of the same disease: the money supply expands out of all proportion to the growth of the economy, inflating asset bubbles. The prime asset bubble is housing, a bubble because it is financed by credit (60% of bank loans use property as collateral) and because much of it is built as a form of investment and may even then sit empty — in 2014, a survey estimated that the previous year, 20% of urban housing stock was vacant. The housing boom was unleashed by two legal changes. First, was the 1988 change in the Constitution that allowed people the right to use the land but not own it — i.e., it could be leased (eventually for up to 70 years for residential housing) and the leasehold could be inherited, bought or sold at market prices. Second, in 1998, the Party decreed that SOEs could no longer provide housing to their employees gratis, but employees could buy housing from their employers at steeply discounted prices. Housing construction took off and soon became the bedrock of the economy,

[7] In 2017, financial services represented 9% of China's GDP, exceeding that of US (7.2% in 2015). McMahon, *Great Wall*, p. 133.

accounting for 20% of GDP by 2013, more than in the US before the subprime crisis. From 2011 to 2013, China poured more concrete than the United States did in the entire 20th century. Construction provided employment for 16% of the urban population. Housing prices spiraled upward from their early bargain price, soon exceeding most people's capacity to purchase. SOEs beset by overproduction ploughed their surplus investment capital into housing projects. The same financialization driven by excessive money with no good place to invest resulted in a stock market boom in 2015, which attracted an estimated US$10 trillion only to see much of it vanish when the market then crashed.

The second difficulty China faces is debt. The impact of the GFC on China's economic locomotive has often been underestimated — exports fell from 20.7% of GDP in 2007 to 7.2% in 2008 and negative 18.3% in 2009 due to the slump in external demand, and both total factor productivity and GDP growth began to decline. When export demand sank, the government in 2009 provided a stimulus of some 4 trillion yuan (about US$586 billion).[8] But these were loans, issued by the banks from depositors' savings, which in principle had to be repaid. Debt continued to rise, outpacing GDP growth for years thereafter. The funds went in the form of loans to SOEs (65%) and to local governments. Between 2007 and 2014, China's companies — both state and private — increased their debt load from $3.5 trillion to $12.5 trillion. By 2017, Chinese firms' debt was equivalent to 160.3% of GDP, up from 120% at the end of 2011 — corporate debt was greater than in Japan (99.9%), the United States (72%), or the Euro-area (103.4%). SOEs accounted for over half of all China's corporate debt, but only contributed to 22% of China's total GDP in 2016. These debts were not government handouts (the government's deficit has remained under control), they were taken from the savings deposits of China's thrifty citizens and in principle must be repaid. Aside from corporate (SOE) loans, much of this debt went to the informal economy, or "shadow banking" sector — to "local

---

[8]The US and Japan pumped a comparatively meager $152 billion and $100 billion, respectively, into their much larger domestic markets.

government financial vehicles" (LGFVs). Why? Because local governments needed funding to achieve their mandated goals (upon which cadre promotions depend) but were ineligible for bank loans. So, the banks colluded with local governments to set up LGFVs on the side.

The problem has been not only higher interest rates but also lack of transparency: not even the central government was sure how much shadow debt existed.[9] The leadership awoke to the problem in 2017, establishing a high-level commission on the financial sector and launching a deleveraging campaign. Since 2017, the authorities have seesawed between maintaining 6% GDP growth and deleveraging. China's total debt has continued to grow (from 246% in 2017 to 248% in 2018). As the trade war suspended deleveraging in 2018, total debt grew the fastest in 10 years, amounting by the beginning of 2019 to ca. US$40 trillion, or 304% of GDP. The mainstay of leverage reduction is the corporate sector, while public and household debt continues to rise. But because the prime target of deleveraging has been shadow banking, it has disproportionately damaged the private economy that relies on it. But the SOEs' bottom line has also been hit, as the gross return on equity and return on assets for SOEs have both significantly declined since 2018. The trade war launched by the United States in July 2018, compounding an overall slowdown in global trade, has cut export revenue and distracted from deleveraging.

Optimists and followers of Modern Monetary Theory believe that concern about China's debt is overblown, because most of the debt is domestic, China has a high savings rate and a huge cache of foreign exchange reserves and can grow itself out of its debts.[10] Higher debt loads have been ubiquitous worldwide since the GFC. But as debt goes up, its production becomes less efficient because of the increasing share of GDP needed to pay debt service. As the incremental capital

---

[9]Moody's estimated at the end of 2015 that the People's Bank of China (PBC) was undercounting shadow banking by 16 trillion yuan, nearly a quarter of GDP.

[10]Government debt and household debt are under control. While Chinese national debt rose to $40 trillion in the first quarter of 2019, US national debt at that time reached an all-time high of $69 trillion.

output ratio (ICOR) goes up (it tripled in China from 2009 to 2017), the amount that a given amount of capital can produce diminishes.

The middle-income trap, as exemplified by say Argentina, consists of the tendency of developing nations to raise their aggregate and per capita GDP to some middling level, but then to remain stuck at that level. If China falls into this trap, it will most likely be by being pushed into a less profitable niche in global supply chains. China's integration into global supply chains was a vital part of its opening to the outside world, contributing mightily to its economic rise. China was thereby able to learn by contributing pieces of a finished product it was not yet able to make. China started out doing a lot of low-value assembly — a piece of electronics would be researched and designed in the US, its expensive high-tech components manufactured in Taiwan or South Korea, and the final product assembled for export in China before being sold and marketed in the US or EU. But China has not been entirely happy with its niche. Though its exports say "made in China," most of the value in these chains was not actually captured by Chinese companies and workers.[11] For instance, the Fung Global Institute and WTO estimated that only about 10% of the US$425 price of a jacket made in China and sold in the United States actually accrues to the Chinese. China leads the world in volume of robot production, yet 75% of precision reduction gears, 80% of submotors, and 80% of controllers are dependent on imports. While China now boasts an indigenous car industry, the import of key parts such as automobile transmissions has increased sharply. The deficit in information technology (IT) trade rose from $137.6 billion in 2011 to $193.3 billion in 2017. (This is known in economics as the smile curve — the workers who occupy the middle of the production process get paid less than the people at either end.) China sees itself not only deprived of the most lucrative links in the chain, but then incurs the ire of importers (such as the US) for contributing to the trade deficit whereas much of the export value is added elsewhere. Unless they can break out of

[11]The Apple I-phone is the best-known example: although some 30% of the value is added in China, it nets only an estimated 3% to 6% of the final price.

these value chains, the Chinese might be consigned to the "middle-income trap."

Xi Jinping's grand design for China to overcome these obstacles is termed "Xi Jinping Thought on socialism with Chinese characteristics in the new era," a unified belief and value system, amplified by a thicket of detailed rules regulating all aspects of organized life and celebrated in songs, pictures, social media and apps sometimes referred to (but not in China) as a personality cult. Although Xi claimed supreme leadership in 2012, his primacy was not fully consolidated until his second term began in 2017, at which point he was able to extend his tenure indefinitely. The substantive content of Xi's Thought is spelled out in a "14-point Basic Policy." Its essence is that the CPC should directly command and control all other hierarchies (as repeated in points 1, 11, and 14). "The leadership of the CPC is the most essential feature of socialism with Chinese characteristics. Party, government, military, civilian and academic; east, west, south, north, center, the Party leads everything," as Xi memorably put it. Xi has devoted very meticulous attention to the drafting of many lists of rules for every conceivable organization and he is unstinting in attending meetings, conferences, to propound these rules — in addition to a frenetic global travel itinerary. The more mundane formulation "new normal," introduced at the 18th Congress, appears only once in his 19th Congress Report.

A sweeping institutional revitalization of the government was introduced in the 13th NPC in March 2018, which attempted to embed the Party firmly in all other organizations. Local politics, the legal system, the media, should break free of factional or private interests and adhere whole-heartedly to CPC leadership, as informed by Xi's Thought. Sophisticated facial recognition and surveillance software facilitate the detection of any deviance. Unnerved by the surge of flight capital after the short-lived experiment with exchange rate liberalization in 2015, the Party-state must also control the financial sector and closely monitor the private economy. When private conglomerates become too large, too indebted, or too autonomous, they may be merged or shut down at state discretion via (1) "instructed" divestment, (2) regulatory takeover (e.g., Anbang Insurance, the

HNA Group), or (3) administrative "guidance" (e.g., the 2016 disappearance of Ye Jianming, erstwhile chairman of CEFC Energy Company, then listed 229th of the global 500 but heavily indebted).

This emphasis on hierarchical discipline and centralization is animated not only by Xi Jinping's subjective predilections but also by two objective considerations. First, "fiscal federalism" and decentralization had caused a lot of problems of corruption, budgetary indiscipline and organizational incoherence.[12] Second, Xi's epoch-making ambitions for China could only be realized by full mobilization of the Party-state apparatus. The market cannot be relied upon to realize such goals because markets are essentially disorganized, while great visions require taut organizations, synchronized to operational goals. State planning has hence made a comeback — the 5-year plans (FYP) continue, now dubbed "guidelines" [*guihua*] instead of plans [*jihua*], but still rigorously enforced as leading key performance indicators (KPI), including targeted annual GDP growth targets (which are rarely missed). The 13th FYP (2016–2020) is but the opening stage of an ambitious "Made in China 2025" plan to transform the country into a production hub for high-tech products like robotics, artificial intelligence, quantum computing, the Internet of things, and new energy vehicles within the coming decade.

But is not China, the "workshop of the world," already an industrial powerhouse? China now produces more steel, aluminum, glass, and cement than the rest of the world combined. No, China relies too much on imported key parts, components, and production equipment, cutting into its profit margins. China wants not just a bigger part of the production network, but a "red supply chain." "Modern technology is the sharp weapon of the modern state," says Xi Jinping, determined to rectify this via an newly industrialized country (NIC)-style industrial policy. Thus, the domestic market

---

[12]See Kang Chen (2019). "The organizational role of the Chinese government: between the centralized Political System and Decentralized Markets," in Yongnian Zheng and Sarah Y. Tong (eds.), *China's Economic Modernization and Structural Changs* (Singapore: World Scientific Publisher), pp. 17–35.

share of Chinese suppliers for "basic core components and important basic materials" is intended to increase to 70% by 2025.

"Made in China 2025," a long-term strategic plan for advanced technological development that is conceived to be "self-reliant," no longer publicly mentioned because of American sensitivities in the trade war but still in effect, sets non-binding targets in three phases: Phase I (2015–2025), Phase II (2025–2035), and Phase III (2035–2045). The emphasis on self-reliance is not only to internalize the supply chain. It is also because, even before the trade war, China was unnerved by such market gyrations as the AFC and the GFC (not to mention domestic stock market crashes in 2008 and 2015). It is also a matter of nationalist pride, an echo of Mao's Great Leap Forward. As Xi Jinping put it in a speech celebrating the bicentennial of the birth of Karl Marx in 2018: "learning from the achievements of human civilization does not mean copying and imitating [*bu dengyu zhaoban zhaochu*]. China's development has not replicated the development model of the West and has not repeated the old path of the West." Speaking at a training session for CPC officials in September 2019, Xi asserted: "For those risks or challenges that jeopardize the leadership of the Communist Party and China's socialist system; for those that endanger China's sovereignty, security and development interests; for those that undermine China's core interests and major principles; and for those that deter China's realization of a great national rejuvenation, we will wage a determined struggle against them as long as they are there. And we must win the struggle."

Xi Jinping's ambitious new era represents a bold departure from Deng Xiaoping's cautious "stepping from stone to stone to cross the stream." Yet, there are also strands of continuity. The strong emphasis on direct, comprehensive Party rule goes back not to Mao, but to Liu Shaoqi.[13] Uneasy with the marketization trend, the slide of property into private hands was halted as was the relaxation of CPC control rights. On edge from the critical foreign reactions to BRI plus the

[13]Cf. Lowell Dittmer (1974). *Liu Shaoqi and the Chinese Cultural Revolution* (Berkeley: University of California Press).

American trade war, the Party also made a spirited bid to control public morality, using advanced technology to monitor the public sphere. Not only Uighur Muslims but Christians and other heterodox belief systems and China's vast non-governmental organization (NGO) sector all endure tightening constraints. The "reform" henceforth is reconstrued to entail a combination of the up-from-behind populism of overcoming a century of Western humiliation with "top-level design" [*dingceng sheji*], formulation of national policy, with upward rather than downward (or sideward) accountability.

How well can it work? It is too soon to say. Although the shift to centralization is understandable in the light of the friction between an authoritarian political system and a decentralized economy, Western economists tend to believe that a more autonomous (and privatized) economy would be more flexible, innovative, and above all efficient in terms of capital allocation and return on assets. Doubts have been raised about the impact of the emphasis on ideological conformity on China's indigenous innovation program. This is even implicitly conceded to be problematic by the Chinese, as indicated in the propensity to copy and reverse engineer foreign technology. "Indigenous innovation" ironically stimulates an upsurge of cyber-espionage, including a "thousand talents" program to lure Western scientists to work in China.

On the other hand, the skepticism of Western critics may be swayed by their own vested ideal interests. Chinese are convinced a strong and stable central government can mobilize and concentrate resources and get things done more quickly than a more pluralistic one. History suggests that innovation can still thrive under authoritarian auspices. The Nazi and Soviet systems both had internationally competitive state-sponsored science and technology programs, particularly in advanced weaponry. Though a champion of free-market innovation, the US itself is no stranger to this approach — the Manhattan Project, the Apollo Project, and the Star Wars Project are proof that, to some extent, technological progress can be planned and state-organized. The Chinese state has intervened in the economy in a variety of ways to promote national technological development and reduce reliance on other countries. China's investment in research and development (R&D) has grown over 20% per year since 1999 and currently accounts for 20% of world R&D funding. Beijing pledged at the delayed 2020 NPC session to spend $1.4 trillion over the next 5 years on advanced technological development. China has succeeded in developing an innovation infrastructure, based *inter alia* on the establishment of over 100 science and technology parks throughout the country, along with encouragement of entrepreneurship outside the state-owned sector. China sent the first expedition to the far side of the moon, built the world's fastest supercomputer and, with six times the number of engineering graduates (in 2015), filed more patents than the US (in 2018). So far it seems however that the most innovative firms have been private ones (Tencent, Baidu, Alibaba) harboring close working relations with Western counterparties.

It may be useful to reconsider the functional relationship between politics and economics. Under Mao, politics, not economics, was "in command." In the Deng era, economics (the "forces of production") took command, and political leaders demanded economic growth to achieve political ends. Now that the Chinese economic miracle has demonstrated its competence, Xi Jinping seems to feel that it is time for economics to serve politics. Thus, China has begun to use its economic capabilities to enhance national power, for example, by refusing to sell rare earth elements to Japan after a Chinese fishing boat captain was arrested for trespassing in Japanese territorial waters, or boycotting Norwegian salmon after Liu Xiaobo was awarded a Nobel Peace Prize. When protests greeted the Chinese procession celebrating the 2008 Beijing Olympics in Paris, Chinese consumers boycotted Carrefour, and when South Korea installed the THAAD anti-missile system that Chinese believed was really targeting Chinese assets, Chinese consumers boycotted Lotte department store, eventually forcing its sale to a Chinese competitor. To be sure, China is not the first or even the most prominent country to resort to economic statecraft, but the world's second largest economy (and soon perhaps the first) will have overweening market power.

Although the motivational logic is clear in some cases, the relationship between economics and politics in China's political economy in the new era is often ambiguous. For example, what was the 2018–2019 Sino-American trade dispute all about? Was it for economic reasons, or political? The public discussion (on both sides) was more about the politics of face than about balance sheets. This also confuses China's trade partners, who do not know whether to view the BRI as a political initiative or an economic venture — economically it would be unacceptably risky, but it could be a geostrategic coup. In the light of *lishu* relations of public–private coordination, the Chinese see no such dilemma. Shut out of politics since Tiananmen, the Chinese public compensatorily invests in economic growth as a symbol of overcoming national humiliation and gaining international legitimacy. As the Chinese economy threatens to surpass the American, this triggers a competitive systemic response from the rival superpower, focusing not on per capita living standards but on measures of collective achievement: can chaotic democratic capitalism compete with a disciplined collectivist alternative? In an era of "National champion" oligopolization, international rivalries replace domestic market competition.

Clearly, the most prominent exercise of economic statecraft under Xi has been the Belt and Road Initiative (BRI), consisting of altogether six main corridors and a number of minor ones, but mainly two, one over land through Central Asia to Europe and one by sea through Southeast Asia and the Indian Ocean to Africa and the Mediterranean. To some extent a rebranding of the 1999 "going out" [*zou chuqu*] policy, both were launched in 2013 in the wake of a hardening of China's territorial claims to the East and South China Seas. Driven by mammoth budgets, not all of the money new (embracing for example the Pakistan economic corridor, and the Myanmar pipeline), the BRI endows heterogeneous projects throughout the developing world with conceptual unity in a grand plan to connect China with global energy and raw material sources, befriend its neighbors, unify Eurasia, export surplus capital and stimulate growth in its own underdeveloped periphery. This trillion dollar scheme is financed not by the Asian Infrastructure Investment Bank, but by the Chinese Development Bank (CDB) and the Export–Import Bank and mostly on commercial terms, now most often on a BOT or BOOT basis. Specific loans are drawn up on bilateral state-to-state terms and then generally contracted to Chinese SOEs. Initially welcomed by over 120 countries in dire need of infrastructure, enthusiasm ebbed somewhat as the consequences of loan defaults became clear and host countries hit their limits.

Since the second BRI conference in April 2019, the policy has hence been adjusted and its financial scope considerably narrowed. According to AEI's China Global Investment Tracker, Chinas outgoing foreign direct investment (COFDI) has declined steeply since 2017. The $27.5 billion spent in the first half of 2019 was only half that of the first half of 2018, a quarter that of the first half of 2017, 20% that of the first half of 2016. COFDI peaked in 2010 (at $124.96 billion) and has declined since, to average around $50 billion per annum, plunging below that in 2019. There are at least three reasons: (1) growing suspicion of Chinese investment in the US, Japan and the EU (all three of which have launched competing infrastructure projects); (2) China's relative shortage of hard currency (because of the anti-corruption campaign, clampdown on capital flight since 2016, trade war impact on exports); (3) clients (e.g., Pakistan) are often overburdened with debt. In addition to economic limitations, there are geopolitical sensitivities: the land route encroaches on Russia's Eurasian Economic Union (EEU), and the maritime route is complicated by New Delhi's opposition and refusal to participate, largely because the CPEC runs through Indian-claimed Kashmir (though India has joined the AIIB, BRICS and the SCO).

But the big geopolitical problem for China is the emergence since around 2010 of growing Sino-American bipolarity. Historically ambivalent, the relationship suddenly shifted from Cold War enmity to strategic alignment in the early 1970s based on two pillars: strategic and economic. For the decade following the ice-breaking Nixon visit in 1972, it was based largely on strategic grounds. Both needed each other, they thought, to counter the looming Soviet threat. With the Soviet–American détente in the Gorbachev era, particularly following dissolution of the Soviet Union in December 1991, this shared threat vanished from the strategic horizon, while the Tiananmen crackdown upset American moral sensibilities. Meanwhile, Deng's opening to the outside world however gave the relationship new footing based on economic complementarity — China needed capital and advanced technology, the US needed cheap consumer imports (and offshore wages) to hold down inflation. Bilateral trade and investment boomed. This mutually profitable interaction accelerated greatly upon China's admission to the World Trade Organization (WTO) in late 2001, immunizing the PRC from any further threat of the most favored nation (MFN) sanctions and establishing "permanent normal trade relations." The objections of American labor unions, human rights advocates and anti-communists were defrayed by the vision of political-economic convergence.

By 2018, both strategic and economic pillars had attenuated, as had American faith in systemic convergence. Strategically, while American relations with an authoritarian Russia cooled after the annexation of Crimea and Russia's 2016 election interference, China was no longer available to balance Russia, now its "comprehensive strategic partner." China was still useful in Asia, tightening sanctions on North Korea after Trump established "fantastic chemistry" with Xi at Mar-a-Lago in April 2017, thereby helping to bring Kim Jung Un to Singapore. But the bilateral economic dialogue they established saw little progress. Having focused on trade deficits for several decades before his vehement 2016 electoral campaign, Trump shocked the world in 2018 by ignoring the WTO and invoking "national security" to impose tariffs on Chinese imports. More shocking still was the apathetic (or even concurring) reaction of China's other trade partners. China's economic opening after admission to WTO had disappointed, imports still constrained by various informal trade barriers and IPR risks. China's global current account surplus mounted annually. In the US, Xi Jinping's grand nationalist "great power" ambitions aroused concern, coupled as they were with his view that Asians no longer needed US protection and should abandon Cold War thinking and security alliances.[14]

[14]See Xi Jinping's speech to the 4th summit of the Conference on Interaction and Security-Building Measures in Asia (CICA), 20–21 May 2014, http://www.china.org.cn/world/node_7206254.htm.

Thus, while the Obama administration's 2015 National Security Strategy welcomed "the rise of a stable, peaceful, and prosperous China" and aimed "to develop a constructive relationship," the Trump administration's 2017 National Security Strategy alleges bluntly that "China ... want[s] to shape a world antithetical to US values and interests."

The large but steeply asymmetrical trade deficit (a US$375.6 in 2017, up from US$103.1 billion in 2002) provided Donald Trump with both financial leverage and plausible grievance. China's foreign exchange surplus comes of course from its export sector, around half of which is produced by FIEs (more in high-tech), seemingly providing a sound footing for economic cooperation with the West.[15] Yet, Trump's abrupt announcement of trade sanctions in the spring of 2018 did not generate the chorus of protest from the China-engaged business community that had thwarted Clinton's earlier attempt to use trade to induce human rights reform. A Pew report in March 2020 (based on a survey at the end of 2019) disclosed that 66% of Americans had an unfavorable view of China (up from 47% just the year before) and only 26%, a favorable one. This was China's worst showing since the survey's inception in 2005. China's ambitious 2025 modernization plans previewed a shift to import substitution, as China morphed from trade partner to high-tech competitor with diminishing interest in pampering foreign investors. In November 2013, there were 57,200 foreign-invested enterprises (FIEs) in China, but by November 2016 the number had shrunk by 10%: among the firms planning to relocate Chinese manufacturing sites were Nikon, Nitto, Samsung, Olympus, Omron, Adidas, Uniqlo, Foxconn, Intel, LG, and Nokia.[16] This was not just the trade war:

---

[15]Foreign companies account for less than 3% of the total companies in China, but they contributed over 50% of China's foreign trade volume in 2017, 25% of profit, and 20% of China's tax income. The private and foreign-invested enterprises accounted for 46.5% and 43.2%, respectively, of China's foreign trade surplus in 2017, while state-owned enterprises (SOEs) accounted for only 10.3%.

[16]Three major reasons why foreign companies have left China are: the real estate bubble, increases in wages and operating costs, and the tariff war.

fixed capital investment by foreign companies shrank from $508.7 billion in 2011 to $214.6 billion in 2017, a reduction of 57.8% in just 6 years. Nearly 100 annual bilateral negotiating forums had not brought the two sides closer to agreement on either China's expanded East Asian strategic role or its neo-mercantilist economic policies.

In 2018–2019, the US imposed tariffs on altogether around $250 billion of Chinese imports, while China reciprocated with tariffs on around $110 billion of US imports (up to 72%, on pork). Additional US tariffs on $300 billion were scheduled to take effect in January 2020, but then rescinded as a "first stage" interim deal was announced in December 2019. The agreement would have Beijing purchase an additional $200 billion of US goods and services (compared to 2017) over the next 2 years, while the US agreed not to impose the $300 billion in tariffs scheduled for January 1 and to reduce tariffs on $120 billion in Chinese imports from 15% to 7.5%. China agreed to further open its markets, strengthen intellectual property rights protection, get rid of forced technological transfers and increase the transparency of its exchange rate policy. In return, the United States would cut half the tariffs it imposed in 2019, while keeping the 2018 tariffs intact. Equivalent to 1% of US GDP, a US$200 billion increase in exports to China would certainly boost Trump's chances of re-election. Critics belittled an outcome that might have been had at the outset, but this was only Phase I, to be followed by further talks on SOEs, planning, subsidies, and other structural issues.

The confrontation has been damaging to both economies: bilateral trade plunged by almost 88% from 2016 to 2018, still further in 2019, as did the bilateral trade deficit, while America's overall trade deficit went up (from $544 billion in 2016 to $641 billion in the 12 months ending in October 2019), as other (untariffed) exporters such as Vietnam took China's place. Bilateral investment also slowed, Chinese FDI in the US especially, now constrained by a beefed up Commission on Foreign Investment in the US (CFIUS). Though China made most of the concessions, arousing considerable skepticism about whether they would fill import purchasing targets, the deal could provide the needed respite for an improvement in relations after a difficult 2 years.[17] The confrontation did push Chinese economic reform, resulting in a new foreign investment law, banning forced technological transfers and allowing wholly foreign-owned financial institutions to operate in the country.[18] If China indeed purchases $200 billion US imports (1% of GDP), that would probably boost Trump's election prospects and deepen economic ties between the two nations — indeed, Chinese imports would double, eliminating the trade imbalance entirely. For the US, to fulfill its side of the deal (most of which is actually manufactures) that would boost employment appreciably. Should the "war" resume, China is more vulnerable in the short term given the continuing trade imbalance (by June 2020 China was again America's leading trade partner), but the risk to America is that China survives the trade war and increases its trade with the rest of the world while only the US misses out on a future China import boom. Meanwhile, the "tech war" that began by putting ZTE and Huawei on an "entities list" may continue. China seems likely in that case to develop its own chips and other software and roll up global tech markets the way high-speed rail transformed Chinese transportation.

To Trump, China was viewed as a threat primarily to US economic hegemony — he has rarely alluded publicly to security threats

---

[17]Cf Yao Yang (2020), "US–China trade rapprochement round one," *East Asia Forum*, 19 January 2020, https://www.eastasiaforum.org/?p=228636?utm_source=newsletter&utm_medium=email&utm_campaign=newsletter2020-01-19.

[18]The new foreign investment law that came into effect in January 2020 seeks to level the playing field between FIEs and Chinese enterprises. Effective 30 July 2019, the Special Administrative Measures (Negative List) for Foreign Investment Access (2019 Edition) (National Negative List) and the Special Administrative Measures (Negative List) for Foreign Investment Access in Pilot Free Trade Zones (2019 Edition) (FTZ Negative List), which set out sectors with restrictions on foreign investment in the Mainland nationally and the Free Trade Zone regions, respectively, were shortened. Compared to the 2018 Editions, the 2019 Editions reduced the number of restricted items on the National Negative List from 48 to 40, and from 45 to 37 on the FTZ Negative List. These were substantial reductions from 180 items in 2011 on the National Negative List and 190 items in 2013 on the FTZ Negative List. New pilot FTZs were also added, in one of which (Shanghai) the services sector would be liberalized to permit foreign competition.

in the Pacific or to human rights violations — but his hyperbolic rhetoric, and his sustained trade offensive, has mobilized a "whole nation" concern with the China challenge. "Decoupling" or trade diversification was raised as a final solution, but that would be costly in view of the degree of economic integration — some 51,000 factories worldwide rely on parts or equipment made in Wuhan, 4 million indirectly. The American share of global high-tech exports has fallen from just below 20% in 1999 to barely over 5% in 2014, while China's share has risen from 3% to 26%. How many would join the US in decoupling from their largest trade partner? On the other hand, if the East Asian network of value chains were cut off from its richest consumers, could China with a per capita income one-fifth of America's and one-fourth of Europe's replace those markets?

The year 2019 found the world in equipoise. In China, though Xi Jinping wants to move his nation from undecipherable market logic to one tightly controlled by regulatory and supervisory networks descending from the Party Center, he is constrained by the need for employment and economic efficiency. Trump's trade war was domestically popular as a corrective to an engagement many felt had slipped out of control, but his remedy was costly and unsustainable. Thus, Phase I could be considered an imperfect but welcome hiatus. Yet, the ink was scarcely dry when the accord was hit by three major headwinds: the novel coronavirus epidemic (COVID-19) originating in Wuhan, the democratic upheaval in Hong Kong, and finally the American presidential election.

The novel coronavirus made its first appearance in Wuhan in the fall of 2019 and by early January 2020 had begun to spread; apparently the virus was similar to the SARS encountered in 2002–2003, less deadly but much more infectious. The Chinese leadership, no doubt concerned about disruption of the economy, Chinese New Year festivities and other ongoing activities sought to smother news of the contagion, assuring the outside world all was in hand, reinforced by a gullible World Health Organization. Thus, when the virus very quickly spread throughout the world, many countries were caught unprepared and tended to blame China's secrecy-mongering. From all available information (which China remains wary of sharing)

China's technologically enhanced authoritarian system proved extremely adept at containing the domestic spread of the virus, and in March was among the first countries to reopen its economy: China's official manufacturing purchasing managers index (PMI) and the Caixin China manufacturing PMI in May 2020 both reported three straight months of expansion, with factory activity jumping to a 4-month high of 50.7 from 49.4 in April. But China's publication of its triumphant rebound while its more pluralist counterparts remained mired in disease (10 million cases and nearly 500,000 deaths world-wide as of 28 June) fell on deaf ears.[19]

The economic impact of the pandemic has been to disrupt global value chains (GVCs) and slow trade and GDP growth, generally exacerbating trends sparked by the trade war. Countries suddenly discovered that much of their medical equipment was in short supply with refills manufactured only in China (e.g., 80% of American antibiotics); nearly 90 governments blocked the export of medical goods to preserve supplies for their citizens, while 29 did the same with food. Governments resolved to "reshore" various strategically vital industries, such as medical equipment or high technology. French President Macron pledged "full independence" in crucial medical supplies by year end. Japan, South Korea and Taiwan are providing subsidies for companies to come home. In April 2020, Modi invited multinationals in China or Hong Kong to relocate in India.[20]

The evidence is still ambiguous about how many will do so. If they are producing for the China market, they have reason to stay, while if they are primarily exporting, they may seek greener pastures. An EU Chamber of Commerce issued a Business Conference Survey in February 2020 finding that 11% were considering shifting to other

---

[19] Early in the panic, the EU provided some 60 tons of medical equipment to China, often from national strategic stockpiles — discreetly, at Beijing's request. But when the EU was then impacted and China offered to give (or sell) sometime defective equipment back, calling for public expressions of gratitude, the Europeans were not amused.

[20] As of April 16, Taipei had approved 180 Taiwan companies to invest $25B in reshoring manufacturing back from China since the beginning of 2019, getting the Taiwan government's help in procuring land, water, electricity, labor and financing.

markets, while a synchronic American Chamber of Commerce survey found 9% were locating and 8% considering doing so. Kearney (a global business consultancy) released its seventh annual Reshoring Index in May showing what it called a "dramatic reversal" of a 5-year trend as domestic US manufacturing in 2019 commanded a significantly greater share versus 14 Asian exporters tracked in the study. Manufacturing imports from China were the hardest hit. The main beneficiaries were Southeast Asia and Mexico.

There have been several protest movements in Hong Kong since it was returned to China in 1997, and the core issue has remained resistance to China's attempts to integrate the Special Administrative Region (SAR) more securely into the mainland political-economic system. Seemingly, the largest of these movements started in June 2019 in response to the government's introduction of a bill introduced to permit extradition of criminals from Hong Kong to the mainland for trial. This evoked widespread concern largely because of the mainland's more politicized definition of criminal activity. On 4 September, after 13 weeks of protests, Lam finally promised to withdraw the bill, and on 23 October this was done. By this time, however, protests had gained momentum (and become more destructive, involving, for example, the use of Molotov cocktails), demanding additional concessions, the gist of which called for a continuation of the political liberalization process that had since 2014 been suspended. The police cracked down hard, making nearly 9,000 arrests. The deadlock however continued until pandemic quarantines slowed momentum in February.

Meanwhile, Beijing quietly resolved in October 2019 to employ firmer measures. These took the form of a draft National Security Law (NSL) presented at the delayed National People's Congress in May. The law prohibits subversion, secession, terrorism, and collusion with foreign powers. To enforce these prohibitions, Chinese security officials will staff a National Security Office in Hong Kong to "supervise, guide and coordinate" implementation, also to collect and analyze relevant intelligence information and deal with criminal cases under the auspices of the NPC Standing Committee; the Hong Kong Government will also set up a National Security Commission (with a mainland advisor). Provision is made for a "small minority" of criminal cases to be extradited to mainland courts. The Hong Kong Chief Executive will appoint NSL judges with preliminary jurisdiction over NSL violations.

The economic impact of this Procrustean legislation is yet unclear, at this writing the full text is not available. Presentation of the draft was greeted by the largest protest demonstrations since the start of the pandemic. The economic recession deepened in the first quarter of 2020, with real GDP contracting by 8.9% from a year earlier, the steepest for a single quarter on record. Unemployment reached 5.9%, the highest in 15 years, and the real GDP growth forecast for 2020 as a whole is a negative 6–7%. The international reaction was generally critical of the NSL for its circumvention of the 1984 Sino-British Joint Declaration, an international treaty that promised a "high degree of autonomy" for 50 years. Hong Kong relies on international trade, with a trade-to-GDP ratio of 293% in 2019, so if it loses the qualities that distinguish it from other mainland cities — the rule of law, a clean and efficient bureaucracy and civic culture — it would no longer thrive as an international financial hub. An AmCham poll of the foreign business community conducted in late May found that 53.5% were very or moderately concerned by the NSL and that 30% would consider relocating. The American Secretary of State on 27 May certified to Congress that "Hong Kong does not continue to warrant treatment under United States laws in the same manner as US laws were applied to Hong Kong before July 1997. No reasonable person can assert today that Hong Kong maintains a high degree of autonomy from China."[21] President Trump announced he would "begin the process of eliminating policy exemptions that give Hong Kong different and special treatment."

Hong Kong's fate hangs on three interlinked questions: will the draft NSL be approved and implemented as is; will the US, the EU

---

[21] Michael R. Pompeo, Secretary of State, "Press Statement: P.R.C. National People's Congress Proposal on Hong Kong National Security Legislation," Department of State, 27 May 2020, https://www.state.gov/prc-national-peoples-congress-proposal-on-hong-kong-national-security-legislation/.

and the outside world then treat Hong Kong no differently than the Chinese mainland (thereby removing its special customs status); and if so, how will this affect the future economic well-being of Hong Kong and China? One line of thinking is that China is indifferent; after all, the whole thrust of the mainland's tightening grip on the SAR has been to eliminate its special status and integrate it into the mainland economy. At the time of the handover, Hong Kong's GDP was 18% that of the mainland, while by 2019 it was only 3%. Beijing has since elevated Shanghai and Dalian to duplicate Hong Kong's financial functions, and created the Greater Bay Area to fold it into southern China along with Macao, Shenzhen, and the Pearl River Delta as an agglomerated high-tech financial center.

Time can only tell of course, but up to now Hong Kong provides services it will be hard to duplicate. The bulk of foreign direct investment (FDI) in China continues to be channeled through the city. According to China's Ministry of Commerce, over 58% (around US$70 billion) of China's non-financial outbound direct investment (ODI) went to Hong Kong in 2018. Much of this Chinese investment does not remain in Hong Kong, it is either repatriated to China as profits or round-trip investments or sent elsewhere. Much of what remains goes into the stock market (Stock Exchange of Hong Kong, SEHK) or into real estate. Many of China's biggest firms are listed in Hong Kong. In 2019, Chinese companies raised $64.2 billion globally — almost a third of the worldwide total — via initial public offerings (IPOs). Of the 10 largest IPOs raised by Hong Kong — listed companies since 1986, nine are Chinese, including eight SOEs. The SEHK is now home to 250 H-share Chinese companies and another 171 "red chip" firms controlled by the Chinese state. The combined 421 China-related companies have a total market capitalization of nearly US$1.54 trillion, more than one-third of SEHK's total market capitalization. This is likely to increase, particularly if the American stock market evicts Chinese firms that fail to meet SEC auditing requirements (as is threatened by pending legislation). Chinese businesses also tapped Hong Kong's debt market for 33% of their $165.9 billion in offshore US dollar funding in 2019. In 2018, around 8% of China's exports to the US and 6% of imports were routed through

Hong Kong; if the SAR's special status is revoked, they will be subject to the same tariffs as Chinese merchandise. In sum, it looks as if the premature *de facto* elimination of "one country, two systems" could be quite costly to an already slowing Chinese economy, particularly to its international financial standing.

Finally, the American election in November 2020 seems likely to turn more than normally on foreign policy issues. The American economy, like much of the rest of the world, will still be in relatively bad shape. Trump's plan in 2019 was to run on a strong economy bolstered by a great first-stage China deal that would correct the trade imbalance and bolster domestic employment and GDP. That plan was shattered by COVID-19, and Trump will blame China and try to tie his opponent to a pre-Trump appeasement policy. To evade that brand, Biden too will run against China. So, regardless who wins, China seems destined to get hit with a lot of "China threat" invective.

https://doi.org/10.1142/9789811226588_bmatter

Index

T

www.ingramcontent.com/pod-product-compliance
Lightning Source LLC
LaVergne TN
LVHW011701200926
848484LV00004B/1017